DANIEL HERAUD

The Canadian Used Car Guide 2002-2003

Daniel Heraud

CREDITS

The photographs appearing on the cover and inside pages were provided by the manufacturers' press services and Daniel P. Heraud.

Project Manager:	Daniel LAFRANCE
Chief Editor:	Daniel HERAUD
Assistant:	Julien CHAMPAGNE
Coordinator:	Lyse HERAUD
Proofreaders:	Claude BOUCHER, Michel DOYON

All rights reserved.
No part of this publication may be reproduced, stored in a retrieval system, or transmitted in any form or by any means, electronic, mechanical, photocopying, recording or otherwise, without the prior written consent of the editor.
The information in this book is true and complete to the best of our knowledge. All recommendations are made without any guaranty on the part of the editor and his collaborators. They disclaim all liability in connection with the use of this information.

"Le Guide Des Autos Usagées" and "Canadian Used Car Guide" are registered trademarks.
Legal deposit: First quarter of 2002
Bibliothèque nationale du Québec
National Library of Canada
ISBN: 1-895729-42-4

Printed and bound in Canada

HOW TO USE THIS GUIDE

The whole purpose of this book is to inform you of the dramatic differences that can exist between brand new cars and these same cars when they're put on the market as used vehicles. However one evaluates a used vehicle, be it in regard to safety features, handling capabilities, over-all performance, upkeep or repairs, the approach or emphasis is quite different from the flashy descriptions one is used to reading about when it comes to brand new vehicles. For example, you'll see that we've added those notorious recall campaigns, which say a great deal about the quality of some components and about chronic reliability problems that have persisted over the years.

This little guide is one of a kind, both on the Canadian and American publications market. It informs you in a concise and clear way of everything you should know in order to make the best possible purchase choice.

I hope you will enjoy browsing through this book and that you will find the best used car out there that money can buy.

Daniel HERAUD

ABBREVIATIONS

	ENGINE TYPES
H	Horizontal engine
L	In-line cylinders
V	V-shaped cylinders
R	Rotary piston
Cyl	Cylinder
L.	Capacity in liters
hp	Horsepower

	CARBURATION
SOHC	Single overhead cam
DOHC	Double overhead cam
OHV	Overhead valve
T.	Turbocharger
C.	Supercharged

	TRANSMISSIONS
M4	Manual 4-speed
M5	Manual 5-speed
M6	Manual 6-speed
A3	Automatic 3-speed
A4	Automatic 4-speed
A5	Automatic 5-speed

	MODELS
con	Convertible
cpe	Coupe
sdn	Sedan
a.p.v	All-purpose vehicle

wgn	Station wagon
m.v.	Mini-van
p.u.	pickup truck
2dr	2-door
3dr	3-door
4dr	4-door
5dr	5-door
2x4 or 2WD	2-wheel drive
4x4 or 4WD	4-wheel drive
AWD	permanent 4-wheel drive

	MEASURES
mm	Milimetre
kg	Kilogram
km/h	Kilometers per hour
l./100 km	Liters per 100 km

	OTHERS
NA	Not available
Cd	Coefficient drag
dc	Disc
dr	Drum
r&p.	Rack & Pinion
bal.	Recirculating balls
w&r	Worm & Roller
fr.	Front
rr.	Rear
pwr.	Power assistance
ABS	Anti-lock brake system

INDEX

Credits	2
Foreword/Abbreviations	3
Index	4-5
A few tips	6
How to use this guide	7

ACURA
CL	8
EL	10
Integra	12
MDX	14
RL	16
TL	18

AUDI
A4	20
A6/S4/S6	22
A8	24
Allroad	26
TT	28

BMW
3 Series	30
5 Series	34
7 Series	36
8 Series	38
X5	40
Z3	42

BUICK
Century (A)	104
Century (W)	144
Le Sabre	118
Park Avenue	108
Regal	144
Riviera	110
Roadmaster	106
Skylark	132

CADILLAC
Escalade	150
Catera	142
DeVille	122
Eldorado/Seville	122

CHEVROLET
Astro	130
Beretta	124
Blazer S-10	114
Camaro	112
Caprice	106
Cavalier	120
Corsica	124
Corvette	148
Impala	144
Impala SS	106
Lumina	144
Lumina APV/Minivan	136
Malibu	126
Metro	128
Monte Carlo	144
Suburban	150
Tahoe	150
Tracker	314
Venture	138

CHRYSLER
Cirrus	48
Concorde	50
Intrepid	52
Neon	60
New Yorker/LHS/300M	52
PT Cruiser	54
Sebring	46
Town & Country	58

DAEWOO
Lanos	64
Leganza	66
Nubira	68

DODGE
Avenger	46
Caravan	56
Durango	44
Grand Caravan	58
Intrepid	50
Neon	60
Stratus	48

EAGLE
Talon	62
Vision	50

FORD
Aerostar	70
Aspire	72
Contour	74
Crown Victoria	76
Escape	78
Escort	80
Excursion	82
Expedition	84
Explorer	86
Focus	88
Mustang	90
Probe	92
Taurus	94
Thunderbird	96
Windstar	102
ZX2	80

GEO
Metro	128
Tracker	302

GMC
Jimmy S-15	114
Safari	130
Suburban	156
Yukon	150
Yukon XL	150

HONDA
Accord	152
Civic	154
CR-V	156
del Sol	158
Insight	160
Odyssey	162
Prelude	164
S2000	166

HYUNDAI
Accent	168
Elantra	170
Santa Fe	172
Sonata	174
Tiburon	176
XG300	178

INFINITI
G20	180
I30	182
J30	184
Q45	186
QX4	188

ISUZU
Rodeo	190
Trooper	192

JAGUAR
S-Type	194
XJ	196
XJS	198
XK8	200

INDEX

JEEP
Cherokee	202
Grand Cherokee	204
YJ-TJ	206

KIA
Rio	208
Sephia	210
Sportage	212

LADA
Niva	214
Samara	216

LEXUS
ES	218
GS	220
LS	222
LX	224
RX	226
SC	222

LINCOLN
Continental	228
LS	230
Mark VIII	232
Navigator	234
Town Car	236

MAZDA
Miata	238
Millenia	240
MPV propulsion	242
MPV traction	244
MX-3 Precidia	246
Protegé	248
626/MX-6	250
Tribute	252

MERCEDES-BENZ
C Class	254
CLK	256
E Class	258
M Class	260
S Class	262
SL-CL	264
SLK	266

MERCURY
Cougar XR7	96
Cougar	98
Grand Marquis	76
Mystique	74
Sable	94
Villager	100

NISSAN
Altima	268
Maxima	270
Pathfinder	272
Quest	274
Sentra	276
Xterra	278
200SX	276
240SX	280
300ZX	282

OLDSMOBILE
Achieva	132
Alero	132
Aurora	116
Cutlass Ciera	104
Cutlass Supreme	144
Intrigue	144
Silhouette	138
88	118
98	108

PLYMOUTH
Breeze	48
Grand Voyager	58
Neon	60
Voyager	56

PONTIAC
Aztek	140
Bonneville	118
Firebird	112
Firefly	128
Grand Am	132
Grand Prix	144
Montana	138
Sunfire	120
Sunrunner	302
Trans Sport 1996	136
Trans Sport 97-01	138

SAAB
900-9^3	284
9000-9^5	286

SATURN
L	288
S	290

SUBARU
Forester	292
Impreza	294
Legacy	296
SVX	298

SUZUKI
Esteem	300
Sidekick	302
Swift	304
Vitara-Grand Vitara	306
X-90	308

TOYOTA
Avalon	310
Camry	312
Celica	314
Corolla	316
Echo	318
Highlander	320
Paseo	334
Previa	322
Prius	324
RAV4	326
Sequoia	328
Sienna	330
Solara	312
Supra	332
Tercel	334
4Runner	336

VOLKSWAGEN
Eurovan	338
Golf	340
Jetta	342
New Beetle	344
New Golf	346
New Jetta	348
New Passat	350
Passat	352

VOLVO
40 Series	354
60 Series	356
70 Series	358
80 Series	360
850 Series	362
900/90 Series	364

A FEW TIPS ON BUYING A USED CAR

WHERE CAN YOU FIND THE BEST BARGAINS?

- At dealerships which offer the best choice of recent model vehicles, with low kilometrage, but available at higher prices.
- At independent resellers, but beware of those who have no repair facilities on the premises or who offer recent model vehicles with high kilometrage.
- Through individuals, where prices are more affordable, but where no other warranties are available except the remainder of the vehicle's original warranty.
- In all cases, make sure that the vehicle's origin is correctly stipulated on the documents supplied to you, that the maintenance record is up-to-date and that copies of all major repair bills have been supplied.

VEHICLE INSPECTION

- Check the body in full daylight, look for repainting, any indication of previous accidents and make a detailed evaluation of the degree of rust present, especially on doors and the trunk lid.
- Wear patterns on tires are an indication whether balancing is good, tar residues on the end of the exhaust pipe indicates that the engine is burning oil because valves or other parts need replacement. Test shock absorbers by leaning hard on the vehicle, which should not bounce more than twice, and examine the exhaust system.

TEST DRIVING THE VEHICLE

- After examining the vehicle while it is standing still, you should insist on test driving it yourself. Take someone with you and have them sit in the back of the vehicle to detect any suspicious noises. As a first step, press down on pedals before starting the engine. The gas pedal and the clutch pedal should be firm and should return quickly to their normal position when released. Verify controls and dials on the instrument panel, check inside lights, headlights, and taillights: everything should be in good working order.
- The engine should start smoothly, with no unusual noises, knocking, whistling or rattling. Engage the handbrake and try to accelerate. The vehicle should go forward slightly, if not, the clutch or the transmission needs adjusting. When in motion, gear shifting should be smooth on automatic transmissions. It should be easy and precise on manual transmissions and the clutch pedal should not need excessive pressure.
- Use a clear area to apply brakes at 50 km/h; they should respond energetically and the vehicle should not deviate from its trajectory. On an incline, it should not move any further when the handbrake is engaged.
- When you return from the test drive, let the engine idle for a few minutes, move the vehicle forward, and check the ground for evidence of leaks.

THINGS TO REMEMBER

- Verify the origin of the vehicle with the manufacturer and with your insurance agent.
- When purchasing a privately owned vehicle, draw up a sales contract and include all pertinent details: the names and addresses of both parties, the vehicle's description, its serial number, the price you have actually paid.
- After the purchase, in writing, notify the manufacturer that you are the new owner of the vehicle and include its serial number; this will ensure that you can take advantage of the remainder of the original warranty and that you will receive notice of any future recalls.

IMPORTANT

Minimum and maximum price quotations provided in this Guide reflect the condition of cars built between 1996 and 2001, at the time of the purchase transaction.
The lowest value quoted applies to a vehicle in poor condition and the highest value quoted applies to a vehicle in the best possible condition.
The average of these two values can be considered to apply to a vehicle in normal condition given its age.
1) Average annual kilometrage is less than 20,000 km.
2) The body and mechanical system should not require any major repairs, nor should painting be necessary.
3) All accessories included as equipment should be in good working order.
4) Tires, shock absorbers and brake linings should have a potential that is equal to or greater than 50%.
5) If in doubt, have a professional proceed with a detailed evaluation to determine the true value of the vehicle you are considering.
Depending on the case, adjust the value using the following charts:

ADJUST THE PRICES ACCORDING TO THE KILOMETRAGE						
Km	2001	2000	1999	1998	1997	1996
ADD IN $						
10 000	225	370	475	625	770	850
20 000	0	275	375	550	650	750
30 000	375	175	250	375	475	550
40 000	500	0	175	275	400	500
50 000	650	300	125	225	325	425
60 000	850	450	0	150	225	350
70 000	1100	650	275	125	175	275
80 000	1275	825	450	0	125	225
90 000	1400	1100	600	250	100	175
100 000	1575	1250	950	400	0	125
110 000	1750	1300	1025	600	225	100
120 000	2000	1525	1125	750	475	0
130 000	2100	1725	1300	925	600	175
140 000	2300	2000	1400	1100	650	300
150 000	2525	2100	1650	1250	875	500
DEDUCT IN $						

EQUIPMENT
ADD IN $ IF NOT DELIVERED STANDARD

Equipment	1996	1997	1998	1999	2000	2001
Automatic transmission	225	325	475	625	800	900
Cruise control	75	100	125	150	175	200
Air conditioning	425	525	650	750	850	950
Electric windows	75	100	125	150	175	200
Electric door locks	100	125	150	175	200	225
Electric seats	100	125	150	175	200	225
Leather seats	175	225	275	325	400	500
Radio-cassette	175	200	225	250	275	325
CD player	225	250	275	325	350	425
Sunroof or T-top	325	425	525	675	750	800
Light alloy wheels	200	225	250	275	300	325

The Canadian Used Car Guide 2002-2003

ACURA CL

1999 ACURA 2.3 CL

The Acura CL is sold in a single two-door 2+2 body style, in either base or De Luxe 2.3 trim levels. The 2.3CL is powered by a 2.3L 4-cylinder engine and the 3.0CL is powered by a 3.0L V6 engine.

PROS
- **Streamlined style** with a futuristic look, especially the taillamps. The over-all effect is quite elegant, more so than are most of its rivals.
- **Comfortable drive**. The cabin seats four passengers with room to spare, but head room is a bit tight. The suspension handles big road faults like a charm, even though there's only average wheel travel.
- **A lot of commodities**, on a car of this like. The trunk is a nice size, and there's plenty of storage space everywhere.
- **Driving** is pleasant even with the 4-cylinder, the car makes quick moves and the suspension really controls car path. Steering is great, it's clean, though slightly firm and benefits from a good reduction ratio.
- **The cabin interior** is quite classy with the wood appliqués, leather trim seats, meticulous finish details and nice plastic trim that for once looks really neat.
- **The V6 engine** is smooth and quiet, puts out very good accelerations and pick-up, but it doesn't really move like a Sportscar.
- **Brakes** are good and firm, ABS helps achieve emergency stops of around 40 meters and are easy to apply.

CONS
- **The 4-cylinder engine** is a wimp, it's so smooth that it purrs like a big tabby, it never achieves the speed you'd expect on a sports coupe in this price category.
- **Maneuverability** isn't great with a 11.9m steer angle diameter and you have to take several cracks at most moves.
- **Rigidity isn't enough**, with the groans and rattles we heard on our two test cars when we hit the rippled road section on our test course.
- **The trunk** isn't convertible, it only connects to the cabin via a ski-sized pass-through and the trunk door is pretty narrow.
- **ABS** is somewhat unpredictable, sometimes it's slow on the trigger, and wheel lock occurs over several meters.
- **Unbelievable**: front seat belts that aren't height-adjustable and the standard sound system that, as they say, sucks.

CONCLUSION
All in all, this sports coupe is built more for civilized comfort than for wild sporty behavior.

RECALLS
None over this period.

CL   ACURA

RELIABILITY PROBLEMS

	1996	1997	1998	1999	2000	2001
Engine:		-	-	-	-	-
Transmission:		X	-	-	-	-
Suspension:		-	-	-	-	-
Steering:		-	-	-	-	-
Brakes:		-	-	-	-	-
Electricity:		X	X	-	-	-
Body:		X	X	-	-	-
Accessories:		X	-	-	-	-
Fit/finish:		X	-	-	-	-

POWERTRAIN

Year	Type/ L/Camshaft/bhp	Drivetrain & gearbox	Acceler. 0/100 sec.	Top speed km/h	Ave. Fuel consp. l./100 km
1997	L4/2.2/SOHC/145	front-M5	9.0	190	9.5
		front-A4	10.0	180	10.5
98-99	L4/2.3/SOHC/150	front-M5	9.0	190	9.6
		front-A4	10.0	180	10.4
97-99	V6/3.0/SOHC/200	front-A4	8.5	200	12.0
2001	V6/3.2/SOHC/225	front-A5	8.2	200	12.0
	V6/3.2/DOHC/260	front-A5	7.5	220	12.2

PERFORMANCE

SPECIFICATIONS

Model	Wlb. mm	Lght. mm	Cb.wt kg	Brakes fr/rr	Steering type	Standard tires
cpe. 2dr. 2.2	2715	4826	1365	dc/ABS	pwr.r&p.	205/55R16
cpe. 2dr. 2.3	2715	4830	1362	dc/ABS	pwr.r&p.	205/55R16
cpe. 2dr. 3.0	2715	4830	1466	dc/ABS	pwr.r&p.	205/55R16
cpe. 2 dr. 3.2	2715	4877	1574	dc/ABS	pwr.r&p.	205/60R16
cpe. 2 dr. 3.2 S	2715	4877	1592	dc/ABS	pwr.r&p.	215/50R17

PRICES

Model / version		1996	1997	1998	1999	2000	2001
cpe. 2dr. 2.2	mini		13850				
	maxi		16050				
cpe. 2dr. 2.2 Prem	mini		14800				
	maxi		17200				
cpe. 2dr. 2.3	mini				18500	20250	
	maxi				20150	23100	
cpe. 2dr. 3.0	mini			16150	19750	22350	
	maxi			18800	22050	25200	
cpe. 2dr. 3.2	mini						29700
	maxi						32550
cpe. 2dr. Type S	mini						31000
	maxi						33600

See page 7 to adapt these figures.

2001 ACURA 3.2 CL

ACURA EL

ACURA EL 2001

The Acura EL is supposed to attract buyers who can't afford an Integra. In fact, it is a dressed up Honda Civic loaded with equipment. It is a four-door sedan in base, Sport and Premium trim levels. It's powered by a 1.6L engine.

PROS

- **Roadhandling** benefits from the excellent original tires and 15-inch wheels. Equipped with two standard stabilizer bars, the EL models take curves very nicely and they're quite agile on slalom runs.
- **Comfort** is good because the suspension handles bumps beautifully and there's less engine roar and vibration. Seats offer good support, but the upholstery is firm.
- **The VTEC engine** is fuel-efficient for normal driving, for the performance it delivers.
- **Commodities**, the trunk is roomy enough when at full passenger capacity and it can also be extended. There are a goodly number of storage compartments in the cabin, but they aren't terribly generous.
- **Build quality** and finish details are scrupulously executed and the cabin interior is spiffy, especially the seat coverings and plastic trim on the dashboard that's the same as on the Civic.
- **This car has inherited** some nice features from the Civic: an ergonomic dashboard, clear outward view and simple gauges and controls.
- **These cars** are really plush-looking, even with the nothing-new body design. Dressed up in certain colors, the EL looks like a little gem.

CONS

- **Performance** are so-and-so because of vehicle weight, due to the rich equipment and safety-oriented vehicle rigidity.
- **Brakes** on the base model are poor, because they aren't linked to ABS, front wheels lock on emergency stops.
- **The EL body** design isn't unattractive, but it's just as nondescript as that of the Civic.
- **The engine** isn't at all well-mannered, it screeches and snorts whenever your toe touches the gas pedal.
- **The automatic shifter** is jumpy and cuts out a few precious horsepower, especially when the air conditioner is functioning.

CONCLUSION

The Acura EL isn't a bad idea in this day and age when everyone wants to drive a ritzy car, but can't always afford one.

RECALLS

96-98 Right frontal air bag needs to be repaired.
2001 Corroded fuel pump and loose hose clamp will be checked by dealers.

EL ACURA

RELIABILITY PROBLEMS

	1996	1997	1998	1999	2000	2001
Engine:		X	X	X	-	-
Transmission:		-	-	-	-	-
Suspension:		X	-	-	-	-
Steering:		-	-	-	-	-
Brakes:		X	-	-	-	-
Electricity:		-	-	-	X	X
Body:		X	X	X	-	-
Accessories:		-	-	X	X	X
Fit/finish:		-	-	-	-	-

POWERTRAIN

Year	Type/ L/Camshaft/bhp	Drivetrain & gearbox	Acceler. 0/100 sec.	Top. speed km/h	Ave. Fuel consp. l./100 km
97-00	L4/1.6/SOHC/127	front-M5	8.8	190	8.3
		front-A4	10.0	180	9.1
2001	L4/1.7/SOHC/127	front-M5	9.5	190	7.7
		front-A4	10.5	185	8.0

SPECIFICATIONS

Model	Wlb. mm	Lght. mm	Cb.wt kg	Brakes fr/rr	Steering type	Standard tires
97-00						
sdn. 4dr.base/SE	2620	4478	1124	dc/dr	pwr.r&p.	195/55R15
sdn. 4dr. Sport	2620	4478	1144	dc/dr/ABS	pwr.r&p.	195/55R15
sdn. 4dr. Prem.	2620	4478	1162	dc/dr/ABS	pwr.r&p.	195/55R15
2001						
ber. 4 p. Tour.	2620	4488	1155	dc/dr/ABS	pwr.r&p.	185/65R15
ber. 4 p. Prem.	2620	4488	1172	dc/dr/ABS	pwr.r&p.	185/65R15

PRICES

Model / version		1996	1997	1998	1999	2000	2001
sdn. 4dr.	mini		10800	12200			
	maxi		12600	13950			
sdn. 4dr. SE	mini				13450	15750	
	maxi				15200	17850	
sdn. 4dr. Sport	mini		11850	13200	14500	16800	
	maxi		13650	14700	16300	18900	
sdn. 4dr. Premium	mini		12900	14300	15550	18400	20250
	maxi		14700	16050	17300	20500	22600
sdn. 4dr. Touring	mini						18900
	maxi						21000

See page 7 to adapt these figures.

2000 ACURA EL

ACURA   Integra

2000 ACURA Integra

The Acura Integra was first sold in Canada in 1987 and its body design got the latest face-lift in '94.

PROS
- **Top-notch** reliability, akin to that of Honda products.
- **The 1.8L engine** is more muscular than the former generation 1.6L, especially the latest Type-R's which its 195-hp offers some rather exotic accelerations.
- **Sportscar-like handling** is great with the well-adjusted suspension.
- **The comfy cluster** of seat, steering wheel and instrument panel makes for pleasant driving.
- **The 4-disc brakes** are very effective.
- **Rack and pinion** steering is precise, well-calibrated and has a good reduction ratio.
- **Equipment** is more complete on the LS and GS models.
- **The modular rear seatbench** allows for trunk extension and for greater luggage capacity.

CONS
- **Rear seats** on the coupes are snug and hard to get to.
- **The sedan** body design is too blah and run-of-the-mill for a car of this class.
- **Some trim** materials look chintzy.
- **The automatic gear box** siphons off a lot of power and makes the engine roar and sputter.
- **The sporty suspension** isn't terribly smooth.
- **Soundproofing** on lower-end models isn't what it should be.
- **The poorly upholstered seats** are a pain on long trips.
- **The high trunk** opening doesn't make for easy luggage handling.

CONCLUSION
The Integra, a reliable, economical car with a Sportscar character, doesn't depreciate or lose its stylish charm as much as its main rivals.

RECALLS
None over this period.

Integra   ACURA

RELIABILITY PROBLEMS

	1996	1997	1998	1999	2000	2001
Engine:	-	-	-	-	-	-
Transmission:	-	-	-	-	-	-
Suspension:	-	-	-	-	-	-
Steering:	-	-	-	-	-	-
Brakes:	-	X	X	X	X	-
Electricity:	X	-	-	-	X	-
Body:	X	X	-	-	-	-
Accessories:	X	X	X	X	-	X
Fit/finish:	X	X	-	-	-	-

POWERTRAIN

Year	Type/ L/Camshaft/bhp	Drivetrain & gearbox
96-01	L4/1.8/DOHC/130-139	front-M5
		front-A4
	L4/1.8/DOHC/170	front-M5
		front-A4
98-01	L4/1.8/DOHC/195	front-M5

PERFORMANCE

Acceler. 0/100 sec.	Top. speed km/h	Ave. Fuel consp. l./100 km
8.8	200	9.3
9.6	190	9.8
7.5	210	9.3
8.6	200	9.5
7.0	220	9.5

SPECIFICATIONS

Model 1996	Wlb. mm	Lght. mm	Cb.wt kg	Brakes fr/rr	Steering type	Standard tires
sdn. 4dr. RS	2620	4525	1172	dc/dc	pwr.r&p.	195/60R14
cpe. 2dr. LS	2620	4525	1205	dc/dc	pwr.r&p.	195/60R14
sdn. 4dr. LS	2620	4525	1243	dc/dc	pwr.r&p.	195/60R14
96-00						
cpe. 2dr.RS/SE	2570	4380	1147	dc/dc	pwr.r&p.	195/60R14
cpe. 2dr. LS	2570	4380	1170	dc/dc	pwr.r&p.	195/60R14
cpe. 2dr. GS	2570	4380	1197	dc/ABS	pwr.r&p.	195/55R15
cpe. 2dr. GS-R	2570	4380	1214	dc/ABS	pwr.r&p.	195/55R15
cpe. 2dr. Type R	2570	4380	1161	dc/ABS	pwr.r&p.	195/55R15

PRICES

Model / version		1996	1997	1998	1999	2000	2001
sdn. 4 dr. RS	mini	10200					
	maxi	12200					
sdn. 4 dr. LS	mini	11150					
	maxi	13200					
sdn. 4 dr. SE	mini	12200					
	maxi	14050					
cpe. 2 dr. RS	mini	9700	11850	13200			
	maxi	11950	13650	15000			
cpe. 2 dr. LS	mini	10900	13950				
	maxi	13000	15750				
cpe. 2 dr. GS	mini		15000	15850	17650	18400	21500
	maxi		16800	17650	19400	20500	23600
cpe. 2 dr. SE	mini	12200			15000	15750	17300
	maxi	14100			16800	17850	19400
cpe. 2 dr. GS-R	mini	12700	16050	16800	18700	20500	23100
	maxi	14600	17850	18700	20500	22600	25800
cpe. 2dr. Anniv.Ed	mini		12400				
	maxi		14300				
cpe. 2 dr. Type R	mini		19200	20600	22350	23600	25700
	maxi		21600	22900	24150	25700	27800

See page 7 to adapt these figures.

ACURA MDX

2001 ACURA MDX

Acura took its sweet time to develop its high-end sport-utility vehicle. The result is than much more competitive.

PROS
- **The sober and classic lines** are nevertheless modern and will pass the test of time better than some of its competitors that are already outdated.
- **The MDX has enough interior room** to accommodate seven people in three rows of seats; this makes it about as roomy as a compact minivan.
- **The very sophisticated engine** cranks out brilliant performance, and Honda is the only one to know its secrets since it also equips the Odyssey.
- **The brakes** are powerful, efficient and perfectly balanced. As a result, the hefty MDX comes safely to a stop over short distances. However, fade resistance could be improved.
- **The MDX** is closer to an automobile than a utility vehicle when it comes to ride comfort, because it benefits from a supple suspension as well as efficient shock absorbers and soundproofing.
- **The bin** housed in the floor under the luggage compartment is useful to keep valuables away from prying eyes.

CONS
- **The rear seats** are not comfortable because the benches' cushions are very short, the seatbacks too flat and rear legroom is at a premium.
- **The windshield wipers** are terribly slow and are unable to provide adequate visibility in pouring rain.
- **The plastic materials** look rather cheap; they have a utilitarian look to them that sticks out like a sore thumb in a vehicle of this status and price.
- **Front-seat access** is hindered by the lack of grab handles. Acura could have installed some on the A pillars as most of the competition does.
- **The ridiculous compact spare tire** has no place on a vehicle of such luxury. Here again, Acura shows a lack of judgement in a market segment where competition is fierce.

VERDICT
Technically speaking, the MDX is a remarkable SUV, but its equipment is unfortunately tarnished by certain annoying details.

RECALLS
None over this period.

MDX   ACURA

RELIABILITY PROBLEMS

	1996	1997	1998	1999	2000	2001
Engine:						
Transmission:						
Suspension:						
Steering:						
Brakes:			Insufficient data			
Electricity:						
Body:						
Accessories:						
Fit/finish:						

POWERTRAIN   PERFORMANCE

Year	Type/ L/Camshaft/bhp	Drivetrain & gearbox	Acceler. 0/100 sec.	Top. speed km/h	Ave. Fuel consp. l./100 km
2001	V6/3.5/SACT/240	all-A5	8.5	185	14.0

SPECIFICATIONS

Model 2001	Wlb. mm	Lght. mm	Cb.wt kg	Brakes fr/rr	Steering type	Standard tires
wgn. 4 dr.	2700	4789	1965	dc/ABS	pwr.r&p.	235/65R17

PRICES

Model / version		1996	1997	1998	1999	2000	2001
wgn. 4 dr.	mini						42500
	maxi						46000

See page 7 to adapt these figures.

2001 ACURA MDX

ACURA   RL

2000 ACURA 3.5RL

Put on the market in 1987, the Legend was the very first Japanese luxury car. It underwent some design modifications in 1991 and in 1996, when it was named the RL.

PROS
• **It is one of the most reliable** car on the market.
• **Its body design** is elegant, but it doesn't have an ounce of character.
• **Driving** is much more enjoyable at the wheel of a coupe powered by a manual transmission.
• **The driver is really spoiled** with such a good driver's position, convenient instrument panel and clear all-round visibility.
• **Build quality** is top-notch.
• **Handling** is generally clean and crisp.
• **Driving** is cushy in such a quiet, spacious interior; there's no vibration whatsoever and seats are well-designed.
• **Fuel consumption** is very reasonable for a car of such displacement and size.

CONS
• **Even the new 210-bhp** V6 engine only yields fair to middling power and torque, it's really quite gutless.
• **Braking power** is generally rather poor because of vehicle weight but stops are mostly straight or predictable, thanks to the ABS.
• **The automatic** siphons off engine output and shifting speeds can be pretty rough and uneven; the 6-speed manual is imprecise and nothing special, given the speed limits that have to be respected by law-abiding citizens.
• **Steering** is over-assisted and crippled by a too high reduction ratio.
• **The terribly** "synthetic"-looking instrument panel on the RL.
• **Trunk capacity** isn't proportional to interior cabin space.
• **The seats** aren't terribly comfortable, for they're poorly contoured and upholstered, and the seat on the seatbench is too short.

CONCLUSION
The Legend-RL models really lack charisma and character and they trail far behind their Lexus and Infiniti rivals, as far as luxury, comfort or power go.

RECALLS
96-98 Front suspension lower ball joints may prematurely wear out.

RL — ACURA

RELIABILITY PROBLEMS

	1996	1997	1998	1999	2000	2001
Engine:	X	X	-	-	-	-
Transmission:	-	-	-	-	-	-
Suspension:	X	X	X	-	-	-
Steering:	-	-	-	-	-	-
Brakes:	-	-	-	X	-	-
Electricity:	X	-	X	X	X	-
Body:	X	X	X	-	-	-
Accessories:	X	-	X	X	X	X
Fit/finish:	-	-	-	-	-	-

POWERTRAIN

Year	Type/ L/Camshaft/bhp	Drivetrain & gearbox
96-01	V6/3.5/SOHC/210	front-A4

PERFORMANCE

Acceler. 0/100 sec.	Top. speed km/h	Ave. Fuel consp. l./100 km
8.5	200	12.6

SPECIFICATIONS

Model 96-01	Wlb. mm	Lght. mm	Cb.wt kg	Brakes fr/rr	Steering type	Standard tires
sdn. 4dr. RL	2910	4995	1655	dc/ABS	pwr.r&p.	215/60R16

PRICES

Model / version		1996	1997	1998	1999	2000	2001
sdn. 4dr. RL	mini	16900	20250	25800	28550	33600	44600
	maxi	20350	23700	29100	32550	37300	48300

0

See page 7 to adapt these figures.

1998 ACURA 3.5RL

ACURA TL

2001 ACURA 3.2TL Type S

Built on the Honda Accord platform, the Vigor just hasn't found its niche in the luxury compact market. It became the TL in 1996 and was equipped with the V6 Legend engine. The Type S version was introduced in 2001.

PROS

- **Its clean, classic body** design isn't sensational, but it never goes out of style.
- **The 3.2L V6 engine** has sure added character to the TL, due to a better power to weight ratio.
- **Handling is fine**, but the supple suspension doesn't make for crisp Sportscar moves or maneuvers.
- **Build quality**, fit and finish and materials are absolutely top-notch.
- **Well-designed** suspension and soundproofing make long drives enjoyable and fatigue-free.
- **A rigid frame** resists impact and enhances safety features.
- **The sequential automatic gearbox** that equipped the 99 TL, logically delays upshifting when climbing an incline and applies braking effect by automatically downshifting when going downhill.

CONS

- **The 5-cylinder** engine is a real wimp compared to the V6.
- **Cabin space** is snug, especially in the rear seats where there isn't much head room or leg room.
- **Steering** the Vigor-TL makes you feel like you're driving one of those big American cars of the '70's, for it's over-assisted and has too high a reduction ratio.
- **Vehicle weight** really affects engine performance, especially with four passengers aboard and a trunk chock-full of luggage.
- **Brakes lack** gripping power, the pedal is soft and takes a while to get used to.
- **Aerodynamic efficiency** is disappointing (0.37), given that the car was designed in the nineties.

CONCLUSION

Like the Vigor, the TL hasn't been a smashing success, for there's nothing special about it, nothing to make it stand out among so many other models in the same category.

RECALLS

1998 Front suspension lower ball joints may prematurely wear out.

TL   ACURA

RELIABILITY PROBLEMS

	1996	1997	1998	1999	2000	2001
Engine:	X	X	-	-	-	-
Transmission:	-	-	-	-	-	-
Suspension:	X	-	X	-	-	-
Steering:	-	-	-	-	-	-
Brakes:	X	-	-	-	-	-
Electricity:	-	X	-	X	X	-
Body:	-	X	X	-	-	-
Accessories:	X	-	X	X	X	-

POWERTRAIN

Year	Type/ L/Camshaft/bhp	Drivetrain & gearbox
96-98	L5/2.5/SOHC/176	front-A4
96-00	V6/3.2/SOHC/200-225	front-A4
2001	V6/3.2/DOHC/225 (S)	front-A5

PERFORMANCE

Acceler. 0/100 sec.	Top. speed km/h	Ave. Fuel consp. l./100 km
9.3	200	11.9
8.6	220	12.3
7.2	220	13.4

SPECIFICATIONS

Model	Wlb. mm	Lght. mm	Cb.wt kg	Brakes fr/rr	Steering type	Standard tires
96-98						
sdn. 4dr. 2.5TL	2840	4865	1480	dc/ABS	pwr.r&p.	205/60R15
98-01						
sdn. 4dr. 3.2TL	2745	4900	1565	dc/ABS	pwr.r&p.	205/60R16
2001						
sdn. 4dr. 3.2TLS	2745	4900	1614	dc/ABS	pwr.r&p.	215/50R17

PRICES

Model / version		1996	1997	1998	1999	2000	2001
sdn. 4dr. 2.5	mini	10600	15550	18900			
	maxi	13650	18500	21850			
sdn. 4dr. 3.2	mini	12700	17650	21500	23950	26250	31000
	maxi	15750	20600	23950	26800	28900	34100
sdn. 4 dr. 3.2 S	mini						34100
	maxi						39400

See page 7 to adapt these figures.

1998 ACURA 2.5 TL

The Canadian Used Car Guide 2002-2003

AUDI A4

1997 AUDI A4

The A4 that came out in 1996 had what was missing in the 90, in other words, it had a very winsome and charming look, but was still equipped with most of the mechanical features of its predecessor.

PROS
- **A nicely shaped**, striking body design.
- **With the right tires**, the Quattro all-wheel drive makes for safer handling in winter conditions, and the A4 really holds the road in most cases.
- **Engine performance** are impressive, thanks to a good power to weight ratio and to a well-suited 5-speed automatic gear box.
- **The build is very rigid**, fit and finish are meticulous and materials are top-notch, and reliability is no longer a problem.
- **Monocoque body** is made entirely of galvanized steel, so it provides one of the best warranty in the world to win the war against rust.
- **Overall comfort** is great due to a supple suspension, contoured and well-cushioned seats and effective soundproofing that blocks out engine and road noise.
- **A comfortable driver's position**, good visibility and a straightforward and practical instrument panel make for pleasant driving.
- **There are plenty** of good-sized storage compartments and the trunk is expandable and of easy access with its large opening.

CONS
- **Price tag** isn't too popular and the V6 sure guzzles the gas and of course, upkeep and repairs can cost an arm and a leg.
- **Cabin space** is quite snug in the rear seat, there's more head room and hip room, but leg room is quite tight.
- **Steering** is a bit over-assisted and becomes light and sensitive at high speeds. Luckily the body isn't sensitive to wind.
- **The typically European** controls take getting used to.
- **The Audi service** network is quite limited, which makes upkeep a bit touchy.

CONCLUSION
People who are out to impress others will opt for this high-tech sophisticated model, but their choice won't be cheap...

RECALLS
96-97 Airbags are defective.
1996 Intermittent horn malfunction.
1998 Air flow meter's screen is defective.
97-99 Possible loss of power brake assist at low temperatures.

A4 — AUDI

RELIABILITY PROBLEMS

	1996	1997	1998	1999	2000	2001
Engine:	X	X	-	-	-	-
Transmission:	X	X	X	-	-	-
Suspension:	-	-	-	-	-	-
Steering:	-	-	-	-	-	-
Brakes:	-	X	-	X	X	-
Electricity:	-	X	X	X	X	X
Body:	X	-	-	-	-	-
Accessories:	X	X	X	X	X	X
Fit/finish:	-	-	-	X	-	-

POWERTRAIN

Year 96-2000	Type/ L/Camshaft/bhp	Drivetrain & gearbox
1.8	L4T/1.8/DOHC/150	front-M5
		front-A5
1.8 q.	L4T/1.8/DOHC/150	all-M5
		all-A5
2.8	V6/2.8/DOHC/172-190	front-M5
		front-A4
2.8 q.	V6/2.8/DOHC/172-190	all-M5
		all-A5

PERFORMANCE

Acceler. 0/100 sec.	Top speed km/h	Ave. Fuel consp. l./100 km
8.8	210	10.2
9.6	200	11.3
9.0	200	13.2
10.0	200	12.1
8.7	210	11.7
9.7	200	12.9
10.0	200	12.2
10.5	190	13.5

SPECIFICATIONS

Model	Wlb. mm	Lght. mm	Cb.wt kg	Brakes fr/rr	Steering type	Standard tires
sdn. 4dr. 1.8	2617	4522	1305	dc/ABS	r&p.r&p.	205/60R15
sdn. 4dr. 1.8 q.	2607	4522	1420	dc/ABS	r&p.r&p.	205/60R15
sdn. 4dr. 2.8	2617	4522	1400	dc/ABS	r&p.r&p.	205/55R16
sdn. 4dr. 2.8 q.	2607	4522	1505	dc/ABS	r&p.r&p.	205/55R16

PRICES

Model / version		1996	1997	1998	1999	2000	2001
sdn. 4dr. 1.8T	mini		16275	18600	21700	27800	32550
	maxi		19300	21700	24900	30750	35200
sdn. 4dr. 1.8T Q.	mini		16800	19500	22700	30450	35200
	maxi		19950	22800	25900	33400	37800
sdn. 4dr. 2.8	mini	14700	18900	21500	24700	29900	34650
	maxi	17850	22450	24900	28000	32850	36750
sdn. 4dr. 2.8 Q.	mini	15550	19950	22450	25600	33000	37800
	maxi	18900	23500	25900	29000	36000	40400

See page 7 to adapt these figures.

AUDI A6/S4-S6

1997 AUDI A6

The A6, redesigned in '95, is available with front-wheel drive or Quattro all-wheel drive and are driven by the 2.8L V6, while the sporty S4 is powered by a 2.2L 5-cylinder. The A6 was renewed in 1998 and a 2.7 V6 Turbo and a V8 engines where added in 2000.

PROS

- **The Quattro system** provides excellent traction in all kinds of weather, which makes for remarkable handling, especially in snow.
- **The sporty S4/S6/2.7/4.2** models are thrilling to drive and they are real spoilers too, because they are so plush.
- **In some respects**, build quality and fit and finish are superior to that of BMW and Mercedes cars.
- **The body shape** of the 1998 A6 is classic yet has a lot more character than its predecessors.
- **The cabin comfortably** seats five adults and the trunk is spacious and of easy access, even if it isn't expandable.
- **Equipment** is very lush and a real treat.
- **The 6-cylinder** engine is smooth, powerful and economical.
- **As far as rust goes**, you don't have a care in the world with a completely galvanized steel body. A world first.

CONS

- **With such a heavy vehicle**, the V6 seems to strain and sputter and performance is at the base limit of what you'd expect for a model of this price...
- **Steering** is terribly over-assisted, so you have to really keep an eye on it.
- **The suspension** is too flexible and causes a lot of sway.
- **Some of the controls** are quite unconventional and require getting used to.
- **Maintenance** isn't cheap when the warranty runs out and resale value plummets, so you don't see too many of these cars on the road.

CONCLUSION

In spite of its high-tech features, build quality and reliability, this model isn't too popular as a new or used car because of consumer mistrust of Audi products.

RECALLS

96-97 Airbags are defective.
1998 Air flow meter's screen is defective.
98-00 Defective fuel tank sensors give false indications about the real amount of fuel.

A6/S4-S6 — AUDI

RELIABILITY PROBLEMS

	1996	1997	1998	1999	2000	2001
Engine:	X	X	X	X	-	-
Transmission:	X	X	-	-	X	X
Suspension:	-	-	X	X	-	-
Steering:	-	-	X	X	-	-
Brakes:	-	-	X	X	-	-
Electricity:	X	X	X	X	X	X
Body:	-	-	-	-	-	-
Accessories:	X	X	X	X	X	-
Fit/finish:	-	-	-	-	-	X

POWERTRAIN

Year	Type/ L/Camshaft/bhp	Drivetrain & gearbox
96-97		
base	V6/2.8/SOHC/172	front-A4
quat.	V6/2.8/SOHC/172	all-A4
S4-S6	L5T/2.3/SOHC/227	all-M5
98-01		
base	V6/2.8/DOHC/193-200	front-A5
quat.	V6/2.8/DOHC/193-200	all-A5
00-01		
2.7T	V6T/DOHC/250	all-A5
4.2	V8/4.2/DOHC/300	all-A5

PERFORMANCE

	Acceler. 0/100 sec.	Top. speed km/h	Ave. Fuel consp. l/100 km
	10.0	210	13.3
	11.2	210	12.6
	7.0	210	12.7
	9.6	230	13.4
	11.0	225	13.8
	7.2	210	13.5
	6.7	210	14.0

SPECIFICATIONS

Model	Wlb. mm	Lght. mm	Cb.wt kg	Brakes fr/rr	Steering type	Standard tires
96-97						
sdn. 4dr.	2692	4892	1535	dc/ABS	pwr.r&p.	195/65R15
sdn. 4dr. q.	2692	4892	1665	dc/ABS	pwr.r&p.	195/65R15
wgn. 4dr.	2692	4892	1685	dc/ABS	pwr.r&p.	195/65R15
sdn. 4dr. S4	2692	4892	1715	dc/ABS	pwr.r&p.	225/50R16
sdn. 4dr. S6	2692	4892	1715	dc/ABS	pwr.r&p.	225/50R16
98-01						
sdn. 4dr.	2760	4878	1575	dc/ABS	pwr.r&p.	205/55R16
sdn. 4dr. q.	2759	4878	1680	dc/ABS	pwr.r&p.	205/55R16
wgn. 4dr. q.	2759	4878	1749	dc/ABS	pwr.r&p.	195/65R15
00-01						
sdn. 4dr. 2.7 q	2760	4878	1705	dc/ABS	pwr.r&p.	205/55R16
sdn. 4dr. 4.2 q	2759	4912	1825	dc/ABS	pwr.r&p.	235/50R16

PRICES

Model / version		1996	1997	1998	1999	2000	2001
A6							
sdn. 4dr.	mini	17650		28350	32550	34550	40400
	maxi	21200		32350	36550	38850	43350
sdn. 4dr. quat.	mini	19200	24900	29400	33600	37150	43600
	maxi	23300	28750	33400	37600	42000	46500
sdn. 4dr. 2.7 q.	mini					41900	47800
	maxi					46200	50700
sdn. 4dr. 4.2 q.	mini					53100	59300
	maxi					57550	62250
wgn. 4dr.	mini	18300					
	maxi	22300					
wgn. 4dr. q.	mini	21200	26750				
	maxi	25400	30650				
wgn. 4dr. q. IV	mini				35200	39800	45650
	maxi				39150	44100	48600
S4							
sdn. 4dr. 2.7 q.	mini					44800	51450
	maxi					48600	54400
S6							
sdn. 4dr.	mini	21000	29400				
	maxi	25400	33600				

See page 7 to adapt these figures.

AUDI — A8

1999 AUDI A8 4.2

The first V8-powered Audi came on the market towards the end of 1992, whereas the A8 has been sold since 1997 and makes more than one dream about. The S8 version was introduced in 2001.

PROS

- **Roadability** with the exclusive Torsen quattro system is super, especially in winter conditions.
- **The remarkable V8** engine pumps out real sporty zoom, yet these roomy sedans are luxurious and practical.
- **The 4.2L** engine is smooth and zippy and fuel consumption is reasonable with the front-wheel drive mode.
- **Four-disc brakes** provide honorable braking, but linings wear out quickly and have to be replaced often.
- **The cabin comfortably** seats five passengers and the trunk holds quite a bit of luggage.
- **Steering** is smooth and precise.
- **The galvanized** steel body on the first models or aluminum body on the more recent models holds up well against rust.
- **The array** of equipment is lush and refined.

CONS

- **Maintenance and repairs** are pricy, so the privilege of driving such a high-tech vehicle doesn't come cheap.
- **Driving pleasure** is a mixed bag with the A8, due to the prim and proper behavior of such a perfect specimen that seems to lack soul.
- **Body and cabin design** are rather blah, which doesn't quite match the modern engineering that comes with the package.
- **The quattro versions** are gas guzzlers due to the hefty weight and its all-wheel drive mechanism.
- **These heavy, bulky cars** can't boast of athletic agility on slalom runs.

CONCLUSION

The innovative features of the V8-powered Audi cost a bundle when it comes to upkeep and repairs. Best to think twice before making such an investment.

RECALLS

1997 Airbags are defective.

A8   AUDI

RELIABILITY PROBLEMS

	1996	1997	1998	1999	2000	2001
Engine:						
Transmission:						
Suspension:						
Steering:						
Brakes:			Insufficient data			
Electricity:						
Body:						
Accessories:						
Fit/finish:						

POWERTRAIN / PERFORMANCE

Year	Type/ L/Camshaft/bhp	Drivetrain & gearbox	Acceler. 0/100 sec.	Top. speed km/h	Ave. Fuel consp. l./100 km
97-01	V8/4.2/DOHC/300-310	all-A5	7.5	210	14.0
2001	V8/4.2/DOHC/360 S8	all-A5	6.5	240	16.0

SPECIFICATIONS

Model	Wlb.	Lght.	Cb.wt	Brakes	Steering	Standard
97-01						
sdn. 4dr. A8	2882	5034	1770	dc/ABS	pwr.r&p.	225/60R16
00-01						
sdn. 4dr. A8L	3010	5164	1885	dc/ABS	pwr.r&p.	225/60R16
2001						
sdn. 4dr. S8	2880	5034	1845	dc/ABS	pwr.r&p.	245/45R18

PRICES

Model / version		1996	1997	1998	1999	2000	2001
sdn. 4dr. q. A8	mini		36750	41500	48800	53200	61600
	maxi		40900	45600	53550	57750	64600
sdn. 4dr. q. S8	mini						79300
	maxi						82200

See page 7 to adapt these figures.

1998 AUDI A8 4.2

The Canadian Used Car Guide 2002-2003

AUDI Allroad

2001 AUDI Allroad

The Allroad is based on the A6 Avant and equipped with a height-adjustable suspension that enables it to travel "somewhat" off the beaten path, somewhat being the key word because it's not a true all-terrain vehicle.

PROS
- The model is a shining example of **active and passive safety**, a rarity among multi-purpose vehicles.
- **It's remarkably versatile**, combining luxury and utility features.
- **Assembly and finish quality** are remarkable, and the Audi even outclasses its reputed German rivals in this respect.
- **The twin-turbo V6** cranks out high performance and makes this luxurious utilitarian feel like an exotic.
- **The generous cabin and cargo bay** make it possible for five people to travel aboard in full comfort and bring their luggage along with them.
- **The extended warranty** will keep bad surprises due to defects at bay for original owners.
- **Audi models' resale value** is progressing quite well, but many potential buyers fear the high repair costs associated with these technological marvels.

CONS
- This luxury car comes with a **high price tag** and commands expensive maintenance costs, placing it out of the financial reach of most buyers.
- **The Allroad's off-road capabilities** are limited, and it's far from being a real all-terrain vehicle.
- **The turbocharger** is plagued by an annoyingly long turbo lag; making the most of the engine's power therefore takes some getting used to.
- **The Tiptronic shifter** is not as practical to use as other similar systems on the market.
- **The harsh suspension** and extremely firm seats are not very comfortable but typical of German automobiles.
- **The steering** is too light and fuzzy because it's overassisted. Drivers must exercise caution when travelling in strong crosswinds or on slippery surfaces.
- **The windshield wipers** are terribly slow and do not provide adequate visibility in heavy rain.
- **The digital information display** housed in the middle of the instrument panel is completely impossible to decipher during the day.

VERDICT
The Allroad remains a marginal model that will interest only the make's fanatics, because other auto makers offer models that are just as good but less expensive.

RECALLS
None over this period.

Allroad AUDI

RELIABILITY PROBLEMS

	1996	1997	1998	1999	2000	2001
Engine:						
Transmission:						
Suspension:						
Steering:						
Brakes:			Insufficient data			
Electricity:						
Body:						
Accessories:						
Fit/finish:						

POWERTRAIN

Year	Type/ L/Camshaft/bhp	Drivetrain & gearbox
2001	V6T/2.7/DOHC/250	all-M6

PERFORMANCE

Acceler. 0/100 sec.	Top. speed km/h	Ave. Fuel consp. l./100 km
7.5	210	15.0

SPECIFICATIONS

Model	Wlb. mm	Lght. mm	Cb.wt kg	Brakes fr/rr	Steering type	Standard tires
wgn. 4dr.	2757	4810	1890	dc/ABS	pwr.r&p.	225/55R17

PRICES

Model / version		1996	1997	1998	1999	2000	**2001**
wag. 4dr. Quat.	mini						41500
	maxi						44600

See page 7 to adapt these figures.

2001 AUDI Allroad

AUDI TT

2000 AUDI TT convertible

Derived from the A4, the TT coupe, which is equipped with a 1.8-liter engine, compete with the BMW Z3 and the Mercedes SLK.

PROS
- **The bulky style** of this speedster that looks solid as a rock.
- **Safety** is insured by the extremely stiff body and front and side-impact airbags.
- **Performance** of the base engine are fun but its 225 hp version seems sometimes too powerful...
- **Handling** of the quattro version is impressive, because the car seems to be literally glued to the road.
- **Brakes** are easy to adjust, grip smoothly and progressively. Stopping distances are short and fade resistance very good.
- **The suspension** isn't really too supple, but it benefits from enough travel to take a bruising from the bumps, without jostling occupants.
- **Cabin design** is gorgeous since it imitates race car stylistics with all this polished metal inserts.
- **High quality** of engineering, assembly and finish which is simply flawless.
- **Convenient** storage bins and the regular shapes of the trunk.

CONS
- **Steering** system springs and lacks of accuracy on FWD.
- **Visibility** isn't ideal because the seating position is low, the body belt high and roof pillars are very thick.
- **Access** to the rear seats is no picnic and their use is very limited.
- **Center console** gobbles up a lot of space, especially the aluminum bar that forms a handle that you're always hitting your knee against.
- **Remote-control** switches to open the rear hatch door, gas tank filler hole cap and to deactivate the alarm system are hard to reach, hidden in a compartment at the extremity of the center console.

CONCLUSION
Against its competitors the TT coupe offers the advantage of year-round driveability thanks to a very reliable quattro AWD system.

RECALLS
1999 The highly sensible steering system hampered stability in curves on the FWD version.

TT — AUDI

RELIABILITY PROBLEMS

	1996	1997	1998	1999	2000	2001
Engine:						
Transmission:						
Suspension:						
Steering:						
Brakes:			Insufficient data			
Electricity:						
Body:						
Accessories:						
Fit/finish:						

POWERTRAIN

Year	Type/ L/Camshaft/bhp	Drivetrain & gearbox
00-01	L4/1.8/DOHC/180	front-M5
	L4/1.8/DOHC/180	all-M5
	L4T/1.8/DOC/225	all-M5

PERFORMANCE

Acceler. 0/100 sec.	Top speed km/h	Ave. Fuel consp. l./100 km
8.4	200	11.0
9.0	190	11.5
7.8	210	12.0

SPECIFICATIONS

Model 00-01	Wlb. mm	Lght. mm	Cb.wt kg	Brakes fr/rr	Steering type	Standard tires
cpe. 2dr. FWD	2429	4041	1325	dc/ABS	pwr.r&p	205/55R16
cpe. 2dr. AWD	2429	4041	1485	dc/ABS	pwr.r&p.	225/45R17
conv. 2dr. FWD	2429	4041	1420	dc/ABS	pwr.r&p	205/55R16
conv. 2dr. AWD	2429	4041	1575	dc/ABS	pwr.r&p.	225/45R17

PRICES

Model / version		1996	1997	1998	1999	2000	2001
cpe. 2dr. Quat.1.8	mini					36750	44300
	maxi					40950	47200
cpe. 2dr. Quat.2.2	mini						46200
	maxi						48300
cpe. 2dr. Rdstr1.8	mini						46700
	maxi						48800
cpe. 2dr. Rdstr2.2	mini						48300
	maxi						51450

See page 7 to adapt these figures.

2000 AUDI TT coupe

BMW 3 Series

2000 BMW 325ix

The 3 Series is the bread and butter of BMW. Last revamped in 1999 brings 2.5 and 3.0L engines and, since then, the model range has widened considerably.

PROS
- **Handling** on s and M3 models is much more stable than on the basic i model whose rear end tends to swing.
- **The engines** are really gutsy and silky smooth except for the 1.8L.
- **The M3 sports** model is incredible and worth every cent.
- **Brakes** are absolutely sensational, for they're powerful and stop on a dime.
- **You can't beat** the fun of driving with such a good seating position and a well-organized instrument panel at your fingertips.
- **The well-adjusted** suspension and plush seats make for a great blend of Sportscar capabilities and luxury sedan comfort.

CONS
- **The really snug** rear seat on the 94 models and predecessors.
- **Overall build** quality isn't as good as for other cars available in this model range.
- **The trunk** isn't too roomy and is hard to get to because of the high opening.
- **Whistling** wind noise around the windshield and sunroof.
- **Plastic trim** on the instrument panel looks pretty chintzy.

CONCLUSION
The 3 Series is the most affordable BMW vehicle for Sportscar enthusiasts who never give up on their dream of owning such a car...

RECALLS
1996 Faulty left airbag hookup.
1997 Cruise control is defective.
1999 Airbag control module must be reprogrammed to avoid inadvertent side airbags and head protection system.
The retaining clip that secures the brake booster pushrod to the brake pedal arm may be incompletely seated.
2001 Some defective rims will be checked by dealers.

3 Series — BMW

RELIABILITY PROBLEMS

	1996	1997	1998	1999	2000	2001
Engine:	X	X	X	X	X	-
Transmission:	-	-	-	-	-	-
Suspension:	-	-	-	-	-	-
Steering:	-	-	-	-	-	-
Brakes:	-	-	-	X	-	-
Electricity:	X	-	X	X	X	X
Body:	-	X	X	X	-	-
Accessories:	X	X	X	X	X	X
Fit/finish:	-	-	-	-	-	-

POWERTRAIN

Year	Type/ L/Camshaft/bhp	Drivetrain & gearbox
96-99	L4/1.9/DOHC/138 (318)	rear-M5
98-01	L6/2.5/DOHC/168 (323)	rear-M5
96-00	L6/2.8/DOHC/190 (328)	rear-M5
1997	L6/3.2/DOHC/321 (M3)	rear-M5
98-99	L6/3.2/DOHC/240 (M3)	rear-M5
2001	L6/2.2/DOHC/168	rear-M5
	L6/3.0/DOHC/225 (ix)	rr./all-M5

PERFORMANCE

Acceler. 0/100 sec.	Top. speed km/h	Ave. Fuel consp. l./100 km
9.8	187	10.2
NA	NA	11.6
8.0	206	11.9
6.0	230	13.0
7.0	220	11.8
NA	NA	11.5
8.5	205	12.0

SPECIFICATIONS

Model	Wlb. mm	Lght. mm	Cb.wt kg	Brakes fr/rr	Steering type	Standard tires
96-98						
cpe. 2dr. 318i	2700	4210	1260	dc/dr/ABS	pwr.r&p.	185/65R15
sdn. 4dr. 318is	2700	4433	1300	dc/ABS	pwr.r&p.	205/60R15
sdn. 4dr. 320i	2700	4433	1370	dc/ABS	pwr.r&p.	205/60R15
sdn. 4dr. 323i	2725	4471	1430	dc/ABS	pwr.r&p.	195/65R15
cpe. 2dr. 325is	2700	4433	1370	dc/ABS	pwr.r&p.	205/60R15
sdn. 4dr. 325i	2700	4433	1405	dc/ABS	pwr.r&p.	205/60R15
sdn. 4dr. 328i	2725	4471	1450	dc/ABS	pwr.r&p.	205/55R16
cpe. 2dr. M3	2710	4433	1440	dc/ABS	pwr.r&p.	225/45R17
sdn. 4dr. M3	2700	4433	1440	dc/ABS	pwr.r&p.	225/45R17
99-01						
sdn. 4dr. 320i	2725	4471	1440	dc/ABS	pwr.r&p.	195/65R15
sdn. 4dr. 325i	2725	4471	1470	dc/ABS	pwr.r&p.	205/55R16
cpe. 2dr. 325iCi	2725	4471	1490	dc/ABS	pwr.r&p.	205/55R16
sdn. 4dr. 330i	2725	4471	1505	dc/ABS	pwr.r&p.	205/50R17
conv. 2dr. 330Ci	2725	4488	1645	dc/ABS	pwr.r&p.	205/50R17

2000 BMW 325 cabriolet

BMW (cont.) 3 Series

BMW 330ix 2001

PRICES

Model / version		1996	1997	1998	1999	2000	2001
cpe. 2dr. 318i	mini	8800	11200	13650	15750		
	maxi	10800	13650	16300	18400		
cpe. 2dr. 318S	mini	13650	16500	20500	21500		
	maxi	16400	19200	23100	24150		
cpe. 2dr. 318ti	mini	10600	12600	15200	16800		
Active	maxi	13000	14700	17300	18900		
cpe. 2dr. 318ti	mini	12200	13350	17650	18800		
Sport	maxi	14600	15750	20150	21000		
con. 2dr. 318C	mini	18000	22000	26250	29400		
	maxi	22000	26250	29900	33500		
cpe. 2dr. 323i	mini			20500			
	maxi			24150			
cpe. 2dr. 323	mini					31000	
	maxi					35200	
con. 2dr. 323Ci	mini			28900	33000	38300	
	maxi			32550	36750	42500	
cpe. 2dr. 323iS	mini				29200		
	maxi				37800		
cpe. 2dr. M	mini				41450	47800	
	maxi				45150	52000	
cpe. 2dr. M3	mini		33600	40100	44100		64000
	maxi		37600	44100	48000		67700
con. 2dr. M3	mini						73500
	maxi						77200
cpe. 2dr. 325Ci	mini						35700
	maxi						39000
con. 2dr. 325Ci	mini						47200
	maxi						50900

3 Series (cont.) BMW

PRICES

Model / version		1996	1997	1998	1999	2000	2001
cpe. 2dr. 328iS	mini	19300	22900	27000	30750		
	maxi	23950	27000	31200	34650		
cpe. 2dr. 328Ci	mini					39400	
	maxi					43600	
con. 2dr. 328Ci	mini	25850	29700	35700	41250		
	maxi	29800	33900	40100	45150		
cpe. 2dr. 330Ci	mini						43000
	maxi						46700
con. 2dr. 330Ci	mini						57750
	maxi						61400
sdn. 4dr. 318i	mini	12400	15200	19750			
	maxi	15000	18000	22350			
sdn. 4dr. 320i	mini						27300
	maxi						30900
sdn. 4dr. 323i	mini				28550	29700	
	maxi				32450	33800	
sdn. 4dr. 325i	mini						33000
	maxi						36750
sdn. 4dr. 328i	mini	17950	22000	25700	31800	36750	
	maxi	22000	26200	29700	35700	40900	
sdn. 4dr. 330i	mini						41500
	maxi						45150
sdn. 4dr. M3	mini		33600	40200			
	maxi		37600	44100			

See page 7 to adapt these figures.

2000 BMW 325I convertible

BMW 5 Series

1997 BMW 540i

The 5 Series ranks between the lower-end 3 Series and the upper-end 7 Series. The last generation was born in 1996 when the V8 engine was available along with the traditional 6-cylinder engine. Since 1999, two new and improved wagons were introduced, powered by either a 6 or a 8 cylinders.

PROS

- **The clean**, classic look is elegant and even the station wagon has a charming design.
- **The engines** have gutsy get up and go, especially the V8 or the M5 model, which even at normal speeds, make for a really thrilling ride.
- **This car** is state-of-the-art high-tech, body is robust and rustproof.
- **The car handles** smoothly and evenly and traction is sensational for these rear-wheel drive vehicles, even on slippery roads.
- **Comfort** is getting cushier and cushier, with smoother suspensions and plusher seats and the interior cabin design has improved.
- **Steering** and brakes are simply perfect and completely reliable.
- **The interior cabin** is less plain than on the former 500 Series, build quality and fit and finish are clean as a whistle.
- **The trunk** is roomy and nicely shaped and the cabin has lots of well-designed storage compartments.

CONS

- **Vehicle weight**, price tag and high cost of upkeep.
- **The manual transmissions** are poorly calibrated for they're geared to driving at top speeds on the "autobahn", which really affects torque at low rpm.
- **The cabin** is still snug even with the bigger body.
- **Fuel consumption** varies according to the engine performance: so the 525i/ 528i are the most economical models to run.

CONCLUSION

Even used, 5 Series cars are pretty pricy and you should think twice about investing in one.

RECALLS

1996 Faulty left airbag hookup.
1998 Transmission gear position switch is defective (528i).
Some defective differential assemblies must be replaced.

5 Series — BMW

RELIABILITY PROBLEMS

	1996	1997	1998	1999	2000	2001
Engine:	-	-	X	X	X	-
Transmission:	X	-	X	-	-	-
Suspension:	-	-	-	-	-	-
Steering:	-	-	-	-	-	-
Brakes:	-	-	-	X	-	-
Electricity:	-	-	X	-	X	X
Body:	X	-	X	-	-	-
Accessories:	X	-	X	X	X	-
Fit/finish:	-	-	-	-	-	-

POWERTRAIN

Year	Type/ L/Camshaft/bhp	Drivetrain & gearbox	Acceler. 0/100 sec.	Top. speed km/h	Ave. Fuel consp. l./100 km
2001	L6/2.5/DOHC/184(525i)	rear-M5	8.6	206	11.5
97-00	L6/2.8/DOHC/190 (528i)	rear-M5	8.0	206	11.9
2001	L6/3.0/DOHC/225(530i)	rear-M5	8.0	206	12.0
99-01	V8/4.4/DOHC/282 (540i)	rear-M6	6.7	250	15.5
00-01	V8/5.0/DOHC/400 (M5)	rear-M6	5.5	250	15.0

SPECIFICATIONS

Model 97-01	Wlb.	Lght.	Cb.wt	Brakes	Steering	Standard
sdn. 4dr. 525i	2830	4775	1575	dc/ABS	pwr.bal.	225/55R15
sdn. 4dr. 528i	2830	4775	1585	dc/ABS	pwr.bal.	225/60R15
sdn. 4dr. 530i	2830	4775	1600	dc/ABS	pwr.bal.	225/66R16
sdn. 4dr. 540i	2830	4775	1700	dc/ABS	pwr.bal.	235/45R15
wgn. 4dr. 525il	2830	4805	1690	dc/ABS	pwr.bal.	225/60R15
wgn. 4dr. 528iT	2830	4805	1690	dc/ABS	pwr.bal.	225/60R16
wgn. 4dr. 540iT	2830	4805	1840	dc/ABS	pwr.bal.	225/55R16
00-01						
sdn. 4dr. M5	2830	4785	1720	dc/ABS	pwr.bal.	245/40R18 275/35R18

PRICES

Model / version		1996	1997	1998	1999	2000	2001
sdn. 4dr. 525i	mini						47250
	maxi						50900
wag. 4dr. 525T	mini						47800
	maxi						51450
sdn. 4dr. 528iA	mini		26250	30350	37800	42700	
	maxi		30450	32550	42000	44400	
wgn. 4dr. 528iT	mini				38300	44300	
	maxi				42500	49150	
sdn. 4dr. 530i	mini						54900
	maxi						58800
sdn. 4dr. 540iA	mini		31300		42000	49000	64800
	maxi		35700		47450	54900	68800
sdn. 4dr. M5	mini					77700	82950
	maxi					84800	89250
wgn. 4dr. 540iT	mini				43000	51450	66700
	maxi				48500	57200	70350

See page 7 to adapt these figures.

BMW 7 Series

1998 BMW 750IL

Launched in 1986, the 7 Series vehicles come in short or long body styles, driven by a 6-cylinder in-line engine, a V8 or a V12. They were redesigned in 1995.

PROS
- **State-of-the-art technology** is the name of the game, like the anti-skid system, the electronically controlled suspension and other expensive high-tech items that are simply amazing.
- **Engine performance** are awesome, especially with the V12 that takes you away into another dimension.
- **Handling** is just sensational and works like a charm, no matter what the driving style.
- **Driving** is safe and sure, thanks to near-perfect steering and clean, crisp brakes.
- **The electronically controlled** suspension, plush seats and quiet as a mouse soundproofing make for a regal ride.
- **Equipment** is very extensive and includes various sophisticated devices.

CONS
- **The high price** tag and expensive upkeep after the warranty runs out.
- **Vehicle weight** and size are awkward at times and affect maneuverability.
- **Pick-up** is pretty soft and lazy with the automatic, and gears take quite a while to wake up and kick in.
- **Some of the controls** are unusual and/or complicated and take time getting used to.

CONCLUSION
The BMW 7 Series is the top-end and top-price model range produced by the carmaker. Yet, you have to be wary of buying one of the older models that cost a small fortune to keep in good running order.

RECALLS
- **1996** Faulty hookup of impact sensors on left airbag.
- **96-97** Defective front suspension springs.
- **1998** Some defective differential assemblies must be replaced.

7 Series — BMW

RELIABILITY PROBLEMS

	1996	1997	1998	1999	2000	2001
Engine:	X	X	X	X	-	-
Transmission:	-	X	-	-	-	-
Suspension:	-	-	X	X	-	-
Steering:	-	-	-	-	-	-
Brakes:	-	X	X	X	-	-
Electricity:	-	-	X	X	X	X
Body:	X	X	-	-	-	-
Accessories:	-	X	X	X	X	X
Fit/finish:	-	-	-	-	-	-

POWERTRAIN

Year	Type/ L/Camshaft/bhp	Drivetrain & gearbox
96-01	V8/4.4/DOHC/282 (740)	rear-A5
	V12/5.4/SOHC/322 (750)	rear-A5

PERFORMANCE

Acceler. 0/100 sec.	Top. speed km/h	Ave. Fuel consp. l./100 km
8.5	206	13.9
7.8	206	16.2

SPECIFICATIONS

Model 96-01	Wlb. mm	Lght. mm	Cb.wt kg	Brakes fr/rr	Steering type	Standard tires
sdn. 4dr.740i	2930	4984	1930	dc/ABS	pwr.bal.	235/60HR16
sdn. 4dr.740iL	3070	5124	1945	dc/ABS	pwr.bal.	235/60HR16
sdn. 4dr.750iL	3070	5124	2068	dc/ABS	pwr.bal.	235/60HR16

PRICES

Model / version		1996	1997	1998	1999	2000	2001
sdn. 4dr. 740i	mini		36550	41600	49000	58800	67900
	maxi		38850	46200	54600	64600	71900
sdn. 4dr. 740iL	mini	30900	37000	43700	52000	60900	71200
	maxi	35000	41600	48300	57400	66600	75000
sdn. 4dr. 750iL	mini	49550	56200	65800	73500	83700	96000
	maxi	57200	63800	73200	81600	91800	99900

See page 7 to adapt these figures.

1999 BMW 740iL

BMW 8 Series

1997 BMW 850i

Built on the 7 Series platform and sharing the same mechanical features, the 8 Series is an exotic GT cocktail.

PROS
- **An upper-crust** model belonging to a very select club of cars driven by a V12 (850).
- **The body design** isn't too bold and brassy and hasn't really gone out of style.
- **Engine performance** are pretty impressive, considering vehicle weight and size.
- **High-tech features** provide top-notch control and handling.
- **Road stability** is just outstanding in most situations, but these coupe are more suited to highway driving.
- **It's really a thrill to drive** a vehicle dressed up with such extensive and high-tech equipment.
- **Driving** is quite comfortable, even with the snug interior, stiff suspension and a higher noise level than on a 750 sedan.
- **With such a top-notch design**, build and finish quality and such lavish materials, the vehicle is, of course, quite pricy.

CONS
- **Sky-high costs** go with the territory, for depreciation is high and it costs an arm and a leg to run, maintain and repair such a vehicle, so much so that even the most enthusiastic potential buyers might walk away from it.
- **Maneuverability** isn't really great, given vehicle weight and size.
- **Sportscar performance** aren't up to par on curved roads and the 850 just doesn't go through the paces it should, which takes all the fun out of being at the wheel.
- **Rear seats** are cramped and hard to get to, head room and leg room are tight.
- **There aren't enough** storage compartments in the cabin interior and the trunk is low and quite small.

CONCLUSION
The 840 / 850 coupe have never been too popular and aren't the best used car buy either, for the most affordable among them aren't really a steal, because they'll rob your pocketbook.

RECALLS
1996 Faulty hookup of impact sensors on left airbag.
96-97 Defective cruise control.

8 Series — BMW

RELIABILITY PROBLEMS

	1996	1997	1998	1999	2000	2001
Engine:	-	X				
Transmission:	X	-				
Suspension:	-	-				
Steering:	-	-				
Brakes:	-	X				
Electricity:	X	-				
Body:	X	-				
Accessories:	X	X				
Fit/finish:	-	-				

POWERTRAIN

Year	Type/ L/Camshaft/bhp	Drivetrain & gearbox
96-97	V8/4.4/DOHC/285	rear-A5
	V12/5.4/SOHC/322	rear-A5

PERFORMANCE

Acceler. 0/100 sec.	Top. speed km/h	Ave. Fuel consp. l./100 km
7.8	250	14.4
6.5	250	17.1

SPECIFICATIONS

Model	Wlb. mm	Lght. mm	Cb.wt kg	Brakes fr/rr	Steering type	Standard tires
cpe. 2dr. (840)	2684	4780	1870	dc/ABS	pwr.bal.	235/50R16
cpe. 2dr. (850)	2684	4780	1950	dc/ABS	pwr.bal.	235/50R16

PRICES

Model / version		1996	1997	1998	1999	2000	2001
cpe. 2dr. 840i	mini	24000	30100				
	maxi	30900	37400				
cpe. 2dr. 850i	mini	44700	48500				
	maxi	52500	56300				

See page 7 to adapt these figures.

1996 BMW 850i

BMW X5

2000 BMW X5 4.0i

Keeping in step with Mercedes-Benz, BMW has come up with its own all-terrain SUV in the form of the X5, a car specifically designed for the North American market which is also built in North America.

PROS
- **Aesthetically**, the X5 is a sure-fire hit and its flamboyant presentation contrasts a great deal with that of the more reserved Mercedes ML.
- **The V8 engine** churns out sports-car performance; full-stop and passing accelerations are quite impressive.
- **The brakes** are very efficient and bite into the pavement when pushed hard. In emergency situations, they quickly bring the X5 to a perfectly controlled stop.
- **The X5 handles** extremely well for a vehicle of this sort, despite its high center of gravity and bulky weight.
- **The HDC** (Hill Descent Control) system replaces the low first gear when descending a steep grade without applying the brakes.
- **Getting into** the X5 is easy despite its generous road clearance.
- **Its interior** is just as luxurious as that of any BMW automobile.
- **The extensive equipment** list compares well with that of the automobiles produced by the Munich-based manufacturer.
- **Practical storage** space abounds in front.
- **The exhaust note** resembles that of a sports coupe.

CONS
- **The high sticker price**, of this vehicle which is a gas guzzler and costs a fortune in maintenance.
- **The ideal driving position** is low and hard to find.
- **The dashboard** is not very ergonomic on center.
- **The two-part liftgate** is not very practical to use.
- **The roof pillars** are devoid of access handles.

CONCLUSION
The X5 is more synonymous with luxury than utilitarianism and—just as is the case with BMW automobiles—it targets an elite clientele who has the financial means of keeping it on the road. . .

RECALLS
2000 The steering rack input shaft collar will be inspected and repositioned if necessary.
2001 Steering spindlewill be inspected and fastening bolt replaced. Some safety belt lower anchorage may not have been secured. The nut that secures the axialjoint of the left steering rod may not have been tightened properly.

X5 — BMW

RELIABILITY PROBLEMS

	1996	1997	1998	1999	2000	2001
Engine:					-	-
Transmission:					X	-
Suspension:					-	-
Steering:					-	-
Brakes:					-	-
Electricity:					X	-
Body:					-	-
Accessories:					X	-
Fit/finish:					-	-

POWERTRAIN / PERFORMANCE

Year	Type/ L/Camshaft/bhp	Drivetrain & gearbox	Acceler. 0/100 sec.	Top. speed km/h	Ave. Fuel consp. l./100 km
2001	L6/3.0/DOHC/225	all-A5	9.5	190	14.0
		all-M5	8.8	200	13.8
00-01	V8/4.4/DOHC/282	all-A5	8.3	200	17.0

SPECIFICATIONS

Model 2000-01	Wlb. mm	Lght. mm	Cb.wt kg	Brakes fr/rr	Steering type	Standard tires
wgn. 4dr. 3.0i	2820	4667	2050	dc/ABS	pwr.r&p.	235/65R17
wgn. 4dr. 4.0l	2820	4470	2175	dc/ABS	pwr.r&p.	255/55R18

PRICES

Model / version		1996	1997	1998	1999	2000	2001
wgn. 4dr. 3.0	mini					56200	61900
	maxi					60900	69300
wgn. 4dr. 4.4	mini						72400
	maxi						78700

See page 7 to adapt these figures.

2000 BMW X5 4.0i

BMW Z3

1998 BMW Z3 M Roadster

In 1996, BMW came up with a roadster derived from the 3 Series platform. The base model offers a 4-cylinder 1.9L engine, the 2.8L and M 3.2L a 6-cylinder engine. In 99, a 2.5L replaced the 1.9L and a M coupe is available as a special order.

PROS

- **Its bold and lively** body design is a looker, yet it's nice and traditional with those little retro grilles along the fenders.
- **It is fun driving** this car, for engine response is clean and crisp and you feel like you're king of the road with the wind and exhaust roaring.
- **The 6-cylinder** engines, especially the M version's, makes for a much more exciting driving experience than the 4-cylinder offers.
- **Power steering** is smooth and right on with such a good reduction ratio and small steer angle diameter.
- **Handling** is terrific and taking those curves is a real thrill with so much grip and power at your fingertips.
- **Brakes are impressive**, making for smooth, straight, short stops, and they don't heat up with intensive use.
- **Driving comfort** is quite good for a vehicle of this type, the suspension is smooth and noise level is at a minimum.
- **Wind isn't a problem** with the top down, thanks to a net placed vertically behind the passengers' heads.
- **The convertible top** is a breeze to open and close and bolts clamp down easily.
- **The trunk** is practical, even if it's smallish.

CONS

- **The price tag**, given the poor quality of the original equipment.
- **Engine performance** of the 1.9L are very run-of-the-mill and similar to those of the Miata.
- **The convertible top** isn't lined, it isn't too rain-proof (above the side windows) and the rear panel is made of plastic.
- **Some of the controls** aren't within easy reach, like the power window locks located on the center console and especially the steering column that stays just where it is, because you can't adjust it even an inch!
- **Seats are flat** and don't provide much lateral support.
- **Overall quality** could be ritzier, considering the price.

CONCLUSION

BMW really didn't make a good move by first putting on the market a lower-end roadster which is really nothing special.

RECALLS

96-97 Defective cruise control.

Z3 — BMW

RELIABILITY PROBLEMS

	1996	1997	1998	1999	2000	2001
Engine:	X	X	X	X	X	X
Transmission:	-	-	-	-	-	-
Suspension:	X	-	X	-	-	-
Steering:	-	-	X	-	-	-
Brakes:	-	-	-	-	-	-
Electricity:	X	X	X	X	X	X
Body:	X	-	X	-	-	-
Accessories:	X	X	X	X	X	X
Fit/finish:	-	-	-	-	X	-

POWERTRAIN

Year	Type/ L/Camshaft/bhp	Drivetrain & gearbox
96-98	L4/1.9/DOHC/138	rear-M5
99-01	L6/2.5/DOHC/168	rear-M5
97-00	L6/2.8/DOHC/189	rear-M5
2001	L6/3.0/DOHC/225	rear-M5
98-01	L6/3.2/DOHC/240	rear-M5

PERFORMANCE

Acceler. 0/100 sec.	Top. speed km/h	Ave. Fuel consp. l./100 km
9.0	190	10.2
8.0	200	11.6
6.7	210	12.3
7.5	206	11.5
5.4	220	11.8

SPECIFICATIONS

Model 96-01	Wlb. mm	Lght. mm	Cb.wt kg	Brakes fr/rr	Steering type	Standard tires
con. 2dr. 1.9	2445	4025	1210	dc/ABS	pwr.r&p.	225/50R16
con. 2dr. 2.3-2.5	2445	4025	1220	dc/ABS	pwr.r&p.	225/50R16
con. 2dr. 2.8-3.0	2445	4025	1300	dc/ABS	pwr.r&p.	225/45R17
con. 2dr. 3.2	2445	4025	1350	dc/ABS	pwr.r&p.	245/40R17

PRICES

Model / version		1996	1997	1998	1999	2000	2001
2dr. 1.9	mini	19400	21500	25800			
	maxi	23500	25800	29700			
2dr. 2.3	mini				28650	33000	
	maxi				32500	37300	
2dr. 2.5	mini						38600
	maxi						42000
2dr. 2.8	mini		25200	32550	34650	39400	
	maxi		29400	36500	38500	43600	
2dr. 3.0	mini						48300
	maxi						51450
2dr. 3.2	mini			37400	41250	46700	
	maxi			41500	45150	50900	

See page 7 to adapt these figures.

1997 BMW Z3

CHRYSLER D Series   DODGE Durango

2000 DODGE Durango

The Durango is a 4-door rear or all-wheel drive multi-purpose vehicle, derived from the Dakota pickup, equipped with a 3.9L V6 or a 5.2L and 5.9L V8.

PROS

• A great-looking design with a zoomy, virile character is a definite ace in the hand.
• Cabin space is remarkable since the Durango is the only vehicle in its category to be able to accommodate eight passengers.
• Its mid-size format between that of the Blazer-Explorer and Tahoe-Expedition seems ideal for available engine power.
• Load and trailering capabilities are almost equivalent to those of an Expedition, yet it's less cumbersome.
• Build is definitely solid all-round and the stiff chassis makes for super-smooth handling prowess.
• The suspension is cushy in spite of its rustic leaf springs and it provides ride comfort comparable to that inside a minivan.
• The dashboard is neat and logical, but it's rather basic and home-spun.
• Nice feature: modular seatbenches and trunk located under the cargo hold floor.

CONS

• Fuel consumption is never cheap even with the base model V6, since this vehicle weighs well over 2 tons when at full load capacity.
• Brakes aren't at all up to snuff, either when slowing down in normal conditions or in emergency situations, causing vehicle lurch and sway.
• Front seats are barely contoured and rear seats are awfully flat and thinly upholstered.
• Recirculating ball steering on the 4X4 model is vague and lacks spontaneity due to the big, springy tires.
• Technical features seem a bit too bare-boned basic for such a recent vehicle

CONCLUSION

The Durango is more of a workhorse than a luxury all-terrain vehicle. Regular use should depend on its load and trailering capabilities, for fuel consumption is far from frugal.

RECALLS

1998 The fasteners which secure the alternator and the battery cables may have insufficient clamp load.
2001 Defective electric shift transfer case on 4-wheel drive models.

DODGE Durango   D Series CHRYSLER

RELIABILITY PROBLEMS

	1996	1997	1998	1999	2000	2001
Engine:			-	X	-	-
Transmission:			X	-	-	-
Suspension:			-	-	-	-
Steering:			-	-	-	-
Brakes:			-	-	-	-
Electricity:			X	X	-	X
Body:			-	X	X	-
Accessories:			X	X	X	X
Fit/finish:			X	X	X	-

POWERTRAIN

Year	Type/ L/Camshaft/bhp	Drivetrain & gearbox
98-00	V6/3.9/OHV/175	rear/all
	V8/5.2/OHV/230	rear/all
00-01	V8/4.7/SOHC/235	ar./toutes
98-01	V8/5.9/OHV/245	rear/all

PERFORMANCE

Acceler. 0/100 sec.	Top. speed km/h	Ave. Fuel consp. l./100 km
12.0	150	15.4
9.5	185	17.8
10.5	175	18.5
9.3	180	20.5

SPECIFICATIONS

Model 98-01	Wlb. mm	Lght. mm	Cb.wt kg	Brakes fr/rr	Steering type	Standard tires
wgn. 4dr. 4x2	2944	4910	1932	dc/dr/ABS	pwr.r&p.	235/75R15
wgn. 4dr. 4x4	2944	4910	2112	dc/dr/ABS	pwr.bal.	235/75R15

PRICES

Model / version		1996	1997	1998	1999	2000	2001
wgn. 4dr. SLT	mini			21800	25200	27600	33600
	maxi			24000	27300	30150	37800
wgn. 4dr. SLT+	mini			23100	27000		
	maxi			25200	29100		
wgn. 4dr. Sport	mini					26250	27800
	maxi					28900	31000

See page 7 to adapt these figures.

1998 DODGE Durango

CHRYSLER FG Series

CHRYSLER Sebring
DODGE Avenger

2001 CHRYSLER Sebring

These 1995 coupes replaced the former Le Baron and Daytona. They're built in the United States by Mitsubishi and equipped with a 2.0L or 2.4L 4-cylinder engine or with a 2.5L V6. The Sebring convertible that was launched in 1996 is also derived from the Cirrus-Stratus.

PROS
- **Their attractive look** with their hulky, bold shape up front reminiscent of the Viper.
- **The cabin comfortably** seats 4 adults with plenty of head room and leg room. Rear seats are quite high, but lean too far back.
- **Driving** is fine rather than fun, for you don't get that zesty, spirited Sportscar feeling with such smooth power steering and brakes.
- **The ergonomic instrument** panel is straightforward. It's actually the Eagle Talon design that the Sebring-Avengers share along with many other features.
- **The top** on the convertible is well-designed for it handles well and its glass rear window comes with an electric defroster.

CONS
- **The V6** just doesn't cough up the goods compared to the 4-cylinder Neon, even if the power to weight ratio in both cases is affected by heavy vehicle weight.
- **The interior cabin** design is terribly blah and not even the imitation wood trim on the Sebring can liven things up.
- **Outward view** is only fair because of the low front seat, high trunk, minuscule rearview mirror up front and C-pillar which affects rearward view at quarterback.
- **If you want to store things**, there's the reasonably sized glove box, but the door side-pockets are hard to reach and the compartment on the center console is tiny.
- **To be improved upon**: climate control venting system strains in extreme temperatures, rear windows don't open and there's quite a bit of body rattle and chatter.

CONCLUSION
These models have an attractive body design, but the cabin design is quite colorless. There's nothing sporty about them, except for the name, for none of the engines really have the muscle that Sportscar dreams are made of...

RECALLS
1996 Poorly installed brake fluid outlet pipe on the power brake. (on the convertible)
Possible short circuit due to defective power mirror switch on the convertible.
Damaged rubber boot on the lower lateral ball joint may cause an extraordinary wear on the ball joint and a possible separation.
96-97 Defective control arm ball joint due to loss of lubrication.
1997 Headrest support bracket weld might fail on some vehicles.
1998 Failing aspirator system increases nitrous oxide emissions.
Dash panel may sag and interfere with the accelerator pedal.
Safety belts anchors may have not been properly installed.
Shift lever lock mecanism may get stuck.

CHRYSLER Sebring / DODGE Avenger — FG Series CHRYSLER

2001 On some vehicles the passenger side airbag module may not retain the airbag door during deployment.
The automatic transmission cooler hoses may not meet winner wall thickness requirements.
Crankshaft position sensor wiring harness must be rerouted.
Dealers must inspect fuel return hose date code and replace it if required.

RELIABILITY PROBLEMS

	1996	1997	1998	1999	2000	2001
Engine:	X	X	-	-	X	-
Transmission:	X	X	-	-	-	-
Suspension:	-	-	-	-	-	-
Steering:	-	-	X	-	-	-
Brakes:	X	X	X	X	X	-
Electricity:	X	X	-	-	-	X
Body:	X	-	X	X	X	-
Accessories:	-	X	X	X	X	X
Fit/finish:	-	-	X	-	X	X

POWERTRAIN

Year	Type/ L/Camshaft/bhp	Drivetrain & gearbox
96-99	L4/2.0/DOHC/140	front-M5
		front-A4
96-01	L4/2.4/DOHC/150	front-A4
96-00	V6/2.5/SOHC/163-168	front-A4
00-01	V6/2.7/SOHC/198	front-A4

PERFORMANCE

Acceler. 0/100 sec.	Top speed km/h	Ave. Fuel consp. l./100 km
10.5	165	10.8
11.8	160	11.1
10.7	170	11.3
10.2	175	12.2
9.0	180	12.5

SPECIFICATIONS

Model	Wlb. mm	Lght. mm	Cb.wt kg	Brakes fr/rr	Steering type	Standard tires
Sebring						
cpe. 2dr. LX	2635	4850	1346	dc/dr	pwr.r&p.	195/70R14
cpe. 2dr. LXi	2635	4850	1453	dc/dc	pwr.r&p.	215/50R17
con. 2dr. JX	2692	4893	1511	dc/dr	pwr.r&p.	205/65R15
con. 2dr. JXi	2692	4893	1534	dc/dr/ABS	pwr.r&p.	215/55R16
con. 2dr. JXiLTD	2692	4893	1545	dc/ABS	pwr.r&p.	215/55R16
sdn. 4dr. LX	2743	4844	1479	dc/dr	pwr.r&p.	205/65R15
sdn. 4dr. LXI	2743	4844	1504	dc	pwr.r&p.	205/60R16
Avenger						
cpe. 2dr. base	2635	4830	1314	dc/dr	pwr.r&p.	195/70R14
cpe. 2dr. ES	2635	4830	1359	dc/dc	pwr.r&p.	205/55R16

PRICES

Model / version		1996	1997	1998	1999	2000	2001
Sebring							
cpe. 2dr. LX	mini	7900	10500	11550	13450	16300	19400
	maxi	10800	13200	14500	16300	19400	22600
cpe. 2dr. LXi	mini	9750	11350	13000	15550	18400	22600
	maxi	12600	14300	16000	18400	21500	24700
con. 2dr. JX	mini	10800	12400	14200	18150	20500	
	maxi	13650	15300	16600	21000	23600	
con. 2dr. JXi	mini	12600	14200	16400	20250	22600	
	maxi	15200	17300	19000	23100	25700	
con. 2dr. LX	mini						24700
	maxi						27800
con. 2dr. LXi	mini						26750
	maxi						27800
con. 2dr. Ltd	mini						30450
	maxi						33600
sdn. 4dr. LX	mini						18900
	maxi						22000
sdn. 4dr. LXi	mini						21000
	maxi						24150
Avenger							
cpe. 2dr. base	mini	7350	9250	11150	12600		
	maxi	10000	11950	13650	15200		
cpe. 2dr. ES	mini	8900	10800	12600	14700		
	maxi	11550	13650	15200	17300		

See page 7 to adapt these figures.

CHRYSLER JA Series

CHRYSLER Cirrus
DODGE Stratus
PLYMOUTH Breeze

1999 CHRYSLER Cirrus

The Cirrus-Stratus models replaced the Le Baron-Acclaim's in 1995. They're driven by a 2.0L or 2.4L 4-cylinder engine, or by a 2.5L V6.

PROS

• **Advanced technical** features such as rigid build, MacPherson suspensions that muffle wheel vibration and superb rear end follow-through, as well as state-of-the-art engines.
• **Original design** and resemblance to other members of the Chrysler car family.
• **Good handling**, in spite of the sensitive suspension, for there isn't much sway or body roll.
• **The cushy suspension** and comfy, well-shaped seats that provide good support.
• **The interior cabin** is really much nicer than that of their direct rivals, the Contour-Mystique's, for even tall rear seat passengers have enough head room and leg room.

CONS

• **The V6 engine** isn't as muscular as that of the competition.
• **The 4-speed automatic** is a hassle because the shifter design doesn't provide any real braking effect.
• **Stops** are very long, but they're smooth and straight with ABS.
• **Some trim materials** and poor fit of some components aren't up to par for such a car.
• **Rearward visibility** is poor because of the high, narrow rear window.
• **Soundproofing** could be beefed up, for there's a lot of road and wind noise.
• **The instrument panel** deck reflects too much into the windshield and blinds the driver in bright sun.

CONCLUSION

These are good cars that made more of a splash before they hit the market than since, because of certain inconsistencies. Basic models are the best buy.

RECALLS

96-97 Defective control arm ball joint due to loss of lubrication.
96-98 Safety pin in the automatic transmission shift lever may break.
1996 Powertrain control module is miscalibrated and may not control CO emissions adequately.

CHRYSLER Cirrus
DODGE Stratus
PLYMOUTH Breeze

JA Series CHRYSLER

96-97 Oil leakage on cylinder head.
Premature rusting on the ABS unit.
Risk of possible brake fluid leakage on master cylinder.
1997 Defective primary & secondary hood latch spring.
1998 Premature failure of the catalytic converter assembly.
2000 A brake line bracket will be added to the right front brake tube, because of a defective weld.
Incorrect child lock instruction label.

RELIABILITY PROBLEMS

	1996	1997	1998	1999	2000	2001
Engine:	X	-	-	-	-	-
Transmission:	X	X	-	X	X	-
Suspension:	X	-	X	-	-	-
Steering:	-	-	-	-	-	-
Brakes:	-	-	X	-	X	-
Electricity:	X	X	X	-	X	-
Body:	X	X	-	-	-	-
Accessories:	-	X	X	X	-	-
Fit/finish:	-	-	-	-	-	-

POWERTRAIN

Year	Type/ L/Camshaft/bhp	Drivetrain & gearbox	Acceler. 0/100 sec.	Top. speed km/h	Ave. Fuel consp. l./100 km
96-00	L4/2.0/SOHC/132	front-M5	11.3	165	8.7
		front-A4	12.0	160	10.4
	L4/2.4/DOHC/150	front-A4	10.4	175	11.3
	V6/2.5/SOHC/168	front-A4	9.7	180	12.2

SPECIFICATIONS

Model	Wlb. mm	Lght. mm	Cb.wt kg	Brakes fr/rr	Steering type	Standard tires
Cirrus						
sdn. 4dr.LX	2743	4750	1395	dc/dr/ABS	pwr.r&p.	195/65R15
sdn. 4dr.LXi	2743	4750	1428	dc/ABS	pwr.r&p.	195/65R15
Stratus						
sdn. 4dr.base	2743	4725	1325	dc/dr	pwr.r&p.	195/70R14
sdn. 4dr.ES	2743	4725	1391	dc/dr/ABS	pwr.r&p.	195/65R15
Breeze						
sdn. 4dr.	2743	4742	1327	dc/dr	pwr.r&p.	195/70R14

PRICES

Model / version		1996	1997	1998	1999	2000	2001
Cirrus							
sdn. 4dr. LX	mini	6500	8200		10800	12600	
	maxi	9450	11000		13650	15200	
sdn. 4dr. LXi	mini	7900	9750	10500	12400	14700	
	maxi	10900	12600	13450	15200	17300	
Stratus							
sdn. 4dr. base	mini	5350	7150	8900	10500		
	maxi	8300	10000	11850	13650		
sdn. 4dr. ES	mini	6900	8700	10400	12100		
	maxi	9850	11550	13100	14700		
Breeze							
sdn. 4dr.	mini	5550	7150	9000	10400		
	maxi	8400	10000	11550	13100		

See page 7 to adapt these figures.

CHRYSLER LH Series

CHRYSLER Concorde
DODGE Intrepid
EAGLE Vision

1999 CHRYSLER Intrepid

The Chrysler Concorde, Intrepid and Eagle Vision were first sold in 1993 and share the same platform and mechanical features. In 1998, a facelift was given to the Chrysler and Dodge but the Eagle didn't make it and has been terminated in 1997.

PROS
- **The unique style** of the latest Concorde, sporting a more retro look, and the Intrepid's daring panache.
- **The cab forward design** that was first used on these models has since been copied by many competitors.
- **The cabin** is akin to that of a luxury car, which is a nice surprise for a mid-size car.
- **The rigid frame**, dual airbags and on the upper-end model, 4-disc brakes with ABS, are excellent safety features.
- **The adaptive suspension**, well-cushioned seats and superb sound-proofing make for a smooth ride.
- **Handling** is stable and neutral in most situations, as long as the car is equipped with good-quality tires.
- **Engine performance** are quite good especially given the fact that fuel consumption is reasonable for the vehicle size.
- **Build quality** and tight fit and finish are on a par with Japanese products sold at similar or higher prices.
- **Convenient**: huge trunk and scads of storage compartments.

CONS
- **The automatic shifter** that doesn't come through with vital braking effect and whose unreliability made for lots of repairs under warranty.
- **The plastic materials** used for the dash board seem a little cheap for models in this price range.
- **Rear drum brakes** on the base model Intrepid make for longer stops and don't hold up as well.
- **To be improved upon**: no headrests in the rear, seatbench that can't be folded down, hand-brake located under the instrument panel and poor headlights on the Intrepid.

CONCLUSION
The LH Series models have a lot of good features: an attractive body, tight fit and finish, a roomy cabin, all at an affordable price. They're popular cars and don't depreciate too much.

RECALLS
96-97 Rubber compound rings on the fuel injector feed may leak.
1998 Airbag module's initiator is incomplete and may not work.
99-00 A defective adjustable turning loop on the shoulder belt will be replaced.
2000 Defective master cylinder will be replaced on some vehicles. Left front retractor assemblies will be replaced on some vehicles.

CHRYSLER Concorde
DODGE Intrepid
EAGLE Vision

LH Series CHRYSLER

RELIABILITY PROBLEMS

	1996	1997	1998	1999	2000	2001
Engine:	X	X	X	X	-	-
Transmission:	X	X	X	X	X	-
Suspension:	-	-	X	-	X	-
Steering:	X	X	-	-	-	-
Brakes:	-	-	X	-	-	-
Electricity:	-	-	X	X	X	X
Body:	-	-	X	X	-	-
Accessories:	X	X	X	X	X	X
Fit/finish:	-	-	X	-	X	-

POWERTRAIN

Year	Type/ L/Camshaft/bhp	Drivetrain & gearbox
96-97	V6/3.3/OHV/161	front-A4
	V6/3.5/SOHC/214	front-A4
98-01	V6/2.7/DOHC/200	front-A4
	V6/3.2/SOHC/225	front-A4

PERFORMANCE

Acceler. 0/100 sec.	Top. speed km/h	Ave. Fuel consp. l./100 km
10.8	175	12.4
9.0	210	13.7
10.5	180	11.3
9.3	220	12.6

SPECIFICATIONS

Model 96-97	Wlb. mm	Lght. mm	Cb.wt kg	Brakes fr/rr	Steering type	Standard tires
Concorde						
sdn. 4dr. LX	2870	5119	1584	dc/ABS	pwr.r&p.	225/60R16
sdn. 4dr. LXi	2870	5119	1611	dc/ABS	pwr.r&p.	225/60R16
Intrepid						
sdn. 4dr. base	2870	5126	1549	dc/dr	pwr.r&p.	205/70R15
sdn. 4dr. ES	2870	5126	1599	dc/ABS	pwr.r&p.	225/60R16
Vision						
sdn. 4dr. ESi	2870	5121	1563	dc/dc	pwr.r&p.	205/70R15
sdn. 4dr. TSi	2870	5121	1600	dc/ABS	pwr.r&p.	225/60R16
98-01						
Concorde						
sdn. 4dr. LX	2870	5311	1563	dc	pwr.r&p.	205/70R15
sdn. 4dr. LXi	2870	5311	1613	dc/ABS	pwr.r&p.	225/60R16
Intrepid						
sdn. 4dr. base	2870	5175	1552	dc	pwr.r&p.	205/70R15
sdn. 4dr. ES	2870	5175	1596	dc/ABS	pwr.r&p.	225/60R16

PRICES

Model / version		1996	1997	1998	1999	2000	2001
Concorde							
sdn. 4dr. LX	mini	6700	9250	11550	14300	16600	19400
	maxi	9850	12200	14500	16800	19400	22000
sdn. 4dr. LXi	mini	8500	10800	13250	16800	18700	21500
	maxi	11450	13650	16000	19400	21500	24150
Intrepid							
sdn. 4dr. base	mini	5800	7650	10100	12600	15000	
	maxi	8700	10500	13100	15200	17850	
sdn. 4dr. ES	mini	7150	9250	11550	14800	17100	19400
	maxi	10100	12100	14700	17300	19950	22600
sdn. 4dr. R\T	mini					18150	20500
	maxi					21000	23600
sdn. 4dr. SE	mini						17300
	maxi						20500
Vision							
sdn. 4dr. ESi	mini	6400	8700				
	maxi	8800	11550				
sdn. 4dr. TSi	mini	8200	10300				
	maxi	11150	13250				

See page 7 to adapt these figures.

CHRYSLER New Yorker-LHS-300M

1999 CHRYSLER LHS

Designed in 1994, these deluxe Chrysler sedans were built on the LH series platform. The New Yorker and LHS are quite similar but they have a different body design and array of equipment. The 300M joined the last LHS in 1999.

PROS
- **The sensational body design**, especially the rear window design, reminiscent of upper-crust models; more particularly the 300M look.
- **Price, upkeep and fuel** consumption are very reasonable.
- **The spacious cabin** seats five passengers and the huge trunk can hold all their luggage.
- **Handling** is cool and smooth with such a well-balanced vehicle that moves all of a piece and engine performance are really quite impressive. The 300M is a lot of fun to drive with its roaring 253-bhp.
- **Well-contoured** and cushioned seats, a smooth as silk suspension and superb soundproofing put you on cloud nine.
- **Build quality**, fit and materials are top-notch.
- **Equipment is extensive**, both safety-wise and convenience-wise for there are a reasonable number of storage compartments.

CONS
- **The shifter** on the automatic doesn't provide for anywhere near enough braking effect and has caused a lot of hassles.
- **The body is starting** to show its age for there's quite a bit of wind noise blowing about (except for the 300M).
- **The cruise control** button isn't conveniently located and the shape of the steering wheel doesn't allow for resting one's hands on the spokes.
- **Some finish** details could be improved upon.
- **Storage compartments** are small, the glove compartment is tiny and there's no compartment in the rear elbowrest.
- **There aren't any headrests** in the rear.

CONCLUSION
These cars are a good buy, for they're lavish, comfortable and quite economical.

RECALLS
1999 Wrong Vehicle Emission Control Information (VECI) label.
2000 Left front retractor assemblies will be replaced on some vehicles.

New Yorker-LHS-300M — CHRYSLER

RELIABILITY PROBLEMS

	1996	1997	1998	1999	2000	2001
Engine:	-	-		-	-	-
Transmission:	X	X		-	-	-
Suspension:	-	-		-	-	-
Steering:	X	-		X	-	-
Brakes:	X	X		X	-	-
Electricity:	X	X		X	X	X
Body:	-	-		-	X	-
Accessories:	-	-		X	-	-
Fit/finish:	X	-		X	X	-

POWERTRAIN

Year	Type/ L/Camshaft/bhp	Drivetrain & gearbox	Acceler. 0/100 sec.	Top. speed km/h	Ave. Fuel consp. l./100 km
96-97	V6/3.5/SOHC/214	front-A4	9.2	200	13.7
99-01	V6/3.5/SOHC/253	front-A4	8.5	220	13.3

SPECIFICATIONS

Model	Wlb. mm	Lght. mm	Cb.wt kg	Brakes fr/rr	Steering type	Standard tires
New Yorker sdn. 4dr.	2870	5268	1629	dc/ABS	pwr.r&p.	225/60R16
LHS sdn. 4dr.	2870	5276	1623	dc/ABS	pwr.r&p.	225/55R17
300M sdn. 4dr.	2870	5023	1618	dc/ABS	pwr.r&p.	225/55R17

PRICES

Model / version		1996	1997	1998	1999	2000	2001
New Yorker sdn. 4dr.	mini	10100					
	maxi	13000					
LHS sdn. 4dr.	mini	9000	10800		19100	24150	27800
	maxi	11950	14300		22550	27300	30950
300M sdn. 4 dr.	mini				22900	27300	30950
	maxi				25700	30450	34100

See page 7 to adapt these figures.

2001 CHRYSLER 300M

CHRYSLER — PT Cruiser

2001 CHRYSLER PT Cruiser Limited

The PT Cruiser is difficult to fit into an one category: it's a versatile 4-door wagon based on the Neon's platform and equipped with the base Sebring's mechanical components.

PROS

- **This vehicle's irresistible styling** explains half of its success. Combining modern and retro styling cues, it's unique on the North American market.
- The other half of the PT Cruiser's success can be attributed to its **versatility**. The front portion of the cabin is highly modular and easy to adapt according to the circumstances.
- **The PT Cruiser drives** with surprising aplomb, despite its higher-than-average center of gravity. It could even be considered sporty if its engine were more powerful.
- **The base model packs plenty of equipment** for the price and is an affordable small utility vehicle.
- **The cabin** will seat 4 adults comfortably, and room is ample in all directions. Furthermore, cabin access is made easy by the large doors that open wide.
- **With loads of storage space** and a shelf that can be installed in various ways and even be used as a picnic table, this car has an undeniably practical side.

CONS

- **With the timid performance** of the automatic version, due to a poor weight-to-power ratio, it's a shame that a small V6 engine (2.5 L) is not available.
- **Rearward visibility** is hindered by the headrests and narrow rear window.
- **Some of the ergonomics** need improving.
- **The automatic version** is not as maneuverable as the manual, whose turning radius is narrower.
- **The mechanical components** are almost inaccessible, which makes basic maintenance and simple repairs difficult. Indeed, there's hardly a square inch of unused space under the hood.

VERDICT

The PT Cruiser is a marketing phenomenon that also has the advantage of being practical and sure-footed.

RECALLS

None over this period.

PT Cruiser — CHRYSLER

RELIABILITY PROBLEMS

	1996	1997	1998	1999	2000	2001
Engine:						
Transmission:						
Suspension:						
Steering:						
Brakes:			Insufficient data			
Electricity:						
Body:						
Accessories:						
Fit/finish:						

POWERTRAIN / PERFORMANCE

Year	Type/ L/Camshaft/bhp	Drivetrain & gearbox	Acceler. 0/100 sec.	Top. speed km/h	Ave. Fuel consp. l./100 km
2001	L4/2.4/SOHC/150	front-M5	10.5	175	12.5
		front-A4	11.7	170	12.0

SPECIFICATIONS

Model 2001	Wlb. mm	Lght. mm	Cb.wt kg	Brakes fr/rr	Steering type	Standard tires
wgn. 4dr.	2616	4288	1421	dc/dr	pwr.r&p.	195/65R15
wgn. 4dr. Limited	2616	4288	1448	dc/dr	pwr.r&p.	205/55R16

PRICES

Model / version		1996	1997	1998	1999	2000	2001
sdn. 5dr.	mini						23800
	maxi						27000
sdn. 5dr. Ltd	mini						24900
	maxi						28000

See page 7 to adapt these figures.

2001 CHRYSLER PT Cruiser Limited

CHRYSLER S Series

DODGE Caravan
PLYMOUTH Voyager

1996 DODGE Caravan Sport

Chrysler minivans opened up a new and highly successful market segment in the '80's and '90's. Driven by 4 and 6-cylinder engines, they hail back to 1984, were upgraded in 1991 and 1994, and completely redesigned in 1996 to offer the «first» second sliding door on the market for this type of vehicle.

PROS
- **Wide choice** range of models and mechanical features at a competitive price.
- **Their varied uses** have made all sorts of people very happy.
- **The driver's position** is reassuring for it provides an excellent outward view and makes for virtually fatigue-free driving on long hauls.
- **With its front-wheel** and all-wheel drive, it handles safely and surely, especially in winter conditions.
- **It's a comfortable** vehicle with such a roomy interior, smooth suspension, well-upholstered seats and good soundproofing.

CONS
- **Its leaf springs** and rigid axle rear suspension are jumpy and bumpy on rough pavement and can be quite unpleasant.
- **Limited maneuverability** on extended models due to a large turning radius.
- **The frame** rattles and chatters, especially when it comes to the touchy sliding doors.
- **Headlights** don't have good luminosity or reach.
- **Limited load** and pulling capabilities in spite of the V6.
- **The weak 4-cylinder** engines and their automatic gear boxes.
- **To be improved upon**: emergency brake and next to no storage compartments.

CONCLUSION
The basic models are the best buy and the 3.0L V6 coupled with a 3-speed automatic is the most reliable combination.

RECALLS
1996 Electrostatic charge building up in gas tank and line may cause a fire.
Faulty bolts on built-in child's seat.
Risk of gas leakage near check valve.
Faulty bolts on rear seatbench mounts.
96-00 An external seal will prevent fuel leakage that could occur as the «O-Ring» degradation.
1997 Tires on vehicles with steel road wheels may have been damaged during mounting.
Master cylinder of the brakes is defective.
1998 Seat belt not properly installed on child's seats and locking mechanism may malfunction.
2000 Left front retractor assemblies will be replaced on some vehicles.
2001 Dealers will replace the lower control arm bolts and nuts.
On some vehicles the daylight running lamps do not function when the switch is in the park lamp position.

DODGE Caravan
PLYMOUTH Voyager

S Series CHRYSLER

RELIABILITY PROBLEMS

	1996	1997	1998	1999	2000	2001
Engine:	X	X	X	X	-	-
Transmission:	-	X	-	-	-	-
Suspension:	-	X	-	X	X	-
Steering:	X	-	-	X	-	-
Brakes:	-	X	X	-	-	-
Electricity:	-	-	-	X	X	X
Body:	-	-	-	X	-	-
Accessories:	X	X	X	X	X	X
Fit/finish:	X	-	-	X	-	-

POWERTRAIN

Type/ L/Camshaft/bhp	Drivetrain & gearbox	Acceler. 0/100 sec.	Top. speed km/h	Ave. Fuel consp. l./100 km
96-01 L4/2.4/DOHC/150	front-A3/A4	NA	NA	11.8
V6/3.0/OHC136-150	front-A3/A4	12.0	165	12.7
V6/3.3/OHV/150-180	front-A4	11.7	170	13.3
V6/3.8/OHV/162-215	front-A4	11.0	175	13.8

PERFORMANCE Year

SPECIFICATIONS

Model	Wlb. mm	Lght. mm	Cb.wt kg	Brakes fr/rr	Steering type	Standard tires
Caravan/Voyager 96-00						
m.v. 4dr.	2878	4733	1682	dc/dr/ABS	pwr.r&p.	215/65R15
Caravan 2001						
m.v. 4dr.	2878	4803	1755	dc/dr/ABS	pwr.r&p.	215/70R15

PRICES

Model / version		1996	1997	1998	1999	2000	2001
Caravan/Voyager							
m.v. 4dr. 5 st.	mini	6300	7550	11000	13350	16400	
	maxi	8400	10200	13100	15200	18050	
m.v. 4dr. 5 st. SE	mini	7350	9450	13000	15300	18900	
	maxi	9450	11550	15100	17300	21200	
m.v. 4dr. 5 st. LE	mini	9660	13000	16700			
	maxi	12000	14900	17300			
m.v. 4dr. 5 st. LX/ES	mini	10800	13950				
	maxi	13000	16050				
m.v. 5dr. 5 st. SE	mini						22550
	maxi						25700
m.v. 5dr. 5 st. Sport	mini						24150
	maxi						26550
m.v. 4dr. 7 st. SE	mini	7650	9750	11550	13850	17000	
	maxi	9750	11850	13650	15750	18700	
m.v. 4dr. 7 st. LE	mini	9950	13350	14600	15850	19550	
	maxi	12300	15200	16700	17850	23950	
m.v. 4dr. 7 st. ES	mini	11150	14300				
	maxi	13350	16400				
m.v. 5dr. 7 st. SE	mini						23100
	maxi						26250
m.v. 5dr. 7 st. Sport	mini						24800
	maxi						27200
AWD							
m.v. 4dr. 7 st. SE	mini		10800	12800	15100	18500	
	maxi		12900	14900	17000	20150	
m.v. 4dr. 7 st. LE	mini		14400	15750	17100	21000	
	maxi		16250	17850	19100	25400	
m.v. 4dr. 7 st. ES	mini		15350				
	maxi		17450				
m.v. 5dr. 7 st. SE	mini		13350	13350	15650	18900	24650
	maxi		14400	15450	17550	20700	27800
m.v. 5dr. 7 st. LE	mini		14900	16250	17650	21500	
	maxi		16800	18350	19650	21750	
m.v. 5dr. 7 st. Sport	mini						27300
	maxi						28850

See page 7 to adapt these figures.

CHRYSLER S Series

CHRYSLER Town & Country
DODGE Grand Caravan
PLYMOUTH Grand Voyager

2001 CHRYSLER Town & Country

Chrysler minivans opened up a new and highly successful market segment in the '80's and '90's. Driven by 4 and 6-cylinder engines, they hail back to 1984, were upgraded in 1991 and 1994, and completely redesigned in 1996 to offer the «first» second sliding door on the market for this type of vehicle.

PROS
- **Wide choice** range of models and mechanical features at a competitive price.
- **Their varied uses** have made all sorts of people very happy.
- **The driver's position** is reassuring for it provides an excellent outward view and makes for virtually fatigue-free driving on long hauls.
- **With its front-wheel** and all-wheel drive, it handles safely and surely, especially in winter conditions.
- **It's a comfortable** vehicle with such a roomy interior, smooth suspension, well-upholstered seats and good soundproofing.

CONS
- **Its leaf springs** and rigid axle rear suspension are jumpy and bumpy on rough pavement and can be quite unpleasant.
- **Limited maneuverability** on extended models due to a large turning radius.
- **The frame** rattles and chatters, especially when it comes to the touchy sliding doors.
- **Headlights** don't have good luminosity or reach.
- **Limited load** and pulling capabilities in spite of the V6.
- **To be improved upon**: emergency brake and next to no storage compartments.

CONCLUSION
The basic models are the best buy and the 3.0L V6 coupled with a 3-speed automatic is the most reliable combination.

RECALLS
1996 Electrostatic charge building up in gas tank and line may cause a fire.
Faulty bolts on built-in child's seat.
Risk of gas leakage near check valve.
Faulty bolts on rear seatbench mounts.
1997 Tires on vehicles with steel road wheels may have been damaged during mounting.
Cylinder of the brakes master is defective.
1998 Seat belt not properly installed on child's seats and locking mechanism may malfunction.
96-00 An external seal will prevent fuel leakage that could occur as the «O-Ring» degradation.
2000 Left front retractor assemblies will be replaced on some vehicles.
2001 Dealers will replace the lower control arm bolts and nuts.
On some vehicles the daylight running lamps do not function when the switch is in the park lamp position.

CHRYSLER Town & Country
DODGE Grand Caravan
PLYMOUTH Grand Voyager

S Series CHRYSLER

RELIABILITY PROBLEMS

	1996	1997	1998	1999	2000	2001
Engine:	X	X	X	X	X	-
Transmission:	X	-	-	-	-	-
Suspension:	X	-	X	X	-	-
Steering:	X	X	-	X	X	-
Brakes:	-	-	X	-	-	-
Electricity:	X	-	-	-	X	X
Body:	X	-	-	-	-	-
Accessories:	-	X	X	X	X	X
Fit/finish:	-	X	-	-	-	-

POWERTRAIN

Year	Type/ L/Camshaft/bhp	Drivetrain & gearbox	Acceler. 0/100 sec.	Top. speed km/h	Ave. Fuel consp. l./100 km
96-00	V6/3.0/OHC/136-150	front-A3/A4	12.0	165	12.7
	V6/3.3/OHV/150-158	front-A4	11.7	170	13.3
	V6/3.8/OHV/162-180	front-A4	11.0	175	13.8

SPECIFICATIONS

Model 96-00	Wlb. mm	Lght. mm	Cb.wt kg	Brakes fr/rr	Steering type	Standard tires
Town & Country						
m.v. 4dr. base	2878	4735	1795	dc/dr/ABS	pwr.r&p.	215/65R16
m.v. 4dr. AWD	3030	5073	1971	dc/ABS	pwr.r&p.	215/65R16
Gd Caravan-Gd Voyager						
m.v. 4dr. base	2853	4468	1499	dc/dr/ABS	pwr.r&p.	195/75R14
m.v. 4dr. SE/LE	2853	4468	1515	dc/dr/ABS	pwr.r&p.	195/75R14
Gd Caravan/Gd Voyager						
m.v. 4dr. SE/LE	3030	5070	1671	dc/dr/ABS	pwr.r&p.	215/70R15
m.v. 4dr. ES	3030	5070	1837	dc/dr/ABS	pwr.r&p.	215/60R17
Gd Caravan 2001						
m.v. 4dr. base	3030	5070	1671	dc/dr/ABS	pwr.r&p.	215/70R15

PRICES

Model / version		1996	1997	1998	1999	2000	2001
Gd Caravan/Gd Voyager							
m.v. 4dr. 7 st.	mini	7350	9650	12600	14400	18600	
	maxi	9450	11550	14900	16500	20700	
m.v. 4dr. 7 st. SE	mini	9000	11000	14700	16600	19750	
	maxi	11000	13100	17000	18600	22000	
m.v. 4dr.7 st. LE	mini	11950	14150	17450	20150	21500	
	maxi	14150	16250	19650	22000	23950	
m.v. 4dr. 7 st. ES	mini	13650	15550	18600	20900	24150	
	maxi	15750	17750	21200	23100	26750	
m.v. 4dr. 7 st. SE AWD	mini		12100	15950	17850	21000	
	maxi		14150	18250	19850	23300	
m.v. 4dr. 7 st. LE AWD	mini		15250	18700	21400	22800	
	maxi		17300	20900	23300	25200	
m.v. 4dr. 7 st. ES AWD	mini		16600	20150	22000	25400	
	maxi		18800	22450	24350	28000	
m.v. 5dr. 7 st.	mini	7850	10200	13250	15000	19300	
	maxi	9950	12100	15550	16900	21400	
m.v. 5dr. 7 st. SE	mini	9550	11550	15200	17100	20500	
	maxi	11550	13650	17650	19200	22800	
m.v. 5dr. 7 st. LE	mini	12500	14700	17950	20800	22200	
	maxi	14700	16800	20150	22700	24600	
m.v. 5dr. 7 st. ES	mini	14200	16000	19550	21500	24900	34500
	maxi	16250	18250	21850	23700	27500	37300
m.v. 5dr. 7 st. Sport	mini						27200
	maxi						29900
m.v. 5dr. 7 st. SE AWD	mini		12800	16500	18400	21900	
	maxi		14900	18900	20500	24150	
m.v. 5dr. 7 st. LE AWD	mini		15950	19200	22000	23750	
	maxi		18000	21400	23900	26150	
m.v. 5dr. 7 st. ES AWD	mini		17300	20800	22800	26250	36100
	maxi		19550	23100	25000	29000	38850
m.v. 5dr. 7 st. Sport AWD	mini						28750
	maxi						31500
Town & Country							
m.v. 5dr. 7 st. LXi	mini	13650	17100	20250	23850	27200	30150
	maxi	16000	19100	22800	26250	29900	33100
m.v. 5dr. 7 st. LXi AWD	mini		18000	21500	25000	28750	31700
	maxi		20100	24000	27300	31400	34650
m.v. 5dr. 7 st. LTD	mini				25700	29100	34300
	maxi				28350	32000	37300

See page 7 to adapt these figures.

CHRYSLER TL Series
CHRYSLER-DODGE-PLYMOUTH Neon

2001 DODGE Neon R/T

After retiring the Colt, the Neon is now the smallest model in the Chrysler line. It is available either as a 4-door sedan with a 2.0L 130-hp or a 2-door coupe with 150-hp.

PROS
• **The amusing looks** which have contributed significantly to its success.
• **Efficient handling** due to moderate lean and good quality shocks.
• **The power steering**, precise and direct, which makes driving much nicer than with the manual found in the older base model.
• **The decent performance**, in spite of a larger engine and greater fuel consumption than the average.
• **The interior space** which is decent, although it does lack leg room in the rear.
• **The price** of the base model, the only one which is really attractive.

CONS
• **The 2.0L engine** which is rough, noisy and lacks refinement. In addition, we are not sure it produces the advertised power.
• **The price** of the Highline version which isn't a miracle car and is as expensive as some competitive models.
• **The firm rear suspension** with limited wheel movement.
• **The average brakes** which lack stability without the ABS and the spongy pedal which makes precise braking difficult.
• **The overall quality** which still isn't as good as Japanese products.
• **The front seats** which are uncomfortable for big people and in the rear, the bench is short and lacks padding.
• **A note**: the steering wheel is not very practical and visibility to the front is affected by dashboard reflection in the front windshield.

CONCLUSION
The Neon isn't the miraculous vehicle that Chrysler had originally announced. Simply put, it is an honest and reliable mode of transportation.

RECALLS
1996 Possible short-circuit on the engine cables.
1997 Defective circuit design may cause inadvertent airbag deployment.
1998 Engine's fan is malfunctioning.
Rear suspension crossmember may be missing spot welds.
2001 Brake booster hose may swell and loosen from the intake manifold.
Some vehicles may have wrong tire label.

CHRYSLER-DODGE-PLYMOUTH Neon

TL Series CHRYSLER

RELIABILITY PROBLEMS

	1996	1997	1998	1999	2000	2001
Engine:	X	X	X	X	X	-
Transmission:	X	X	-	-	-	-
Suspension:	-	X	X	-	-	-
Steering:	-	-	-	-	-	-
Brakes:	-	X	X	X	-	-
Electricity:	X	X	X	X	-	-
Body:	X	X	-	X	X	X
Accessories:	-	X	X	X	X	X
Fit/finish:	X	X	X	X	-	-

POWERTRAIN

Year	Type/ L/Camshaft/bhp	Drivetrain & gearbox	Acceler. 0/100 sec.	Top. speed km/h	Ave. Fuel consp. l./100 km
96-01	L4/2.0/SOHC/132	front-M5	9.5	185	8.2
		front-A3	10.6	180	10.1
	L4/2.0/DOHC/150	front-M5	8.5	195	9.1
		front-A3	9.4	190	9.8

SPECIFICATIONS

Model 96-99	Wlb. mm	Lght. mm	Cb.wt kg	Brakes fr/rr	Steering type	Standard tires
cpe. 2dr. base	2642	4364	1082	dc/dr	pwr.r&p.	185/65R14
cpe. 2dr. Sport	2642	4364	1120	dc/dr	pwr.r&p.	185/65R14
cpe. 2dr. R/T	2642	4364	1120	dc/dc	pwr.r&p.	185/65R14
sdn. 4dr. base	2642	4364	1063	dc/dr	pwr.r&p.	185/65R14
sdn. 4dr. High	2642	4364	1096	dc/dr	pwr.r&p.	185/65R14
sdn. 4dr. Sport	2642	4364	1137	dc/dr	pwr.r&p.	185/65R14
00-01						
sdn. 4dr.	2667	4430	1164	dc/dr	pwr.r&p.	185/65R14
sdn. 4dr. R/T	2267	4430	1229	dc/ABS	pwr.r&p.	195/50R16

PRICES

Model / version		1996	1997	1998	1999	2000	2001
cpe. 2dr.	mini	3150	4500	5250			
	maxi	5800	6950	7750			
cpe. 2dr. Highline	mini	3700	5000		7150		
	maxi	6300	7350		9450		
cpe. 2dr. EX	mini			5900	7650		
	maxi			8200	10000		
cpe. 2dr. Sport	mini	4200	5550	6400	8200		
	maxi	6800	8000	8700	10500		
cpe. 2dr. Compet.	mini			7150	8700		
	maxi			9250	11000		
cpe. 2dr. R/T Expr.	mini			7450	9250		
	maxi			9750	11550		
sdn. 4dr.	mini	3550	4700	5600			
	maxi	6000	7150	8000			
sdn. 4dr. Highline	mini	3900	5250		7600		
	maxi	6500	7550		9850		
sdn. 4dr. EX	mini			6200	8100		
	maxi			8500	10400		
sdn. 4dr. Sport	mini	4400	5750	6700	8600		
	maxi	7000	8200	9000	10900		
sdn. 4dr. Compet.	mini			7450	9000		
	maxi			9500	11450		
sdn. 4dr. R/T Expr.	mini			7800	9650		14700
	maxi			10100	12000		17850
sdn. 4dr. LE	mini					10500	12600
	maxi					13100	15750
sdn. 4dr. LX	mini					11550	13650
	maxi					14200	16800

See page 7 to adapt these figures.

EAGLE   Talon

1997 EAGLE Talon ESi

The Talon sports model coupes, the first vehicles to be equipped with all-wheel drive, were built on the Mitsubishi Galant platform. They were designed by Chrysler and have been built by Diamond Star in Illinois since 1990.

PROS
- **Such a bold**, gutsy look has a lot to do with vehicle sales.
- **What you get** for your money goes a long way: the TSi Turbo 4WD model is less expensive than rival imports.
- **Handling** on the all-wheel drive model is clean as a whistle with the high-tech rear suspension and large tires.
- **The 2.0L Turbo** is a mean engine, and with the well-adjusted suspension as a sidekick, the sky's the limit.
- **The ride** is quite smooth, for the suspension never bounces and the front contour seats are comfortable.

CONS
- **There's a heck of a torque** wallop on the Turbo-driven 4X4's when you gun it.
- **Rear passengers** suffer from cramped head and leg room.
- **The noise level** is more noticeable on more recent models.
- **Only tall passengers** will be really comfortable in the front because seats are low and the body frame is high.
- **The trunk** on the AWD model is small and hard to get to.
- **The second generation** car interiors are plain and colorless.

CONCLUSION
These sports model coupes have been a smashing success because of all-wheel drive and because they're relatively cheap to buy and keep in good running order.

RECALLS
96-98 On AWD models, the oil level of the transfer case may be too low resulting in seizure and wheel lock-up.
Damaged rubber boot on the lower lateral ball joint may cause an extraordinary wear on the ball joint and a possible separation.
1998 Dash panel may sag interfering with the accelerator pedal. (on the Talon).

Talon EAGLE

RELIABILITY PROBLEMS

	1996	1997	1998	1999	2000	2001
Engine:	X	X	X			
Transmission:	X	X	-			
Suspension	-	-	-			
Steering:	X	-	-			
Brakes:	-	X	X			
Electricity:	X	X	-			
Body:	-	-	-			
Accessories:	X	X	X			
Fit/finish:	-	-	X			

POWERTRAIN

Year	Type/ L/Camshaft/bhp	Drivetrain & gearbox
96-98		front/all-A4
ESi	L4/2.0/DOHC/141	front-M5
		front-A4
TSi	L4T/2.0/DOHC/210	front/all-M5
		front/all-A4

PERFORMANCE

Acceler. 0/100	Top. speed	Ave. Fuel consp.
7.2	215	12.0
9.5	175	9.0
10.8	170	10.0
7.0	225	11.0
7.2	215	12.0

SPECIFICATIONS

Model	Wlb.	Lght.	Cb.wt	Brakes	Steering	Standard
96-98						
cpe. 3dr. ESi	2510	4340	1286	dc/dc	pwr.r&p.	195/70R14
cpe. 3dr. TSi	2510	4340	1315	dc/dc	pwr.r&p.	205/55R15
cpe. 3dr. TSi/AWD	2510	4340	1470	dc/dc	pwr.r&p.	215/55R17

PRICES

Model / version		1996	1997	1998	1999	2000	2001
EAGLE Talon							
cpe. 3dr. base	mini		9450	12200			
	maxi		12200	14700			
cpe. 3dr. TSi AWD	mini	13450	15550	18500			
	maxi	16300	18500	21500			
cpe. 3dr. ESi	mini	9450	11550	13650			
	maxi	12200	14300	16300			

See page 7 to adapt these figures.

1996 EAGLE Talon ESi

DAEWOO   Lanos

2000 DAEWOO Lanos

The Lanos is the smallest Daewoo commercialized in North America. It is available as a 2-door coupe and 4-door sedan.

PROS

• **Its attractive asking price** encourages consumers to disregard its limited equipment level. This in turn gives the Lanos an edge over its Korean and Japanese competitors.
• **Its body** features flowing lines and has an original shape.
• **The engine** is surprisingly modern, the controls enjoyably accurate and the handling pleasantly composed for a car in this price range.
• **With good quality tires**, the Lanos provides good handling despite its smooth suspension.
• **The well-gauged suspension** and properly padded seats combine to produce quite a comfortable ride.
• Even without ABS, the **brakes** bring the Lanos to a stable and straight stop; also, the pads are quite durable and resist well to fading.
• **The rigorous quality**, attention to detail, and materials used are attractive to the eye and the touch.
• **The well-proportioned trunk** can fit a good amount of luggage.

CONS

• **Stopping distances** are above-average, because of the threshold braking system designed to prevent the wheels from locking.
• **Acceleration** and pick-up are both laborious when the vehicle is fully loaded.
• **The engine** and tires are loud, and wind leaks can be heard around the windshield.
• **The suspension** is too soft on smooth roads and has a tendency to go wild on rough surfaces, which in turn creates some jumping.
• **The rear seats** are minuscule and hard to access, and the storage space is limited to a cup holder. . .
• **Performance** is compromised by the gap between the second and third gears on the automatic transmission.
• **A few drawbacks** worth pointing out are the fact that the instrument panel is not equipped with an indicator to show which gear the automatic transmission is in, the huge blind spot created by the windshield wipers and the lack of storage space.

CONCLUSION

While the Lanos still needs a few improvements here and there, it's a good bargain and is sure to shake things up a bit.

RECALLS

99-00 Wheel bolt torque will be increased to 88 lb/pi.
2001 Extra protection will be applied to the ECM wiring harness which will be rerouted too.

Lanos — DAEWOO

RELIABILITY PROBLEMS

	1996	1997	1998	1999	2000	2001
Engine:				-	-	-
Transmission:				-	-	-
Suspension:				-	-	-
Steering:				-	-	-
Brakes:				-	-	-
Electricity:				X	-	-
Body:				X	X	X
Accessories:				X	-	-
Fit/finish:				-	X	-

POWERTRAIN

Year	Type/ L/Camshaft/bhp	Drivetrain & gearbox
99-01	L4/1.6/DOHC/105	front-M5
		front-A4

PERFORMANCE

Acceler. 0/100 sec.	Top. speed km/h	Ave. Fuel consp. l./100 km
11.2	165	9.2
12.3	160	10.4

SPECIFICATIONS

Model 99-01	Wlb. mm	Lght. mm	Cb.wt kg	Brakes fr/rr	Steering type	Standard tires
cpe. 2 dr.	2520	4076	1110	dc/dr	pwr.r&p.	185/60R14
sdn. 4 dr.	2520	4237	1144	dc/dr	pwr.r&p.	185/60R14

PRICES

Model / version		1996	1997	1998	1999	2000	2001
cpe. 2dr. S	mini				7900	8900	10100
	maxi				10300	11450	12600
cpe. 2dr. SX	mini				9000	11000	11200
	maxi				11550	12600	13800
sdn. 4dr. S	mini				8100	8900	10300
	maxi				10500	11550	12800
sdn. 4dr. SX	mini				9450	10500	11550
	maxi				12100	13200	14200

See page 7 to adapt these figures.

1999 DAEWOO Lanos

The Canadian Used Car Guide 2002-2003

DAEWOO — Leganza

2000 DAEWOO Leganza

The Leganza is Daewoo's luxury model in North America. It is a 4-door sedan available in two versions.

PROS
- **The lines** are elegant and reserved.
- **The CDX version** features all of the equipment typical of a luxury car.
- **The Leganza is fun to drive** because of its precise steering system, good braking power that's easy to gauge and impeccable ergonomics.
- **Performance** levels are comparable to the Infiniti G20's, and acceleration and pick-up are strong enough.
- **The car is stable** on the road in spite of its mediocre tires.
- **The volume** of the cabin and trunk can easily accommodate four adults and their luggage.
- **The rear seats** are easy to get into thanks to long doors that open wide, and the windows roll all the way down.
- **The comfort level** is decent for a car of this calibre, and the noise level remains reasonable even on the highway.
- **The lightweight panels** are carefully assembled and the finish is impeccable, with several unusual features for a car sold at this price.
- **The full-size spare wheel** and the quality of the Sony radio-cassette player with multiple speakers.

CONS
- **The seats** are insufficiently padded, and the front seat adjustments are very strange. Furthermore, the ideal driving position is hard to find.
- **The Korean tires** that equip the Leganza have a long way to go before equalling the quality of their American or European counterparts.
- **Storage spaces** are few and far between in the rear, where even cup holders are lacking.
- **Oversights**: the windshield wipers have a hard time handling heavy rain and the headlights are not bright enough.

CONCLUSION
Daewoo has innovated and deserves its share of success if product reliability and service quality are part of the bargain.

RECALLS
2001 Dealers will install padding to A-pillar to reduce the risk of injury in case of a crash.

Leganza — DAEWOO

RELIABILITY PROBLEMS

	1996	1997	1998	1999	2000	2001
Engine:				-	-	-
Transmission:				-	-	-
Suspension:				-	-	-
Steering:				-	-	-
Brakes:				X	-	-
Electricity:				X	X	X
Body:				X	-	-
Accessories:				-	X	-
Fit/finish:				-	-	-

POWERTRAIN

Year	Type/ L/Camshaft/bhp	Drivetrain & gearbox
99-01	L4/2.2/DOHC/131	front-A4

PERFORMANCE

Acceler. 0/100 sec.	Top. speed km/h	Ave. Fuel consp. l./100 km
11.5	175	12.0

SPECIFICATIONS

Model 99-01	Wlb. mm	Lght. mm	Cb.wt kg	Brakes fr/rr	Steering type	Standard tires
sdn. 4dr. SX	2670	4671	1415	dc/dc	pwr.r&p.	200/60R15
sdn. 4dr. CDX	2670	4671	1420	dc/ABS	pwr.r&p.	200/60R15

PRICES

Model / version		1996	1997	1998	1999	2000	2001
sdn 4dr. SX	mini				13650	14700	15750
	maxi				16800	18000	19950
sdn 4dr. CDX	mini				15200	16600	17850
	maxi				17850	19300	22000

See page 7 to adapt these figures.

2000 DAEWOO Leganza

DAEWOO   Nubira

2000 DAEWOO Nubira

The Nubira is the mid-range model in Daewoo's line-up. It is sold as a 4-door sedan and a wagon, both models sharing the same mechanical components.

PROS

- **The engine** is a real workhorse and both acceleration and pick-up are more than satisfactory. However, certain passing maneuvres will need to be planned well in advance.
- **Braking** is among the most efficient in this class: stopping distances are short and power is well-balanced and easy to gauge.
- **The passenger compartment** is roomy enough to accommodate four adults comfortably, and access to the front and rear seats is easy.
- **The dash** is conservatively presented, controls are ergonomic and materials generally look good.
- While very detailed on CDX versions, **the equipment** is very adequate on the SX models, which feature power controls and a good quality radio.
- **The Nubira is fun to drive** because it reacts quickly and consistently. Braking is reassuring and the precise steering system produces a car that is easy to handle.
- Despite being equipped with average quality tires, the Nubira offers **good road stability** and corners with only moderate roll.
- **The wagon's trunk** features many compartments around the emergency wheel. It also includes a baggage cover.

CONS

- **The suspension** is harsh even though its travel and smoothness are average and shock absorption is effective.
- **Engine and road noise** is omnipresent, pointing to a serious lack of soundproofing especially in the case of the wagon.
- **Storage space** is kept to a minimum, both in front and back.
- **The wagon's bench seat** is positively rustic; its cushion is short, padding is minimal and the back is almost perfectly vertical.
- **The radio** is maddeningly busy and controls are microscopic and hard to master.
- **The reliability** of these new models remains to be proven.
- **The network** is currently under development, which may hinder these models' popularity and complicate their scheduled maintenance.

CONCLUSION

The Nubira is surprisingly composed and solidly built. What remain to be known is how well it will fare with the competition and whether will maintain enough of its value over the longer term.

RECALLS

None over this period.

Nubira DAEWOO

RELIABILITY PROBLEMS

	1996	1997	1998	1999	2000	2001
Engine:						
Transmission:						
Suspension:						
Steering:						
Brakes:			Insufficient data			
Electricity:						
Body:						
Accessories:						
Fit/finish:						

POWERTRAIN

Year	Type/ L/Camshaft/bhp	Drivetrain & gearbox
99-01	L4/2.0/DOHC/129	front-M5
		front-A4

PERFORMANCE

Acceler. 0/100 sec.	Top. speed km/h	Ave. Fuel consp. l./100 km
9.5	170	11.0
10.7	165	11.0

SPECIFICATIONS

Model 99-01	Wlb. mm	Lght. mm	Cb.wt kg	Brakes fr/rr	Steering type	Standard tires
sdn. 4 dr.	2750	4470	1165	dc/dr/ABS	pwr.r&p.	185/65R14
wgn. 4 dr.	2750	4514	1222	dc/dr/ABS	pwr.r&p.	185/65R14

PRICES

Model / version		1996	1997	1998	1999	2000	2001
sdn. 4dr. SX	mini				10000	11350	13100
	maxi				13650	15200	16600
sdn. 4dr. CDX	mini				12600	13850	14700
	maxi				15500	17300	17850
wgn. 4dr. SX	mini				10500	11750	14500
	maxi				14200	15900	17600
wgn. 4dr. CDX	mini				12600	14500	15900
	maxi				15750	18100	18900

See page 7 to adapt these figures.

2000 DAEWOO Nubira

FORD Aerostar

1997 FORD Aerostar

This minivan was first available in 1985. It comes in base, extended and 4WD models, powered by 3.0L and 4.0L V6 engines.

PROS
- **Its body** mounted on an H-frame provides a good cargo capacity or pulling power for heavy loads.
- **The ride** is smooth, more so on the highway than on bumpy roads, because of the rigid rear axle.
- **The instrument panel** is practical, the driver's position is comfortable and the digital gauges are convenient.
- **Steering** is clean and crisp.
- **Noteworthy**: a really huge baggage compartment on the extended model, adjustable bucket seats and optional «captain's chairs», convenient hand-brake and sliding side windows.

CONS
- **Hit and miss** reliability on the first models.
- **High fuel bills** because of excessive vehicle weight.
- **Handling** is pretty sloppy with all that swing and sway, and the ride is bumpy with the rigid rear axle and poor-quality shock absorbers.
- **The thick A-pillar** obstructs peripheral vision, rearview mirrors are tiny and those small triangular windows up front are a pain.
- **Cabin space** is cluttered with the large seatbenches and low ceiling clearance.
- **Body height** makes parking a problem, if you try to park in a private garage or in some indoor public parking lots.
- **Brakes** are sluggish and unreliable because of chronic front-wheel lock.
- **Things to be considered**: some inconveniently located controls, the cumbersome shifter on the floor, hard-to-get-to mechanical components and very heavy rear hatch.

CONCLUSION
The Aerostar is a sturdy all-purpose vehicle, whose 4WD extended model is a good buy if you need to tow heavy loads.

RECALLS
1996 Malfunctioning power door lock on driver's side.
Faulty mass airflow sensor.
96-97 Possibility of transmission case assembly failure on all-wheel drive vehicles.
A short circuit could occur at the accessory terminal in the ignition switch when it is in the "on" position causing overheating and the potential for a vehicle fire.

Aerostar — FORD

RELIABILITY PROBLEMS

	1996	1997	1998	1999	2000	2001
Engine:	X	X				
Transmission:	-	-				
Suspension:	-	-				
Steering:	X	-				
Brakes:	-	-				
Electricity:	X	X				
Body:	X	X				
Accessories:	X	-				
Fit/finish:	X	-				

POWERTRAIN

Year	Type/ L/Camshaft/bhp	Drivetrain & gearbox	Acceler. 0/100 sec.	Top. speed km/h	Ave. Fuel consp. l./100 km
96-97	V6/3.0/OHV/140	rear-A4	12.7	160	13.7
	V6/4.0/OHV/152	rear-A4	10.0	175	14.4
		all-A4	11.2	165	15.6

SPECIFICATIONS

Model	Wlb. mm	Lght. mm	Cb.wt kg	Brakes fr/rr	Steering type	Standard tires
m.v. 4dr.short	3020	4442	1545	dc/dr	pwr.r&p.	215/70R14
m.v. 4dr.AWD short	3020	4442	1570	dc/dr/ABS	pwr.r&p.	215/70R14
m.v. 4dr.long	3020	4834	1655	dc/dr	pwr.r&p.	215/75R14
m.v. 4dr.AWD long	3020	4834	1695	dc/dr/ABS	pwr.r&p.	215/75R14

PRICES

Model / version		1996	1997	1998	1999	2000	2001
4x2							
m.v. 4dr. XLT 7st.	mini	5450	6500				
	maxi	7350	8600				
m.v. 4dr.XLT lwb 7st.	mini	6300	7750				
	maxi	8600	10000				
4x4							
m.v. 4dr.XLT 7st.	mini	6500	7550				
	maxi	8400	9650				
m.v. 4dr.XLT lwb 7st.	mini	7350	8800				
	maxi	8600	11000				

See page 7 to adapt these figures.

1997 FORD Aerostar

FORD Aspire

1996 3-door FORD Aspire

The ancestor of the Aspire, the Festiva that first sold in 1989, was built in Korea by Kia, an unknown manufacturer for the North Americans at that time. It was replaced in '94 by the Aspire that is equipped with the same mechanical features.

PROS
- **Dual airbags** and more rigid body are great safety features.
- **The cabin interior** is quite spacious and the rear seatbench can be lowered to extend trunk size.
- **The Aspire models** are much more equipped than the former Festiva models.
- **The 1.3L engine** is really quite impressive, even with the automatic, because the vehicle is light as a feather.
- **Driving is safe** and sure, and understeering isn't really a problem, because it's easily controlled.
- **Brakes grip well**, but front wheels tend to lock.
- **Build quality** is quite good, but some parts of the bodywork seem pretty fragile.
- **Small vehicle size** and crisp steering make for slick city maneuvres.

CONS
- **Sluggish performance** of the 5 doors sedan are due to excessive vehicle weight and a too small horsepower engine.
- **The over-sensitive** shock absorbers and small wheels sure take the suspension for a rough ride.
- **Torque** give quite a wallop when you really accelerate and crosswind effect on handling. And gauges are hard to read at night.
- **To keep in mind**: rear windshield wiper and side rearview mirror on the right aren't standard equipment. Moreover, the optional rear spoiler is probably the ugliest one of this kind in the world.

CONCLUSION
The tiny Aspire is a real city slicker. It's a lot fun to drive and overall it is a safe one.

RECALLS
None over this period.

Aspire — FORD

RELIABILITY PROBLEMS

	1996	1997	1998	1999	2000	2001
Engine:	X	-				
Transmission:	X	-				
Suspension:	-	-				
Steering:	-	-				
Brakes:	X	-				
Electricity:	-	-				
Body:	-	-				
Accessories:	X	X				
Fit/finish:	X	-				

POWERTRAIN

Year	Type/ L/Camshaft/bhp	Drivetrain & gearbox
Aspire		
96-97	L4/1.3/SOHC/63	front-M5
		front-A3

PERFORMANCE

Acceler. 0/100 sec.	Top. speed km/h	Ave. Fuel consp. l./100 km
12.5	150	6.5
13.7	140	7.0

SPECIFICATIONS

Model 96-97	Wlb. mm	Lght. mm	Cb.wt kg	Brakes fr/rr	Steering type	Standard tires
Aspire						
sdn. 3dr.	2304	3881	909	dc/dr	r&p.	165/70SR13
sdn. 3dr. SE	2304	3881	909	dc/dr	r&p.	165/70SR13
sdn. 5dr.	2333	3960	931	dc/dr	pwr.r&p.	165/70SR13

PRICES

Model / version			1996	1997	1998	1999	2000	2001
sdn. 3dr.		mini	1900	2850				
		maxi	4200	5400				
sdn. 3dr. SE		mini	2850					
		maxi	5400					
sdn. 5dr.		mini	2400	3350				
		maxi	4700	5750				

See page 7 to adapt these figures.

1997 FORD Aspire

FORD-MERCURY Contour-Mystique

1998 FORD Contour LX

The Contour-Mystique replaced the Tempo-Topaz models in 1995. They're more high-tech 4-door sedans that come in GL, LX and SE trim levels at Ford and in GS and LS trim levels at Mercury.

PROS
- **A rugged build** provides good passenger protection and excellent road stability.
- **Construction quality** is solid, fit and finish are meticulous and materials and parts are top-notch.
- **The 4-cylinder** engine and the SVT model are really quite powerful.
- **The "oh so" charming SVT** with its daring look and buffed up engine letting out a very noticeable purr.
- **The SE** has the best braking system of the lot, thanks to 4-disc brakes, but stops are more predictable with ABS.
- **You can be sure** of a regal ride with such a smooth suspension, well-contoured seats and low noise level.
- **The car handles** beautifully, it stays good and neutral before going into understeer, which is easy to readjust.
- **The instrument panel** is ergonomic and has a good lay-out, with a style midway between Ford European and American cars.
- **Good fuel economy** with the reasonably powerful 4-cylinder engine, especially when it's coupled to a manual transmission.
- **Bonus points** for some practical items like the inside door handles that light up and are easy to find at night, and the rear seatback control located in the trunk.

CONS
- **Snug room** in the rear seats, both head and leg room are cramped, which is surprising for this type of car, especially when compared to its Cirrus-Stratus rivals.
- **The V6 engine** performance are pretty disappointing, for both accelerations and pick-up are no more muscular than those of the 4-cylinder engine which doesn't burn as much gas.
- **The awkward maneuverability** of the SE model due to its large steer angle.
- **These cars aren't stunning** enough to attract much notice in this day and age, when body design is such a decisive purchase factor.

CONCLUSION
The Contour-Mystique are solid and safe. But it's too bad the rear seats are so cramped...

Contour-Mystique   FORD-MERCURY

RECALLS
1996 Catalyst and exhaust manifold need to be replaced. (2.5L)
Damaged attachment hardware on front safety belts.
Possible leaks at filler neck seal on gas tank.
96-98 Automatic floor shift control may not correctly indicate the actual gear position.
96-98 Defective headlight switch and wiring harness connectors.
1997 Throttle cables to be replaced. (models with traction control).
1998 A burr on the accelerator cable may cause the accelerator not to return to idle when the pedal is released.
1999 Rear fuel lines may allow dangerous evaporative emissions. Ignition key can be removed from the steering column without the shift lever and transmission being in "PARK".

RELIABILITY PROBLEMS

	1996	1997	1998	1999	2000	2001
Engine:	X	X	X	X		
Transmission:		X				
Suspension:	X	-	-	-		
Steering:	X	X	-	-		
Brakes:	X	-	-	X		
Electricity:	-	X	X	-		
Body:	X	-	-	X		
Accessories:	-	X	X	X		
Fit/finish:	X	X	-	-		

POWERTRAIN

Year	Type/ L/Camshaft/bhp	Drivetrain & gearbox	Acceler. 0/100 sec.	Top. speed km/h	Ave. Fuel consp. l./100 km
96-99	L4/2.0/DOHC/125	front-M5	10.0	175	9.6
		front-A4	11.1	170	9.9
	V6/2.5/DOHC/170	front-M5	8.8	180	11.5
		front-A4	9.4	175	10.9
98-99	V6/2.5/DOHC/200 (SVT)	front-M5	7.7	220	11.9

SPECIFICATIONS

Model	Wlb. mm	Lght. mm	Cb.wt kg	Brakes fr/rr	Steering type	Standard tires
Contour						
sdn. 4dr. GL	2705	4671	1256	dc/dr	pwr.r&p.	185/70R14
sdn. 4dr. LX	2705	4689	1256	dc/dr	pwr.r&p.	185/70R14
sdn. 4dr. SE	2705	4689	1285	dc/dc	pwr.r&p.	185/70R14
sdn. 4dr. SVT	2705	4671	1392	dc/dc/ABS	pwr.r&p.	215/50ZR16
Mystique						
sdn. 4dr. GS	2705	4694	1272	dc/dr	pwr.r&p.	185/70R14
sdn. 4dr. LS	2705	4694	1272	dc/dc	pwr.r&p.	205/60R15

PRICES

Model / version		1996	1997	1998	1999	2000	2001
Contour							
sdn. 4dr.	mini		6100	7350			
	maxi		9000	10300			
sdn. 4dr. GL	mini	4950	6600	8000			
	maxi	7750	9450	10700			
sdn. 4dr. LX	mini	5450	7650	8500	9750		
	maxi	8400	10500	11350	12600		
sdn. 4dr. SE	mini	6500	8200	8900	10300		
	maxi	9450	11000	11750	13100		
sdn. 4dr. LX V6	mini			9450			
	maxi			12400			
sdn. 4dr. SE V6	mini			10100			
	maxi			12800			
sdn. 4dr. SVT V6	mini			11150	11750		
	maxi			13850	14700		
Mystique							
sdn. 4dr.	mini		6300	7550			
	maxi		9250	10500			
sdn. 4dr. GS	mini	5150	6800	8700	10000		
	maxi	8000	9650	11650	12800		
sdn. 4dr. LS	mini	5900	7900	9150	10500		
	maxi	9900	10700	11950	13350		

See page 7 to adapt these figures.

FORD-MERCURY

**Crown Victoria
Grand Marquis**

1997 FORD Crown Victoria

Launched in 1978, these models were redesigned in 1991 and got a face-lift in 1992 and 1997. In 1999, the antilock braking device becomes standard feature on these rear wheel-drive vehicles.

PROS
- **The cabin** is really roomy and can accommodate up to six adults and the huge trunk can gobble up all their luggage.
- **Their rather fluid** and flowing body design is sure more striking than those on the defunct GM rivals...
- **Standard dual airbags** and rigidified body structure are good preventive safety features.
- **The smooth suspension** gently rocks passengers in the quiet, calm cabin interior where next to no noise can creep in.
- **Engine performance** are quite impressive and out of the ordinary for such heavy cars.
- **The newly designed Intech engine** is more economical on gas than were its gas-guzzling predecessors.
- **The plush ride** you've come to expect in such luxury cars.

CONS
- **The jumpy rear axle** is an indicator that mechanical components are a bit out-dated and on bad roads, wheels bounce a lot.
- **Steering** is quite vague and is problematic in crosswinds and on slippery roads.
- **Brakes** just don't grip as they should, even with 4-disc brakes, and long stops are proof positive of same.
- **The suspension** with such flexible wheel travel causes quite a sway, but it's really more annoying than dangerous.
- **The seats** are nicely shaped, but they don't provide much lateral or lumbar support.

CONCLUSION
These cars are the last living specimens of a dying breed, but they still provide a very cushy form of travel.

RECALLS
96-99 Eventual cracking of the lower control arm ball joints.
1996 Steering arms weren't greased when assembled.
Malfunctioning power door lock on driver's side.
98-00 Replacement of the label regarding the jacking operation of the car, by a more detailed one.
2000 Inspection and if necessary replacement of the wiper control module on some vehicles.
2001 Dealers will inspect RCM, side and front crash sensor and replace them if necessary.
Restraint Control Module will be replace.

Crown Victoria
Grand Marquis

FORD-MERCURY

RELIABILITY PROBLEMS

	1996	1997	1998	1999	2000	2001
Engine:	X	-	X	X	-	-
Transmission:	X	-	X	X	-	-
Suspension:	-	-	-	X	X	-
Steering:	X	X	X	X	-	-
Brakes:	X	X	X	X	-	-
Electricity:	X	X	X	X	X	X
Body:	-	X	-	X	X	X
Accessories:	X	-	X	-	X	X
Fit/finish:	-	X	X	X	X	-

POWERTRAIN

Year	Type/ L/Camshaft/bhp	Drivetrain & gearbox
96-01	V8/4.6/OHC/175-215	rear-A4

PERFORMANCE

Acceler. 0/100 sec.	Top. speed km/h	Ave. Fuel consp. l./100 km
8.8	175	13.5

SPECIFICATIONS

Model 96-97	Wlb. mm	Lght. mm	Cb.wt kg	Brakes fr/rr	Steering type	Standard tires
sdn. 4dr. base	2906	5395	1713	dc/dc	pwr.bal.	215/70R15
sdn. 4dr. LX/LS	2906	5395	1750	dc/dc	pwr.bal.	215/70R15
98-01						
sdn. 4dr. base	2913	5385	1776	dc/ABS	pwr.bal.	225/60SR16
sdn. 4dr. LX/LS	2913	5385	1781	dc/ABS	pwr.bal.	225/60SR16

PRICES

Model / version		1996	1997	1998	1999	2000	2001
Crown Victoria							
sdn. 4dr. base	mini	8500	11850	15350	18700	21000	24150
	maxi	11550	14700	18150	21500	24150	27300
sdn. 4dr. LX	mini	9550	12900	16800	20250	23100	26250
	maxi	12600	15750	19750	22900	26250	29400
Grand Marquis							
sdn. 4dr. GS	mini	8800	12200	15750	19000	22000	25200
	maxi	11850	15000	18350	21850	25200	28350
sdn. 4dr. LS	mini	10100	13450	17100	20450	24150	27300
	maxi	13000	16250	20150	23100	27300	30450

See page 7 to adapt these figures.

1998 MERCURY Grand Marquis

FORD   Escape

2001 FORD Escape

The identical twin of the Mazda Tribute, the Escape arrived just at the right time to complete Ford's lineup and allay suspicion from the Explorer's setbacks. At once compact and modern, the Escape is a good choice in mechanical terms.

PROS
- **The compact size** is current and practical, and the youthful styling is highly successful within the otherwise very conservative lineup.
- **The Escape handles** as safely as a car, to the great delight of female drivers.
- **The overall comfort** level is quite adequate for a utility vehicle, thanks to efficient seats and soundproofing.
- **The brakes** are powerful and easy to modulate. Stops are short and straight, even without ABS.
- **The V6** cranks out honorable performance levels, and output is quite reasonable under load.
- The simple and efficient **all-wheel traction system** requires no driver intervention.
- **The Escape's off-road capabilities** are adequate to allow it to travel over quite hilly terrain, but it's not a real 4x4.
- **The powerful headlights** provide good visibility even in poor weather.

CONS
- **The 4-cylinder's** limited performance is adequate only with front-wheel drive and the manual transmission.
- **Rear-seat** roominess is limited. Indeed, rear accessibility and legroom are at a premium.
- **The standard tires** are of poor quality because their provide mediocre grip even on dry roads.
- **The suspension** reacts harshly on poor roads where the occupants get jostled around without mercy.
- **Ford's plastics** look very cheap and give the dashboard a very utilitarian look to it.
- **The windshield wipers** operate too slowly to ensure adequate visibility in rainy conditions.

VERDICT
The Escape is a very successful compact vehicle that will represent for many a more realistic alternative to the purchase of an Explorer . . .

RECALLS
None over this period.

Escape   FORD

RELIABILITY PROBLEMS
                     1996 1997 1998 1999 2000 2001

Engine:
Transmission:
Suspension:
Steering:
Brakes: Insufficient data
Electricity:
Body:
Accessories:
Fit/finish:

POWERTRAIN   PERFORMANCE

Year	Type/ L/Camshaft/bhp	Drivetrain & gearbox	Acceler. 0/100 sec.	Top. speed km/h	Ave. Fuel consp. l./100 km
2001	L4/2.0/SOHC/125	av./all-M5	12.0	160	10.0
	V6/3.0/OHV/200	av./all-A4	10.0	175	13.0

SPECIFICATIONS

Model 2001	Wlb. mm	Lght. mm	Cb.wt kg	Brakes fr/rr	Steering type	Standard tires
wgn. 4dr. 4x2	2618	4395	1390	dc/dr	pwr.r.&p.	225/70R15
wgn. 4dr. 4x4	2618	4395	1568	dc/dr	pwr.r.&p.	235/70R15

PRICES

Model / version		1996	1997	1998	1999	2000	2001
wgn. 4dr. XLS	mini						26600
	maxi						28000
wgn. 4dr. XLT	mini						28350
	maxi						31500

See page 7 to adapt these figures.

2001 FORD Escape

FORD-MERCURY — Escort

1997 FORD Escort

The last Escorts have been singularly improved. Unlike their predecessor, they owe less to the Mazda 323-Protegé and have unveiled a new 2.0L engine before their retirement. The ZX2 coupe derived from the Escort has been produced between 1998 and 2000.

PROS

- **Handling** is more sure and stable than on former models because of smoother suspension, greater wheel travel and upgraded shock absorbers.
- **These models** are more reliable, which may not mean much, given the plethora of problems that afflicted their predecessors.
- **Cabin space** and trunk capacity are roomier, which puts these models in the upper-crust compact car range.
- **The 1.8L engine** is gustier with its improved torque and power.
- **Brakes are easier** to control and are sturdier than before.
- **Comfort** on the road is more noticeable on the latest models whose suspension absorbs shocks better and the front seats are more stuffed and comfy.

CONS

- **Assembly quality** is still the pits, for body fit is far from tight or straight and materials aren't ritzy-looking at all, quite the contrary.
- **Speeding along** in a GT model isn't always care-free on poor roads, for road stability is a bit iffy.
- **The 1.9L and 1.8L engines** coupled to the automatic aren't lively at all and performance can be quite inconsistent, so driving becomes a real drag.
- **Brakes** are quite poor, achieving only long stopping distances.

CONCLUSION

Escort sales are really quite good, because the Escort is what you could call the typical economical family car.

RECALLS

1999 Belt buckle assemblies will be inspected and replaced if necessary.

Escort   **FORD-MERCURY**

RELIABILITY PROBLEMS

	1996	1997	1998	1999	2000	2001
Engine:	X	X	X	X	-	
Transmission:	-	-	-	-	-	
Suspension:	X	-	-	X	-	
Steering:	-	X	-	-	-	
Brakes:	-	-	X	-	X	
Electricity:	X	X	X	X	X	
Body:	X	-	X	X	-	
Accessories:	X	-	X	X	-	
Fit/finish:	-	-	-	-	-	

POWERTRAIN

Year	Type/ L/Camshaft/bhp	Drivetrain & gearbox
1996		
base	L4/1.9/SOHC/88	front-M5
		front-A4
others	L4/1.8/DOHC/127	front-M5
		front-A4
97-00	L4/2.0/SOHC/110	front-M5
		front-A4

PERFORMANCE

Acceler. 0/100 sec.	Top. speed km/h	Ave. Fuel consp. l./100 km
10.0	165	8.0
11.3	160	9.0
8.7	185	9.5
10.2	180	10.0
10.0	175	8.4
11.0	170	9.3

SPECIFICATIONS

Model	Wlb. mm	Lght. mm	Cb.wt kg	Brakes fr/rr	Steering type	Standard tires
1996						
sdn. 3dr. LX	2500	4317	1049	dc/dr	r&p.	175/70R13
sdn. 3dr. GT	2500	4317	1115	dc/dc	pwr.r&p.	185/60HR15
wgn. 5dr. LX	2500	4352	1094	dc/dr	r&p.	175/70R13
97-99						
sdn. 4dr. base	2499	4428	1119	dc/dr	pwr.r&p.	185/65R14
sdn. 4dr. LX/LS	2499	4428	1121	dc/dr	pwr.r&p.	185/65R14
wgn. 5dr. LX/LS	2499	4386	1148	dc/dr	pwr.r&p.	185/65R14
98-00						
cpe. 2dr. ZX2	2499	4450	1124	dc/dr	pwr.r&p.	185/65R14

PRICES

Model / version		1996	1997	1998	1999	2000	2001
Escort							
cpe. 2dr. ZX2 cool	mini			8050	9750		
	maxi			11000	12600		
cpe. 2dr. ZX2 hot	mini			8500	10300	11550	
	maxi			11550	13100	14700	
sdn. 3dr. LX	mini	3900					
	maxi	6700					
sdn. 4dr. LX	mini	4400	6100	6950	8700		
	maxi	7350	9000	9750	11550		
sdn. 4dr.GL	mini		5550				
	maxi		8500				
sdn. 4dr. SE	mini			7350	9750		
	maxi			10300	12600		
sdn. 5dr. LX	mini	4400					
	maxi	7250					
wgn. 4dr. LX	mini	5450	6600				
	maxi	7850	9550				
wgn. 5dr. SE	mini			8000	10300		
	maxi			11000	13100		

See page 7 to adapt these figures.

FORD   Excursion

2000 FORD Excursion

A champion of the sport-utility market, Ford wanted to crown its success by creating the ultimate SUV ever marketed. Derived from the Super-Duty pickup, the Excursion comes in XLT and Limited trim levels and is available with a RWD or AWD transmission.

PROS
- **The ultimate expression** of the largest civilian vehicle on the market after the Hummer.
- **A large choice** of mechanical components makes it possible to tailor the vehicle's performance to specific uses.
- **The cavernous cabin**—with its three rows of seats—and baggage compartment can fit up to eight people and their luggage.
- **The load and traction capacities** allow it to carry or pull heavy loads.
- **The rear hatch** features an original design that makes it practical and easy to handle.
- **The thickly upholstered seats**—is comfortable, and the soundproofing is effective even with the diesel engine aboard.
- **The dashboard** is nevertheless ergonomic and provides ample storage space.

CONS
- **This vehicle's overall dimensions** and hefty weight limit its use in both on- and off-road conditions.
- **Maneuverability** is hindered by the wide steer angle diameter.
- **The different engines** are veritable gas guzzlers, because of the indecent weight and size of the Excursion.
- **The hefty weight** translates into wimpy performance levels. Accelerations and pick-up are more of a chore, and the driver must plan passing maneuvres well in advance.
- **Braking is mediocre**, with emergency stop distances that are longer than average. This in turn requires the driver to adopt a defensive driving style.
- **Reselling** the Excursion will be problematic in regions where gasoline does not come cheap.

CONCLUSION
The out-of-the-ordinary Excursion is the fare of the professional crowd given the amount of cash it takes to buy and operate this vehicle.

RECALLS
None over this period.

Excursion — FORD

RELIABILITY PROBLEMS

	1996	1997	1998	1999	2000	2001
Engine:						
Transmission:						
Suspension:						
Steering:						
Brakes:			Insufficient data			
Electricity:						
Body:						
Accessories:						
Fit/finish:						

POWERTRAIN

Year	Type/ L/Camshaft/bhp	Drivetrain & gearbox
00-01	V8/5.4/SOHC/255	rr./all-A4
	V10/6.8/OHC/310	rr./all-A4
	V8TDI/7.3/OHC/250	rr./all-A4

PERFORMANCE

Acceler. 0/100 sec.	Top. speed km/h	Ave. Fuel consp. l./100 km
14.5	165	17.0
12.5	175	20.0
16.0	165	18.0

SPECIFICATIONS

Model 00-01	Wlb. mm	Lght. mm	Cb.wt kg	Brakes fr/rr	Steering type	Standard tires
wgn. 4dr. 4x2	3480	5758	3016	dc/ABS	pwr.ball	LT265/75R16
wgn. 4dr. 4x4	3480	5758	3487	dc/ABS	pwr.ball	LT265/75R16

PRICES

Model / version		1996	1997	1998	1999	2000	2001
wgn. 4dr. XLT	mini					32550	35700
	maxi					34100	37800
wgn. 4dr. LTD	mini					35700	38850
	maxi					38000	41450

See page 7 to adapt these figures.

2000 FORD Excursion

FORD   Expedition

1997 FORD Expedition

The Expedition is a RWD or AWD sport utility vehicle that comes as a large 4-door station wagon XLT or Eddie Bauer.

PROS
- **The spacious cabin** can welcome six, even seven passengers aboard and if the middle individual seats are replaced by a seatbench, an eighth passenger can be accommodated.
- **You'll be amazed** at the cool comfort you get in this sport ute. The suspension is silky smooth even on the 4X4 models. The thickly upholstered seats are comfortable, though cushions are a bit short and soundproofing provides a nice, quiet travel environment.
- **Maneuverability** is amazing for such a humungous vehicle and with such a short turning diameter.
- **Handling** is a breeze with the new sophisticated front suspension and steering is slick, clean and benefits from a good reduction ratio.
- **The rear hatch** is fitted with a window that opens for handier cargo area access, so you don't have to open the hatch door to load or unload various and sundry objects inside the cabin.
- **The drive is super-comfy**, controls and responses are incredibly smooth, the quiet ride is soothing and handling is a piece of cake.
- **Kudos for**: the simple Control-Trac control that's equipped with a 4X4 automatic function and for the safer, lit-up running boards and the sound system and climate control dials in the rear seat area.
- **Workmanship** is very good for a domestic product. The build is robust, clean finish details and trim materials are as classy.

CONS
- **Fuel consumption** is far from frugal, as is to be expected on such a heavyweight that can tow a trailer weighing up to 8,000 lb. But the gas tank capacity does allow for good road autonomy.
- **Brakes** aren't the best with those long emergency stops.
- **Parking** such a big brute in the city isn't a treat, when parking spots are in shrink mode.
- **Pick-up** isn't as peppy as accelerations and so you have to be pretty careful when passing because this maneuver takes more room.
- **The poorly** designed third seatbench isn't too comfy and it's tough as heck getting to it.

CONCLUSION
This vehicle is as civilized as a limo and yet super-practical and really versatile.

RECALLS
1997   Inaccurate vehicle identification number.
Transmission shifter cable must be inspected and reinstalled.
97-99   The lug nuts of the wheels must be inspected and replaced.
1999   Missing or partially installed retainer clip that holds the master cylinder pushrod to the brake pedal arm.
Defective fuel line assemblies that could develop a leak.
17-inch chrome steel wheels can separate from the vehicle due to insufficient wheel contact area with the hub and lack of lug nuts torque.
2001   Driver airbag module can be defective and will be replaced.
The wiper motor gear case will be inspected and replaced on suspect time frame vehicles.

Expedition   FORD

RELIABILITY PROBLEMS

	1996	1997	1998	1999	2000	2001
Engine:	-	-	-	-	X	-
Transmission:		X	-	X	-	-
Suspension:		-	-	X	-	-
Steering:		X	-	-	-	-
Brakes:		X	-	X	-	-
Electricity:		X	X	X	X	X
Body:		-	-	X	X	-
Accessories:		X	X	X	X	X
Fit/finish:		X	X	X	X	-

POWERTRAIN

Year	Type/ L/Camshaft/bhp	Drivetrain & gearbox
97-01	V8/4.6/SOHC/214-240	rear/all-A4
	V8/5.4/SOHC/235-260	rear/all-A4

PERFORMANCE

Acceler. 0/100 sec.	Top. speed km/h	Ave. Fuel consp. l./100 km
11.5	170	16.9
11.0	175	18.2

SPECIFICATIONS

Model 4x2	Wlb. mm	Lght. mm	Cb.wt kg	Brakes fr/rr	Steering type	Standard tires
wgn. 4dr. XLT	3025	5197	2199	dc/ABS	pwr.bal.	255/70R16
wgn. 4dr. E.B	3025	5197	2220	dc/ABS	pwr.bal.	255/70R16
4x4						
wgn. 4dr. XLT	3025	5197	2300	dc/ABS	pwr.bal.	255/70R16
wgn. 4dr. E.B	3025	5197	2350	dc/ABS	pwr.bal.	265/70R17

PRICES

Model / version		1996	1997	1998	1999	2000	2001
4x2							
wgn. 4dr. XLT	mini		19200	22900	25400	28000	32750
	maxi		22000	25400	28000	30950	35700
wgn. 4dr. E.B.	mini		22250	25950	28750	33100	37800
	maxi		25200	28350	31500	36200	40950
4x4							
wgn. 4dr. XLT	mini		23600	24450	27300	30150	34100
	maxi		27800	27000	29900	33100	37800
wgn. 4dr. E.B.	mini		23850	27500	30450	34100	39900
	maxi		26750	29900	33300	38300	43000

See page 7 to adapt these figures.

1998 FORD Expedition

FORD Explorer

1996 FORD Explorer

The Explorer replaced the Bronco II in 1991. It's an all-purpose sports vehicle that comes in 2 or 4-door body styles, with 2WD or 4WD.

PROS
- **Its more modern look** has a lot to do with its popularity.
- **The interior cabin** is very much like that of a car.
- **Road stability** on straight runs and overall handling are better on the 4-door model with its longer body frame.
- **The 5.0L V8** engine is super with its surging torque and power.
- **This vehicle** is more comfortable because of its longer wheelbase and better designed soundproofing.
- **Reliability** is better than most of its competitors.

CONS
- **The hefty price** of the Eddie Bauer and Limited models that cost as much as upper-end luxury cars.
- **Touch and go handling** on the 2-door model in crosswinds.
- **The ride** in the base models is as smooth or as rough as the road you're travelling on.
- **Brakes** could be improved, stops are long and unpredictable and brake pads don't have too much lasting power.
- **The manual shifter** is imprecise and quite unpleasant to use.
- **The driver's position** is far from perfect with the long steering column, high instrument panel and low-slung seat. Besides, the windshield pillars obstruct visibility on both sides.
- **Rear seats** are tough to get to without a step to climb up on, because of high ground clearance.

CONCLUSION
The Explorer is more refined than the Bronco II, for handling and comfort are of higher caliber, but by opting for luxury, it's become an expensive vehicle to run.

RECALLS
1996 Defective power door lock on driver's side.
Welds on the bracket that attaches the liftgate are undersized.
96-97 Ice may form around the throttle plate while driving at temperatures under 29°C and at highway speeds.
Antipollution device does not correspond to established standards
97-98 Fuel line may be damaged if used as ground while jump starting the vehicle.
1998 Warning chime for opened doors may not work on some vehicles.
98-99 Speed control cable may interfere with the servo pulley and not allow the throttle to return to idle when disengaging the unit.
Secondary hood latch may corrode and cause a hood fly-up.
1999 Right front brake line attachment may separate from the ABS hydraulic control unit resulting in a loss of brake pressure.
2000 Belt buckle assemblies will be inspected and replaced if necessary.
Dealers will install a relay and wring on affected vehicles.
Side crash sensor will be replaced with a revised design.
Dealers will insta a resistor on GEM (Generic Electronic Module) to prevent electronic noise.
2001 Dealers will install a revised seat back hinge.

Explorer — FORD

RELIABILITY PROBLEMS

	1996	1997	1998	1999	2000	2001
Engine:	-	X	X	X	-	-
Transmission:	X	X	-	-	-	-
Suspension:	X	X	-	-	X	-
Steering:	X	-	-	-	-	-
Brakes:	-	-	X	-	-	-
Electricity:	X	-	-	X	X	X
Body:	-	-	-	-	-	-
Accessories:	X	X	X	X	X	X
Fit/finish:	X	-	-	-	X	-

POWERTRAIN

Year	Type/ L/Camshaft/bhp	Drivetrain & gearbox
96-97	V8/5.0/OHV/210-215	rear/all-A4
96-01	V6/4.0/OHV/145-210	rear/all-M5
		rear/all-A4/5

PERFORMANCE

Acceler. 0/100 sec.	Top. speed km/h	Ave. Fuel consp. l./100 km
10.0	175	17.7
9.0	170	15.1
8.5	175	15.5

SPECIFICATIONS

Model Explorer	Wlb. mm	Lght. mm	Cb.wt kg	Brakes fr/rr	Steering type	Standard tires
wgn. 2dr. 4x2	2583	4893	1667	dc/ABS	pwr.bal.	235/70R15
wgn. 2dr. 4x4	2583	4893	1765	dc/ABS	pwr.bal.	225/70R15
wgn. 4dr. 4x2	2835	4844	1775	dc/ABS	pwr.bal.	225/70R15
wgn. 4dr. 4x4	2835	4844	1880	dc/ABS	pwr.bal.	255/70R16

PRICES

Model / version		1996	1997	1998	1999	2000	2001
4x2							
wgn. 2dr. XL	mini	7350	10500				
	maxi	10900	12600				
wgn. 2dr. XL Sport	mini	8900	11550	15000	16800	19950	22000
	maxi	12600	13850	17000	19000	22600	25200
wgn. 4dr. XL	mini	9350	12000	15450	16700		
	maxi	13000	14400	17650	18800		
wgn. 4dr. XLT	mini	10500	13350	17450	17750	23750	25700
	maxi	14400	15750	19650	20500	26250	28850
wgn. 4dr. E.B.	mini	12900	17550	18900	21850	25200	27300
	maxi	16800	19950	21300	24000	27800	30450
wgn. 4dr. LTD	mini	14700	19400	20600	22900	26250	28350
	maxi	18700	21950	22900	25100	28850	31500
wgn. 4dr. XLS	mini					21650	23600
	maxi					24150	26800
4x4							
wgn. 2dr. XL	mini	8400	11750				
	maxi	11950	13850				
wgn. 2dr. XL Sport	mini	9950	12800	16300	18000	21600	23600
	maxi	13650	15100	18400	20250	24150	26750
wgn. 4dr. XL	mini	10400	13350	16700	17950		
	maxi	14000	15650	18900	20000		
wgn. 4dr. XLT	mini	11550	14600	18700	19000	25200	27300
	maxi	15450	17000	20900	21700	27800	30450
wgn. 4dr. E.B.	mini	14000	18800	20150	23100	26750	28850
	maxi	17850	21200	22550	25300	29400	32000
wgn. 4dr. LTD	mini	15750	20700	21850	24150	27800	29900
	maxi	19750	23100	24150	26250	30450	33100
wgn. 4dr. XLS	mini					24650	
	maxi					27800	
wgn. 4dr. XLT V8	mini	12600	15000	19750	20500	26250	28350
	maxi	15750	17650	21950	23100	28850	31500
wgn. 4dr. E.B. V8	mini	15000	19300	21500	24150	27800	29900
	maxi	18900	22000	23600	26250	30450	33000
wgn. 4dr. LTD V8	mini	16800	21500	23600	25200	28850	30950
	maxi	20800	24150	25200	27300	31500	34100
Sport Trac							
wgn. 4dr. 2WD	mini						25200
	maxi						28850
wgn. 4dr. 4WD	mini						28350
	maxi						32000

See page 7 to adapt these figures.

FORD   Focus

2001 FORD Focus wagon

The Focus replaced the Escort in 2000 and is available as a 3-door coupe, a 4-door sedan and a wagon. It shares its mechanical components with its predecessor.

PROS
- **The Focus is competitively priced**, but to the detriment of its equipment and the fact that a number of practical features haven't been included.
- **Rounded lines** and other styling touches make the Focus look bigger than most of its rivals.
- **Stopping distances** are short, power is progressive and easy to gauge. The brake pads resist well to heat.
- **The Zetec engine** offers better performance.
- **The Focus handles** with assurance and efficiency, and is well-balanced in curves when equipped with good quality tires.
- **The trunk** can take on a fair amount of baggage, but its narrow opening makes it hard to load large items.
- **The quality** of the radio on our test drive models was remarkable, especially when compared with other equipment that was mediocre at best.

CONS
- **The dashboard's tortured lines** make it a nightmare to look at, and it is already seriously outdated.
- **The disappointing quality** of the finish and the quality of materials, fabrics and plastics create an overall look that is decidedly inexpensive.
- **The rear seats** are hard to get into because of limited space and the narrow opening of the doors.
- **The base engine** provides mediocre performance, especially when coupled with the automatic transmission. Also, it produces as much noise as it does vibration.
- **The suspension** is too soft, and the poor shock absorbers cause the front wheels to hop on bad road surfaces.
- **Visibility** is not ideal because of the thick A-and C-pillars; the small triangular windows are a further drawback.
- **Major road, wind and engine noise** points to very poor soundproofing.
- **A number of practical features have been left out**: the driver has no dummy pedal, there is no gear indicator for the automatic transmission, and rear-seat passengers have no headrests or storage spaces.

CONCLUSION
Like the Escort, the Focus is relatively inexpensive, but it is not worth much more.

RECALLS
2000 Speed control cable will be inspected and replaced if necessary. Vehicles will be inspected and rear wheel hub assembly replaced if necessary.
Dealers will replace the IPS (Injector Pressure Sensor) on some vehicles.
2001 Seat back recliner handle spring will be replaced on both front seats.

Focus FORD

RELIABILITY PROBLEMS

	1996	1997	1998	1999	2000	2001
Engine:					X	-
Transmission:					-	-
Suspension:					-	-
Steering:					-	-
Brakes:					X	X
Electricity:					X	-
Body:					-	-
Accessories:					X	-
Fit/finish:					X	-

POWERTRAIN

Year	Type/ L/Camshaft/bhp	Drivetrain & gearbox	Acceler. 0/100 sec.	Top. speed km/h	Ave. Fuel consp. l./100 km
00-01					
LX/SE	L4/2.0/SOHC/110	front-M5	11.2	170	8.5
		front-A4	12.0	165	9.2
ZX3/	L4/2.0/DOHC/130	front-M5	9.5	180	9.2
ZTS		front-A4	10.5	175	9.6

SPECIFICATIONS

Model 00-01	Wlb. mm	Lght. mm	Cb.wt kg	Brakes fr/rr	Steering type	Standard tires
cpe. 2 dr.	2616	4270	1157	dc/dr	pwr.r&p.	175/70R14
sdn. 4 dr.	2616	4526	1163	dc/dr	pwr.r&p.	195/60R15
wgn. 4 dr.	2616	4526	1232	dc/dr	pwr.r&p.	195/60R15

PRICES

Model / version		1996	1997	1998	1999	2000	2001
cpe. 3dr. ZX3	mini					12300	14500
	maxi					15450	17550
sdn. 4dr. LX	mini					11250	13350
	maxi					14400	16700
sdn. 4dr. S	mini					12300	14500
	maxi					15450	17750
sdn. 4dr. ZTS	mini					13350	15450
	maxi					16500	18900
wgn. 4dr. Se	mini					13850	15950
	maxi					17000	19400

See page 7 to adapt these figures.

2000 3-door FORD Focus

FORD   Mustang

FORD Mustang GT 1996

Renewed in 1994, the latest Mustang is offered with a V6 or V8 engine, as a coupe or a convertible, as a base version, a GT and, since 1997, as a Cobra with a blasting 305-hp. To celebrate its 35th anniversary in 1999, a new body design has been introduced.

PROS

- **The sassy body** design is a winner for the young and young at heart.
- **The V6 and V8 engines** are quite different one from the other, but they put a lot of fun and frolic into driving.
- **The latest generation** vehicle is more stable because of its beefed up body.
- **Brakes are gutsy** and stop-on-a-dime dependable, but they're over-assisted so they can be a bit tricky.
- **Driving** is a treat with such spirited, straight-on steering and clean gears.
- **More recent models** are more comfy for there's more room in the rear seat, the suspension is never brutal and there are just enough decibels to add zest to the drive.

CONS

- **Road stability** can be touch and go on slippery roads, for wheels skid and the rigid rear end gives you a Jolly Jumper workout.
- **Steering** is fine at low speeds, but it becomes vague and out of touch at high speeds, so the driver has to watch what he's doing.
- **Fuel consumption** is high with all engine models.
- **The 3.8L engine** doesn't have much get up and go, so driving becomes rather dull and run-of-the-mill.
- **The really stiff suspension** and seats, along with high noise level, make for pretty tiring trips in the older GT.
- **Rear seat** access is awkward and the trunk is hard to get to as well.
- **The trunk** on the convertible model is pretty small.

CONCLUSION

The Mustang is a versatile and affordable Sportscar that's way ahead in the race against its rivals, yes, even when it comes to the Probe...

RECALLS

1996   Hood is defective and might separate itself.
1998   The 4.6L engine's fuel rail could separate.
98-99 Speed control cable may interfere with the servo pulley and not allow the throttle to return to idle.
2001   Dealers will modify the parking brake to control the self adjustment mechanism.

Mustang   FORD

RELIABILITY PROBLEMS

	1996	1997	1998	1999	2000	2001
Engine:	X	X	X	X	-	-
Transmission:	-X	X	-	X	-	-
Suspension:	X	X	X	X	X	X
Steering:	-	-	-	-	-	-
Brakes:	-	X	X	X	-	-
Electricity:	X	X	X	-	-	-
Body:	X	X	X	X	X	-
Accessories:	X	X	X	X	X	X
Fit/finish:	-	X	-	X	-	-

POWERTRAIN

Year	Type/ L/Camshaft/bhp	Drivetrain & gearbox
96-01	V6/3.8/OHV/145-190	rear-M5
		rear-A4
	V8/4.6/SOHC/215-250	rear-M5
		rear-A4
96-99	V8/4.6/DOHC/305	rear-M5

PERFORMANCE

Acceler. 0/100 sec.	Top. speed km/h	Ave. Fuel consp. l./100 km
8.2	170	11.6
9.0	165	12.3
6.7	190	13.7
7.5	180	13.7
6.0	225	13.4

SPECIFICATIONS

Model	Wlb. mm	Lght. mm	Cb.wt kg	Brakes fr/rr	Steering type	Standard tires
96-01						
con. 2dr.	2573	4653	1392	dc/dc	pwr.r&p.	205/65R15
cpe. 2dr.	2573	4653	1456	dc/dc	pwr.r&p.	205/65R15
96-99						
cpe. 2dr. Cobra	2573	4610	1540	dc/ABS	pwr.r&p.	245/45ZR17
con. 2dr. Cobra	2573	4610	1600	dc/ABS	pwr.r&p.	245/45ZR17

PRICES

Model / version		1996	1997	1998	1999	2000	2001
cpe. 2dr.	mini	6100	8700	11150	13450	15200	17650
	maxi	8900	11550	13950	16300	18400	21000
cpe. 2dr. GT	mini	11150	12900	14700	18150	20500	23400
	maxi	14000	15750	17650	20800	23600	26750
cpe. 2dr. Cobra	mini	15350	18150	19950	23400		30750
	maxi	18250	21000	22900	26250		34100
con. 2dr.	mini	10100	12200	13650	15550	18350	20800
	maxi	13000	14700	16600	18400	21500	24150
con. 2dr. GT	mini	14300	16000	17850	21300	23600	26550
	maxi	16800	18900	20800	24150	26750	29900
con. 2dr. Cobra	mini	17450	20250	22000	25550		32850
	maxi	20350	23100	25000	28350		38300

See page 7 to adapt these figures.

FORD   Probe

1997 FORD Probe GT

Of Ford and Mazda design, the Probe coupe shares its platform and mechanical components with the MX-6. It was touched up in '93 along the same lines. The former conventional and Turbo 2.2L and the 3.0L V6 engines were later replaced by the 2.0L 4-cylinder and 2.5L V6.

PROS
- **Its unique design** once created quite a sensation.
- **The nicely designed** cockpit is the icing on the cake when you're at the wheel of such a fun vehicle.
- **The V6 engines** are thrilling with the manual transmission.
- **Road stability** is better on the GT models, because shock absorbers are better adjusted than on the base models, and these models stay neutral longer.
- **Fuel consumption** is economical if you're not too rough and ready a driver.
- **This is a pretty comfortable** sportswear, even with the stiff suspension and it can accommodate four adults, even with the low ceiling clearance in the rear seat.

CONS
- **Excessive vehicle weight** explains why the base engine model isn't too spirited.
- **Rear seats** are quite cramped on the latest model.
- **The muscular V6 accelerations** can cause walloping torque, which can be hazardous on slippery roads.
- **Brakes** on the base model are definitely less effective than those on the GT that comes equipped with rear disc-brakes.
- **The narrow windows** obstruct vision and the driver is seated low, so it's hard to get a good outward view.
- **The high trunk** opening doesn't make luggage handling easy.

CONCLUSION
The Probe coupe doesn't have what it takes any more, for former owners are now buying multi-purpose sports vehicles that better meet their varied needs.

RECALLS
96-97 Fuel cap must be replaced to prevent fuel vapor leak.
1997 2.0L engine timing belt auto tensioner may break resulting in possible engine stalling.

Probe — FORD

RELIABILITY PROBLEMS

	1996	1997	1998	1999	2000	2001
Engine:	X	X				
Transmission:	X	-				
Suspension:	X	X				
Steering:	-	-				
Brakes:	-	-				
Electricity:	-	-				
Body:	-	-				
Accessories:	X	-				
Fit/finish:	X	-				

POWERTRAIN

Year	Type/ L/Camshaft/bhp	Drivetrain & gearbox	Acceler. 0/100 sec.	Top. speed km/h	Ave. Fuel consp. l./100 km
96-97	L4/2.0/DOHC/118	front-M5	9.9	180	9.2
		front-A4	11.0	175	10.5
	V6/2.5/DOHC/164	front-M5	7.9	210	11.4
		front-A4	8.8	200	11.8

SPECIFICATIONS

Model 96-97	Wlb. mm	Lght. mm	Cb.wt kg	Brakes fr/rr	Steering type	Standard tires
cpe. 3dr.base	2611	4539	1220	dc/dr	pwr.r&p.	195/65R14
cpe. 3dr.GT	2611	4559	1325	dc/dc	pwr.r&p.	225/50R16

PRICES

Model / version		1996	1997	1998	1999	2000	2001
cpe. 3dr. base	mini		7650				
	maxi		10500				
cpe. 3dr. GT	mini	8400	10300				
	maxi	11450	13250				
cpe. 3dr. SE	mini	5900					
	maxi	8800					

See page 7 to adapt these figures.

1996 FORD Probe

FORD-MERCURY — Taurus-Sable

2000 FORD Taurus

The Taurus and Sable are the most popular cars in North America. Launched on the market in 1986, they were redesigned ten years later and got a serious remodeling in 1998 and 2000.

PROS
- **Sumptuous,** clean lines that are just a bit sassy.
- **With such firm shock** absorbers and such a smooth independent suspension, road stability is just great.
- **The ride is silky** smooth, thanks to well-adjusted suspension, cushy seats and dead on soundproofing.
- **The SHO engine** is thrilling and has great thrust, power steering is smooth and clean as a whistle and the tires are perfect for Sportscar maneuvers.
- **Finish is spiffy** and construction build is tight, yet some of the plastic moldings are really quite awful-looking.

CONS
- **The first generation models** weren't always reliable and build quality was never quite top-notch.
- **The 3.0L engine** puts out only fair to middling performance.
- **The models equipped** with rear drum brakes are iffy when it comes to clean stops or right-on road stability because ABS is only standard on SHO models.
- **Items to consider**: the impractical parking brake, poor maneuverability, rearward vision on the station wagons, not enough and weirdly designed storage compartments and the smaller trunk on the latest models.

CONCLUSION
The Taurus-Sable have a fresh body design, are really good cars and are still quite affordable.

RECALLS
1996 Faulty parking mechanism on transmission that may disengage, causing car to roll.
Defective catch that may stop shifter from going into park.
Defective fuel pressure regulator (SHO engine).
Brake fluid gauge may fail.
Vapour control valves may not operate properly.
Some fuel tanks are defective.

97-98 Transaxle's cover can separate while car is being driven.

1998 Attaching stud on front seat belt buckle defective.

2001 Brake lamp will be replaced and excess grease wiped off the adjustable pedal assembly.
Dealers will install a jumper/resistor assembly at the spoiler.
Dealers will replace driver and front passenger seat belt buckles.

Taurus-Sable — MERCURY-FORD

RELIABILITY PROBLEMS

	1996	1997	1998	1999	2000	2001
Engine:	X	X	-	X	X	-
Transmission:	X	X	X	-	-	-
Suspension:	-	-	-	-	X	-
Steering:	-	-	-	X	X	-
Brakes:	-	-	-	-	-	-
Electricity:	-	X	-	-	X	X
Body:	X	X	X	X	X	X
Accessories:	X	X	-	-	X	-
Fit/finish:	X	X	X	X	-	-

POWERTRAIN

Year	Type/ L/Camshaft/bhp	Drivetrain & gearbox
96-99	V6/3.0/OHV/145	front-A4
	V6/3.0/DOHC/200	front-A4
	V8/3.4/DOHC/235	front-A4
00-01	V6/3.0/OHV/145	front-A4
	V6/3.0/DOHC/200	front-A4

PERFORMANCE

Acceler. 0/100 sec.	Top. speed km/h	Ave. Fuel consp. l./100 km
10.6	165	12.4
9.4	175	12.7
8.0	200	14.2
10.2	165	12.5
9.0	175	12.8

SPECIFICATIONS

Model	Wlb. mm	Lght. mm	Cb.wt kg	Brakes fr/rr	Steering type	Standard tires
96-99						
sdn. 4dr. GL/GS	2756	5017	1510	dc/dr	pwr.r&p.	205/65R15
sdn. 4dr. SHO	2756	5039	1504	dc/ABS	pwr.r&p.	225/55ZR16
wgn. 4dr. LX/LS	2756	5070	1579	dc/dr	pwr.r&p.	205/65R15
00-01						
sdn. 4dr.	2756	5019	1550	dc/dr	pwr.r&p.	205/65R15
wgn. 4dr.	2756	5022	1585	dc/dr	pwr.r&p.	205/65R15

PRICES

Model / version		1996	1997	1998	1999	2000	2001
Taurus							
sdn. 4dr. GL	mini	4950	6600				
	maxi	7750	9650				
sdn. 4dr. LX	mini	6000	7650	8400	9750	12600	15000
	maxi	8800	10700	11550	12600	15750	18350
sdn. 4dr. SHO	mini	9650	12400	15200	18700		
	maxi	11950	14900	18350	21500		
sdn. 4dr. SE	mini			9450	11350	14700	17100
	maxi			12600	14150	17850	20450
sdn. 4dr. SEL	mini					15750	18350
	maxi					18900	21500
wgn. 4dr. GL	mini	6000	7150				
	maxi	8800	10200				
wgn. 4dr. LX	mini	7450	8700				
	maxi	9850	11750				
wgn. 4dr. SE	mini			10500	12400	15200	17650
	maxi			13650	15200	18400	21000
wgn. 4dr. SEL	mini					16250	18700
	maxi					19400	22550
Sable							
sdn. 4dr. GS	mini	5250	6900	8600	10300		
	maxi	8100	10000	11750	13100		
sdn. 4dr. LS	mini	6300	8000	9650	11550		
	maxi	9150	11000	12900	14500		
wgn. 4dr. GS	mini	5750	7350				
	maxi	8600	10500				
wgn. 4dr. LS	mini	7650	9000	11700	12600		
	maxi	10200	12100	13950	15550		

See page 7 to adapt these figures.

FORD-MERCURY

Thunderbird Cougar XR7

1997 MERCURY Cougar

These mid-size coupes that hail way back to 1954 have had quite an erratic and bumpy career. They were last revamped in '89 in a still very large format before disappearing in '98 due to poor sales. In 99, the Cougar is re-introduced on the market but this time, in a much smaller format and in a very different style; all of this based on the Contour-Mystique platform.

PROS

- **Lots of folks are still wild** about their clean and classic body design while the dynamic lines inspired by the "Edge design" school of thought will appeal to the younger buyers.
- **A comfortable ride** with spacious cabin, sensitive suspension, well-upholstered seats and low noise level.
- **Muscular accelerations** and pick-up on the SuperCoupe and XR7 with supercharged engine. With regards of the 99 Cougar, the V6 engine is much healtier than the inline 4-cylinder but cannot match by far the performance and the drive sensation obtained by the older Cougar nor the Probe that it is replacing.
- **Handling** is good with the independent rear suspension and good-sized original tires.
- **Steering is quick**, crisp and smooth.
- **There are lots of storage** compartments and the trunk holds an amazing amount of luggage. On the '99, the trunk is also expandable.
- **Solid construction** quality and cleaner finish on the latest models.

CONS

- **High fuel consumption**, especially with the Thunderbird's V8.
- **Maneuverability** and ability to make quick moves aren't perfect because of vehicle size and very large steer angle.
- **The cabin interior** is rather dull and some items just aren't the right design for a so-called Sportscar. At the other end, the design of the '99 Cougar is somewhat so excessive that it can easily go out of style.
- **Brakes are smooth**, but they don't have much lasting power and emergency stops are too long.
- **No shifter position** indicator among the instruments and poorly located air-conditioner controls.
- **The sound level** monitored in the '99 Cougar is one of the highiest found on a similar type of car.

CONCLUSION

Even though they're quite winsome, these models have fewer and fewer takers, because engine performances aren't really of Sportscar caliber. If only their famous name can evoke more than good old memories...

Thunderbird / Cougar XR7 — MERCURY-FORD

RECALLS
1996 Defective semi-automatic temperature control unit on heater system.
Faulty power door-lock on driver's side.

RELIABILITY PROBLEMS

	1996	1997	1998	1999	2000	2001
Engine:	X	X		X	-	
Transmission:	-	-		-	-	
Suspension:	-	-		X	-	
Steering:	X	X		-	-	
Brakes:	X	-		X	X	
Electricity:	-	-		X	X	
Body:	X	-		-	-	
Accessories:	-	-		X	-	
Fit/finish:	X	X		X	-	

POWERTRAIN

Year	Type/ L/Camshaft/bhp	Drivetrain & gearbox
96-97	V6/3.8/OHV/140	rear-A4
96-97	V8/4.6/SOHC/205	rear-A4

PERFORMANCE

Acceler. 0/100 sec.	Top. speed km/h	Ave. Fuel consp. l./100 km
11.5	165	11.0
9.0	195	13.0

SPECIFICATIONS

Model	Wlb. mm	Lght. mm	Cb.wt kg	Brakes fr/rr	Steering type	Standard tires
cpe. 2dr. LX	2870	5047	1641	dc/dr	pwr.r&p.	205/70R15
cpe. 2dr. SC	2870	5047	1728	dc/ABS	pwr.r&p.	225/60R16
Cougar / XR7						
cpe. 2dr. XR7	2870	5047	1739	dc/ABS	pwr.r&p.	225/60R16
Cougar 99-00						
cpe. 2dr. 2+2 I4	2703	4699	1312	dc/dr	pwr.r&p.	205/70R15
cpe. 2dr. 2+2 V-6	2703	4699	1363	dc/dr	pwr.r&p.	205/60R15

PRICES

Model / version		1996	1997	1998	1999	2000	2001
Thunderbird							
cpe. 2dr. LX	mini	7550	9450				
	maxi	9850	12200				
Cougar / XR7							
cpe. 2dr. XR7	mini	7450	9250				
	maxi	10500	12600				

See page 7 to adapt these figures.

1996 FORD Thunderbird

MERCURY Cougar

2001 MERCURY Cougar

The compact Cougar was introduced to the market in 1999. It's a completely different model from the one that bore the same name for a long time in Mercury's lineup. Its platform and mechanical components are derived from the defunct Contour/Mystique.

PROS

- **The modern styling** of the first model was slightly exaggerated, but it has since been slightly redesigned and has become more sober.
- **The compromise** between comfort and handling is unusual for a car whose intentions are sporty, because the suspension, seats and sound level are surprisingly civilized.
- **The large modular trunk** is a very appreciated practical touch in an era where versatility is a must for any vehicle.
- **The well-contoured front seats** provide great lateral and lumbar support, and they are consistently padded.
- **The V6** engine's sporty exhaust note makes driving this car addictive.
- **The equipment** list is extensive, despite a few oddities.

CONS

- **The V6's performance** is disappointing; the Cougar accelerates no quicker that the former Contour/Mystique. Ford could have given it more character by entrusting it to its SVT guys.
- **The manual gearbox** is fuzzy and does not encourage sporty driving. This is in direct contradiction with the vehicle's mission.
- **Torque steer** becomes a problem when accelerating and can prove to be downright dangerous on slippery roads.
- The irrational equipment list contains many oddities, but there is no tilt steering column or ABS.
- **The rear seats** are rather useless, as is often the case in such coupes. Only small children or pets will have enough room in back.
- **Rearward visibility** is greatly hindered because of the small exterior mirrors, sharp slope of the rear window and thickness of the B and C pillars.
- **The high trunk** sill seriously complicates the loading and unloading of luggage.

VERDICT

Ford failed to seize a great opportunity to launch an interesting vehicle. It missed its target market and chose components that produce a vapid cocktail.

RECALLS

None over this period.

Cougar — MERCURY

RELIABILITY PROBLEMS

	1996	1997	1998	1999	2000	2001
Engine:				X	X	-
Transmission:				-	-	-
Suspension:				X	-	-
Steering:				-	X	-
Brakes:				X	X	X
Electricity:				X	X	X
Body:				-	-	-
Accessories:				X	X	-
Fit/finish:				X	-	-

POWERTRAIN

Year	Type/ L/Camshaft/bhp	Drivetrain & gearbox
99-00	L4/2.0/DOHC/125	front-M5
99-01	V6/2.5/DOHC/170	front-M5
		front-A4

PERFORMANCE

Acceler. 0/100 sec.	Top. speed km/h	Ave. Fuel consp. l./100 km
11.0	175	9.7
9.0	185	12.0
10.4	180	11.4

SPECIFICATIONS

Model 99-01	Wlb. mm	Lght. mm	Cb.wt kg	Brakes fr/rr	Steering type	Standard tires
cpe. 2dr. 2+2 I4	2703	4699	1312	dc/dr	pwr.r.&p.	205/70R15
cpe. 2dr. 2+2 V6	2703	4699	1363	dc/dr	pwr.r.&p.	205/60R15

PRICES

Model / version		1996	1997	1998	1999	2000	2001
cpe. 2dr. I4	mini				12600	14200	
	maxi				15200	17300	
cpe. 2dr. V6	mini				15200	16800	17100
	maxi				17850	19400	21000
cpe. 2dr. V6-S	mini						19750
	maxi						23600

See page 7 to adapt these figures.

2001 MERCURY Cougar

FORD-MERCURY — Villager

1999 MERCURY Villager

Designed by Nissan and built by Ford, these two front-wheel drive minivans are inspired and built along the same lines as the former Maxima. They were first sold in 1993, the instrument panel got a new look in 1996 and its body a redesign in '99 with the addition of a second sliding door. Since then, these minivans are equipped with a 170-bhp 3.3L V6 powerteam.

PROS
- **They look great** both inside and out and the body design is clean and elegant.
- **Modular rear seatbenches** are unique and cleverly designed and besides, they're easy to adjust.
- **Driving comfort** is enhanced by a well-adjusted combination of springs and shock absorbers and by good rear end follow-through.
- **Handling** is stable even though there's some sway due to the soft suspension and rustic rear axle design.
- **Safety features** are great with such a rigid cabin frame, standard airbags and headrests as well as standard ABS on Ford products and on the Nissan GXE.
- **Build and finish** quality and spiffy materials are more like those of a luxury car rather than a sports utility vehicle.
- **These two models** come loaded with a lot of standard equipment, which explains why they're pricier than the equivalent competitor models.

CONS
- **Excessive vehicle weight** affects engine performance and fuel consumption.
- **Brakes** don't have much grip or lasting power, because it is not equipped with 4-disc brakes, like its Japanese counterpart the Quest.
- **Engine performance** is weak when vehicle is loaded or when pulling a trailer.
- **Trunk and rear seat** area are cramped with seven passengers aboard.
- **Maneuverability** isn't great with such a large steer angle.
- **Better soundproofing** would make for a more comfortable ride.
- **Some of the controls** and storage areas are inconvenient.

CONCLUSION
These vehicles are perfect for people looking for the kind of space and comfort that you used to get in the large station wagons no longer on the market.

RECALLS
1996 Risk of leakage near four small housing ducts located on the gas tank.
1997 Defective battery.

Villager — MERCURY-FORD

RELIABILITY PROBLEMS

	1996	1997	1998	1999	2000	2001
Engine:	X	X	X			
ansmission:	-	X	-			
Suspension:	X	-	-			
Steering:	-	X	X			
Brakes:	X	-	-			
Electricity:	-	X	X			
Body:	-	X	X			
Accessories:	X	X	X			
Fit/finish:	X	X	X			

POWERTRAIN

Year	Type/ L/Camshaft/bhp	Drivetrain & gearbox
96-98	V6/3.0/SOHC/151	front-A4
1999	V6/3.3/SOHC/170	front-A4

PERFORMANCE

Acceler. 0/100 sec.	Top. speed km/h	Ave. Fuel consp. l./100 km
12.0	180	13.0
11.0	180	13.8

SPECIFICATIONS

Model 96-98	Wlb. mm	Lght. mm	Cb.wt kg	Brakes fr/rr	Steering type	Standard tires
m.v. 4dr. GS	2850	4831	1810	dc/dr/ABS	pwr.r&p.	205/75R15
m.v. 4dr. LS	2850	4831	1848	dc/dr/ABS	pwr.r&p.	205/75R15
m.v. 4dr. Nautica	2850	4831	1848	dc/dr/ABS	pwr.r&p.	205/75R15
1999						
m.v. 4dr. Estate	2850	4945	NA	dc/dr	pwr.r&p.	225/60R16

PRICES

Model / version		1996	1997	1998	1999	2000	2001
m.v. 4dr. GS	mini	6500	8900	12400			
	maxi	8400	10900	13850			
m.v. 4dr. LS	mini	7850	10800	14700			
	maxi	10500	13450	16600			
m.v. 4dr. Nautica	mini	10000	14200	15950			
	maxi	11550	16150	18100			

See page 7 to adapt these figures.

1996 MERCURY Villager LS

FORD Windstar

2001 FORD Windstar SEL

It took Ford ten years to come up with a front-wheel drive minivan with a long wheelbase and driven by a V6 engine. Remolded in '99, it offers a left side sliding door to follow the competition.

PROS
- **It's well-designed** to accommodate seven passengers and the huge baggage compartment holds all their luggage.
- **Brakes are effective**, emergency stops are normal, ABS comes as standard equipment and the brake pedal is responsive and smooth.
- **The 3.8L V6** engine puts out 200-bhp and far outstrips performance of its main rivals.
- **The ride** is cushy with such a smooth suspension, thickly upholstered seats and low noise level.
- **The elegant**, even though a bit blah, look and spiffy design down to the smallest details.
- **Fuel consumption** is quite economical even with the muscular 3.8L engine that isn't too gas-thirsty.
- **Driving is pleasant** with such crisp steering, smooth engine and good road stability, even though there is a bit of sway.
- **Build is solid**, fit and finish are clean and tight, materials are nice and the overall design is simple and straightforward.
- **Convenient**: the well-designed hand brake and rear hatch handle.

CONS
- **Its bland body** design and conventional technical features put the Windstar far behind in the race against its Chrysler and GM rivals (no second sliding door before 1999, no short body style model, etc.)
- **The far-fetched** instrument panel is neither convenient nor ergonomic.
- **Seatbenches** are heavy and hard to handle, the seat is short but there are standard headrests.
- **There aren't enough** storage compartments in the front seat area.
- **To be improved upon**: the off-center rear windshield wiper and it isn't intermittent either.

CONCLUSION
The Windstar is a solid and powerful (3.8L engine) minivan, but its design and equipment aren't at all interesting or innovative.

RECALLS
1996 Defective catch may stop shifter from going into park. Bolts holding the driver's seat in place improperly tightened.
96-98 May have faulty front brake rotors and pads.
96-99 The brake fluid warning statement embossed on the reservoir is not clearly visible by direct view. New label required.
97-98 Transaxle's cover can separate while car is being driven.
1998 Headrest's lock defective on second row bench seat. Rack and pinion steering gears may be damaged.

Windstar — FORD

2001 Dealers will inspect the Restraint Control Module or crash sensors and if necessary replace them.
Dealers will replace both front driver and passenger floormat of some vehicles equipped with adjustable pedal option.

RELIABILITY PROBLEMS

	1996	1997	1998	1999	2000	2001
Engine:	X	X	X	X	X	-
Transmission:	X	X	-	X	-	X
Suspension:	X	X	X	X	X	-
Steering:	X	-	-	-	-	-
Brakes:	X	X	X	X	X	X
Electricity:	X	X	-	-	-	X
Body:	-	X	-	X	-	-
Accessories:	X	X	X	X	X	X
Fit/finish:	X	X	X	X	X	-

POWERTRAIN

Year	Type/ L/Camshaft/bhp	Drivetrain & gearbox
96-99	V6/3.0/OHV/150	front-A4
96-01	V6/3.8/OHV/155-200	front-A4

PERFORMANCE

	Acceler. 0/100 sec.	Top. speed km/h	Ave. Fuel consp. l./100 km
	NA	NA	NA
	9.8	175	13.6

SPECIFICATIONS

Model 96-01	Wlb. mm	Lght. mm	Cb.wt kg	Brakes fr/rr	Steering type	Standard tires
m.v. 4dr. 3.0	3066	5103	NA	dc/dr/ABS	pwr.r&p.	205/70R15
m.v. 4dr. LX	3066	5103	1671	dc/dr/ABS	pwr.r&p.	215/70R15
m.v. 4dr. GL	3066	5110	1681	dc/dr/ABS	pwr.r&p.	215/70R15
m.v. 4dr. LTD	3066	5110	NA	dc/dr/ABS	pwr.r&p.	225/60R16
m.v. 4dr. SE	3066	5103	NA	dc/dr/ABS	pwr.r&p.	215/70R15
m.v. 4dr. SEL	3066	5103	NA	dc/dr/ABS	pwr.r&p.	225/60R16

PRICES

Model / version		1996	1997	1998	1999	2000	2001
m.v. 4dr. 7 st. 3.0	mini			11000	13250		
	maxi			13350	15750		
m.v. 4dr. 7 st. GL	mini	7350	9450	12300			
	maxi	9450	11550	14600			
m.v. 4dr. 7 st. LX	mini	8900	13100	15200	16300	17300	23300
	maxi	11000	15250	17650	18600	19850	25950
m.v. 4dr. 7 st. LTD	mini			18000			
	maxi			20450			
m.v. 4dr. 7 st. SE	mini				17200		
	maxi				19650		
m.v. 4dr. 7 st. SEL	mini				20350	21750	28350
	maxi				22800	24150	30950
m.v. 4dr. 7 st. Sport	mini						25500
	maxi						28000
m.v. 5dr. 7 st. LX	mini					17850	23850
	maxi					20350	26450
m.v. 5dr. 7 st. SEL	mini					22250	28850
	maxi					24650	31500
m.v. 5dr. 7st. LTD	mini					25500	31700
	maxi					28000	34350
m.v. 5dr. 7st. Sport	mini						26000
	maxi						28550

See page 7 to adapt these figures.

GM A Series

BUICK Century
OLDSMOBILE Cutlass Ciera

1996 BUICK Century

The Century and Cutlass Ciera have been on the market since 1982 and the station wagon was first sold in 1984. They're powered by a 2.2L 4-cylinder or a 3.1L V6 engine.

PROS

- **This is the best buy** for your money on the market, for these models are tried and true and haven't had to undergo any modifications for a heck of a long time.
- **The cabin and trunk** are roomy enough to easily accommodate six passengers and all their luggage.
- **The car handles well**, for there isn't much sway, especially with the reinforced optional suspension.
- **Driving** is a dream with the smooth as silk V6 engine, convenient controls and excellent all-round view.
- **Reliability** has greatly improved over the years and availability of parts is a plus when it comes to maintenance and repairs, for there are still a lot of these cars around.

CONS

- **The 4-cylinder** engine isn't gutsy enough to really put these vehicles through the paces and it guzzles as much gas as the V6, something potential buyers think twice about.
- **Steering** is light because it's over-assisted, which cuts down on fluid vehicle movement.
- **Handling** on the base model isn't the greatest because there's a lot of sway due to the overly soft suspension and it's pretty jumpy and jerky when it hits road surface irregularities.
- **To be avoided**: the base model with its lean equipment and wimpy engine, which make it hard to resell as a used vehicle.
- **The high trunk** opening and scarce storage compartments.

CONCLUSION

These cars are ideal station wagons, for they've got loads of room, they're quite economical to run and repair and they seem to never go out of style...

RECALLS

None over this period.

BUICK Century
OLDSMOBILE Cutlass Ciera
A Series GM

RELIABILITY PROBLEMS

	1996	1997	1998	1999	2000	2001
Engine:	X					
Transmission:	-					
Suspension:	-					
Steering:	-					
Brakes:	X					
Electricity:	-					
Body:	X					
Accessories:	X					
Fit/finish:	X					

POWERTRAIN

Year	Type/ L/Camshaft/bhp	Drivetrain & gearbox
1996	L4/2.2/SOHC/110-120	front-A3
	V6/3.1/OHV/140-160	front-A4

PERFORMANCE

Acceler. 0/100 sec.	Top. speed km/h	Ave. Fuel consp. l./100 km
13.6	155	11.5
12.0	165	12.0

SPECIFICATIONS

Model 1996	Wlb. mm	Lght. mm	Cb.wt kg	Brakes fr/rr	Steering type	Standard tires
BUICK Century						
sdn. 4dr.	2664	4803	1338	dc/dr	pwr.r&p.	185/75R14
wgn. 4dr.	2664	4849	1393	dc/dr	pwr.r&p.	185/75R14
OLDSMOBILE Cutlass Ciera						
sdn. 4dr.	2664	4834	1306	dc/dr	pwr.r&p.	185/75R14
wgn. 4dr.	2664	4937	1397	dc/dr	pwr.r&p.	185/75R14

PRICES

Model / version			1996	1997	1998	1999	2000	2001
Century								
sdn. 4dr. Special		mini	7550					
		maxi	9850					
wgn. 4dr. Special		mini	8000					
		maxi	10500					
Cutlass Ciera								
sdn. 4dr. SL		mini	6800					
		maxi	8800					
wgn. 4dr. SL		mini	6800					
		maxi	10000					

See page 7 to adapt these figures.

GM B Series

BUICK Roadmaster 1996
CHEVROLET Caprice/Impala 1996

1996 CHEVROLET Caprice

The Chevrolet Caprice and the Buick Roadmaster were revamped in 1991 on the earlier model platform and share the same mechanical features.

PROS
- **The spacious cabin** interior and trunk can accommodate six passengers and all their luggage.
- **Highway driving** is very comfy with the soft suspension and low noise level.
- **Handling** on the Buick Roadmaster is great, thanks to its more effective Dynaride suspension.
- **The sleek Impala SS** model whoops a lot of power and it handles beautifully.
- **The upper-end Estate and LS models** have more extensive equipment and they sure look more spiffy.
- **Extremely reliable** and durable, and availability of parts make them immortal...
- **Impressive towing** capacity and they can pull heavy trailers with no trouble at all.

CONS
- **The excessive weight** and bulk of these huge cars of another era make maneuverability a chore.
- **Faithful customers** of this type of car have complained about its clumsy, hulky look and have gone out and bought a Ford instead.
- **Gas consumption** is pretty high with all engine models.
- **Sway and roll** because of too soft a suspension.
- **The poorly designed** seats on the Caprice don't provide good support or posture, making long trips very tiring indeed.
- **Steering** is light and suffers from too high a reduction ratio, so the driver is really out of touch with road conditions; this, along with rear-wheel drive, makes winter driving hazardous.
- **Brakes** are terribly ineffective and unreliable on sudden stops.
- **Assembly** is sloppy and fit and finish are loose and untidy.

CONCLUSION
Even if GM has stopped making these cars because of lower demand, they're still good, useful vehicles, but in very particular situations.

RECALLS
1996 The bolts on the wheels were not tightened correctly.

BUICK Roadmaster 1996
CHEVROLET Caprice/Impala 1996

B Series GM

RELIABILITY PROBLEMS

	1996	1997	1998	1999	2000	2001
Engine:	X					
Transmission:	-					
Suspension:	X					
Steering:	X					
Brakes:	-					
Electricity:	-					
Body:	X					
Accessories:	X					
Fit/finish:	X					

POWERTRAIN / PERFORMANCE

Year	Type/ L/Camshaft/bhp	Drivetrain & gearbox	Acceler. 0/100 sec.	Top. speed km/h	Ave. Fuel consp. l./100 km
1996	V8/5.0/OHV/170	rear-A4	12.5	170	13.5
	V8/5.7/OHV/180-260	rear-A4	11.0	175	14.0

SPECIFICATIONS

Model 1996	Wlb. mm	Lght. mm	Cb.wt kg	Brakes fr/rr	Steering type	Standard tires
sdn. 4dr.	2945	5481	1842	dc/dr	pwr.r&p.	205/75R15
wgn. 4dr.	2945	5524	1975	dc/dr	pwr.r&p.	225/75R15

PRICES

Model / version		1996	1997	1998	1999	2000	2001
Buick Roadmaster							
sdn. 4dr.	mini	10700					
	maxi	14300					
wgn. 4dr. LTD	mini	11750					
	maxi	15100					
wgn. 4dr. Estate	mini	12800					
	maxi	16150					
Chevrolet Impala SS							
sdn. 4dr.	mini	17850					
	maxi	20900					

See page 7 to adapt these figures.

1996 BUICK Roadmaster

GM C Series

BUICK Park Avenue
OLDSMOBILE 98

1996 OLDSMOBILE 98

These cars are the cream of the crop at GM. They're loaded luxury vehicles and their design is ultra-discrete.

PROS
- **Advanced technical** features, because these front-wheel drive vehicles have independent suspensions and standard ABS.
- **Five passengers** can be comfortably seated in the cabin and the trunk sure holds a lot of luggage.
- **The ride is regal** when you're seated in such plush seats, rocked by the soft suspension and soothed by ultimate quiet.
- **The V6 engines** are adequate and gas consumption is reasonable.
- **The Park Avenue Ultra** engine with supercharger has the vim and vigor of the V8 Cadillac engine...
- **If you're looking for space** and comfort at an affordable price, these reliable and durable cars are the answer.

CONS
- **The overly soft** suspension makes for a pretty rock 'n roll ride (except on the Ultra).
- **Brakes** aren't too smooth and they fizzle out with intensive use.
- **Seats are straight** and the lumbar section isn't adjustable.
- **Power steering** is too over-assisted and you don't have a clue as to what the road is like and there's generally poor maneuverability with these cars.
- **High depreciation** of such big cars doesn't make for a good investment.

CONCLUSION
These Buick and Oldsmobile cars are elegant and they work like a charm if they're properly maintained.

RECALLS
1996 Backfire may damage manifold. (Park Avenue)
Defective seat belt buckles.
Bolts anchoring the rear-central safety belt are not tight enough.
1997 Brake's electronic command module is defective.
1998 Powertrain control module is miscalibrated.
2000 The hydraulic modulator of the ABS system will be inspected and replaced if necessary.
2001 Dealers will replace the windshield wiper motor cover which contains the microprocessor.

BUICK Park Avenue / OLDSMOBILE 98 — C Series GM

RELIABILITY PROBLEMS

	1996	1997	1998	1999	2000	2001
Engine:	X	X	-	-	X	-
Transmission:	-	-	X	X	-	-
Suspension:	X	X	-	-	-	-
Steering:	-	-	-	-	-	-
Brakes:	X	X	X	X	X	X
Electricity:	X	X	X	X	X	X
Body:	-	X	-	-	X	-
Accessories:	X	X	X	X	X	-
Fit/finish:	X	-	-	X	-	-

POWERTRAIN

Year	Type/ L/Camshaft/bhp	Drivetrain & gearbox
96-01	V6/3.8/OHV/170-205	front-A4
	V6C/3.8/OHV/205-240	front-A4

PERFORMANCE

Acceler. 0/100 sec.	Top. speed km/h	Ave. Fuel consp. l./100 km
9.5	180	13.0
8.5	200	13.5

SPECIFICATIONS

Model	Wlb. mm	Lght. mm	Cb.wt kg	Brakes fr/rr	Steering type	Standard tires
Park Avenue 96-01						
sdn. 4dr. Ultra	2891	5253	1762	dc/ABS	pwr.r&p.	225/60R16
98/Regency Elite 1996						
sdn. 4dr.	2814	5227	1636	dc/dr/ABS	pwr.r&p.	205/70R15

PRICES

Model / version		1996	1997	1998	1999	2000	2001
BUICK Park Avenue							
sdn. 4dr. base	mini	9000	12400	15750	19100	22550	27100
	maxi	13650	16400	19750	23100	26750	31000
wgn. 4dr. Ultra	mini	11150	14500	18500	20800	25200	29900
	maxi	15100	17850	22000	24700	29400	33600
OLDSMOBILE 98							
sdn. 4dr. Elite	mini	7550					
	maxi	12600					

See page 7 to adapt these figures.

1998 BUICK Park Avenue

GM E Series — BUICK Riviera

1999 BUICK Riviera

This big coupes have always been prized by a very specific clientele that has dwindled over the years, who are looking for a vehicle of the same look and dimensions as their family yacht.

PROS
- **Four adults** can be comfortably seated in the cabin and the trunk can handle all their luggage.
- **The supercharged** engines are very spirited, but they don't have the guts or gusto of real Sportscars.
- **Driving one** of these cars is like being on cloud nine with the supple suspension, deep, cushy seats and really top-notch soundproofing.
- **The car holds** the road, thanks to well-adjusted shock absorbers.
- **Brakes** are powerful brutes, with or without ABS.
- **The 3.8L V6** engine is quite easy on gas, given the vehicle weight.
- **The instrument panel** on the latest generation models is straightforward and convenient, but some people don't like all the round motifs.

CONS
- **Riviera is a big boat** by today's standards.
- **Steering** is pretty touch and go, and you really have to keep an eye on it if you want to keep on track.
- **Outward visibility** isn't great with the low-slung driver's seat and the relatively high body frame.
- **The electronic instruments** on some models can be terribly distracting for the driver and they cost an arm and a leg to repair.
- **On some models**, trunk capacity has been cut down to accommodate the rear end body design, and it doesn't hold what it should for a vehicle this size.
- **To be improved upon**: rear windows that don't open and the awkward steering column which, even when adjusted, doesn't allow for a comfortable driving position.

CONCLUSION
These coupes are still quite unique and they don't appeal to everyone. They're rare and if they're in good shape, they're a good investment.

RECALLS
None over this period.

BUICK Riviera — E Series GM

RELIABILITY PROBLEMS

	1996	1997	1998	1999	2000	2001
Engine:	X	X	X	X		
Transmission:	X	X	X	-		
Suspension:	X	X	-	X		
Steering:	-	-	-	-		
Brakes:	X	X	X	X		
Electricity:	X	X	X	X		
Body:	X	-	-	-		
Accessories:	X	X	X	-		
Fit/finish:	-	-	X	X		

POWERTRAIN

Year	Type/ L/Camshaft/bhp	Drivetrain & gearbox
96-98	V6/3.8/OHV/170-205	front-A4
96-99	V6C/3.8/OHV/225-240	front-A4

PERFORMANCE

Acceler. 0/100 sec.	Top. speed km/h	Ave. Fuel consp. l./100 km
9.5	190	12.0
7.8	180	13.5

SPECIFICATIONS

Model Riviera	Wlb. mm	Lght. mm	Cb.wt kg	Brakes fr/rr	Steering type	Standard tires
cpe. 2dr.	2891	5263	1684	dc/ABS	pwr.r&p.	225/60R16

PRICES

Model / version		1996	1997	1998	1999	2000	2001
Riviera							
cpe. 2dr.	mini	11550	13450	15350	18700		
	maxi	15350	16800	19750	23100		

See page 7 to adapt these figures.

1996 BUICK Riviera

GM F Series

CHEVROLET Camaro
PONTIAC Firebird

1999 CHEVROLET Camaro Z28

The Camaro-Firebird models, launched in 1966-67, are now in their fifth generation model range and are available as coupes or convertibles.

PROS
- **Their bold** and brassy look appeals to the young and young at heart.
- **You get a lot for your money** and it's a good buy because of reasonably low maintenance bills.
- **Road stability** on the latest generation models is steadier because of the beefed up reinforced body.
- **The V8** engine takes your breath away, but the V6 is a wiser and more economical choice.
- **Passenger safety** is assured with standard ABS and dual airbags.
- **The instrument panel** on the latest model is more practical.
- **The well-designed** convertible top is a breeze.

CONS
- **Driving on curved roads** can be tricky because of excessive weight.
- **The drive can be a drag** with the Jack-in-the-box suspension, stiff seats and high noise level with all engine models.
- **Visibility isn't great** with the low-slung driver's seat and the blind spots with the convertible top.
- **Steering is over-assisted** and far too sensitive.
- **Brakes lack grip**, but with ABS, they're more reliable.
- **Gas consumption** is never really economical particularly with a V8 engine.
- **Fit and finish** and trim materials aren't what you'd expect on such a vehicle.
- **The catalytic converter** bump under the front passenger's legs can be quite annoying on long trips.

CONCLUSION
Only dyed-in-the-wool fanatics will be willing to spend the cash it takes to keep these beasts on the road and these days, there are fewer and fewer takers...

RECALLS
1996   Faulty front shoulder belt guide loop on convertibles.
1998   Exhaust gas recirculation valve may fail.

CHEVROLET Camaro / PONTIAC Firebird — F Series GM

RELIABILITY PROBLEMS

	1996	1997	1998	1999	2000	2001
Engine:	X	X	X	X	-	-
Transmission:	-	-	-	-	-	-
Suspension:	X	-	X	-	-	-
Steering:	X	X	-	-	-	-
Brakes:	X	X	X	X	X	X
Electricity:	X	X	X	X	X	-
Body:	X	X	-	-	-	X
Accessories:	X	X	X	X	X	X
Fit/finish:	X	-	-	-	-	-

POWERTRAIN

Year	Type/ L/Camshaft/bhp	Drivetrain & gearbox
96-01	V6/3.8/OHV/200	rear-M5
		rear-A4
	V8/5.7/OHV/240-320	rear-M5/M6
		rear-A4

PERFORMANCE

Acceler. 0/100 sec.	Top. speed km/h	Ave. Fuel consp. l./100 km
9.0	185	12.2
9.8	180	12.4
5.3	230	14.5
6.0	220	14.0

SPECIFICATIONS

Model	Wlb. mm	Lght. mm	Cb.wt kg	Brakes fr/rr	Steering type	Standard tires
Camaro 96-01						
cpe. 2dr. base	2568	4907	1500	dc/ABS	pwr.r&p.	215/60R16
con. 2dr. base	2568	4907	1588	dc/ABS	pwr.r&p.	215/60R16
cpe. 2dr. Z28	2568	4907	1560	dc/ABS	pwr.r&p.	235/55R16
con. 2dr. Z28	2568	4907	1622	dc/ABS	pwr.r&p.	235/55R16
Firebird 96-01						
cpe. 2dr. base	2568	4910	1507	dc/ABS	pwr.r&p.	215/60R16
con. 2dr. base	2568	4910	1543	dc/ABS	pwr.r&p.	215/60R16
cpe. 2dr. Formula	2568	4910	1515	dc/ABS	pwr.r&p.	245/50ZR16
con. 2dr. Formula	2568	4912	1584	dc/ABS	pwr.r&p.	245/50ZR16
cpe. 2dr. T.A.	2568	4920	1541	dc/ABS	pwr.r&p.	245/50ZR16
con. 2dr. T.A.	2568	4920	1594	dc/ABS	pwr.r&p.	245/50ZR16

PRICES

Model / version		1996	1997	1998	1999	2000	2001
Camaro							
cpe. 2dr. base	mini	7550	9250	11100	13950	17300	20800
	maxi	10100	12200	13950	16800	20500	24700
cpe. 2dr. Z28	mini	11100	12900	15300	18150	21500	25000
	maxi	14300	15750	18150	21000	24700	28900
con. 2dr.	mini	10710	12400	14700	17650	21000	
	maxi	13550	15300	17650	20500	24150	
con. 2dr. Z28	mini	13200	15550	18500	21300	24700	28150
	maxi	16150	18500	21300	24150	27800	32000
Firebird							
cpe. 2dr.	mini	10100	11350	13200	17100	20500	24700
	maxi	13000	14300	16050	19950	23600	27800
cpe. 2dr. Formula	mini	12000	12900	14700	18700		29200
	maxi	14600	15750	17650	21500		32550
cpe. 2dr.Trans Am	mini	13300	16050	18500	24450	25700	29700
	maxi	16150	18900	21300	25200	28900	33100
con. 2dr.	mini	11200	13950	16400	20250	23600	
	maxi	15100	16800	19200	23100	26800	
con. 2dr.Trans Am	mini	14300	17100	20600	24450	27800	32850
	maxi	17200	19950	23400	27300	31000	35200
con. 2dr. Formula	mini	13300	16050				
	maxi	16150	18900				

See page 7 to adapt these figures.

GM F/UT Series

CHEVROLET Blazer S-10
GMC Jimmy S-15

1996 CHEVROLET Blazer

These sport utility vehicles are more and more popular since they were put on the market in 1982. They were modified in 1995 and driven by a 4.3L V6 engine. A luxurious version of the Jimmy, the Envoy, is available since 1998.

PROS
• **The 4.3L V6** engine has power and torque to burn, so it can pull a heavy load or head out to explore rough terrain whenever it pleases.
• **These vehicles** are more comfortable with their improved suspension, big tires that don't bounce too much and better-contoured seats.
• **Handling** on the latest generation models is more crisp and clean because of the reinforced frame.
• **These vehicles** are much more reliable, but «we reckon they still have a ways to go» to beat the Ford Explorer...

CONS
• **The manual transmission** shifter is stiff, steering is over-assisted and all over the map.
• **Handling** off-the-road is pretty rough, because of poor shock absorbers and by the less than sturdy body (before '95).
• **Brakes** lack grip, lasting power and reliability on sudden stops.
• **These vehicles** are expensive to run, whether it be at the pump, at the insurance company office or at the good local garage.
• **Access** to rear seats is not easy on two-door models.
• **The big tires** make quite a racket, as does the engine at the least acceleration.
• **Storage compartments** are scarce and the split rear hatch door complicates access to the baggage compartment.

CONCLUSION
The Jimmy-Blazer's sell and resell well for they're more affordable than their main rivals. The reason for this is their less robust build, a less spit and polish finish and lower-quality materials.

RECALLS
1996	4WD vehicles driven in the 2-wheel drive position can experience increased stopping distances during ABS stops due to a defective switch. Leaking fuel line.
96-97	Front outboard seatbelt webbing could separate on frontal impact.
1998	The right-hand rear brake may wear itself out.
2000	Some seatbelts doesn't satisfied strenght regulations. Payload informations can be wrong and label replaced.

CHEVROLET Blazer S-10
GMC Jimmy S-15

F/UT Series GM

RELIABILITY PROBLEMS

	1996	1997	1998	1999	2000	2001
Engine:	X	X	X	-	X	-
Transmission:	X	X	-	X	X	-
Suspension:	X	-	-	-	-	-
Steering:	-	-	-	-	-	-
Brakes:	X	-	-	-	-	-
Electricity:	X	X	X	X	X	X
Body:	X	X	-	-	X	X
Accessories:	-	X	X	X	X	X
Fit/finish:	X	X	-	X	-	-

POWERTRAIN

Year	Type/ L/Camshaft/bhp	Drivetrain & gearbox
96-01	V6/4.3/OHV/160-190	rear/all-M5
		rear/all-A4

PERFORMANCE

	Acceler. 0/100 sec.	Top. speed km/h	Ave. Fuel consp. l./100 km
	9.6	175	17.2
	9.9	185	15.4

SPECIFICATIONS

Model 96-01	Wlb. mm	Lght. mm	Cb.wt kg	Brakes fr/rr	Steering type	Standard tires
Blazer-Jimmy						
wgn. 2dr. 4x2	2553	4491	1596	dc/ABS	pwr.bal.	205/75R15
wgn. 2dr. 4x4	2553	4491	1746	dc/ABS	pwr.bal.	205/75R15
wgn. 4dr. 4x2	2718	4656	1666	dc/ABS	pwr.bal.	205/75R15
wgn. 4dr. 4x4	2718	4656	1837	dc/ABS	pwr.bal.	205/75R15

PRICES

Model / version		1996	1997	1998	1999	2000	2001
Jimmy / Blazer 4x2							
wgn. 2dr.base/SL	mini	6800	10100	12600	14200	16700	22050
	maxi	10200	12200	14400	16300	19100	24700
wgn. 2dr. LS/SLS	mini	7150	11000	14100	15100	17750	23100
	maxi	10500	13200	15950	17200	20150	25700
wgn.4dr. base/SL	mini	8400	12800	15100	17100		
	maxi	12300	14900	17000	19400		
wgn. 4dr. LT/SLT	mini	11550	15450	17200	20450	25400	32000
	maxi	15450	17300	19100	22800	28050	33900
wgn. 4dr. LS/SLS	mini	9750	14150	16150	18700	22900	29600
	maxi	13650	16150	18050	21000	25400	32550
wgn. 4dr. SLE	mini					24150	29200
	maxi					26250	31500
Jimmy / Blazer 4x4							
wgn. 2dr. base/SL	mini	7850	11350	14200	15750	18800	24150
	maxi	11250	13450	15950	17850	21200	26750
wgn. 2dr. LS/SLS	mini	8200	12500	15650	16700	19850	25200
	maxi	11550	14500	17550	18800	22250	27800
wgn. 4dr.base/SL	mini	9450	14300	16700	18700		
	maxi	13350	16150	18600	21000		
wgn. 4dr. LT/SLT	mini	12600	16700	18800	22550	27500	34100
	maxi	16500	18600	20900	24350	30150	36000
wgn. 4dr. LS/SLS	mini	10800	15450	17750	20250	25000	31700
	maxi	14700	17450	19650	22600	27500	34650
wgn. 4dr. Envoy	mini				18900	23600	25400
	maxi				21000	25700	30150
wgn. 4dr.TrailBlazer	mini					26750	32000
	maxi					29400	35150
wgn. 4dr. SLE	mini					26250	31300
	maxi					28350	33600

See page 7 to adapt these figures.

GM G Series — OLDSMOBILE Aurora

2001 OLDSMOBILE Aurora

This deluxe sedan powered by a V8 was launched in early '94 as the '95 model. It's an elaborately equipped 4-door model that comes in a single trim level.

PROS

- **It's competitively** priced in comparison with its smaller and less zippy rivals.
- **Its sleek**, aerodynamic design is just sensational.
- **It's solidly built**, finish is clean and tight, overall design is terrific and trim materials look great.
- **The interior cabin** design is unique and very spiffy.
- **The car handles** well in most situations, but it doesn't have an ounce of Sportscar zoom and zest.
- **Gas consumption** is quite low, given the good power to weight ratio.
- **This is a comfy car** equipped with a smooth suspension, nicely upholstered and contoured seats and excellent soundproofing.
- **There are sufficient storage** compartments, and they're convenient too, which is rare for a GM product!

CONS

- **Brakes** of the first models are inadequate because of vehicle weight and they heat up in no time flat.
- **Steering** is over-assisted and so it's over-sensitive, and besides it has a large steer angle diameter and high reduction ratio, which is no picnic when you're at the wheel of such a big car.
- **Visibility** is obstructed by the thick roof supports.
- **Accelerations** and pick-up are only adequate for engine weight is pretty hefty and the engine rarely really puts out 250-bhp.
- **Some equipment** items have been overlooked or botched up, for example, there's no shifter indicator on the instrument panel and seat belt buckles are poorly designed.
- **Getting to the trunk** of the first Aurora isn't easy with such a high, narrow opening.

CONCLUSION

The Aurora has a good reliability record so far and there haven't been any recalls, which is a good sign, and so we recommend it as a good used car purchase.

RECALLS

None over this period.

OLDSMOBILE Aurora — G Series GM

RELIABILITY PROBLEMS

	1996	1997	1998	1999	2000	2001
Engine:	X	X	-	-		-
Transmission:	-	-	-	-		-
Suspension:	-	-	-	-		-
Steering:	-	-	-	-		-
Brakes:	-	X	X	X		-
Electricity:	X	-	-	-		-
Body:	-	X	-	-		-
Accessories:	X	X	X	X		-
Fit/finish:	-	X	X	X		-

POWERTRAIN

Year	Type/ L/Camshaft/bhp	Drivetrain & gearbox
96-99	V8/4.0/DOHC/250	front-A4
2001	V6/3.5/SOHC/215	front-A4
	V8/4.0/DOHC/250	front-A4

PERFORMANCE

Acceler. 0/100 sec.	Top. speed km/h	Ave. Fuel consp. l./100 km
9.0	215	13.5
8.5	200	13.3
8.0	215	13.5

SPECIFICATIONS

Model	Wlb. mm	Lght. mm	Cb.wt kg	Brakes fr/rr	Steering type	Standard tires
96-99						
sdn. 4dr.	2891	5217	1799	dc/ABS	pwr.r&p.	235/60R16
2001						
ber. 4 p. 3.5	2850	5062	1645	dc/ABS	pwr.r.&p.	225/55R17
ber. 4 p. 4.0	2850	5062	1725	dc/ABS	pwr.r.&p.	235/55R17

PRICES

Model / version		1996	1997	1998	1999	2000	2001
sdn. 4dr.	mini	10300	12600	15750	19200		
	maxi	14600	16800	19750	23200		
sdn. 4dr. 3.0	mini						30450
	maxi						34100
sdn. 4dr. 4.0	mini						33600
	maxi						37250

See page 7 to adapt these figures.

1996 OLDSMOBILE Aurora

GM H Series

**BUICK LeSabre,
OLDSMOBILE 88
PONTIAC Bonneville**

1999 BUICK LeSabre Limited

Introduced in 69 as full-size vehicles, they became pared down front-wheel drive in 86. The unavoidable V6 is the only option available, even on the Pontiac Bonneville SSE and on the Oldsmobile 88 LSS both assisted with a Roots compressor.

PROS

- **Performance** is good, thanks to the reasonable weight/power ratio and the venerable V6 is up to the task assigned to it.
- **Driving pleasure** comes from wide visibility, a well-geared steering system and efficient brakes that are easy to gauge.
- **Comfort** resulting from a smooth suspension and a discreet mechanical system make these cars perfect for long highway journeys.

CONS

- **Lines** on the Bonneville SSE are much too complex.
- **Weight** is way too high and prevents the Bonneville SSE from giving the performance expected from its compressor-powered engine.
- **Interior design** is uninspired, the instrument panel is frustrating, storage spaces are all but nonexistent.
- **Seats** are badly shaped and provide little support, something strange in cars designed primarily for comfort.
- **The base suspension** is excessively smooth and shock absorbers are unable to filter out road surface irregularities; the «Heavy Duty» option is advisable.
- **Steering** is over-assisted and requires a lot of concentration on the part of the driver.

CONCLUSION

Roomy, easy to maintain and well-equipped, these intermediate sedans are reliable and available at a reasonable price.

RECALLS

1996	Defective seatbelt buckles.
	Backfire that could damage the exhaust manifold.
1998	Powertrain control module is miscalibrated.
98-99	Defective chrome plated aluminum wheels that might have not been machined properly can separate from the vehicle.
	Incorrect emission control labels.
1999	Driver's indication "PRNDL" state may differ from the hydraulic state of the transmission due to a loose retaining clip.
2000	The hydraulic modulator of the ABS system will be inspected and replaced if necessary.

**BUICK LeSabre,
OLDSMOBILE 88
PONTIAC Bonneville**

H Series GM

RELIABILITY PROBLEMS

	1996	1997	1998	1999	2000	2001
Engine:	X	X	X	-	-	-
Transmission:	-	-	-	X	-	-
Suspension:	X	-	-	-	-	-
Steering:	-	-	-	-	-	-
Brakes:	X	X	-	-	-	-
Electricity:	X	-	X	X	X	X
Body:	X	X	X	X	X	X
Accessories:	X	X	X	X	-	-
Fit/finish:	X	X	-	-	-	-

POWERTRAIN

Year	Type/ L/Camshaft/bhp	Drivetrain & gearbox	Acceler. 0/100 sec.	Top. speed km/h	Ave. Fuel consp. l./100 km
96-01	V6/3.8/OHV/165 -205	front-A4	8.2	180	12.4
	V6C/3.8/OHV/205-240	front-A4	7.7	200	13.3

SPECIFICATIONS

Model	Wlb. mm	Lght. mm	Cb.wt kg	Brakes fr/rr	Steering type	Standard tires
LeSabre 96-01						
sdn. 4dr. Custom	2814	5100	1562	dc/dr/ABS	pwr.r&p.	205/70R15
sdn. 4dr. Limited	2814	5100	1573	dc/dr/ABS	pwr.r&p.	205/70R15
88 96-99						
sdn. 4dr. base	2814	5090	1567	dc/dr/ABS	pwr.r&p.	205/70R15
sdn. 4dr. LS	2814	5090	1569	dc/dr/ABS	pwr.r&p.	215/65R15
sdn. 4dr. LSS	2814	5090	1609	dc/dr/ABS	pwr.r&p.	225/60R16
Bonneville 96-01						
sdn. 4dr. SE	2814	5093	1563	dc/dr/ABS	pwr.r&p.	215/65R15
sdn. 4dr. SSEi	2814	5133	1627	dc/dr/ABS	pwr.r&p.	225/60R16

PRICES

Model / version		1996	1997	1998	1999	2000	2001
LeSabre							
sdn. 4dr. Custom	mini	8900	11350	13450	16400	17850	21850
	maxi	12500	14700	16800	19200	22050	25700
sdn. 4dr. LTD	mini	10500	12900	15550	17850	20450	23400
	maxi	14050	16400	18900	21300	24150	27300
88							
sdn. 4dr. LS	mini	7350	9250	11550	13950		
	maxi	10500	12200	14500	16800		
sdn. 4dr. LSS	mini	8400	11350	13650	15750		
	maxi	12050	14300	17650	18350		
sdn. 4dr. 50th Ann.	mini				16250		
	maxi				18900		
Bonneville							
sdn. 4dr. SE	mini	8900	10300	12600	14900	18350	22550
	maxi	11550	13650	15750	17850	21500	25700
sdn. 4dr. SSE	mini	10500	12050	15220	17650	21000	25200
	maxi	13100	15220	18350	20450	24150	28350
sdn. 4dr. SSEi	mini	11750	13650	17300	19950	23600	27800
	maxi	14050	16250	19950	23100	26750	30950

See page 7 to adapt these figures.

GM J Series

CHEVROLET Cavalier
PONTIAC Sunfire

1996 PONTIAC Sunfire GT

These compact cars have nothing spectacular about them, but they are economical and reliable. Positioned as the most widely sold in Canada, few vehicles can rival with the Cavalier-Sunbird models.

PROS
- **Model range** is wide, with a chance for everyone to find something within their budget.
- **Performance** with the V6 and the A3 transmission are the best.
- **Price** is affordable and results from the minimal design and mechanical changes made over the years.
- **The passenger compartment** on the sedans and wagons can accommodate five adults and the trunk is large enough for their baggage.
- **The suspension** is firm but counters road defects effectively.

CONS
- **Steering:** the manual is spongy and the power system is over-assisted.
- **Fuel consumption** with the V6 isn't at all economical.
- **The four-cylinder engine** is listless, noisy and vibrates noticeably.
- **The trunk** is tiny on the convertible version and offers few storage capacity.
- **Driving pleasure** on base models is absent because of bad quality tires and shock absorbers.
- **Reliability** is precarious and even the latest generation suffers from mechanical problems and the early onset of rust.

CONCLUSION
The Cavalier-Sunbird models are good bargains as long as driven kilometers aren't too high. Beware of sports versions that may have suffered abuse at the hands of their previous owners.

RECALLS
1996 Moisture entering the powertrain control module as a result of corrosion can cause the engine to run rough and stall.
Defective emergency lights that won't light up.
Fuel vapor leakage around the injection system.
Lamp control module is defective. (Sunfire)
96-97 Airbag control module must be recalibrated.
Weak rear suspension trailing arm fasteners.
1997 The rim of the spare tire doesn't match the actual size of the tire, which could cause the tire to separate itself from the rim.
Welding might be necessary on side doors.

CHEVROLET Cavalier / PONTIAC Sunfire — J Series GM

RELIABILITY PROBLEMS

	1996	1997	1998	1999	2000	2001
Engine:	X	X	X	X	X	X
Transmission:	-	-	-	-	-	-
Suspension:	-	X	X	-	-	-
Steering:	-	-	-	-	-	-
Brakes:	X	X	X	X	X	X
Electricity:	X	X	X	X	X	X
Body:	X	X	-	-	-	-
Accessories:	X	X	X	X	X	X
Fit/finish:	X	X	X	X	X	-

POWERTRAIN

Year	Type/ L/Camshaft/bhp	Drivetrain & gearbox
95-01	L4/2.2/SOHC/95-130 (115 in 1999)	front-M5 / front-A3/4
95-96	L4/2.3/DOHC/150	front-M5 / front-A4
97-01	L4/2.4/DOHC/150	front-M5 / front-A4

PERFORMANCE

Acceler. 0/100 sec.	Top speed km/h	Ave. Fuel consp. l/100 km
10.0	165	9.7
11.2	160	10.0
9.0	175	10.0
9.8	170	11.0
8.0	180	10.2
8.8	175	10.7

SPECIFICATIONS

Model 96-01	Wlb. mm	Lght. mm	Cb.wt kg	Brakes fr/rr	Steering type	Standard tires
Cavalier						
cpe. 2dr. base	2644	4590	1188	dc/dr/ABS	pwr.r&p.	195/70R14
cpe. 2dr. RS	2644	4590	1191	dc/dr/ABS	pwr.r&p.	195/65R15
cpe. 2dr. Z24	2644	4590	1247	dc/dr/ABS	pwr.r&p.	205/55R16
con. 2dr. Z24	2644	4590	1288	dc/dr/ABS	pwr.r&p.	195/65R15
sdn. 4dr. base	2644	4590	1214	dc/dr/ABS	pwr.r&p.	185/75R14
sdn. 4dr. LS	2644	4590	1235	dc/dr/ABS	pwr.r&p.	195/65R15
Sunfire						
cpe. 2dr. SE	2644	4620	1193	dc/dr/ABS	pwr.r&p.	195/70R14
cpe. 2dr. GT	2644	4620	1280	dc/dr/ABS	pwr.r&p.	205/55R16
sdn. 4dr. SE/GT	2644	4615	1211	dc/dr/ABS	pwr.r&p.	195/70R14

PRICES

Model / version		1996	1997	1998	1999	2000	2001
Cavalier							
cpe. 2dr. base	mini	3900	5100	6300	8200	10300	12600
	maxi	7100	7550	8600	10800	13450	16300
cpe. 2dr. Z24	mini	5450	7150	8200	10500	12600	14700
	maxi	8900	10200	11250	13100	15750	18400
con. 2dr. LS	mini	7800	8800				
	maxi	10500	12100				
con. 2dr. Z24	mini			10800	13650	15350	
	maxi			13550	16300	18400	
sdn. 4dr.	mini	4200	5200	6600	8400	10500	13650
	maxi	6500	7900	8900	11000	13650	17300
sdn. 4dr. LS	mini	4950	6300	7350	9450	11550	
	maxi	7350	8900	10000	12100	14700	
sdn. 4dr. VL	mini						9450
	maxi						13100
sdn. 4dr. VLX	mini						13100
	maxi						16300
Sunfire							
cpe. 2dr.	mini						12600
	maxi						16300
cpe. 2dr. SE	mini	4100	4800	6100	8400	10500	
	maxi	7100	7800	8400	11250	13650	
cpe. 2dr. GT	mini	5700	6300	7900	10500	12800	14700
	maxi	9150	10000	10500	13350	15900	18400
con. 2 dr. SE	mini	8000	8900	11000			
	maxi	10700	11550	13650			
con. 2 dr. GT	mini				13450	15200	
	maxi				16500	18600	
sdn. 4dr. SE	mini	4400	5450	6300	8700	10700	
	maxi	6700	8100	8600	11550	13850	
sdn. 4dr. GTX	mini						15200
	maxi						18900
sdn. 4dr. SL	mini						10000
	maxi						13200
sdn. 4dr. SLX	mini						13650
	maxi						16800

See page 7 to adapt these figures.

GM K Series

CADILLAC DeVille Eldorado/Seville

1999 CADILLAC DeVille

The DeVille was first available in 1970, the Eldorado in 1968 and the Seville in 1979, but since 1994, these models have come equipped with the famous Northstar engine. Recently, GM has introduced on these models their first GPS "OnStar" navigational system.

PROS
- **These cars easily** accommodate five adults and all their belongings.
- **The V8 Northstar** engine really makes these cars go away fast.
- **The flexible suspension**, thickly cushioned seats and superb soundproofing make for a really comfortable ride.
- **Handling** is predictable with such well-adjusted shock absorbers.
- **Brakes grip** but lack real power, for stops are long due to excessive vehicle weight, but thanks to ABS, stops are nice and stable.
- **Car design** has become more classic and elegant over the years, especially the Seville that has acquired a truly international look.

CONS
- **Maneuvering** the DeVille isn't the best since it got a rejuvenating face-lift...
- **The base model suspension** is really too flexible, so all the swing and sway can make you feel seasick after a while.
- **Seats** aren't too firm and don't provide much support, something you wouldn't expect on luxury cars.
- **Steering** is over-assisted and far too light and it doesn't give you a real feel for the road.

CONCLUSION
These are nice upper-crust, comfortable American-style cars that are more affordable than their imported counterparts.

RECALLS
1996 Analog instrument cluster may short-circuit and go out.
The assist catch on some hoods is poorly aligned and isn't functional. (DeVille/Concours)
1997 Brakes' electronic command module is defective.
The evaporative emissions harness is misrouted.
1998 Hood hinge pivot bolts may break. (DeVille)
Faulty windshield wiper motor microprocessor. (Seville)
1999 A rectifier bridge short may develop in the generator even when the engine is off, causing an engine compartment fire.
2000 The ABS hydraulic modulator must be inspected and replaced if it leaks. (DeVille)
Remplacement of the crankshaft position sensor and verification of the torque of the bolts on the rear link assembly. (Eldorado-Seville)

CADILLAC DeVille Eldorado/Seville — K Series GM

RELIABILITY PROBLEMS

	1996	1997	1998	1999	2000	2001
Engine:	X	X	X	X	X	X
Transmission:	-	X	X	-	-	-
Suspension:	X	-	-	X	-	-
Steering:	-	-	-	-	-	-
Brakes:	X	X	X	X	X	X
Electricity:	X	X	X	X	X	X
Body:	X	X	X	-	-	-
Accessories:	X	X	X	X	X	X
Fit/finish:	X	X	-	X	X	X

POWERTRAIN

Year	Type/ L/Camshaft/bhp	Drivetrain & gearbox
96-01	V8/4.6/DOHC/270-300	front-A4

PERFORMANCE

Acceler. 0/100 sec.	Top. speed km/h	Ave. Fuel consp. l/100 km
8.0	240	14.2

SPECIFICATIONS

Model	Wlb. mm	Lght. mm	Cb.wt kg	Brakes fr/rr	Steering type	Standard tires
DeVille 96-99						
sdn. 4dr.	2891	5330	1820	dc/ABS	pwr.r&p.	225/60R16
sdn. 4dr. Concours	2891	5330	1843	dc/ABS	pwr.r&p.	225/60R16
sdn. 4dr. Elegance	2891	5330	1838	dc/ABS	pwr.r&p.	225/60R16
DeVille 00-01						
sdn 4dr.	2929	5270	1820	dc/ABS	pwr.r&p.	225/60R16
sdn. 4dr. DHS	2929	5270	1843	dc/ABS	pwr.r&p.	225/60R16
sdn. 4dr. DTS	2929	5270	1838	dc/ABS	pwr.r&p.	225/60R16
Eldorado/Seville 96-01						
cpe. 2dr.	2743	5095	1743	dc/ABS	pwr.r&p.	225/60R16
sdn. 4dr.	2819	5177	1688	dc/ABS	pwr.r&p.	225/60R16
sdn. 4dr. 98-99	2850	5105	1815	dc/ABS	pwr.r&p.	235/60R16

PRICES

Model / version		1996	1997	1998	1999	2000	2001
CADILLAC DeVille							
sdn. 4dr.	mini	10500	14200	21000	25900	35700	44100
	maxi	11000	18900	25200	28900	39400	48300
sdn. 4dr. Concours	mini	13100	18400	25700	30900	45100	53550
DTS	maxi	17850	23100	28900	34100	48800	57700
sdn. 4dr. D'Elegance	mini		16300	24150	27800	44100	52500
DTS	maxi		21000	27300	31000	47750	56700
Eldorado.							
cpe. 2dr.	mini	11750	16300	23600	31000	37800	46200
	maxi	16150	21000	29400	34600	42000	52000
cpe. 2dr. Touring	mini	13900	18400	24700	32000	39900	
	maxi	18300	23100	30450	36750	44100	
Seville							
sdn. 4dr. STS	mini	13650	15750	24700	35150	38300	46200
	maxi	17850	21000	31500	39900	45700	53550
sdn. 4dr. SLS	mini	14700	16800	25700	36700	38850	47200
	maxi	18900	22000	32000	41450	46800	54600

See page 7 to adapt these figures.

GM L Series — CHEVROLET Beretta - Corsica

1996 CHEVROLET Beretta

Replacing the defunct Citation and Omega, the Corsica sedan borrows its frame and engines straight from the Skylark, Calais and Grand Am.

PROS
- **Their prices** are their most attractive factor, especially for used cars.
- **Lines** are modern, rounded and timeless.
- **Steering**, a GM role model, is precise and well-geared.
- **Construction** is sturdy and the body is fairly rigid.
- **Performance** with the V6 and QuadFour engines are uplifting.
- **Road adherence** is grippy on the Z26 version, equipped with a more technologically advanced suspension than the base models.

CONS
- **Maintenance problems** are a frequent occurrence and the number of recalls are proof of these models' inferior quality. An in-depth inspection is advisable before going ahead with a purchase.
- **Comfort** is laughable, seats cave in and the suspension is awful.
- **The instrument panel** is weird and controls are badly positioned.
- **Fit and finish** as well as the quality of some materials are noticeably inferior.
- **The four-cylinder engine**, a 2.2L, is rough when combined with the automatic transmission; moreover, the air-conditioned system is inefficient.
- **Braking** is inadequate, even with an anti-lock system, where the only advantage is more stability during emergency stops.

CONCLUSION
These two models are interesting when new, but they age prematurely and cause a wide range of small problems.

RECALLS
1996 Lamp control module is defective.

CHEVROLET Beretta - Corsica — L Series GM

RELIABILITY PROBLEMS

	1996	1997	1998	1999	2000	2001
Engine:	X					
Transmission:	-					
Suspension:	-					
Steering:	-					
Brakes:	X					
Electricity:	X					
Body:	X					
Accessories:	X					
Fit/finish:	X					

POWERTRAIN / PERFORMANCE

Year	Type/ L/Camshaft/bhp	Drivetrain & gearbox	Acceler. 0/100 sec.	Top. speed km/h	Ave. Fuel consp. l./100 km
1996	L4/2.2/SOHC/95-110	front-M5	12.8	160	8.5
		front-A3-A4	14.0	150	9.5
	V6/3.1/OHV/140	front-M5	9.7	180	10.5
		front-A3-A4	10.6	175	11.5

SPECIFICATIONS

Model	Wlb. mm	Lght. mm	Cb.wt kg	Brakes fr/rr	Steering type	Standard tires
cpe. 2dr.	2626	4658	1202	dc/dr	pwr.r&p.	195/70R14
sdn. 4dr.	2626	4658	1197	dc/dr	pwr.r&p.	185/75R14

PRICES

Model / version			1996	1997	1998	1999	2000	2001
Beretta								
cpe. 2dr. base	mini		4950					
	maxi		8400					
cpe. 2dr. Z26	mini		6720					
	maxi		9450					
Corsica								
sdn. 4dr. base	mini		5450					
	maxi		7800					

See page 7 to adapt these figures.

1996 CHEVROLET Corsica

GM L Series — CHEVROLET Malibu

1998 CHEVROLET Malibu LS

In 1997 the Malibu replaced the Corsica. It's driven by a 2.4L and 3.1L 4 or 6-cylinder engine, providing both the same bhp.

PROS

- **Overall value** for your buck is good, considering the rich equipment, which makes the Malibu highly competitive with some Asian models.
- **The flowing lines** are reminiscent of other slick model designs.
- **The generous cabin and trunk** can really and truly accommodate five passengers and all their luggage.
- **Performance** are a pleasant surprise with both engines that provide zippy accelerations and pick-up, thanks to a favorable power to weight ratio.
- **Ride comfort** is amazing for a popular model. The suspension irons out road faults and seats provide the occupants with effective support.
- **Handling** is crisp and clean even with the iffy-quality original tires. The Malibu takes all kinds of curves with assurance and remains nice and even on emergency maneuvers.
- This car is **passenger-friendly**. There are enough storage compartments, especially for front seat passengers.

CONS

- **A high noise level** is an indication that soundproofing isn't what it should be and it sort of takes the pleasure out of the trip.
- **Brakes** don't dig in when applied, no doubt due to poor-quality linings that you need to keep a close eye on.
- **Some plastic trim components** are of dubious quality and they look rather cheap, especially on the dashboard and inner doors.
- **Some items** need to be improved: not quite enough storage spots, no assist grips in the rear seat area and a missing footrest.

CONCLUSION

The Malibu represents GM's neat solution that shines in the race against popular Asian cars, for it offers good-level value for the going price and the dealership network is more widespread than is the case for the competition.

RECALLS

2000   The fuel fill fitting may leaks more than standards allowed. The fuel tank must be inspected and replaced if necessary.

Malibu CHEVROLET — L Series GM

RELIABILITY PROBLEMS

	1996	1997	1998	1999	2000	2001
Engine:		X	X	-	-	-
Transmission:		X	X	-	-	-
Suspension:		X	X	X	-	-
Steering:		X	-	-	-	-
Brakes:		X	X	X	X	-
Electricity:		X	X	X	X	X
Body:		-	X	X	-	-
Accessories:		-	X	X	X	X
Fit/finish:		X	X	X	X	-

POWERTRAIN

Year	Type/ L/Camshaft/bhp	Drivetrain & gearbox
97-01	L4/2.4/DOHC/150	front-A4
	V6/3.1/OHV/150	front-A4

PERFORMANCE

Acceler. 0/100 sec.	Top. speed km/h	Ave. Fuel consp. l./100 km
10.0	170	11.3
9.5	180	12.3

SPECIFICATIONS

Model 97-01	Wlb. mm	Lght. mm	Cb.wt kg	Brakes fr/rr	Steering type	Standard tires
sdn. 4dr. base	2718	4836	1384	dc/dr/ABS	pwr.r&p.	215/60R15
sdn. 4dr. LS	2718	4836	1396	dc/dr/ABS	pwr.r&p.	215/60R15

PRICES

Model / version		1996	1997	1998	1999	2000	2001
sdn. 4dr. base	mini		7900	9000	10800	12600	15750
	maxi		11000	12100	13750	15750	19400
sdn. 4dr. LS	mini		8900	10100	11900	13650	16800
	maxi		12600	13100	14900	16800	21000

See page 7 to adapt these figures.

1998 CHEVROLET Malibu

GM M Series

CHEVROLET Metro
PONTIAC Firefly
GEO Metro

1997 CHEVROLET Metro

Assembled in Canada, the Metro/Sprint/Firefly models are the modern versions of the Chevette/Acadian. They took over in 1985, derived from the Suzuki Forsa frame and, nowadays, they represent the lowest-end products assembled by GM and Suzuki. Throughout the years, this model has been commercialized under different banners bearing multiple body style and powertrains.

PROS
- **Quality** of assembly and finishing is exemplary.
- **Styling** is modern, simple and tasteful. These cars seem to be specifically destined for city driving and the 4-door sedan features original sizing.
- **Handling** is consistent as long as tires and the suspension are in good condition.
- **Fuel consumption** is excellent and one of the lowest on the market.

CONS
- **Comfort** is basic because of an overly firm suspension, poorly padded seats and poor soundproofing.
- **Ride** suffers the effects of side winds and the torque has a strange effect on the steering system during strong accelerations on damp road surfaces. Lastly, gear shifting isn't easy unless the car is well warmed up.
- **Panels** are paper thin, show the scars of even the slightest impacts and fall victim to rust very early on.
- **Roominess** is limited and rear doors are small and limit access.
- **The trunk** on hatchback versions is too small if there are four passengers on board.
- **Storage spaces** are rare and far between on the base model.

CONCLUSION
The Sprint/Firefly/Metro models are pleasant, economical and practical minicars for city driving but their size makes them unsuitable for longer outings. Parts are expensive and users must be vigilant when it comes to maintenance.

RECALLS
1997 Automatic transmission shifter must be replaced on some models.

CHEVROLET Metro
PONTIAC Firefly
GEO Metro

M Series GM

RELIABILITY PROBLEMS

	1996	1997	1998	1999	2000	2001
Engine:	X	X	X	X	X	
Transmission:	X	-	-	X	-	
Suspension:	-	-	-	-	-	
Steering:	-	-	-	-	-	
Brakes:	X	X	X	X	X	
Electricity:	X	-	X	X	-	
Body:	X	-	-	-	-	
Accessories:	X	X	X	X	X	
Fit/finish:	X	X	X	X	X	

POWERTRAIN

Year	Type/ L/Camshaft/bhp	Drivetrain & gearbox
96-00	L3/1.0/SOHC/55	front-M5
	L4/1.3/SOHC/70-79	front-M5
		front-A3

PERFORMANCE

Acceler. 0/100 sec.	Top. speed km/h	Ave. Fuel consp. l./100 km
14.3	145	5.4
13.2	160	6.4
14.0	150	7.7

SPECIFICATIONS

Model 96-00	Wlb. mm	Lght. mm	Cb.wt kg	Brakes fr/rr	Steering type	Standard tires
cpe. 3dr.	2365	3795	860	dc/dr	r&p.	155/80R13
sdn. 4dr.	2365	4166	900	dc/dr	r&p.	155/80R13

PRICES

Model / version Metro/Firefly		1996	1997	1998	1999	2000	2001
cpe. 3dr. & FE	mini	2900	4000	4800	6100	7900	
	maxi	4200	5250	6800	7900	10000	
cpe. 3dr. SE	mini	3200					
	maxi	4700					
sdn. 4dr.	mini	4000	5000	5900	7200	8900	
	maxi	5150	6300	7650	8900	11000	
sdn. 4dr. SE	mini	4400					
	maxi	5700					

Geo/Chevrolet Metro

		1996	1997	1998	1999	2000	2001
sdn. 3dr.	mini	3350	4500	5350	6600	7900	
	maxi	4700	5800	7350	8400	10000	
sdn. 3dr. GSi	mini	3700					
	maxi	5250					
sdn. 4dr.	mini	4500	5450	6000	7700	8900	
	maxi	5700	6800	7350	9450	11000	
sdn. 4dr. LSi	mini	4900					
	maxi	6200					

See page 7 to adapt these figures.

1998 CHEVROLET Metro

GM M-UT Series

CHEVROLET Astro
GMC Safari

2000 CHEVROLET Astro

The rear-wheel drive Astro and Safari minivans were first put on the market in 1985 and all-drive models were available in 1990. They were designed along the same lines as the S-10 pickup truck frame and are equipped with a 4.3L V6 engine.

PROS

• **The V6 engine** has the torque and horsepower you need to haul or pull heavy loads.

• **The driver's seat** is high and with the wide rearview mirrors, visibility is just great.

• **Power steering** is smooth, well-calibrated and amazingly clean and crisp.

• **The look** of these minivans has improved with the style modifications on the front end.

• **Noteworthy**: the more functional '95 instrument panel, the Dutch-style hatch and the rear bumper that serves as a step.

CONS

• **These vehicles** are gas-thirsty even when not carrying a load.

• **It's impossible to park** these high-perched vehicles in a garage or inside some public parking spaces.

• **Handling** can be pretty touch and go on the rear-wheel drive models in winter conditions or on slippery roads.

• **The interior** is quite cramped, for it's hard to get around the seats and leg room is tight in the front passenger seat.

• **To be taken into account**: no standard rear defroster or windshield wipers, complicated instrument clusters that are hard to read night or day, rough shifting on the automatic, inconvenient engine access and scarce storage compartments on some models.

CONCLUSION

In spite of their fancy, dressed-up look, the Astro/Safari minivans are more plain and simple than family-style vans.

RECALLS

None over this period.

CHEVROLET Astro / GMC Safari — M-UT Series GM

RELIABILITY PROBLEMS

	1996	1997	1998	1999	2000	2001
Engine:	X	X	X	X	X	-
Transmission:	X	X	-	-	-	-
Suspension:	X	-	-	X	X	-
Steering:	-	-	-	-	-	-
Brakes:	X	X	X	X	X	X
Electricity:	X	X	X	X	X	X
Body:	X	-	-	-	-	-
Accessories:	X	X	X	X	X	X
Fit/finish:	X	X	-	X	X	-

POWERTRAIN

Year	Type/ L/Camshaft/bhp	Drivetrain & gearbox
96-01	V6/4.3/OHV/150-190	rear-M5
		rear/all-A4

PERFORMANCE

Acceler. 0/100 sec.	Top. speed km/h	Ave. Fuel consp. l./100 km
11.0	170	15.0
11.7	165	15.3

SPECIFICATIONS

Model	Wlb. mm	Lght. mm	Cb.wt kg	Brakes fr/rr	Steering type	Standard tires
4x2						
m.v. 4dr. LWB	2825	4821	1903	dc/dr/ABS	pwr.bal.	215/75R15
4x4						
m.v. 4dr. LWB	2825	4821	2015	dc/dr/ABS	pwr.bal.	215/75R15

PRICES

Model / version		1996	1997	1998	1999	2000	2001
Astro/Safari							
m.v. 4dr. Cargo	mini	5000	7550	9650	10900	13950	16400
	maxi	7900	10000	11750	13000	16400	19100
m.v. 4dr. SLX/CS	mini	6700	9250	12700	14300	16000	18400
	maxi	9650	11750	14900	16400	18500	21000
m.v. 4dr. SLE/CL	mini	8700	11300	13650	15750	17000	19600
	maxi	11750	13800	16000	18000	19400	22600
m.v. 4dr. SLT/LT	mini	10700	12300	15100	17800	19600	22400
	maxi	13850	14700	17550	19950	22000	25200
m.v. 4dr. SL	mini						18700
	maxi						21500
m.v. 4dr. SLT/LT	mini	13800	13350	16200	18800	20900	23600
LWB 4x4	maxi	14900	15750	18600	21000	23300	26400

See page 7 to adapt these figures.

GM N Series

BUICK Skylark
OLDSMOBILE Achieva/Alero
PONTIAC Grand Am

1996 BUICK Skylark GS

These front-wheel drive compact cars were first sold in '85 and there are lots of them, both coupes and sedans, available on the used car market. In 1999, the Achieva has been replaced by the Alero, available in two body styles and powered by either a 2.4L 4-cylinder or a 3.4L V6 engine.

PROS
• **The Alero** is by far the most stunning of these vehicles, followed closely by the Grand Am, which is why it's always been so popular.
• **The V6** engine is a better choice than the QuadFour for any model, especially for the Grand AM, if it was available at that time.
• **The sports models** handle quite well with their stiffer suspension and larger tires.
• **Steering** is sensitive but becomes vague at high speeds.
• **The V6 engine** is more spirited and more fun to run than the 4-cylinder.
• **The latest model** dashboards are nicer looking and are more straightforward and convenient than before.

CONS
• **The cabin** is smaller than that of the competition, especially in the rear seat area of the coupes that is a chore to climb into, and trunk size is skimpy.
• **Comfort** isn't cushy on the sports models because of the rather primitive suspension, firm tires and high noise level.
• **Rearward view** isn't the greatest with the rear panel support and such small rearview mirrors.
• **Assembly** and finish are slipshod and some components, especially the plastic trim, look flimsy and cheap.
• **The manual transmission** is poorly calibrated and the shifter is tricky to use, but the 3-speed automatic is terrible and to be avoided.
• **Brakes are poor**, ABS is pretty rough and rustic, and it takes forever to get any kind of pedal response.
• **Steering** is light and sensitive, because it's over-assisted and the fact that it's so crisp can make some maneuvers difficult.

CONCLUSION
These cars may look good, but they're not too impressive once you get them on the road. Performance are poor, and overall design and build quality are just as unimpressive. The only exception to this rule remains in the Alero which is manufactured so tight that it clearly indicates that the "small" Olds division at GM is managed better than the larger ones in a very significative and lucrative market segment

BUICK Skylark
OLDSMOBILE Achieva/Alero
PONTIAC Grand Am

N Series GM

POWERTRAIN

Year	Type/ L/Camshaft/bhp	Drivetrain & gearbox
96-98	L4/2.4/DOHC/150	front-M5
		front-A4
	V6/3.1/OHV/155-160	front-A4
99-01	L4/2.4/DOHC/150	front-A4
	V6/3.4/OHV/170-175	front-A4

PERFORMANCE

Acceler. 0/100 sec.	Top. speed km/h	Ave. Fuel consp. l./100 km
9.8	180	12.0
10.5	175	10.7
9.0	175	11.8
10.0	175	10.8
8.5	180	12.0

SPECIFICATIONS

Model	Wlb. mm	Lght. mm	Cb.wt kg	Brakes fr/rr	Steering type	Standard tires
Buick Skylark 96-97						
cpe. 2dr.	2626	4806	1269	dc/dr/ABS	pwr.r&p.	185/75R14
sdn. 4dr.	2626	4788	1354	dc/dr/ABS	pwr.r&p.	195/70R14
cpe. 2dr. GS	2626	4806	1290	dc/dr/ABS	pwr.r&p.	205/55R16
sdn. 4dr. GS	2626	4806	1311	dc/dr/ABS	pwr.r&p.	205/55R16
OLDSMOBILE Achieva 96-98						
cpe. 2dr. S	2627	4773	1292	dc/dr/ABS	pwr.r&p.	185/75R14
sdn. 4dr. S	2627	4773	1223	dc/dr/ABS	pwr.r&p.	185/75R14
cpe. 2dr. SC	2627	4773	1255	dc/dr/ABS	pwr.r&p.	195/70R14
sdn. 4dr. SL	2627	4773	1323	dc/dr/ABS	pwr.r&p.	195/65R15
PONTIAC Grand Am 96-01						
cpe. 2dr. SE	2718	4732	1391	dc/dr/ABS	pwr.r&p.	215/60R15
sdn. 4dr. SE	2718	4732	1413	dc/dr/ABS	pwr.r&p.	215/60R15
cpe. 2dr. GT	2718	4732	1402	dc/ABS	pwr.r&p.	225/50R16
sdn. 4dr. GT	2718	4732	1437	dc/ABS	pwr.r&p.	225/50R16
OLDSMOBILE Alero 99-01						
cpe. 2dr.GX/GL	2718	4742	1372	dc/dr/ABS	pwr.r&p.	215/60R15
sdn. 4dr. GLS	2718	4742	1396	dc/dr/ABS	pwr.r&p.	225/50R16

See prices on the following pages

1997 PONTIAC Grand Am GT

GM N Series

**BUICK Skylark
OLDSMOBILE Achieva/Alero
PONTIAC Grand Am**

1999 PONTIAC Grand Am SE

RECALLS

1996 Loose screws on the steering column.
Emergency lights not functionning correctly.
Passenger airbag doesn't deploy properly.
Lamp control module is defective.
1997 Evaporative emission canister built incorrectly.
Protective cover for underhood fuse centre may be missing.
1999 Loose steering wheel retaining nut.
Defective child rear seat tether anchorages.
2001 Defective automatic transmission locking system.

RELIABILITY PROBLEMS

	1996	1997	1998	1999	2000	2001
Engine:	X	X	-	-	-	-
Transmission:	-	-	-	-	-	-
Suspension:	-	X	X	X	-	-
Steering:	-	-	-	-	X	-
Brakes:	X	X	X	X	X	X
Electricity:	X	X	X	X	-	-
Body:	X	X	X	X	X	X
Accessories:	X	X	X	X	X	-
Fit/finish:	-	X	X	X	-	-

1999 OLDSMOBILE Alero GLS

134 The Canadian Used Car Guide 2002-2003

BUICK Skylark
OLDSMOBILE Achieva/Alero
PONTIAC Grand Am

N Series GM

Model / version		PRICES					
		1996	1997	1998	1999	2000	2001
BUICK Skylark							
cpe. 2dr.Custom	mini	5800	7400				
	maxi	8900	10500				
sdn. 4dr. Custom	mini	6000	7550				
	maxi	9000	10800				
OLDSMOBILE Achieva							
cpe. 2dr. SC	mini	5250	6900				
	maxi	8200	9750				
sdn. 4dr. SL	mini	5500	7150				
	maxi	8400	10000				
PONTIAC Grand Am							
cpe. 2dr. SE	mini	6000	7450	9900	12400	14200	16600
	maxi	9100	10300	12900	15000	17300	19950
cpe. 2dr. GT	mini	8400	10600	13250	15550	17300	19600
	maxi	10350	13450	16000	18150	20500	23100
cpe. 2dr. GTi	mini						21000
	maxi						24700
cpe. 2dr. SET	mini						19100
	maxi						22600
sdn. 4dr. SE	mini	6200	7650	10100	12600	14400	16800
	maxi	9250	10500	13100	15200	17500	20150
sdn. 4dr. GT	mini	8600	10800	13400	15750	17500	19950
	maxi	11550	13650	16300	18400	20700	23600
sdn. 4dr. SET	mini						19400
	maxi						23100
sdn. 4dr. GTi	mini						21200
	maxi						25200
OLDSMOBILE Alero							
cpe. 2dr. GX	mini				11000	12600	14900
	maxi				13650	15750	18400
cpe. 2dr. GL	mini				12600	14200	16500
	maxi				15200	17300	20150
cpe. 2dr. GLS	mini				14200	15750	18000
	maxi				16800	18900	21500
sdn. 4dr. GX	mini				11200	12800	15200
	maxi				13850	16000	18900
sdn. 4dr. GL	mini				12800	15000	16800
	maxi				15450	17000	20500
sdn. 4dr. GLS	mini				14400	16000	18400
	maxi				17000	19100	22000

See page 7 to adapt these figures.

GM U Series

CHEVROLET Lumina Van/APV
PONTIAC Trans Sport 1996

1996 PONTIAC Trans Sport

These sci-fi looking minivans were sold in the '90's and were powered by a 3.1L V6 engine putting out 120-bhp. In 1992, a new 3.8L engine capable of yielding 165-bhp was available as an option.

PROS

• **Modular seats** are easy to maneuver and allow for many and sundry cabin arrangements.
• **The polymer body** is resistant to light impact and rust can't touch it.
• **The ride** is really smooth with such a nice, soft suspension and reasonable noise level. The individual seats are well-contoured and they can be adjusted any which way, which is a real plus as far as comfort goes.
• **These vehicles handle** well on the road with the rear suspension that provides for a smooth ride and rear end stability, more so than the competition.

CONS

• **The unusual driver's position** takes some time getting used to, for you're seated so far away from the front end of the vehicle that you can't even see it.
• **The instrument panel** is massive and poorly designed, it's neither convenient nor ergonomic.
• **Cabin space** is somewhat cramped because of the short wheelbase and the disproportionate size of the front and rear seat areas.
• **The baggage compartment** is next to nil when you have a full house.
• **The 3.1L engine** is anemic and the 3-speed automatic is terribly out of date.
• **The sliding door** is narrow and hard to open in the winter, which doesn't help boarding (and the power version isn't always safe).
• **Ineffective headlights** and windshield wipers.

CONCLUSION

These minivans look good and they're affordable, but they're not really too practical and build quality is pretty poor.

RECALLS

None over this period.

CHEVROLET Lumina Van/APV
PONTIAC Trans Sport 1996
U Series GM

RELIABILITY PROBLEMS

	1996	1997	1998	1999	2000	2001
Engine:	X					
Transmission:	-					
Suspension:	-					
Steering:	-					
Brakes:	X					
Electricity:	x					
Body:	X					
Accessories:	X					
Fit/finish:	X					

POWERTRAIN

Year	Type/ L/Camshaft/bhp	Drivetrain & gearbox
1996	V6 3.4/OHV/180	front-A4

PERFORMANCE

Acceler. 0/100 sec.	Top. speed km/h	Ave. Fuel consp. l./100 km
10.5	175	12.1

SPECIFICATIONS

Model 1996	Wlb. mm	Lght. mm	Cb.wt kg	Brakes fr/rr	Steering type	Standard tires
m.v. 4dr. base	2789	4933	1570	dc/dr	pwr.r&p.	205/70R15
m.v. 4dr. LS/LE	2789	4933	1620	dc/dr	pwr.r&p.	205/70R15

PRICES

Model / version		1996	1997	1998	1999	2000	2001
Lumina Van/APV							
m.v. 4dr. base 5st.	mini	6300					
	maxi	8600					
m.v. 4dr. base 7st.	mini	6600					
	maxi	8900					
m.v. 4dr. LS 5st.	mini	7800					
	maxi	10200					
m.v. 4dr. LS 7st.	mini	8100					
	maxi	10500					
Trans Sport							
m.v. 4dr. SE 5st.	mini	8100					
	maxi	10500					
m.v. 4dr. SE 7st.	mini	8400					
	maxi	10800					

See page 7 to adapt these figures.

1996 CHEVROLET Lumina

GM U Series

CHEVROLET Venture
OLDSMOBILE Silhouette
PONTIAC Trans Sport-Montana

1997 CHEVROLET Venture

These vehicles are available in two wheelbase versions, equipped with a 3.4L V6 driven by a 4-speed automatic transmission. In 1998, the Oldsmobile Silhouette entered this market segment and in 1999 the Trans Sport has been renamed Montana.

PROS

- **Highway driving** is a joy due to the smooth suspension, nicely shaped and cushy front seats and sure-proof soundproofing.
- **They can accelerate** to 100 km/hr in about 11 seconds and pick-up is muscular enough to pass on the highway with a good safety margin. Fuel economy is normal achieving around 13L/100 km.
- **The automatic transmission** is a small wonder and you can brake by downshifting while in third or second gear.
- **Handling** is honest in most situations, thanks to vehicle stability, so you can take any curve with assurance and precision.
- **Kudos for:** power sliding door, functional storage compartments, rear bumper that serves as a boarding step, effective wipers that sweep a large section of the windshield in no time flat.

CONS

- **Seats** are quite low, because of tight head room, so they aren't terribly comfortable. Rear seats are flat and hard and the small headrests aren't of much use.
- **Brakes** don't offer enough grip to achieve short stops and the elastic pedal is hard to hit just right.
- **The multi-function** shifter located under the driving wheel is too complicated.
- **The suspension** acts up on rough road surfaces and front wheels bounce a lot because of the low-slung suspension components.
- **Access** to the engine is as tricky as it was on the former model, because the engine is located way back there under the windshield and the dashboard.
- **The bland interior** sure doesn't get spruced up much by the cheap-looking plastic trim.

CONCLUSION

These three vehicles are more competitive with their 2 wheel-bases and left side sliding door. But the carftmanship is not the best of all and safety is less than average.

RECALLS

97-98	Locking mechanisms on bench seats are unprotected. Must be inspected for possible brake fluid line damage.
1997	A brake pipe retainer clip must be installed to the underbody.
1998	Shift cable must be inspected and replaced if necessary. Water may seep into the evaporitive emission canister and may cause an engine malfunction.
1999	Defective left and right front lower cradle to suspension insulators and the attaching bolts.
2000	Some seatbelts doesn't satisfied strenght regulations. Fuel tank with inoperative rollover valve will be changed.
2001	Dealers will install a new power sliding door and latch assembly (Montana).

CHEVROLET Venture
OLDSMOBILE Silhouette
PONTIAC Trans Sport-Montana

U Series GM

RELIABILITY PROBLEMS

	1996	1997	1998	1999	2000	2001
Engine:	-	-	-	X	-	-
Transmission:	-	-	-	-	-	-
Suspension:	-	X	X	X	-	-
Steering:	-	-	-	-	-	-
Brakes:	X	X	X	X	X	X
Electricity:	X	X	X	X	X	X
Body:	X	X	X	X	X	X
Accessories:	X	X	X	X	X	X
Fit/finish:	X	X	X	-	-	-

POWERTRAIN

Year	Type/ L/Camshaft/bhp	Drivetrain & gearbox
97-01	V6/3.4/OHV/180-185	front-A4

PERFORMANCE

Acceler. 0/100 sec.	Top speed km/h	Ave. Fuel consp. l./100 km
11.0	170	13.0

SPECIFICATIONS

Model	Wlb. mm	Lght. mm	Cb.wt kg	Brakes fr/rr	Steering type	Standard tires
m.v. 4dr. short	2845	4760	1699	dc/dr/ABS	pwr.r&p.	205/70R15
m.v. 4dr. long	3048	5116	1788	dc/dr/ABS	pwr.r&p.	215/70R15

PRICES

Model / version		1996	1997	1998	1999	2000	2001
CHEVROLET Venture							
m.v. 4dr. short	mini		9250	12600	14200		
	maxi		11000	15200	16600		
m.v. 5dr. short	mini		10700	13650	15300	18600	21000
	maxi		12600	16000	17750	21000	23700
m.v. 4dr. LWB	mini		10300	14200			
	maxi		12200	16300			
m.v. 5dr. LWB	mini		11550	15200	16700	19200	22000
	maxi		13450	17500	19100	21950	24700
m.v. 5dr. short LS	mini					19600	22250
	maxi					22350	25200
m.v. 5dr LWB LS	mini					20250	23100
	maxi					23000	25700
m.v. 5dr. LWB LT	mini					22600	25200
	maxi					25200	28000
m.v. 5dr. W/Bros.	mini						26200
	maxi						29100
PONTIAC Trans Sport / Montana (1999)							
m.v. 4dr. short	mini		10500	13100	14900		
	maxi		13100	15750	18400		
m.v. 5dr. short	mini			13550	16300		
	maxi			16500	19750		
m.v. 4dr. LWB	mini		15200	14200			
	maxi		15500	16800			
m.v. 5dr. LWB	mini		13450	14700	17300		
	maxi		15750	17300	19950		
PONTIAC Montana							
m.v. 5 dr.	mini					18400	21500
	maxi					20500	25200
m.v. 5dr. SE	mini					20700	24150
	maxi					23600	27700
m.v. 5dr. LWB	mini					20400	23600
	maxi					23100	27300
m.v. 5dr. LWB LE	mini					21500	25200
	maxi					24150	28550
m.v. 5dr. short GT	mini						27300
	maxi						30450
m.v. 5dr. LWB GT	mini						28350
	maxi						31500
m.v. 5dr. VISION	mini					24000	27300
	maxi					26250	30450
OLDSMOBILE Silhouette							
m.v. 5dr. GS	mini			14700	17300		
	maxi			16800	19650		
m.v. 5dr. GL LWB	mini			14400	16000	20500	22000
	maxi			16700	18500	23000	24700
m.v. 5dr. GLS LWB	mini			17850	20500	24700	26700
	maxi			20250	23000	27300	29300
m.v. 5dr. Pr. Ed. LWB	mini					26250	28400
	maxi					29400	31000

See page 7 to adapt these figures.

U Series GM — Aztek

2001 PONTIAC Aztek

The Aztek is a hybrid vehicle that fits midway between a minivan and an SUV. Available with 2- or 4-wheel drive, it's based on the Trans Sport's platform and mechanics.

PROS

- **This vehicle is versatile** and features a modular rear-end assembly. It targets active individuals and sports amateurs.
- **Performance** is respectable with the infamous 3.4-liter V6, whose weight-to-power ratio is quite good.
- **The Aztek is comfortable** and relaxing to drive on the highway thanks to its soft suspension and good soundproofing.
- **The 3.4-liter** is reasonable on fuel; in fact, it's a fuel economy champion and makes the competition look shameful.
- **The interior features** an original presentation and youthful styling that's out of the ordinary.
- **The front seats** are well-designed and provide good support. Also, their adequate padding makes them quite comfortable.
- **The climate control** system works as efficiently in warm as in cold weather, no matter where your expeditions take you.

CONS

- **The controversial styling** is far from pleasing everyone, to the point that GM has decided to redesign future models to avoid catastrophic consequences.
- **The mediocre brakes** produce long stopping distances, but ABS nevertheless enables the Aztek to maintain a straight trajectory.
- **The suspension** is too supple and generates important body motions that are as unpleasant as they are dangerous.
- **The two-part hatchback** is heavy and cumbersome, in that its lower half complicates access to the cargo bay.
- **The transmission** shifts with irregularity and often seems to be searching for the right gear. This makes driving frustrating, especially given the lack of any form of compression braking.
- **Rearward visibility** is hindered by the two-part rear window, whose top section is sharply sloped, as well as by the headrests.
- **The instrument panel** does not feature a gear selector reminder for the automatic transmission.

VERDICT

Most of the Aztek's target clientele will continue to shrug it off because of its unusual styling.

RECALLS

None over this period.

Aztek — GM U Series

RELIABILITY PROBLEMS

	1996	1997	1998	1999	2000	2001
Engine:						-
Transmission:						-
Suspension:						-
Steering:						-
Brakes:						X
Electricity:						X
Body:						-
Accessories:						X
Fit/finish:						-

POWERTRAIN / PERFORMANCE

Year	Type/ L/Camshaft/bhp	Drivetrain & gearbox	Acceler. 0/100 sec.	Top. speed km/h	Ave. Fuel consp. l./100 km
2001	V6/3.4/OHV/185 FWD	front-A4	10.5	170	12.3
	AWD	front-A4	11.0	165	12.7

SPECIFICATIONS

Model 2001	Wlb. mm	Lght. mm	Cb.wt kg	Brakes fr/rr	Steering type	Standard tires
fam. 4 p FWD	2751	4625	1714	dc/dr/ABS	pwr.r.&p.	215/70R16
fam. 4 p. AWD	2751	4625	1834	dc/dr/ABS	pwr.r.&p.	215/70R16

PRICES

Model / version		1996	1997	1998	1999	2000	2001
wgn. 4dr. AWD	mini						31500
	maxi						36750
wgn. 4dr. GT AWD	mini						33600
	maxi						38850

See page 7 to adapt these figures.

2001 PONTIAC Aztek

GM V Series — CADILLAC Catera

1997 CADILLAC Catera

The Catera is a 4-door sedan who is sold in a single trim level equipped with a standard 3.0L V6 driven by an automatic. This German-built import has been available since 1997.

PROS
- **This car** has some class, even though it's so quietly elegant that it can go unnoticed. The cabin is very lovely and lush.
- **A lot of goodies** for your money, compared to direct rivals, for example, there are heated seats both up front and in the rear.
- **This German-built** car is sure-proof safe and it's as solid and heavy as an army tank. Visibility is clear in all directions.
- **Sitting** is royal on plush seats that offer perfect support, carried along by a velvety suspension that absorbs every bump in the road. All this in a quiet atmosphere, thanks to superb soundproofing.
- **Handling** is honest, for the Catera is stable in any situation.
- **The engine** achieves Sportscar capabilities, but when it comes to pick-up, it's more sluggish, because of heavy vehicle weight.
- **Brakes** are powerful, well-balanced and tough, so you can make any number of sudden stops without a hitch...
- **Assembly quality**, trim materials and fit and finish are perfect examples of Germanic car standards.
- **The car maneuvers** superbly because of a good steering ratio and its very short turning diameter.
- **Practicality** like the trunk, who can hold a lot of luggage and it can be extended by lowering one or both sections of the split rear seatback.

CONS
- **Anonymous** looks make it hard to identify easily and don't do much to add pizzazz.
- **Driving** isn't quite what you'd expect, for the engine lacks get up and go in some situations when the car is the least bit loaded with passengers or luggage.
- **The instrument** panel is massive and takes up crucial space needed by front-seat passengers.
- **Winter driving** isn't as safe and sure as with a front-wheel drive, and the traction control do its best to keep the car on course...

CONCLUSION
The small Cadillac is a solid, well-built car that can boast of impressive capabilities, luxurious equipment and cream of the crop comfort.

RECALLS
1997 Defective child seat anchoring.

CADILLAC Catera   V Series GM

RELIABILITY PROBLEMS

	1996	1997	1998	1999	2000	2001
Engine:		X	X	X	-	-
Transmission:		-	X	-	-	-
Suspension:		-	X	X	X	-
Steering:		-	-	-	-	-
Brakes:		X	X	X	X	X
Electricity:		X	X	X	X	X
Body:		-	X	X	X	-
Accessories:		X	X	X	X	X
Fit/finish:		-	-	-	-	-

POWERTRAIN

Year	Type/ L/Camshaft/bhp	Drivetrain & gearbox
97-01	V6/3.0/DOHC/200	front-A4

PERFORMANCE

Acceler. 0/100 sec.	Top. speed km/h	Ave. Fuel consp. l./100 km
9.0	200	12.9

SPECIFICATIONS

Model 97-01	Wlb. mm	Lght. mm	Cb.wt kg	Brakes fr/rr	Steering type	Standard tires
sdn. 4dr.	2730	4928	1710	dc/ABS	pwr.bal.	225/55HR16

PRICES

Model / version		1996	1997	1998	1999	2000	2001
sdn. 4dr.	mini		13100	15750	19950	23100	27300
	maxi		16800	18900	23100	27300	32000

See page 7 to adapt these figures.

1997 CADILLAC Catera

GM W Series

BUICK Century-Regal
CHEVROLET Lumina-Monte Carlo-Impala
OLDSMOBILE Cutlass Supreme-Intrigue
PONTIAC Grand Prix

2000 CHEVROLET Impala

These mid-size front-wheel drive coupes and sedans were first sold in 1989, and the Lumina models were added to the roster in '91. Unfortunately for the people at GM, who wanted these cars to be the flagships of its car fleet, they weren't as popular as hoped. But in '97, the Buick Century came back and one year later the introduction of the Oldsmobile Intrigue has surely helped a lot that platform to get back on track in terms of sales and craftsmanship.

PROS

- **The Pontiac Grand Prix** is by far the most spectacular, with its sensational body design. Although the Intrigue and Regal-Century are charming for they are coated in finesse.
- **Both the 3.4L and 3.8L** engines are quite impressive for they put out more than 200-bhp.
- **The cabin interior** comfortably accommodates five passengers and the nicely shaped trunk can hold all their luggage.
- **The sports models** handle much better because of their higher performance shock absorbers and sturdier springs.
- **The 4-speed automatic** is one of the best on the market, for the shifter is smooth and right on and it provides really good braking effect in 3rd and 2nd gear.
- **Four-disc brakes** are quite stable, even without ABS (optional on the upper-end models during the first few years).
- **Build and finish quality**, as well as materials used, have vastly improved especially on the latest models, notably on the Intrigue.

CONS

- **Excessive vehicle weight** makes gas bills soar sky high.
- **Low-end models** are more suited for highway driving, for their suspension isn't really too firm.
- **Road stability** on base models isn't the greatest because of the overly flexible suspension that causes quite a bit of swing and sway.
- **Things to consider**: poor visibility on the coupes, scarce storage compartments, weak headlights, ineffective windshield wipers and poor ventilation.

CONCLUSION

This large family of cars offers many models to choose from, all equipped with virtually the same mechanical features. Whether it be the popular Lumina or the wild and woolly Grand Prix, car choice only really depends on people's tastes and pocketbooks...

BUICK Century-Regal
CHEVROLET Lumina-Monte Carlo-Impala
OLDSMOBILE Cutlass Supreme-Intrigue
PONTIAC Grand Prix

W Series GM

POWERTRAIN

Year	Type/ L/Camshaft/bhp	Drivetrain & gearbox
96-01	V6/3.1/OHV/140-160	front-A4
	V6/3.8/OHC/170-205	front-M5
		front-A4
	V6C/3.8/DOHC/215-240	front-A4
99-01	V6/3.5/DOHC/215	front-A4
00-01	V6/3.4/OHC/180	front-A4
	V6/3.8/OHC/200 Impala	front-A4

PERFORMANCE

Acceler. 0/100 sec.	Top speed km/h	Ave. Fuel consp. l./100 km
9.8	165	12.3
8.5	200	12.9
8.3	175	12.4
7.2	200	13.2
NA	NA	12.5
9.6	180	11.8
8.5	190	12.5

SPECIFICATIONS

Model	Wlb. mm	Lght. mm	Cb.wt kg	Brakes fr/rr	Steering type	Standard tires
BUICK Century 96-01						
sdn. 4dr.Custom	2769	4943	1521	dc/dr/ABS	pwr.r&p.	205/70R15
sdn. 4dr. LTD	2769	4943	1529	dc/dr/ABS	pwr.r&p.	205/70R15
BUICK Regal 1996						
cpe. 2dr. Cust.	2730	4925	1480	dc/ABS	pwr.r&p.	205/70R15
cpe. 2dr. GS	2730	4925	1490	dc/ABS	pwr.r&p.	225/60R16
sdn. 4dr. Cust.	2730	4920	1512	dc/ABS	pwr.r&p.	205/70R15
sdn. 4dr. Ltd	2730	4920	1570	dc/ABS	pwr.r&p.	205/70R15
sdn. 4dr. LS/GS	2769	4983	1560	dc/ABS	pwr.r&p.	225/60R16
CHEVROLET Impala 00-01						
sdn. 4dr. base	2807	5080	1537	dc	pwr.r&p.	225/60R16
sdn. 4dr. LS	2807	5080	1572	dc/ABS	pwr.r&p.	225/60R16
CHEVROLET Lumina 96-99						
sdn. 4dr. base	2730	5104	1511	dc/dt/ABS	pwr.r&p.	205/70R15
sdn. 4dr. LS	2730	5104	1531	dc/dt/ABS	pwr.r&p.	225/60R16
sdn. 4dr. LTZ	2730	5104	1551	dc/ABS	pwr.r&p.	225/60R16
CHEVROLET Monte Carlo 96-98						
cpe. 2dr. LS	2730	5098	1470	dc/dt/ABS	pwr.r&p.	205/70R15
cpe. 2dr. Z34	2730	5098	1559	dc/ABS	pwr.r&p.	225/60R16
CHEVROLET Monte Carlo 00-01						
cpe. 2dr. LS	2807	5026	1515	dc/dt/ABS	pwr.r&p.	225/60R16
cpe. 2dr. SS	2807	5026	1538	dc/ABS	pwr.r&p.	225/60R16
OLDSMOBILE Cutlass Supreme 96-97						
cpe. 2dr. SL	2730	4926	1489	dc/ABS	pwr.r&p.	205/70R15
sdn. 4dr. S	2730	4921	1537	dc/ABS	pwr.r&p.	215/60R16
sdn. 4dr. SL	2730	4921	1550	dc/ABS	pwr.r&p.	215/60R16
OLDSMOBILE Intrigue 98-01						
sdn. 4dr. base	2769	4976	1555	dc/ABS	pwr.r&p.	225/60R16
sdn. 4dr.GL/GLS	2769	4976	1567	dc/ABS	pwr.r&p.	225/60R16
PONTIAC Grand Prix 96-97						
cpe. 2dr. SE	2730	4948	1471	dc/ABS	pwr.r&p.	215/60R16
cpe. 2dr. GTP	2730	4948	1471	dc/ABS	pwr.r&p.	225/60R16
sdn. 4dr. SE	2730	4950	1505	dc/ABS	pwr.r&p.	205/70R15
sdn. 4dr. GT	2730	4950	1505	dc/ABS	pwr.r&p.	225/60R16
PONTIAC Grand Prix 98-01						
sdn. 4dr. SE	2807	4991	1549	dc/ABS	pwr.r&p.	205/70R15
cpe. 2dr. GT	2807	4991	1540	dc/ABS	pwr.r&p.	225/60R16
sdn. 4dr. GT	2807	4991	1549	dc/ABS	pwr.r&p.	225/60R16

GM W Series

BUICK Century-Regal
CHEVROLET Lumina-Monte Carlo-Impala
OLDSMOBILE Cutlass Supreme-Intrigue
PONTIAC Grand Prix

1997 BUICK Regal GS

RELIABILITY PROBLEMS

	1996	1997	1998	1999	2000	2001
Engine:	X	X	X	X	-	-
Transmission:	-	-	-	-	-	-
Suspension:	X	-	X	X	X	-
Steering:	X	X	-	-	-	-
Brakes:	-	X	X	X	X	X
Electricity:	X	X	X	X	X	X
Body:	-	-	-	-	-	-
Accessories:	X	X	X	X	X	X
Fit/finish:	-	X	X	-	-	-

RECALLS

96-97 Stress cracks in the center rear seat belt's anchor plate. Defective spark plug assembly kit causing rough idle and poor performance.

1996 Badly installed power brakes resulting in longer braking distances. Backfire in the combustion chamber could damage the engine. (Regal) Front left brake line with premature wear. (Regal)

1997 Wiper's power feed wire may separate.

98-99 Incorrect emission control label.(Lumina-Monte Carlo)

1999 Missing heater hose clip that can cause a coolant leak. Possible ABS motor short circuit that can result in a fire.

2000 Some PCM (Power Control Module) from 3.1, 3.8 and 3.8 supercharged V6 engines must be recalibrated to comply emission regulations.

2001 Dealers will replace sensing and diagnostic module. (Monte Carlo)

2001 OLDSMOBILE Intrigue

BUICK Century-Regal
CHEVROLET Lumina-Monte Carlo-Impala
OLDSMOBILE Cutlass Supreme-Intrigue
PONTIAC Grand Prix

W Series GM

RECALLS (continued)

2000 The fuel hose fill neck will be inspected and if necessary tightened or change to prevent any leaks.
On vehicles equipped with rear drum brakes, the bolts of the rear spindle can break and must be replaced.
The hydraulic modulator of the ABS system can leak and must be inspected and if necessary replaced.
Some seatbelts will not withstand the force requirements of the standard regulation.

PRICES

Model / version		1996	1997	1998	1999	2000	2001
BUICK Century							
sdn. 4dr. Custom	mini		9750	11550	13950	15750	17850
	maxi		12600	14500	16300	18400	21000
sdn. 4dr. LTD	mini		10300	13200	15000	16800	18900
	maxi		13650	15550	17300	19400	22050
BUICK Regal							
cpe. 2dr. Custom	mini	8400					
	maxi	11550					
sdn. 4dr. Custom	mini	8000					
	maxi	11000					
sdn. 4dr. LTD	mini	8700					
	maxi	12100					
sdn. 4dr. Gd Sport	mini	10700					
	maxi	14200					
sdn. 4dr. LS	mini		10800	12200	13950	15750	17850
	maxi		13650	15550	17300	18400	22050
sdn. 4dr. GS	mini		13450	14700	16600	18400	20500
	maxi		16300	18150	19750	22050	24700
CHEVROLET Lumina							
sdn. 4dr.	mini	5250	6100	8000	10000		
	maxi	7900	9450	11000	12800		
sdn. 4dr. LS	mini	5800	6800	8700	10500		
	maxi	8400	10000	11550	13100		
sdn. 4dr. LTZ	mini			8200	9650	11550	
	maxi			11600	12600	14200	
CHEVROLET Monte Carlo							
cpe. 2dr. LS	mini	7000	9250	11100	14200	17300	21000
	maxi	10100	12200	14200	16800	20500	24700
cpe. 2dr. Z34	mini	8600	10800	12200	16300	19950	23100
	maxi	11550	14300	15750	18900	22600	27800
CHEVROLET IMPALA 2000							
sdn. 4dr.	mini					16600	21850
	maxi					20500	25200
sdn. 4dr. LS	mini					19750	24450
	maxi					23100	27800
OLDSMOBILE Cutlass Supreme							
cpe. 2dr.	mini	6500	8200				
	maxi	10000	11100				
sdn. 4dr.	mini	6000	7650				
	maxi	8900	10100				
OLDSMOBILE Intrigue							
sdn 4dr.	mini			10600			
	maxi			13650			
sdn 4dr. GL	mini			11550	14700	16300	20500
	maxi			14700	17300	19400	23600
sdn. 4dr. GLS	mini			13200	16300	17850	22050
	maxi			16300	18900	21000	25200
sdn. 4dr. GX	mini					13100	15200	19400
	maxi					15750	18400	25600
PONTIAC Grand Prix							
cpe. 2dr. SE	mini	6700					
	maxi	9650					
cpe. 2dr. GT	mini		12600	14500	16400	18900	21840
	maxi		14900	17300	18400	22000	25200
cpe. 2dr. GTP	mini	9150			18150	20700	23600
	maxi	12200			21000	23950	27000
sdn. 4dr. SE	mini	6500	9250	11550	14100	16300	19200
	maxi	9450	12200	14500	16800	19400	22600
sdn. 4dr. GT	mini	8600	12400	14300	16600	18900	21850
	maxi	11550	14700	17100	19400	22000	25200
sdn. 4dr. GTP	mini				18400	20500	23400
	maxi				22250	23600	26800

See page 7 to adapt these figures.

GM Y Series — CHEVROLET Corvette

1998 CHEVROLET Corvette

The Corvette has become an institution and a legend on four wheels. It celebrated its 30th birthday in '93. It was completely overhauled in '67 and again in '83 and the breathtaking ZR-1 was launched in '89. Since then, it's been successfully remodeled in '98 et the sporty Hard Top trim level has been introduced in '99 and Z06 in 2001.

PROS
- **The** ZR-1 and Z06 performance.
- **Its stunning style** is the stuff that dreams are made of for a lot of fanatics out there.
- **Handling** is just terrific with the firm suspension and very large Z-grade tires.
- **The driver's position** is perfect with all the adjustments and with the firm, contour bucket seats.
- **Steering** is crisp and clean and silky smooth.
- **With the really large disc brakes** and sophisticated ABS, braking this baby is a piece of cake.

CONS
- **Its hefty price** tag has discouraged quite a few potential buyers.
- **Build and finish** quality are sloppy and some trim components are chintzy, which is totally unacceptable on such a pricy car.
- **The V8 engines** drink up a lot of gas, even more so for racy and raucous Sportscar maneuvers.
- **Comfort** isn't a priority, it seems, with such a snug cabin, harsh suspension, poor wheel travel, acrobatic seat access and loud noise that gets on your nerves in no time.
- **Storage compartments** are almost as rare as hen's teeth and what they call the trunk is teeny tiny.
- **Outward view** is iffy with the high body frame, large blind spots caused by the convertible top, the minuscule rearview mirrors and gauges that are impossible to read in direct sunlight.
- **Note:** a winshield display system (Head-Up) is made standard on '99.

CONCLUSION
Most Corvette owners have made their dream come true, but it can become a real nightmare if the car hasn't been maintained as it should be, for reliability isn't a strong suit for this car.

RECALLS
1997	Torn seal between the fuel tank and unit pump.
	Seat belts may not be effective.
	Rear suspension tie rod may fracture.
2000	Some defective guides which can twisted and jammed safety belts will be replaced.

CHEVROLET Corvette — Y Series GM

RELIABILITY PROBLEMS

	1996	1997	1998	1999	2000	2001
Engine:	X	X	X	X	X	-
Transmission:	-	X	-	-	-	-
Suspension:	-	-	-	-	-	-
Steering:	-	X	-	-	-	-
Brakes:	X	X	X	X	X	X
Electricity:	X	X	X	X	X	X
Body:	X	-	X	-	X	-
Accessories:	X	X	X	X	X	-
Fit/finish:	-	-	-	X	X	-

POWERTRAIN

Year	Type/ L/Camshaft/bhp	Drivetrain & gearbox
96-01	V8/5.7/OHV/245-350	rear-M6
		rear-A4

PERFORMANCE

Acceler. 0/100 sec.	Top. speed km/h	Ave. Fuel consp. l./100 km
5.0	270	13.7
5.3	275	14.0

SPECIFICATIONS

Model	Wlb. mm	Lght. mm	Cb.wt kg	Brakes fr/rr	Steering type	Standard tires
96-97						
cpe. 2dr.	2443	4534	1501	dc/ABS	pwr.r&p.	275/40R17
con. 2dr.	2443	4534	1512	dc/ABS	pwr.r&p.	285/40R17
cpe. 2dr. ZR-1	2443	4534	1590	dc/ABS	pwr.r&p.	275/40R17
98-01						315/35R17
cpe. 2dr.	2655	4566	1472	dc/ABS	pwr.r&p.	245/45R17
cpe. 2dr. Hard top	2655	4566	1430	dc/ABS	pwr.r&p.	245/45R17
con. 2dr.	2655	4566	1473	dc/ABS	pwr.r&p.	275/40R18
cpe. 2dr. Z06	2655	4566	1456	dc/ABS	pwr.r&p.	275/40R18

PRICES

Model / version		1996	1997	1998	1999	2000	2001
cpe. 2dr.	mini	26000	33600	39900	46200	54600	60900
	maxi	30450	36750	43000	49350	57750	65100
cpe. 2dr. Hard top	mini				39900	47250	
	maxi				49350	50900	
cpe. 2dr. Z06HT	mini						66150
	maxi						70300
con. 2dr.	mini	28350			45700	52500	59850	66150
	maxi	32550			48800	55650	63500	70300

See page 7 to adapt these figures.

1999 CHEVROLET Corvette

GM VSU

CADILLAC Escalade
CHEVROLET Tahoe & Suburban
GMC Yukon & Yukon XL

GMC Yukon Denali 1999

Stemming from the venerable Suburban, these vehicles truly inaugurated the market for full-size luxury SUVs. They are available as two- and four-wheel drive and were revamped in 2000.

PROS

- **Spacious cabins**: the Tahoe has room for six people, while the Suburban can seat up to nine . . . not to mention their luggage!
- **Performance** akin to those of big passenger cars.
- **The handling** is much more precise than the previous generations' thanks to a more rigid chassis and improved suspension capabilities.
- **Ride comfort** is appreciable at highway cruising speeds, where the suspension and noise level are acceptable.
- **The dashboard** is not a model of ergonomics, but it houses a lot of instruments and storage compartments.
- **These vehicles** boast impressive load and trailering capabilities.
- **The uppercrust** models are luxurious, but buyers must check off a lot of options before having a complete array of equipment.
- **The high driving position**, low frame belt and big mirrors ensure excellent overall visibility.

CONS

- **These models** are nothing short of gas guzzlers.
- **Maneuverability** is hindered by the imposing hulk and wide steer angle diameter of these vehicles.
- **The Escalade's off-road capabilities** are limited by its front and rear cowls.
- **The seat cushions** are too short and do not provide much in terms of lateral support because they are too flat.
- **The rigid rear axle** often slips and slides.
- **Road noise** from the frame builds up over the kilometers.
- **The two rear side-swing doors** block visibility, while the rear door with swing panel makes it difficult to access the luggage compartment.

CONCLUSION

At long last, these big GMs have fallen into step with their competitors. Their modern engines and much more rigid bodies make them a lot more roadworthy.

RECALLS

1996 A portion of the dash will be cut to provide clearance to the throttle cable.
96-97 A protector will be installed over the recliner mechanism of the front seats.
1998 Rear brake pipe positioning clip will be relocated, brake pipe will be inspected and replaced if necessary.
A pinch bolt will be torqued properly to specification.
99-00 Front right hand brake pipe will be inspected and replaced if necessary.
Dealers will instal a jumper harness that turn on the required lamps when fog lamps are activated.
Inspection will be conducted for loose or missing wheelhouse plug and installed if necessary.
2000 Brake vacuum booster supply hose will be rerouted.
2001 Dealers will inspect for loose or missing wheelhouse plugs and install them back if necessary.
Some vehicles may have an internal component in the 2nd and 3rd row outboard seat retractor that could be cracked.

CADILLAC Escalade
CHEVROLET Tahoe & Suburban
GMC Yukon & Yukon XL

GM VSU

RELIABILITY PROBLEMS

	1996	1997	1998	1999	2000	2001
Engine:	X	X	X	X	X	-
Transmission:	X	X	X	X	X	X
Suspension:	-	-	-	-	-	-
Steering:	-	X	-	X	-	X
Brakes:	-	X	-	X	-	X
Electricity:	X	X	X	X	X	-
Body:	-	-	-	-	-	-
Accessories:	X	X	X	X	X	-
Finition:	X	X	X	X	-	-

POWERTRAIN

Year	Type/ L/Camshaft/bhp	Drivetrain & gearbox	Acceler. 0/100 sec.	Top. speed km/h	Ave. Fuel consp. l./100 km
96-99	V8/5.7/OHC/255	rr./all-A4	9.3	175	18.0
	V8TD/6.5/OHC/195	rr./all-A4	13.5	160	16.0
	V8/7.4/OHC/290	rr./all-A4	12.0	180	20.0
00-01	V8/4.8/OHC/270	rr./all-A4	10.0	175	17.0
	V8/5.3/OHC/285	rr./all-A4	9.5	180	18.0
	V8/6.0/OHC/300	rr./all-A4	11.0	175	20.0

SPECIFICATIONS

Model	Wlb. mm	Lght. mm	Cb.wt kg	Brakes fr/rr	Steering type	Standard tires
Escalade						
wgn. 4dr. 4x4	2984	5110	2528	dc/dr/ABS	pwr.ball	275/70R16
Yukon-Tahoe						
wgn. 4dr. 4x2	2832	4775	2053	dc/dr/ABS	pwr.ball	235/75R15
wgn. 4dr. 4x4	2985	5070	2119	dc/dr/ABS	pwr.ball	245/75R16
Suburban-Yukon XL						
wgn. 4dr. 4x2	3340	5575	2187	dc/dr/ABS	pwr.ball	235/75R15
wgn. 4dr. 4x4	3340	5575	2390	dc/dr/ABS	pwr.ball	265/70R17

PRICES

Model / version		1996	1997	1998	1999	2000	2001
CADILLAC Escalade							
wgn. 4dr.	mini				36750	44100	49350
	maxi				40400	46200	54600
CHEVROLET Tahoe/GMC Yukon							
wgn. 2dr. SL/base	mini	11450	14800	17800	20800		
	maxi	13550	17000	19900	23100		
wgn. 2dr. SLE/LS	mini	13850	17300	19850	24100		
	maxi	16200	19400	22000	26400		
wgn. 2dr. SLT/LT	mini	15950	19200	20600	26200		
	maxi	18300	21600	23100	28650		
wgn. 2dr. GT/Sport	mini	14400	17800	21500	23900		
	maxi	16800	20100	23900	26200		
wgn. 4dr. SLE/LS	mini	17400	20500	21800	26900	32400	37300
	maxi	19900	22900	24100	28800	35200	40400
wgn. 4dr. SLT/LT	mini	19100	22250	23700	28500	37700	42500
	maxi	21400	24700	26250	30600	40400	45700
wgn. 4dr. Denau/	mini					38500	46200
Over	maxi					41300	49300
wgn. 4dr. Base/SL	mini					28600	33400
	maxi					30450	35700
wgn. 4dr. Carryover L	mini					34300	
	maxi					37000	
CHEVROLET Suburban/GMC Suburban & Yukon XL							
Série 1500							
wgn. 4dr. SL/base	mini	13650	15300	17200	20700	27300	33200
	maxi	15750	17800	19800	23100	30100	36600
wgn. 4dr. SLE/LS	mini	18600	21000	22400	25100	31400	37100
	maxi	21100	23300	25100	27500	34100	40400
wgn. 4dr. SLT/LT	mini	20300	23100	25000	27300	36200	41800
	maxi	22700	25600	26500	29800	38900	45000
wgn. 4dr. Denau	mini						46500
	maxi						49900
Série 2500							
wgn. 4dr. SL/base	mini	14200	16500	18400	21000	27900	33900
	maxi	16600	18900	20900	23500	30700	36700
wgn. 4dr. SLE/LS	mini	19800	21800	23500	25400	32100	38000
	maxi	21500	24600	26100	27800	34800	41100
wgn. 4dr. SLT/LT	mini	19500	24800	25500	27500	36800	42600
	maxi	22000	26600	28200	30100	40100	46000

See page 7 to adapt these figures.

HONDA Accord

2001 HONDA Accord

First sold in 1981, the Accord rapidly rose to the top of the sales chart in North America. It was modified in 1985, 89, 91, 94 and in 98.

PROS

- **Its nice size** that is exactly like that of the traditional compact station wagon and its cleaner, more recent design with a stronger, reinforced frame.
- **Resale value** remains high, for demand for this model is only affected by its high initial price tag.
- **The cabin** comfortably seats four adults and the fairly roomy trunk holds all their luggage.
- **The well-adjusted** suspension and super, good-sized original tires make for effective road stability.
- **Engines** have great get up and go, even if the gears are a bit slow to kick in.
- **Gas consumption** is quite low, given the vehicle size.
- **Flawless engineering**, assembly and finish quality.
- **The station wagon** is a good alternative to a minivan.

CONS

- **Some models** aren't too flashy or smart looking.
- **Front wheels** skid in no time flat on slippery roads, which is a real worry in the winter.
- **Rear seat** area on earlier models is quite snug.
- **Steering** is quick but over-assisted, more so at higher speeds.
- **Brakes** lack bite and endurance.
- **Awkward rear seat** access on the two-door coupe and the high trunk opening.

CONCLUSION

The Honda Accord has been a smashing success for it's the perfect car for a certain segment of the population, and it's become a sort of prize horse. There are lots of them on the market, so it would be a good idea to have a used car checked out thoroughly before purchase.

RECALLS

96-97   Air conditioner wiring harness must be inspected and rerouted.
1998   Automatic transmission selection may be defective.
Front suspension lower ball joints may prematurely wear out.
2000   The rear suspension lower control arm could break due to improper welding.

Accord — HONDA

RELIABILITY PROBLEMS

	1996	1997	1998	1999	2000	2001
Engine:	X	X	X	X	-	-
Transmission:	-	-	-	X	X	-
Suspension:	X	-	X	-	-	-
Steering:	-	-	-	-	-	-
Brakes:	X	-	X	X	-	-
Electricity:	-	-	X	X	-	-
Body:	X	-	X	X	-	-
Accessories:	X	X	-	X	X	-
Fit/finish:	-	-	X	X	X	-

POWERTRAIN

Year	Type/ L/Camshaft/bhp	Drivetrain & gearbox
96-97	L4/2.2/SOHC/125-130	front-M5
		front-A4
	L4/2.2/SOHC/140-145	front-A4
	V62.7/SOHC/170	front-A4
98-01	L4/2.3/SOHC/135-150	front-M5
		front-A4
	V6/3.0/SOHC/200	front-A4

PERFORMANCE

Acceler. 0/100 sec.	Top speed km/h	Ave. Fuel consp. l./100 km
9.8	195	9.5
11.0	185	10.5
10.0	200	11.0
8.5	200	12.5
9.4	180	9.5
10.0	175	10.5
8.0	200	11.4

SPECIFICATIONS

Model	Wlb. mm	Lght. mm	Cb.wt kg	Brakes fr/rr	Steering type	Standard tires
1996-97						
cpe. 2dr.	2715	4695	1237	dc/dr	pwr.r&p.	185/70R14
sdn. 4dr.	2715	4695	1253	dc/dr	pwr.r&p.	185/70R14
sdn. 4dr. V6	2715	4745	1480	dc/ABS	pwr.r&p.	205/60R15
sdn. 4dr. EX-R V6	2715	4785	1485	dc/ABS	pwr.r&p.	205/60R15
wgn. 5dr.	2715	4770	1365	dc/dr	pwr.r&p.	195/60R15
98-01						
cpe. 2dr. LX	2670	4745	1345	dc/dr/ABS	pwr.r&p.	195/65R15
cpe. 2dr. EX	2670	4745	1365	dc/ABS	pwr.r&p.	195/65R15
cpe. 2dr. EX-V6	2670	4745	1480	dc/ABS	pwr.r&p.	205/60R16
sdn. 4dr. DX	2715	4796	1305	dc/dr	pwr.r&p.	195/70R14
sdn. 4dr. LX	2715	4796	1350	dc/dr/ABS	pwr.r&p.	195/65R15
sdn. 4dr. EX	2715	4796	1305	dc/ABS	pwr.r&p.	195/65R15
sdn. 4dr. EX-V6	2715	4796	1350	dc/ABS	pwr.r&p.	205/65R16

PRICES

Model / version		1996	1997	1998	1999	2000	2001
cpe. 2dr. LX	mini	8000	10800	13700	14700	16300	
	maxi	10000	12600	15700	16600	18400	
cpe. 2dr. EX	mini			15300	17600	19900	21500
	maxi			17300	19400	22000	24100
cpe. 2dr. EX-R	mini	12200	14500				
	maxi	14200	17000				
cpe. 2dr. EX-V6	mini			17900	20250	22600	24700
	maxi			19900	22000	24700	27300
sdn. 4dr. LX	mini	8600	10800	14100	15000	16800	18900
	maxi	10500	12800	15200	16800	18900	22600
sdn. 4dr. EX	mini	10700	12900	15350	18150	20500	24700
	maxi	12600	14900	17300	19900	22600	27300
sdn. 4dr. DX	mini			12200	14000	15750	
	maxi			14200	15700	17850	
sdn. 4dr. SE	mini		13450			18400	
	maxi		14900			20500	
sdn. 4dr. EX-R	mini	12800	14500				
	maxi	14700	16300				
sdn. 4dr. EX ABS	mini	11250					
	maxi	13100					
sdn. 4dr. LX V6	mini						24100
	maxi						26800
sdn. 4dr. EX V6	mini	12300		17450	20150	22600	25200
	maxi	14200		19400	22000	24700	27800
sdn. 4dr. EX-R V6	mini	13200	15000				
	maxi	15350	17000				

See page 7 to adapt these figures.

HONDA   Civic

1996 HONDA Civic

The Civic got an overhaul in 1992 and the new generation models came out in 1996. They still come in sedan or coupe body styles, and are powered by 1.5L or 1.6L 4-cylinder engines. Since 1999, the sporty SiR is available with its 160-bhp engine ready to roar.

PROS
- **Neat-looking and attractive** car over the years, but the latest models tend to have a more conservative look.
- **Late model cars** are more comfortable because of the smoother suspension and they are more spacious and quiet.
- **The 4-door sedan** is just as roomy as a compact car.
- **Well-designed engines** are powerful and quite economical.
- **The model** for young drivers who want to show off like the Sportscar, especially for the SiR with its 15-inch tires, four-disc brakes, CD player and sporty suspension that shouldn't unplease anyone.
- **Clever engineering**, assembly and finish quality put these cars in a class apart.

CONS
- **Bodywork** is still thin and rust-prone.
- **The rear seat** area on the hatchbacks is very cramped and the trunk is very tiny if the rear seatbench isn't folded down.
- **Brakes** could be improved, for the front wheels lock quickly and stops are iffy without ABS.
- **There's a lot of engine** noise due to poor soundproofing on the '94-'95 models.
- **These subcompacts** are really sensitive to high winds and braking effect could be better, even with the manual.

CONCLUSION
The small Civic's are really economical and a lot of fun to drive. But it's too bad they're so vulnerable to impact.

RECALLS
1996 Defective power brake pump valve.
96-98 Passenger airbag module not assembled properly.
2001 Dealers will check the hose clamps for proper torque and tighten them correctly if necessary.
Dealers will inspect the fuel pump. If corrosion is found, the pump electric connector will be replaced.

RELIABILITY PROBLEMS

	1996	1997	1998	1999	2000	2001
Engine:	-	X	-	X	-	-
Transmission:	X	-	-	-	-	-
Suspension:	-	-	-	-	-	-
Steering:	X	-	-	-	-	-
Brakes:	-	-	X	-	-	-
Electricity:	-	-	-	-	-	-
Body:	X	X	X	X	-	-
Accessories:	X	X	-	X	X	-
Fit/finish:	-	-	-	-	-	-

Civic   HONDA

POWERTRAIN / PERFORMANCE

Year	Type/ L/Camshaft/bhp	Drivetrain & gearbox	Acceler. 0/100 sec.	Top. speed km/h	Ave. Fuel consp. l./100 km
96-00	L4/1.6/SOHC/106	front-M5	11.0	175	7.5
		front-A4	12.2	170	8.4
	L4/1.6/SOHC/125-127	front-M5	9.0	190	8.1
		front-A4	10.8	180	9.1
99-00	L4/1.6/SOHC/160	front-M5	NA	NA	NA
2001	L4/1.7/DOHC/115-127	front-M5	9.9	185	7.4

SPECIFICATIONS

Model	Wlb.	Lght.	Cb.wt	Brakes	Steering	Standard
96-00						
cpe. 2dr. DX	2620	4450	1064	dc/dr	pwr.r&p.	185/65R14
cpe. 2dr. Si	2620	4450	1117	dc/dr	pwr.r&p.	185/65R14
sdn. 3dr. CX	2620	4180	1037	dc/dr	crém.	185/65R14
sdn. 4dr. LX-EX	2620	4450	1060	dc/dr	pwr.r&p.	185/65R14
sdn. 4dr. EX-V	2620	4450	1084	dc/dc	pwr.r&p.	185/65R14
99-00						
cpe. 2dr. SiR	2620	4450	1117	dc/dr	pwr.r&p.	195/60R15
2001						
cpe. 2dr. DX	2619	4437	1091	dc/dr	pwr.r&p.	185/65R14
cpe. 2dr. Si	2619	4437	1175	dc/dr	pwr.r&p.	185/65R15
sdn. 4dr. DX-LX	2619	4435	1096	dc/dr	pwr.r&p.	185/70R15

PRICES

Model / version		1996	1997	1998	1999	2000	2001
cpe. 2dr. DX	mini	7100	8700	10100	11350	12100	14200
	maxi	8900	10700	12100	13100	14200	16800
cpe. 2dr. SI	mini	8600	10800	12700	13400	15650	17300
	maxi	10500	12800	14700	15450	17850	19950
cpe. 2dr. DX/ABS	mini	7550	9750				
	maxi	9450	11800				
cpe. 2dr. SI/ABS	mini	9650	11900				
	maxi	11550	13850				
cpe 2dr. DX-G	mini				11150	11850	14200
	maxi				13100	13850	16300
cpe. 2dr. LX	mini						15750
	maxi						18400
cpe. 2dr. Si-G	mini				13200	14500	16800	15750
	maxi				15200	16500	18900	20000
cpe. 2dr. Si-R	mini					15550	17850
	maxi					17800	19900
cpe. 2dr. SE	mini					12600	
	maxi					14700	
cpe. 3dr. CX	mini	5900	7150	8500	9750	11550	
	maxi	7900	9850	10500	11550	13600	
cpe. 3dr. DX	mini			9000	10300	13100	
	maxi			11000	12100	15200	
cpe. 3dr. CX-G	mini	6500	7650				
	maxi	8400	9650				
cpe. 3dr. SE	mini					13650	
	maxi					15750	
sdn. 4dr. LX	mini	6500	8200	9550	11350	13650	
	maxi	8400	10500	11550	13100	15750	
sdn. 4dr. EX	mini	8100	9750	11150	12900	15200	
	maxi	10000	12100	13100	14700	17300	
sdn. 4dr. LX-G	mini				10600	12400	16800
	maxi				12600	14200	19400
sdn. 4dr. EX-G	mini				12200	13400	15750
	maxi				14200	15400	17850
sdn. 4dr. SE	mini					11850	14200
	maxi					13650	16300
sdn. 4dr. LX ABS	mini	7000	9250				
	maxi	8900	11650				
sdn. 4dr. EX ABS	mini	9150	10800				
	maxi	11000	13100				
sdn. 4dr. DX	mini						15200
	maxi						17800
sdn. 4dr. DXG	mini						16300
	maxi						18900

See page 7 to adapt these figures.

HONDA CR-V

1998 HONDA CR-V

The CR-V is a 4-door all-wheel drive sport utility vehicle built on the Civic platform. Since '98, it's offered as an LX model equipped with a manual gearbox or as an EX model that's equipped with an automatic. Both models are driven by a 2.0L 4-cylinder engine.

PROS

• **The concept** is quite unique, for it's a mix of several kinds of vehicles. All-wheel drive with seats straight like in a minivan and it behaves just like a car, when it comes to performance, handling and safety.
• **Driving pleasure** derives from smooth and neat-design, familiar-looking controls and excellent visibility.
• **It's a super-practical vehicle** and you can move easily from front seats to the rear. There are plenty of convenient storage compartments and the fold-up writing pad between the front seats and the picnic table that also serves as cargo area floor liner are unique and simply great.
• **The vehicle handles** like a car, since, even with all the wheel travel, it doesn't sway much and it sticks to the road in curves.
• **Performance** are quite good, due to a reasonable power to weight ratio. Accelerations and pick-up are equivalent to those of much brawnier and less fuel-efficient engines.
• **Maneuverability** is amazing with such a short turning diameter, good reduction ratio and clear visibility.
• **The price** is reasonable, considering its rich range of equipment.
• **Fuel economy** is interesting because the CR-V sips around 13 liters per every 100 km.

CONS

• **Steering** is light and it sometimes gets vague and wandering, which can be pretty unpleasant.
• **Brakes** don't bit enough and sudden stops are long to achieve.
• **Noise level** is high, due to the cabin configuration and lack of soundproofing, so engine roar and road noise are annoying travelling companions.
• **The poor protection** engine and mechanical components; you don't really feel like heading straight into the underbrush.
• **To be improved upon**: shifter and hand brake that are a pain and better tires so you can tackle snow-covered or muddy roads.

CONCLUSION

Honda has just about succeeded in coming up with the perfect vehicle for our era. The CR-V isn't really a true-grit sport utility vehicle, but it's spacious, practical, fun to drive, and safe.

RECALLS

None over this period.

CR-V   HONDA

RELIABILITY PROBLEMS

	1996	1997	1998	1999	2000	2001
Engine:	-	-	-	-	-	-
Transmission:	-	-	-	-	-	-
Suspension:	-	X	-	-	-	-
Steering:	-	-	-	-	-	-
Brakes:	-	-	-	-	-	-
Electricity:	-	-	-	-	-	-
Body:	-	-	X	X	-	-
Accessories:	-	X	-	-	-	-
Fit/finish:	-	-	-	-	-	-

POWERTRAIN

Year	Type/ L/Camshaft/bhp	Drivetrain & gearbox	Acceler. 0/100 sec.	Top. speed km/h	Ave. Fuel consp. l./100 km
97-01	L4/2.0/DOHC/128-146	all-M5	9.5	175	11.5
		all-A4	11.0	170	12.0

PERFORMANCE

SPECIFICATIONS

Model 97-01	Wlb. mm	Lght. mm	Cb.wt kg	Brakes fr/rr	Steering type	Standard tires
wgn. 4dr.	2620	4470	1350	dc/dr/ABS	pwr.r&p.	205/70R15

PRICES

Model / version		1996	1997	1998	1999	2000	2001
wgn. 4dr. LX	mini		13650	15350	17800	20150	22800
	maxi		15750	17600	19950	22600	25700
wgn. 4dr. EX	mini			16800	19100	21400	24800
	maxi			18900	21300	23800	27300
wgn. 4dr. Ltd. Ed.	mini					22700	25500
	maxi					25100	28350

See page 7 to adapt these figures.

1999 HONDA CR-V

HONDA del Sol

1996 HONDA del Sol

This coupe convertible replaced the CRX in 1993. The 1.6L Si model engine puts out 127 bhp and the VTEC engine puts out 160-bhp.

PROS
- **This is a neat car**, combining coupe and convertible features and the idea of storing the top in the trunk is very clever.
- **The VTEC engine** really moves, but it's always at high rpm, that is, at illegal speeds.
- **It's so original** and sharp that you just want to give this toy a whirl.
- **Engines** are economical, even the VTEC that really pumps out the power.
- **The ride** is surprisingly comfy, with such a smooth and civilized suspension.
- **Convertible-style** removable rear window.
- **Original cabin** design that the competition should sit up and take notice of.
- **The price is high**, but the del Sol is a practical and multi-purpose, year-round car.
- **Build quality** and tight fit and finish are superb, but some trim components look chintzy.
- **The trunk is nice** and big, even with top stored inside it.

CONS
- **The frame really shakes**, rattles and rolls, due to inadequate rigidity and the soft suspension on the Si makes driving a bit touch and go.
- **The base engine** is wimpy and a real drag.
- **Brakes on the Si** aren't the greatest without ABS, and sudden stops aren't straight or predictable.
- **Understeering** (Si) is quite a problem and you have to know what you're doing when driving at high speeds on wet pavement.
- **The manual shifter** is sometimes rough upon a cold start.
- **Rearward view** is obstructed at quarterback because of the thick C-pillar.

CONCLUSION
It's a shame that Honda didn't iron out all the small wrinkles early on, for this vehicle is original and cleverly designed.

RECALLS
None over this period.

del Sol — HONDA

RELIABILITY PROBLEMS

	1996	1997	1998	1999	2000	2001
Engine:	-	-				
Transmission:	-	-				
Suspension:	-	-				
Steering:	-	-				
Brakes:	X	X				
Electricity:	X	-				
Body:	-	-				
Accessories:	-	X				
Fit/finish:	-	-				

POWERTRAIN

Year	Type/ L/Camshaft/bhp	Drivetrain & gearbox
96-97	L4/1.6/SOHC/125-127	front-M5
		front-A4
	L4/1.6/DOHC/160	front-M5

PERFORMANCE

Acceler. 0/100 sec.	Top. speed km/h	Ave. Fuel consp. l./100 km
9.5	190	8.5
10.7	180	9.5
8.5	210	9.5

SPECIFICATIONS

Model 96-97	Wlb. mm	Lght. mm	Cb.wt kg	Brakes fr/rr	Steering type	Standard tires
cpe. 2dr. Si	2370	4005	1095	dc/dc	pwr.r&p.	185/60R14
cpe. 2dr. VTEC	2370	4005	1144	dc/ABS	pwr.r&p.	195/60R14

PRICES

Model / version		1996	1997	1998	1999	2000	2001
cpe. 2dr. Si	mini	8600	11000				
	maxi	10500	13100				
cpe. 2dr. VTEC	mini	10000	11550				
	maxi	12100	14700				

See page 7 to adapt these figures.

1997 HONDA del Sol

HONDA Insight

2000 HONDA Insight

To rob Toyota of any eventual claim to the title of manufacturer of North America's first hybrid vehicle, Honda precipitated the launch of its original-design coupe, the environmentally friendly Insight.

PROS
- **The hybrid system** is highly economical, and fuel consumption is minimal in comparison with conventional automobiles.
- **Emissions** are reduced thanks to the closely managed thermal engine.
- **Leading-edge technologies**, such as a lightweight aluminum body, electronic energy management and smaller-sized batteries.
- **The Insight is very maneuverable** and fits anywhere, thanks to its small overall dimensions and tight steer angle diameter.
- **The cabin** has plenty of room for two adults, with ample clearance and long doors that open up wide to facilitate getting in and out of it.
- **The quality** of the design, manufacturing and finish is up to par with what we have come to expect from Honda.

CONS
- **The sale** and resale of this small car are seriously limited by its outrageous price. It has nothing to offer that would justify investing so much money into it, at least for as long as the price of gasoline remains reasonable.
- **Mediocre performance** is the price to pay to benefit from the Insight's parsimonious appetite. Accelerations and pick-up are frustratingly slow.
- **The brakes** perform disappointingly for such a lightweight vehicle, with the ABS system struggling to prevent the wheels from locking.
- **Not a very practical automobile**: it has a minimal amount of storage space and its albeit accessible trunk is way too small.
- **The hard suspension**, flat seats and high noise level due to a lack of soundproofing combine to produce a generally uncomfortable ride.
- **The low driving position**, poor rearward visibility and confusing instrument panel are not very reassuring for drivers.

CONCLUSION
The Insight is not a very realistic automobile; originality has been given priority over practicality and its high price—combined with the mistrust the public usually has in new technologies—will do little to make the Insight an easy car to sell on the used-car market.

RECALLS
None over this period.

Insight — HONDA

RELIABILITY PROBLEMS

	1996	1997	1998	1999	2000	2001
Engine:						
Transmission:						
Suspension:						
Steering:						
Brakes:			Insufficient data			
Electricity:						
Body:						
Accessories:						
Fit/finish:						

POWERTRAIN

Year	Type/ L/Camshaft/bhp	Drivetrain & gearbox
00-01	L3/1.0/DOHC/67 +10 kW electric motor	front-M5

PERFORMANCE

Acceler. 0/100 sec.	Top. speed km/h	Ave. Fuel consp. l./100 km
15.5	160	5.0

SPECIFICATIONS

Model 00-01	Wlb. mm	Lght. mm	Cb.wt kg	Brakes fr/rr	Steering type	Standard tires
cpe. 3dr.	2400	3940	852	dc/dr/ABS	pwr.r&p	165/65R14

PRICES

Model / version		1996	1997	1998	1999	2000	2001
cpe. 3dr.	mini					20600	23100
	maxi					22600	25700

See page 7 to adapt these figures.

2000 HONDA Insight

HONDA Odyssey

1996 HONDA Odyssey

The first Odyssey was mid-way between a minivan and a station wagon. It was designed on the Accord platform and shared its mechanical features, that is, the 2.2L 4-cylinder engine. In 1999, Honda has entirely redesigned it to truly offer a full-size minivan with double sliding doors and equipped with a 3.5L V6 putting out 210-bhp. In one word, everything it badly needed to make the Odyssey incredibly attractive amongst the others.

PROS
- **Its clean, classic look** and successfull new shape. The older ones hide well the fact that it's a bit narrow.
- **Good cabin design** gives comfortable seating for six passengers.
- **Engine performance** are gutsier than expected, but the V6 could be livelier and smoother.
- **The feel of the vehicle** that handles more like a car than a minivan.
- **A smooth and quiet ride**, with such a good suspension, nicely contoured seats and relatively low noise level.
- **The driver's position** is simply perfect, with such a nice environment and clear outward view.
- **Adequate trunk capacity**, even with six passengers aboard.

CONS
- **It's pretty pricy**, given its run-of-the-mill engines, plain and simple equipment and rather basic cabin design.
- **Maneuverability** is no picnic with such a large steer angle diameter.
- **The spare tire** on the first generation is a real pain for one of the remote rear seatbench passengers.
- **The terribly bleak** cabin design that has become par for the course on Honda models.
- **Tight leg room** in remote rear seatbench.
- **Rear doors** of the first generation can be awkward in tight parking spots, but they do provide relatively easy access. On the latest models, the addition of two sliding doors has corrected the problem.

CONCLUSION
The Odyssey isn't for everyone. It's geared for Honda fanatics who are looking for a multi-purpose car rather than an in and out minivan.

RECALLS
1998 Front suspension lower ball joints may prematurely wear out.
1999 Water in the resonator subchamber can freeze and interfere with the throttle plate's return to the idle position.
Sliding door latches and power lock remote control actuators must be replaced to avoid improper latching.
2000 A wire harness may be damaged by contact with metal pipe.
A dash light dimmer circuit may be damaged by heat build-up in the unit.

Odyssey   HONDA

RELIABILITY PROBLEMS

	1996	1997	1998	1999	2000	2001
Engine:	X	-	-	X	-	-
Transmission:	-	-	-	X	-	-
Suspension:	-	X	X	-	-	-
Steering:	-	-	-	-	-	-
Brakes:	-	-	-	X	X	-
Electricity:	X	-	-	X	X	X
Body:	-	X	-	-	-	-
Accessories:	X	-	X	X	X	-
Fit/finish:	X	-	-	X	-	-

POWERTRAIN

Year	Type/ L/Camshaft/bhp	Drivetrain & gearbox
96-98	L4/2.2/SOHC/140	front-A4
99-01	V6/3.5/SOHC/210	front-A4

PERFORMANCE

Acceler. 0/100 sec.	Top. speed km/h	Ave. Fuel consp. l./100 km
10.4	185	12.0
9.6	190	12.0

SPECIFICATIONS

Model	Wlb. mm	Lght. mm	Cb.wt kg	Brakes fr/rr	Steering type	Standard tires
96-98						
m.v. 4dr.	2830	4755	1565	dc/ABS	pwr.r&p.	205/65R15
99-01						
m.v. 4dr. LX/EX	3000	5110	1945	dc/dr/ABS	pwr.r&p.	215/65R16

PRICES

Model / version		1996	1997	1998	1999	2000	2001
m.v. 4dr. 6 st.	mini	10000	12200	13650			
	maxi	12100	14700	15100			
m.v. 4dr. 7 st.	mini	10200	12500	14000			
	maxi	12600	15000	15450			
m.v. 4dr. LX	mini				18900	23400	27300
	maxi				21100	25800	29400
m.v. 4dr. EX	mini				21600	26000	29900
	maxi				23700	28450	31500

See page 7 to adapt these figures.

1999 HONDA Odyssey

HONDA Prelude

2000 HONDA Prelude

When the Prelude coupe was upgraded in 1992, variable valve timing gave it the punch and power it needed.

PROS
- **Its slinky look** is a real winner and reflects its Sportscar character.
- **Engine performance** on the SR and SR-V models are much more spirited than before.
- **Handling** on the SR and SH is clean as a whistle but not as much as on the defunct SR-4WS that was way too expensive at its end.
- **Brakes** are more effective and predictable on the ABS-equipped models than on the base model (1996).
- **Upper-end models** have plush equipment and are worth the going price.
- **The VTEC engine** is amazingly economical at normal speeds.
- **The trunk is adequate** and can be extended by lowering the rear seatbench.
- **Interior design** is more refined and the instrument panel more conventional on the post 1996 versions.

CONS
- **The instrument panel** is a real mess: it's poorly designed, impractical, not at all ergonomic or nice-looking on the 95-96 models.
- **Rear seats** are awful, head and leg room is terribly tight and these seats are really only good for storing luggage, since even children would feel cramped.
- **Steering is vague** and sluggish at low speeds, and at high speed, it gets so light that it's jerky and has a mind of its own.
- **The base model** Prelude isn't too powerful and handling is no fun with such narrow tires.
- **The sound system** is horrible and unworthy of such a high-priced car.

CONCLUSION
The Prelude is a good buy, even with all the technical snags, high-priced tag and expensive insurance premium. But it's a good idea to avoid the nondescript base model that is more of a pain than a pleasure to drive.

RECALLS
None over this period.

Prelude — HONDA

RELIABILITY PROBLEMS

	1996	1997	1998	1999	2000	2001
Engine:	X	X	-	X	-	-
Transmission:	-	-	-	-	-	-
Suspension:	-	-	-	-	X	-
Steering:	-	X	-	X	-	-
Brakes:	X	-	X	X	-	-
Electricity:	X	-	-	X	X	-
Body:	-	-	-	-	-	-
Accessories:	X	X	X	X	X	X
Fit/finish:	-	-	-	-	X	-

POWERTRAIN

Year	Type/ L/Camshaft/bhp	Drivetrain & gearbox
1996	L4/2.3/DOHC/160	front-M5
		front-A4
97-01	L4/2.2/DOHC/200	front-M5
	L4/2.2/DOHC/190	front-A4

PERFORMANCE

Acceler. 0/100 sec.	Top. speed km/h	Ave. Fuel consp. l./100 km
8.2	205	10.0
9.4	200	11.0
7.2	220	10.8
8.5	210	10.9

SPECIFICATIONS

Model	Wlb. mm	Lght. mm	Cb.wt kg	Brakes fr/rr	Steering type	Standard tires
1996						
cpe. 2dr.SR	2550	4440	1300	dc/ABS	pwr.r&p.	205/55R15
97-01						
cpe. 2dr.	2585	4520	1340	dc/ABS	pwr.r&p.	205/50R16
cpe. 2dr.SH	2585	4520	1365	dc/ABS	pwr.r&p.	205/50R16

PRICES

Model / version		1996	1997	1998	1999	2000	2001
cpe. 2dr.	mini		15000	17400	19200	21000	23600
	maxi		18400	20500	22600	24700	27800
cpe. 2dr. SR	mini	11750					
	maxi	14700					
cpe. 2dr. SR-V	mini	12800					
	maxi	15750					
cpe. 2dr. SH	mini		17100	20600	23400	25200	
	maxi		20500	23600	26800	28900	
cpe. 2dr. SE	mini						27800
	maxi						33100

See page 7 to adapt these figures.

2000 HONDA Prelude

HONDA   S2000

2000 HONDA S2000

To mark the beginning of the third millennium, Honda designed this 2.0-liter roadster for high-level performance enthusiasts.

PROS

• **The exciting style** is a radical change from the stereotypes of the past.

• **The engine** begs to run fast and sounds a lot like a race car. The small nimble gear shift lever also makes the S2000 feel like a real racer.

• **The quality** of the development, manufacturing and finish is typical of Honda standards.

• **The cockpit** is a model of logic and ergonomics.

• **The wind** is efficiently channelled when the side windows are up and the wind deflector is in place.

• **The air conditioning** was designed to operate with the top down.

• **The bucket seats** provide effective lateral and lumbar support.

CONS

• **The styling** lacks strength and personality.

• **The engine**—whose power and torque are located at very high rpm—is not well suited to North American driving conditions.

• **The convertible top**'s simplistic design is very disappointing, and it is unacceptable that on a car of this price, it has no lining and no glass rear window or electric defroster.

• **Totaly unpractical**: it has no glove box, no door pockets, a single cup holder and a minuscule central console.

• **The trunk** is minuscule and houses a compact spare wheel.

• **The digital instrument** cluster is not the most attractive and does not look very sporty at all.

• **The steering wheel** cannot be adjusted in any direction, which for some drivers makes it hard to find a comfortable driving position.

• **Visibility** is hindered by the blind spots resulting from the convertible top. A shame!

• **Flaws**: The central tunnel lets it the heat generated by the engine, and the starter button is completely useless.

CONCLUSION

Designed for an elitist crowd, the S2000 roadster will be hard-pressed to find buyers on the used-car market.

RECALLS

None over this period.

S2000   HONDA

RELIABILITY PROBLEMS

	1996	1997	1998	1999	2000	2001
Engine:						
Transmission:						
Suspension:						
Steering:						
Brakes:			Insufficient data			
Electricity:						
Body:						
Accessories:						
Fit/finish:						

POWERTRAIN   PERFORMANCE

Year	Type/ L/Camshaft/bhp	Drivetrain & gearbox	Acceler. 0/100 sec.	Top. speed km/h	Ave. Fuel consp. l./100 km
00-01	L4/2.0/DOHC/240	rear-M6	6.6	235	11.5

SPECIFICATIONS

Model 00-01	Wlb. mm	Lght. mm	Cb.wt kg	Brakes fr/rr	Steering type	Standard tires
con. 2 dr.	2400	4120	1275	dc/ABS	pwr.r&p.	205/55R16 225/50R16

PRICES

Model / version		1996	1997	1998	1999	2000	2001
con. 2dr.	mini					39400	41500
	maxi					42000	45150

See page 7 to adapt these figures.

2000 HONDA S2000

HYUNDAI Accent

2000 HYUNDAI Accent

The Accent replaced the Excel in 1995. There's a wide model choice, including the GT, GS and GSi hatchback coupes, 3-door coupes and 4-door sedans, that come in L and GL trim levels, all powered by 1.5L 4-cylinder engines.

PROS
- **A competitive price**, but initial price doesn't include some vital equipment like airbags and ABS.
- **The cabin** can accommodate four adults and the trunk holds all their luggage.
- **Its more muscular engine** performance (given the displacement and vehicle weight) with the manual than with the automatic, that downshifts at the least hill or incline and has quite a hard time adjusting.
- **Fuel consumption** is economical, but not as much as that of the competition.
- **Power steering** is great, it's clean and quick and makes for good maneuverability.
- **The smooth suspension** and nicely contoured front seats provide for a cushy ride.
- **Handling** is much better on the GL, GT and GSi models equipped with better-sized tires.
- **Construction quality**, fit and finish and materials are far nicer than on the former Excel.

CONS
- **Manual steering** is slow and vague because it suffers from too high a reduction ratio.
- **Engine performance** are rather poor compared to those of Japanese counterparts.
- **Brakes lack** bite and lasting power, but they're less touchy than those on the Excel.
- **High noise level** is a sign of inadequate soundproofing and noisy as heck engine. And even though the body design is aerodynamic, there's whistling wind noise.

CONCLUSION
The Accent beefed up sales for this Korean carmaker that was beginning to drag its feet. But overall quality and reliability aren't on at par with Japanese vehicles.

RECALLS
96-97 Corrosion from winter road salt may cause the breakage of the lower spring coil.
Wiper motor operates irregularly.
1999 Defective pressure control solenoid valve seal in the automatic transmission may affect acceleration.
2000 Driving in extremely cold temperature can freeze the inside throttle body.
The wiper linkage can separate from the motor because a lack of lubrification.
2001 Dealers will install a modified PCV hose and on manual transmission equipped vehicles without air conditioning.

Accent   HYUNDAI

RELIABILITY PROBLEMS

	1996	1997	1998	1999	2000	2001
Engine:	-	X	X	-	-	-
Transmission:	-	X	-	-	-	-
Suspension:	-	X	-	X	X	-
Steering:	X	-	-	-	-	-
Brakes:	X	X	X	X	X	-
Electricity:	X	X	-	-	-	X
Body:	X	X	-	-	-	-
Accessories:	X	-	X	X	X	X
Fit/finish:	X	-	X	X	X	-

POWERTRAIN

Year	Type/ L/Camshaft/bhp	Drivetrain & gearbox
96-01	L4/1.5/SOHC/92	front-M5
		front-A4
	L4/1.5/DOHC/106	front-M5

PERFORMANCE

Acceler. 0/100 sec.	Top. speed km/h	Ave. Fuel consp. l./100 km
11.5	175	8.3
12.8	165	8.8
11.0	180	8.8

SPECIFICATIONS

Model	Wlb. mm	Lght. mm	Cb.wt kg	Brakes fr/rr	Steering type	Standard tires
96-99						
cpe. 3dr. L	2400	4923	953	dc/dr	r&p.	155/80R13
cpe. 3dr. GT	2400	4103	940	dc/dr	r&p.	155/80R13
cpe. 3dr. GL	2400	4103	959	dc/dr	r&p.	175/70R13
cpe. 3dr. GSi	2400	4923	959	dc/dr	pwr.r&p.	175/70R14
sdn. 4dr. L	2400	4117	955	dc/dr	r&p.	155/80R13
sdn. 4dr. GL	2400	4117	961	dc/dr	pwr.r&p.	175/70R14
00-01						
cpe. 3dr. GS	2440	4200	992	dc/dr	r&p.	155/80R13
cpe. 3dr. GSi	2440	4200	992	dc/dr	pwr.r&p.	185/60R14
sdn. 4dr.	2440	4235	1019	dc/dr	pwr.r&p.	175/70R13

PRICES

Model / version		1996	1997	1998	1999	2000	2001
cpe. 3dr. L	mini	3150	4200	5700	6600		
	maxi	4750	5550	7150	7900		
cpe. 3dr. GL	mini	3700	4400				
	maxi	4750	5900				
cpe. 3dr. GS	mini			6100		8400	9450
	maxi			7700		10000	13100
cpe. 3dr. GSi	mini				7700	10000	11550
	maxi				8900	11550	15200
cpe. 3dr. GT	mini	3900	4750				
	maxi	4950	6400				
cpe. 3dr. Sport	mini		4500	6500			
	maxi		6200	8200			
sdn. 4dr. L	mini	4000	5100	6500	7650	10000	11550
	maxi	5050	6800	8200	8900	11550	15200
sdn. 4dr. GL	mini	3800	4500	6100			
	maxi	4850	6100	7650			

See page 7 to adapt these figures.

1996 HYUNDAI Accent

HYUNDAI — Elantra

1997 HYUNDAI Elantra

In 1992, the Elantra, a compact sedan midway between the Excel and the Sonata, was put on the market. In 1996, it was redesigned and a station wagon model was also made available, driven by a 1.8L engine. One year later, the Tiburon's 2.0L makes its debut.

PROS
- **Its shapely body** design is nice and clean and not at all overdone.
- **Power steering** is smooth, crisp and benefits from a good reduction ratio.
- **The Alpha and Beta** 1.8L and especially the 2.0L Hyundai engines have really spiffed up the Elantra image.
- **Handling** is safe and sure, due to a simple but effective suspension and 14-inch tires.
- **Driving one** of these cars is a real pleasure because of the cushy suspension and firm seats that provide good support.
- **The GLS model** is loaded and is easier to resell.

CONS
- **The 1.6L engine** is rough and noisy and in fact drinks up as much gas as the 1.8L engine.
- **Brakes lack grip**, which explains why sudden stops are long, and they're unpredictable without ABS.
- **The hard seats** can be a real pain on long trips.
- **Soundproofing** isn't up to snuff, for there's loud road and engine noise.
- **The interior** on the '95 models is bland and awfully unimaginative.
- **Build quality** is solid, but fit and finish and the look of some trim components aren't what they should be.
- **The big trunk** is convertible, but its small opening makes it impossible to store large items.

CONCLUSION
With each generation, the Elantra is more technically refined, better built and more comfortable, but there's still room for improvement.

RECALLS
96-97 Wiper motor operates irregularly.
1999 Defective pressure control solenoid valve seal in the automatic transmission may affect acceleration.
99-00 Low speed engine stalling can be caused by a defective MAF (Mass Air Flow) sensor.

RELIABILITY PROBLEMS

	1996	1997	1998	1999	2000	2001
Engine:	X	X	X	X	-	-
Transmission:	X	X	-	X	-	-
Suspension:	X	X	-	X	-	-
Steering:	X	X	-	-	-	-
Brakes:	-	-	X	X	X	-
Electricity:	X	-	X	-	X	-
Body:	X	X	-	-	-	-
Accessories:	-	-	X	X	X	-
Fit/finish:	X	-	-	-	-	-

POWERTRAIN / PERFORMANCE

Year	Type/ L/Camshaft/bhp	Drivetrain & gearbox	Acceler. 0/100 sec.	Top. speed km/h	Ave. Fuel consp. l./100 km
96-98	L4/1.8/DOHC/124-130	front-M5	9.5	175	11.0
		front-A4	11.0	170	10.4
99-01	L4/2.0/DOHC/140	front-M5	9.7	175	10.6
		front-A4	11.0	170	10.5

SPECIFICATIONS

Model 96-01	Wlb.	Lght.	Cb.wt	Brakes	Steering	Standard
sdn. 4dr. GL/SE	2550	4420	1144	dc/dr	pwr.r&p.	175/65R14
wgn.4dr. GL/SE	2550	4450	1188	dc/dr	pwr.r&p.	175/65R14
sdn. 4dr. GLS	2550	4420	1173	dc/dr	pwr.r&p.	195/60R14
wgn. 4dr. GLS	2550	4450	1218	dc/dr	pwr.r&p.	195/60R14

PRICES

Model / version		1996	1997	1998	1999	2000	2001
sdn. 4dr. GL	mini	3900	5100	6400	7650	9450	12100
	maxi	5700	6950	8400	9450	11550	14700
sdn. 4dr. GLS	mini	5000	7150	8500	9750		
	maxi	6900	9000	10500	11550		
sdn. 4dr. SE	mini		6100	7450	8700		
	maxi		8000	9000	10500		
sdn. 4dr. VE	mini					11000	14200
	maxi					13100	16800
wgn. 4dr. GL	mini	4400	5550	6900	8200	10000	
	maxi	6300	7450	8900	10000	12100	
wgn. 4dr. GLS	mini	5450	7650	9000	10300		
	maxi	7350	9550	11000	12100		
wgn. 4dr. SE	mini		6600	8000	9250		
	maxi		8500	10000	11000		
wgn. 4dr. VE	mini					11550	
	maxi					13650	

See page 7 to adapt these figures.

HYUNDAI — Santa Fe

2001 HYUNDAI Santa Fe

The Santa Fe was introduced to the market in 2000. This all-road vehicle was designed using the Sonata's platform and mechanical components. It is available with front- or all-wheel drive.

PROS

- **The aggressive styling** is sure to please young drivers, especially former owners of a Tiburon coupe.
- With sure handling and low body roll, the Santa Fe drives more like an automobile than a utility vehicle.
- **Ride comfort** is ensured by the soft suspension and generous wheel travel. As for the seats, the front ones provide better support than the flat rear bench.
- **The average weight-to-power ratio** translates into honest performance figures.
- **The cockpit** is well laid out and has personality. However, it's as busy as the sheet metal.
- **The powerful headlights** provide good visibility in all circumstances, both in low- and high-beam positions.
- **Front and rear storage** spaces abound.
- **The well-adapted tires** provide good levels of traction on dry and slippery pavement as well as on slightly hilly terrain.

CONS

- **The exaggerated styling** will turn off older drivers, unless they are looking for a way to show off their youthful spirit.
- **The brakes** stand to be improved because stopping is not always straight and reassuring without ABS.
- **The seats** are too firmly padded to provide optimal comfort levels on long trips.
- **The cheap-looking plastics** tarnish the interior presentation somewhat.
- **The compact spare tire** makes the Santa Fe look ridiculous in the event of a puncture.
- **The radio's controls** will drive even the most stoic music fan crazy.

VERDICT

The Santa Fe is a serious competitor in the all-road versatile vehicle market and offers remarkable quality for the price, a trait that will leave no one indifferent.

RECALLS

None over this period.

Santa Fe　　　　　　　　　　　　　　　　HYUNDAI

RELIABILITY PROBLEMS

	1996	1997	1998	1999	2000	2001
Engine:						
Transmission:						
Suspension:						
Steering:						
Brakes:			Insufficient data			
Electricity:						
Body:						
Accessories:						
Fit/finish:						

POWERTRAIN　　　　　　　　　　　PERFORMANCE

Year	Type/ L/Camshaft/bhp	Drivetrain & gearbox	Acceler. 0/100 sec.	Top. speed km/h	Ave. Fuel consp. l./100 km
2001	L4/2.4/DOHC/149	FWD avant-M5	ND		
	V6/2.7/DOHC/181	FWD front-A4	11.8	180	12.5
	V6/2.7/DOHC/181	AWD all-A4	12.0	175	12.6

SPECIFICATIONS

Model	Wlb. mm	Lght. mm	Cb.wt kg	Brakes fr/rr	Steering type	Standard tires
wgn. 4dr. FWD	2620	4500	1585	dc	pwr.r.&p.	225/70R16
wgn. 4dr. AWD	2620	4500	1687	dc	pwr.r.&p.	225/70R16

PRICES

Model / version		1996	1997	1998	1999	2000	2001
wgn. 4dr. GLS	mini						25200
	maxi						28150

See page 7 to adapt these figures.

2001 HYUNDAI Santa Fe

The Canadian Used Car Guide 2002-2003

HYUNDAI   Sonata

1996 HYUNDAI Sonata

The Sonata began its career in 1989. This mid-size sedan is powered by a 2.0L 4-cylinder engine or a 3.0L V6. Entirely revamped in 1999, the Sonata has introduced two new engines. The 148-bhp 4-cylinder and a small 163-bhp 2.5L V6.

PROS
- **A more affordable price** than the competition, because of fairly unsophisticated technical features and components.
- **Five passengers** and all their belongings can be accommodated in this car.
- **The relatively lively 4-cylinder** engine is quite economical.
- **The two V6 engines** are much more spirited because of a better power to weight ratio.
- **The lavish GLS sedan** comes loaded with all kinds of equipment and the '99 GLS comes standard with four very handy disc brakes.

CONS
- **Low resale value** that is the upshot of customer mistrust both in regard to vehicle reliability and overall quality.
- **The manual shifter** is rough and inaccurate.
- **The poorly designed** and hard seats are tiring on long hauls.
- **Power steering** is smooth and well-calibrated, but is affected by torque on strong accelerations.
- **The rustic suspension** is harsh when it hits road faults.
- **Wind, road and engine noise** roars away in the cabin.
- **Stops are too long** and the front end locks in no time flat.

CONCLUSION
The Sonata is a good choice if mileage is reasonably low and if it's been meticulously maintained. If in doubt, look elsewhere...

RECALLS
96-97 Wiper motor operates irregularly.
1997 Weak support of frontal shock absorber and headlights.
99-00 Low speed stalling can be caused by a defective Mass Air Flow sensor.

Sonata   HYUNDAI

RELIABILITY PROBLEMS

	1996	1997	1998	1999	2000	2001
Engine:	X	X	X	X	X	-
Transmission:	-	-	-	-	-	-
Suspension:	X	X	-	-	-	-
Steering:	-	-	-	-	-	-
Brakes:	X	X	-	X	X	-
Electricity:	X	-	X	X	X	-
Body:	-	X	-	-	-	-
Accessories:	X	X	X	X	X	-
Fit/finish:	X	X	-	-	-	-

POWERTRAIN

Year	Type/ L/Camshaft/bhp	Drivetrain & gearbox
96-98	L4/2.0/DOHC/126-137	front-M5
		front-A4
	V6/3.0/OHV/142	front-A4
99-01	L4/2.4/DOHC/148	front-A4
	V6/2.5/DOHC/163	front-A4

PERFORMANCE

Acceler. 0/100 sec.	Top. speed km/h	Ave. Fuel consp. l./100 km
10.0	170	10.5
11.0	165	11.0
9.6	180	12.0
11.0	180	11.4
10.0	200	11.7

SPECIFICATIONS

Model	Wlb. mm	Lght. mm	Cb.wt kg	Brakes fr/rr	Steering type	Standard tires
96-98						
sdn. 4dr. GL	2650	4680	1265	dc/dr	pwr.r&p.	185/70R14
99-01						
sdn. 4dr. GL	2700	4710	1409	dc/dr	pwr.r&p.	195/70R14
sdn. 4dr. GLS V6	2700	4710	1409	dc/dc	pwr.r&p.	205/60R15

PRICES

Model / version		1996	1997	1998	1999	2000	2001
sdn. 4dr. base	mini	5450	7350	9100			
	maxi	6800	9000	11000			
sdn. 4dr. GL	mini	6100	7900	10100	11000	13100	16800
	maxi	6800	9550	12100	12800	15200	19400
sdn. 4dr. GLS	mini	6900	8900	11000	13650	17850	
	maxi	8800	10600	13100	15400	19900	
sdn. 4dr. GLX	mini						21500
	maxi						24100

See page 7 to adapt these figures.

1997 HYUNDAI Sonata

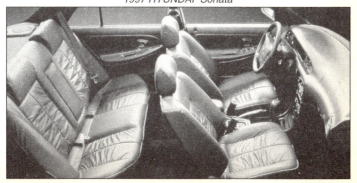

HYUNDAI   Tiburon

1999 HYUNDAI Tiburon

The Tiburon, built on the Elantra platform, replaces the former Scoupe. It's sold in a base model equipped with a 1.8L 4-cylinder engine or in an FX model powered by a 2.0L.

PROS
- **Its bold and brawny** body that seems to have been honed by the wind, its aggressive airscoop, its streamlined curves that give it an unmistakable shark look.
- **Driving** is quite exhilarating on both models, engines are prim and responsive, the car cuts neatly through curves and the accurate steering really makes for slick moves.
- **The 2.0L engine** feels like a Sportscar powerplant, even if accelerations and pick-up are comparable to those of the Elantra.
- **Road adherence** is quite good, due mostly to the finely adjusted suspension designed with Porsche and good standard tires.
- **Ride comfort** is surprising for this type of car, generous cabin space offers lots of room up front, seats offer excellent support and noise level low at cruising speed.
- **The good value** of the FX who gives a good resale dollar.
- **The interior** reminds you a bit of the first Eagle Talon with its off-center dashboard that lets the driver consult white-on-black analog instruments that are easy to read.
- **Cabin size** is quite spacious for the car category, thanks to a long wheelbase and wide wheel tracks.
- **Commodities** are surprising with lots of handy storage spots in the cabin and the convertible trunk can hold quite a bit of luggage.

CONS
- **The dashboard** isn't terribly ergonomic because the radio and climate controls are opposite to normal position.
- **Rear seats** are really more suited to the small fry rather than to full-fledged adults. Knee and head room is very tight and access is rather dangerous.
- **The base model engine** strains a bit, so it's a good idea to stick with the manual gearbox.
- **The dashboard** really reflects into the windshield and into the instrument panel.

CONCLUSION
The Tiburon is a nice proposition to young drivers who are searching for a dramatic look and interesting performance at a bargain price.

RECALLS
96-97   Wiper motor operate irregularly.
1999   Defective pressure control solenoid valve seal in the automatic transmission may affect acceleration.
2000   The day-time running lights doesn't turn off when headlight switch is turned on.

Tiburon — HYUNDAI

RELIABILITY PROBLEMS

	1996	1997	1998	1999	2000	2001
Engine:		X	X	X	X	-
Transmission:		-	-	-	-	-
Suspension:		X	-	-	-	-
Steering:		-	-	-	-	-
Brakes:		X	X	X	-	-
Electricity:		X	X	X	X	-
Body:		X	X	X	-	-
Accessories:		X	X	X	X	-
Fit/finish:		-	-	-	-	-

POWERTRAIN

Year	Type/ L/Camshaft/bhp	Drivetrain & gearbox	Acceler. 0/100 sec.	Top. speed km/h	Ave. Fuel consp. l./100 km
97-01	1.8/DOHC/130	front-M5	9.2	175	10.5
		front-A4	NA	NA	NA
	2.0/DOHC/140 (FX)	front-M5	8.7	185	10.8
		front-A4	9.5	180	11.3

PERFORMANCE

SPECIFICATIONS

Model 97-01	Wlb. mm	Lght. mm	Cb.wt kg	Brakes fr/rr	Steering type	Standard tires
cpe. 2dr. base	2474	4340	1156	dc/dr	pwr.r&p.	195/60R14
cpe. 2dr. FX/SE	2474	4340	1173	dc/dc	pwr.r&p.	195/55R15

PRICES

Model / version		1996	1997	1998	1999	2000	2001
cpe. 2dr. base	mini		7650	9450	11350	13100	14700
	maxi		9650	11550	13100	15200	18400
cpe. 2dr. FX	mini		8700	10000	12400		
	maxi		10700	12100	14200		
cpe. 2dr. SE	mini			10500	13450	15200	16800
	maxi			12600	15200	17300	20500

See page 7 to adapt these figures.

1999 HYUNDAI Tiburon

HYUNDAI   XG300

2001 HYUNDAI XG300

The XG300 became Hyundai's flagship in 2001. It is based on the Korean Dynasty and is equipped with a 3.0-liter V6 mated to a 5-speed automatic transmission.

PROS

• **The price/equipment ratio** is unbeatable for a car capable of competing directly against the likes of the Lexus ES 300 and Infiniti I30.
• **The technical content** and extensive equipment make the XG300 an excellent value, at least on paper.
• **The flattering presentation** lacks neither styling nor personality.
• **Performance** is honest as long as the vehicle is not carrying a full load, in which case the V6 seems to run out of breath somewhat.
• **The generous cabin** and extendable trunk provide roominess for up to five normally sized adults.
• **The careful finish** and quality materials set the XG300 apart from Hyundai's other more utilitarian models.
• **The many practical storage** spaces are efficiently laid out through the cabin.

CONS

• **The windshield wipers** are inefficient and too slow to provide safe visibility in pouring rain.
• **The hefty weight** and simplistic suspension combine to hinder performance in tight turns.
• **The cheap-looking instruments** are out of place and reveal their humble origins.
• Our test model was plagued by **the sound of the wind** swirling above the trunk lid, but we're not sure if this shortcoming is common to all XG300s.
• **The compact spare tire** does not give the XG300 a very flattering look in the event of a puncture.

VERDICT

Hyundai has invested heavily in the affordable luxury-car market by offering a level of value that is sure to entice the competition's clientele.

RECALLS

None over this period.

XG300   HYUNDAI

RELIABILITY PROBLEMS

	1996	1997	1998	1999	2000	2001
Engine:						
Transmission:						
Suspension:						
Steering:						
Brakes:			Insufficient data			
Electricity:						
Body:						
Accessories:						
Fit/finish:						

POWERTRAIN

Year	Type/ L/Camshaft/bhp	Drivetrain & gearbox
2001	V6/3.0/DOHC/192	front-A5

PERFORMANCE

Acceler. 0/100 sec.	Top. speed km/h	Ave. Fuel consp. l./100 km
ND		

SPECIFICATIONS

Model 2001	Wlb. mm	Lght. mm	Cb.wt kg	Brakes fr/rr	Steering type	Standard tires
sdn. 4dr.	2750	4864	1635	dc/ABS	pwr.r.&p.	205/65R15

PRICES

Model / version		1996	1997	1998	1999	2000	2001
sdn. 4dr. GLS	mini						22000
	maxi						25700

See page 7 to adapt these figures.

2001 HYUNDAI XG300

INFINITI   G20

2000 INFINITI G20

The G20 is a lavish compact car with a sporty side that was added to the luxury model range at Nissan in 1991, pulled out in 1997 and re-introduced in 1999 without a lot of major changes.

PROS
- **This solid and sturdy** car really holds to the road.
- **Sportscar handling** is enhanced by the sophisticated suspension and nonslip differential that makes for super wheel function, even on slippery roads.
- **Driving this baby** is a lot of fun, because it's so frisky and gutsy, also because you're comfortable behind the wheel and you have an adequate outward view; besides, steering is crisp and quick as a flash and the brakes have real bite.
- **Solid construction**, tight finish and nice-looking materials, but plain and simple overall design.
- **Longer wheel base**, overall lenght and height of the latest generation provide the driver and the passengers a lot more leg and elbow room.
- **Standard equipment** is very extensive and compares well with rival European counterparts.

CONS
- **There isn't much choice**, since there's only a single body style and a single engine model, and the different body design «t» model only comes equipped with a different suspension.
- **The rather bland look** of the car doesn't reflect its character, especially in regard to its luxury or performance level.
- **A small service network**, even in large cities, complicates things when it comes to upkeep and repairs.
- **The poorly calibrated** automatic transmission doesn't help you get the most out of the engine.

CONCLUSION
The G20 is solidly built, well equipped and reliable, but it just doesn't have the looks of its breed, but it's pleasant to drive and it's economical. Yet, depending on where one lives, its upkeep can be a hassle.

RECALLS
1996   Possible corrosion on the fuel filter tube.

G20 INFINITI

RELIABILITY PROBLEMS

	1996	1997	1998	1999	2000	2001
Engine:	-			-	-	-
Transmission:	X			-	-	-
Suspension:	-			-	-	-
Steering:	-			-	-	-
Brakes:	X			X	-	-
Electricity:	-			X	X	-
Body:	-			-	-	X
Accessories:	X			X	X	-
Fit/finish:	-			-	-	-

POWERTRAIN

Year	Type/ L/Camshaft/bhp	Drivetrain & gearbox
1996	L4/2.0/DOHC/140	front-M5
		front-A4
99-01	L4/2.0/DOHC/140	front-M5
		front-A4

PERFORMANCE

Acceler. 0/100 sec.	Top. speed km/h	Ave. Fuel consp. l./100 km
8.8	195	9.5
9.5	185	10.5
9.0	205	10.5
9.6	200	10.3

SPECIFICATIONS

Model	Wlb. mm	Lght. mm	Cb.wt kg	Brakes fr/rr	Steering type	Standard tires
1996						
sdn. 4dr.	2550	4440	1245	dc/ABS	pwr.r&p.	195/60R14
99-01						
sdn. 4dr.	2600	4509	1332	dc/ABS	pwr.r&p.	195/65R15

PRICES

Model / version			1996	1997	1998	1999	2000	2001
sdn. 4dr.	mini		10800					
	maxi		13650					
sdn. 4dr. Touring	mini		13450			19950	23300	25700
	maxi		15200			22600	26200	29400
sdn. 4dr. Luxury	mini					18900	21700	24100
	maxi					21500	24900	27800

See page 7 to adapt these figures.

1999 INFINITI G20

INFINITI   I30

1996 INFINITI I30

Designed along the lines of the Maxima, the I30 has been on the market since 1996 and is the main rival of the Lexus ES300. It's driven by a 3.0L V6 engine and is equipped with an anti-skating system on the later 1999 model year.

PROS
- **Its unique** classic look is really very different from the Maxima design.
- **Reliability** is top-notch because of build quality, tight finish and top-quality components.
- **Engines** are fairly powerful and economical, but less spirited than the Maxima engine that benefits from a better power to weight ratio.
- **The "Multilink"** rear suspension enhances comfort, which is cushy smooth, as well as handling, that is already neutral.
- **Brakes** are terrific since stopping distances are below 40m. Brakes are also stable and really keep a grip on things.
- **Steering is clean**, quick, well assisted and benefits from a good reduction ratio, but it tends to get light at high speeds.
- **Equipment** is more extensive than on the Maxima, for it includes standard heated front seats.

CONS
- **Seats aren't terribly** comfortable, because they're firmly upholstered and their sunken-in shape doesn't make for good support.
- **The instrument panel** isn't too ergonomic and external rearview mirrors are too small.
- **Trunk size** is fair to middling and the only access from the cabin is the ski slot.
- **Things to consider**: no shifter position indicator on the instrument panel and poor rear windshield wipers and defroster.
- **There are no vents** in the rear seat area, which is often the case on cars of this caliber.

CONCLUSION
Less pricy than the ES300, the I30 is less run-of-the-mill than the Maxima and is just as good a car.

RECALLS
97-98   Damaged alternator diode that could cause the melting of the plastic housing and a possible alternator fire.

I30 — INFINITI

RELIABILITY PROBLEMS

	1996	1997	1998	1999	2000	2001
Engine:	X	-	X	X	X	-
Transmission:	-	-	-	-	-	-
Suspension:	-	-	-	-	-	-
Steering:	-	-	-	-	-	-
Brakes:	X	-	-	-	X	-
Electricity:	-	X	X	X	X	-
Body:	-	-	-	-	-	-
Accessories:	-	X	X	-	-	-
Fit/finish:	-	-	-	-	-	-

POWERTRAIN

Year	Type/ L/Camshaft/bhp	Drivetrain & gearbox
96-01	V6/3.0/DOHC/190-227	front-A4

PERFORMANCE

Acceler. 0/100 sec.	Top. speed km/h	Ave. Fuel consp. l./100 km
8.0	195	11.4

SPECIFICATIONS

Model	Wlb. mm	Lght. mm	Cb.wt kg	Brakes fr/rr	Steering type	Standard tires
96-99						
sdn. 4dr. base	2700	4816	1429	dc/ABS	pwr.r&p.	205/65R15
sdn. 4dr. «t»	2700	4816	1463	dc/ABS	pwr.r&p.	215/55R16
00-01						
sdn. 4dr.	2750	4919	1515	dc/ABS	pwr.r&p.	215/55R16
sdn. 4dr. «t»	2750	4919	1530	dc/ABS	pwr.r&p.	225/50R17

PRICES

Model / version		1996	1997	1998	1999	2000	2001
sdn. 4dr. base	mini	11550	14500	19500	22350		
	maxi	15200	17900	23100	25700		
sdn. 4dr. Touring	mini	12800	16000	22150	23900	28900	32500
	maxi	16800	19500	25700	27300	32500	36700
sdn. 4dr. Luxury	mini					27800	31500
	maxi					31500	35700

See page 7 to adapt these figures.

1999 INFINITI I30

INFINITI J30

1996 INFINITI J30t

Since 1993, the Infiniti J30 has been the main rival of the Lexus GS300. It's a rear-wheel drive vehicle powered by a 3.0L V6 engine designed along the lines of the 300ZX engine.

PROS

- **Its seven-way adjustable** automatic transmission and nonslip differential by viscocoupling make for very impressive road stability and are proof positive that this is a high-tech car.
- **Handling** on the Touring model is more sporty and the car really hugs the road with its four-wheel steering system.
- **Construction quality** and fit and finish are simply perfect.
- **Top-notch comfort** is the result of the ingeniously designed suspension and seats, that are well-contoured, even if not too cushy.
- **The attractive**, ergonomic instrument panel includes all the necessary controls.
- **Equipment is lavish**, but some accessories found on European rivals in the same price range are nowhere to be seen.

CONS

- **Its ovoid design** goes out of style in no time.
- **Engine performance** are pretty wimpy and lack pizzazz.
- **Head and leg** room is very snug in the rear seats and the small doors don't help much when it comes to climbing aboard.
- **ABS system is pretty** rough and ready, causing really serious wheel lock and brakes lack gripping power.
- **Steering** is too light and sensitive because it's over-assisted.
- **The trunk** isn't too big and the opening is too high off the ground.
- **Things to consider**: no on-board computer, tiny rearview mirrors and no heated seats...
- **Low resale value** is a real trap for potential buyers.

CONCLUSION

The J30 is a mixed bag: it's reliable and luxurious, but it's not too practical all-round and it's really no fun to drive.

RECALLS

None over this period.

J30   INFINITI

RELIABILITY PROBLEMS

	1996	1997	1998	1999	2000	2001
Engine:	X	-				
Transmission:	-	-				
Suspension:	-	-				
Steering:	-	-				
Brakes:	-	X				
Electricity:	X	X				
Body:	-	-				
Accessories:	X	X				
Fit/finish:	-	-				

POWERTRAIN

Year	Type/ L/Camshaft/bhp	Drivetrain & gearbox
96-97	V6/3.0/DOHC/210	rear-A4

PERFORMANCE

Acceler. 0/100 sec.	Top. speed km/h	Ave. Fuel consp. l./100 km
8.7	210	12.0

SPECIFICATIONS

Model 96-97	Wlb. mm	Lght. mm	Cb.wt kg	Brakes fr/rr	Steering type	Standard tires
sdn. 4dr.	2761	4859	1576	dc/ABS	pwr.r&p.	215/60R15
sdn. 4dr.Touring	2761	4859	1620	dc/ABS	pwr.r&p.	215/60R15

PRICES

Model / version		1996	1997	1998	1999	2000	2001
sdn. 4dr.	mini	15700	19700				
	maxi	18400	23100				
sdn. 4dr. Touring	mini	17300	21300				
	maxi	21000	24800				

See page 7 to adapt these figures.

1996 NFINITI J30

INFINITI   Q45

1999 INFINITI Q45t

The Q45 is the flagship of the Infiniti fleet. It was launched in 1990, went virtually unnoticed, and was released again in 1997 but sadly remained hidden in the shadows. It's a rear-wheel drive sedan powered by a V8 engine providing an ouput of 266-bhp.

PROS

• **It's a very plush car** with a wonderfully quiet and spacious cabin, and the ride is really smooth, thanks to its suspension.

• **The silky smooth V8** engine and the technically advanced automatic transmission are a great combination, resulting in terrific performance levels.

• **Driving** this car is really safe because of brakes that have real bite, a sturdy frame and dual airbags.

• **Equipment** is lavish and includes all the gadgetry you'd normally expect on a car of this caliber.

• **Now that there's a real grille** up front, the car looks more stylish.

• **It's amazingly reliable**, given its sophisticated mechanical components, and should light the path for European rivals.

CONS

• **High depreciation** because it's a victim of pretty vicious competition in this market segment.

• **The cabin isn't as luxurious** as that of some rivals, for the imitation wood and synthetic leather trim rob it of all class.

• **Vehicle weight** and size make this car moves well-nigh impossible and really affect maneuverability and agility.

• **Some trim details** are in poor taste, like the coffin-style door handles or the crest up front that looks like a cowboy belt buckle on the earlier models...

CONCLUSION

The Infiniti has never won the hearts of those it was set out to court. Its low used car price may look like a bargain, but upkeep can be expensive when the car is no longer under warranty.

RECALLS

97-98 Ignition key can be removed when engine is turn off without placing the transmisssion shift lever in the "Park" position.

Q45 — INFINITI

RELIABILITY PROBLEMS

	1996	1997	1998	1999	2000	2001
Engine:	X	X	X	-	-	-
Transmission:	-	-	X	-	-	-
Suspension:	-	-	-	-	-	-
Steering:	X	-	-	-	-	-
Brakes:	-	X	X	X	-	-
Electricity:	X	-	-	-	-	-
Body:	X	-	-	-	-	-
Accessories:	-	X	X	X	-	-
Fit/finish:	-	-	-	-	-	-

POWERTRAIN

Year	Type/ L/Camshaft/bhp	Drivetrain & gearbox
1996	V8/4.5/DOHC/278	rear-A4
97-01	V8/4.1/DOHC/266	rear-A4

PERFORMANCE

	Acceler. 0/100 sec.	Top. speed km/h	Ave. Fuel consp. l./100 km
1996	7.5	230	14.0
97-01	8.0	230	13.4

SPECIFICATIONS

Model	Wlb. mm	Lght. mm	Cb.wt kg	Brakes fr/rr	Steering type	Standard tires
1996						
sdn. 4dr.	2875	5075	1792	dc/ABS	pwr.r&p.	215/65R15
97-01						
sdn. 4dr.	2830	5060	1765	dc/ABS	pwr.r&p.	215/50R17

PRICES

Model / version			1996	1997	1998	1999	2000	2001
sdn. 4dr.		mini	16300	25700	32500			
		maxi	21500	30900	37800			
sdn. 4dr. Touring		mini	17300	27800	34600	38800		
		maxi	22600	33000	39900	44100		
sdn. 4dr. Anni.Ed.		mini						44100
		maxi						50400

See page 7 to adapt these figures.

1997 INFINITI Q45

INFINITI — QX4

1999 INFINITI QX4

The QX4 is the near-twin, luxury version of the Nissan Pathfinder in the Infiniti model range.

PROS
- **The high-tech** all-wheel drive, akin to that of a racecar, gives the QX4 a highly refined roadability and handling.
- **This lush** utility vehicle's super smooth handling derives from its sturdy body and clean front and rear powertrain guidance.
- **Brakes** are easy to apply as needed and they really dig in, so they can bring this 2.5-ton vehicle to a nice and straight stop.
- **Overall** ride comfort is due to the relatively supple suspensions, thick, cushy seats and effective soundproofing.
- **Build quality**, finish job and trim materials are super, putting this vehicle on a par with its most prestigious rivals.
- **The front end** design is quite fetching and distinguishes the Qx4 from the Pathfinder.

CONS
- **Performance** are somewhat sluggish with such a wimpy engine that's unsuited to this type of vehicle; what's needed is the V8 that powers the Q45.
- **Insufficient** ground clearance really hampers this vehicle's off-the-road prowess, so much so that the chassis sometimes gets a scrape on rough terrain.
- **Snug legroom** in the rear seat sure doesn't help boarding and unboarding.
- **Gas consumption** is completely out of zinc with performance and is a good indication of the trouble this engine has to put the muscle on such a heavy vehicle.
- **The overall design** is rather blah and is too much like that of the Pathfinder.

CONCLUSION
The QX4 is a compact and quite lush vehicle that's pretty reasonably priced. Just what city slickers with an adventurous spirit are looking for.

RECALLS
2001 Defective rear door strut brackets must be replaced. Ignition lock assembly will be inspected and connecting pins replaced if necessary.

QX4   INFINITI

RELIABILITY PROBLEMS

	1996	1997	1998	1999	2000	2001
Engine:		-	-	X	X	-
Transmission:		X	-	X	-	-
Suspension:		X	-	-	-	-
Steering:		-	-	-	-	-
Brakes:		-	X	X	-	-
Electricity:		X	X	X	X	X
Body:		X	X	X	X	-
Accessories:		-	X	X	-	-
Fit/finish:		X	-	-	X	-

POWERTRAIN

Year	Type/ L/Camshaft/bhp	Drivetrain & gearbox
97-01	V6/3.3/SOHC/168	all-A4

PERFORMANCE

Acceler. 0/100 sec.	Top. speed km/h	Ave. Fuel consp. l./100 km
11.2	175	15.7

SPECIFICATIONS

Model 97-01	Wlb. mm	Lght. mm	Cb.wt kg	Brakes fr/rr	Steering type	Standard tires
wgn. 4dr.	2700	4671	1939	dc/dr/ABS	pwr.r&p.	245/70R16

PRICES

Model / version		1996	1997	1998	1999	2000	2001
wgn. 4dr.	mini		21700	25200	28350	32500	39900
	maxi		24100	27500	31400	35300	43500
wgn. 4 dr. (1999.5)	mini				28900		
	maxi				31500		

See page 7 to adapt these figures.

1999 INFINITI QX4

ISUZU   Rodeo

2000 ISUZU Rodeo

Since its introduction back in 1980, the Rodeo has had its ups and downs consequently to its pricing. It is powered by 4 and 6-cylinder engines. Since 1998, the Rodeo has been radically transformed and the luxury version LSE has made its debut in '99.

PROS

- **The cabin interior** is spacious and rear seat access is convenient in spite of high ground clearance, the baggage compartment is quite big and can be extended by lowering the rear seatbench.
- **Passengers** will be comfortable in this vehicle, because the suspension is fairly flexible on the highway, seats are nicely contoured and noise level is quite low.
- **The 3.2L V6** engine is powerful enough to handle rough terrain or pull a trailer.
- **The cockpit** is great with the nicely located steering wheel, seat and pedals and the driver has good all-round visibility.
- **Very dependable** vehicle, as you'd expect, for construction is solid, finish is tight and trim and components are attractive.
- **A good note** for the new and improved rear hatch that gives a lower and easier access to the luggage compartment.

CONS

- **Fuel consumption** is very high because of excessive vehicle weight, high aerodynamic coefficient and especially because of a poor power to weight ratio.
- **Steering** is too light and suffers from a high reduction ratio, so driving is inaccurate and unpredictable in strong crosswinds and the large steer angle diameter really cripples maneuverability.
- **Seats** aren't too well upholstered and don't provide good lateral support.
- **Equipment** on the base model (S) is very basic indeed and yet this model still doesn't come with a lower price tag!
- **Its low resale** price isn't an asset, since it makes potential buyers really stop and think.

CONCLUSION

The Rodeo was very appealing at first, but it losts its charm when prices went sky-high and because the carmaker dragged its feet before making any modifications.

Rodeo — ISUZU

RECALLS
1998 The engine wire harness ground connection terminal may fracture due to improper crimping causing an engine stall.
2001 Dealers will inspect fuel return hose date code and replace it if required.

RELIABILITY PROBLEMS

	1996	1997	1998	1999	2000	2001
Engine:	X	X	-	-	-	-
Transmission:	X	-	X	X	-	-
Suspension:	-	X	X	X	-	-
Steering:	-	-	-	-	-	-
Brakes:	X	-	X	X	X	-
Electricity:	-	X	X	X	X	-
Body:	-	-	-	-	-	-
Accessories:	X	X	X	X	X	-
Fit/finish:	X	X	-	-	-	-

POWERTRAIN

Year	Type/ L/Camshaft/bhp	Drivetrain & gearbox
96-00	V6/3.2/DOHC/175-205	rear/all-M5
		rear/all-A4

PERFORMANCE

Acceler. 0/100 sec.	Top. speed km/h	Ave. Fuel consp. l./100 km
9.0	170	14.4
9.7	165	14.0

SPECIFICATIONS

Model 96-00	Wlb. mm	Lght. mm	Cb.wt kg	Brakes fr/rr	Steering type	Standard tires
wgn. 2dr. 4x2	2760	4690	1583	dc/dr	pwr.bal.	225/75R15
wgn. 2dr. 4x4(S)	2702	4658	1748	dc/ABS	pwr.r&p.	235/75R15
wgn. 2dr. 4x4	2702	4658	1782	dc/ABS	pwr.r&p.	245/70R16

PRICES

Model / version		1996	1997	1998	1999	2000	2001
wgn. 4dr. 4x4 S	mini	7350	10500	13650	14700	16300	19400
	maxi	10000	13100	15450	16300	18900	22000
wgn. 4dr. 4x4 LS	mini	10000	14200	16800	17850	19400	24600
	maxi	12100	16300	19100	20400	22500	27300
wgn. 4dr. 4x4 LSE	mini				20400	24600	30400
Auto	maxi				21900	27800	33100

See page 7 to adapt these figures.

2000 ISUZU Rodeo

ISUZU   Trooper

1997 ISUZU Trooper

The Trooper was rehauled in 1992, then it changed format, style, engine and price, which didn't make for good sales.

PROS

- **Its clean**, classic body design really never goes out of style and the asymmetrical dual-section rear doors are quite original.
- **It's really a multi-purpose** vehicle with its almost minivan-style cabin interior and all-wheel drive that provides for safe driving on slippery roads.
- **Driving** is pleasant with such a comfortable driver's seat, adequate visibility and smooth, accurate controls.
- **Brakes** are more effective on a cold start than when the engine has been running.
- **Solidly built** and components are attractive and tightly fitted, but some color shades of trim materials are rather weird.
- **The huge baggage** compartment is convertible and easy to use, and storage compartments are conveniently located throughout the cabin.

CONS

- **Soft suspension**, there's a lot of swing and sway, and if you don't keep an eye on things, you could lose control of the vehicle.
- **The 24-valve V6** engine is more powerful, but it still isn't as muscular as that of the competition.
- **Excessive vehicle** size and weight affect maneuverability, engine performance and fuel consumption.
- **Fuel consumption** is really pretty high, for the engine yield is never less than 16 L/100 km, whether you're driving in the city or over rough terrain.
- **Safety** isn't a sure thing on some models that aren't equipped with airbags.

CONCLUSION

The Trooper isn't a poor investment, but you have to be willing to put up with its limitations, and a small service network makes for snags when it comes to upkeep and besides, repairs are costly.

Trooper — ISUZU

RECALLS
- **1996** Defective safety belt buckles.
- **96-97** Left frontal brake line built too close to the suspension's control arm.
- **1997** Lock washer and screws missing for bearing adjustement.
- **1998** Lock nuts of the "Torque-On-Demand" 4WD transfer case might not be staked and that may cause the separation of the propeller shaft.
- **2001** Dealers will install a revised fuel hose.

RELIABILITY PROBLEMS

	1996	1997	1998	1999	2000	2001
Engine:	X	X	-	-	-	-
Transmission:	-	X	X	X	X	-
Suspension:	-	-	-	-	-	-
Steering:	X	-	-	-	-	-
Brakes:	X	X	X	X	X	X
Electricity:	X	X	-	X	X	-
Body:	-	-	-	-	-	-
Accessories:	X	-	X	X	X	-
Fit/finish:	-	-	-	-	-	-

POWERTRAIN / PERFORMANCE

Year	Type/ L/Camshaft/bhp	Drivetrain & gearbox	Acceler. 0/100 sec.	Top. speed km/h	Ave. Fuel consp. l./100 km
96-97	V6/3.2/SOHC/175	rear/all-A4	13.5	160	14.5
98-01	V6/3.5/DOHC/215	rear/all-M5	9.0	180	16.1
		rear/all-A4	9.8	175	15.8

SPECIFICATIONS

Model 96-01	Wlb. mm	Lght. mm	Cb.wt kg	Brakes fr/rr	Steering type	Standard tires
wgn. 4dr. S	2760	4670	1991	dc/ABS	pwr.bal.	245/70R16
wgn. 4dr. LS	2760	4670	1995	dc/ABS	pwr.bal.	245/70R16
wgn. 4dr. LTD	2760	4670	2059	dc/ABS	pwr.bal.	245/70R16

PRICES

Model / version		1996	1997	1998	1999	2000	2001
wgn. 4dr. S	mini	6850	9450	10700	15400	17500	22000
	maxi	10500	11550	13100	17850	20500	24700
wgn. 4dr. LS	mini	10000	13650	15750	20700	22800	27300
	maxi	13650	16200	18400	23100	25700	29900
wgn. 4dr. LTD	mini	15750	18900	21000	22100	25800	30400
	maxi	18900	21000	23100	24700	28900	33100

See page 7 to adapt these figures.

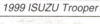

1999 ISUZU Trooper

JAGUAR — S-Type

2000 JAGUAR S-Type

To ensure its presence in market segments that generate higher sales, Jaguar introduced the S-Type to go against the Mercedes-Benz E-Class and BMW 5 Series. It shares its platform and main mechanical components with the Lincoln LS.

PROS

- **The styling** is extremely good and modern. Its powerful lines inevitably conjure up images of the venerable Mark II.
- The S-Type integrates the most **recent technology**: voice-activated systems, Dynamic Stability Control and an adjustable suspension.
- **Driving** this car is a pleasure: the controls are smooth and this model behaves itself as a luxury sedan more than a Sportscar.
- **The V6 engine** is already quite spirited, while the V8 cranks out even more invigorating performance.
- **The interior presentation** is typically British, with decorative leather and wood inlays that set Jaguar apart from its rivals.
- **Comfort** is achieved through well-padded seats and a smooth enough suspension, while the noise level is kept to a minimum.

CONS

- **The S-Type's passenger compartment** is not the roomiest, and rear-seat passengers had best not be too tall to fit comfortably in the space provided.
- **The trunk** lacks height and space given the fact that it also houses a full-size emergency spare and a large battery.
- **The V8 engine** is far from economical; it is not unusual to go beyond 18 L/100 km when driving at faster speeds and the level rarely drops below 16 L/100 km under normal conditions.
- **The designers** could have done a lot more in terms of practicality: the glove box is minuscule, the door pockets are too narrow and the rear-seat passengers have to get by with minimal amenities.

CONCLUSION

The S-Type is a car that is easy to get attached to, but it needs to mature before we are in a position of assessing its reliability and durability.

RECALLS

2001 Belt buckle assembly will be inspected and replaced if necessary.
The front suspension lower balljoint may not have been tightened properly. Its torque will be inspected, tightened or replaced.

S-Type   JAGUAR

RELIABILITY PROBLEMS

	1996	1997	1998	1999	2000	2001
Engine:					X	X
Transmission:					X	-
Suspension:					X	-
Steering:					-	-
Brakes:					-	-
Electricity:					X	X
Body:					X	-
Accessories:					X	-
Fit/finish:					-	-

POWERTRAIN

Year	Type/ L/Camshaft/bhp	Drivetrain & gearbox
00-01	V6/3.0/DOHC/240	rear-A5
	V8/4.0/DOHC/281	rear-A5

PERFORMANCE

Acceler. 0/100 sec.	Top. speed km/h	Ave. Fuel consp. l./100 km
8.5	220	13.0
7.0	240	15.0

SPECIFICATIONS

Model 00-01	Wlb. mm	Lght. mm	Cb.wt kg	Brakes fr/rr	Steering type	Standard tires
sdn. 4dr. 3.0	2909	4860	1656	dc/ABS	pwr.r&p.	225/55R16
sdn. 4dr. 4.0	2909	4860	1710	dc/ABS	pwr.r&p.	225/55R16

PRICES

Model / version		1996	1997	1998	1999	2000	2001
sdn. 4dr. S-Type	mini					34800	45300
3.0	maxi					39000	49500
sdn. 4dr. S-Type	mini					43800	52700
4.0	maxi					47400	56700

See page 7 to adapt these figures.

2000 JAGUAR S-Type

JAGUAR XJ

1999 JAGUAR XJ6

The XJ6 hit the market in 1986 and was powered by a 3.6L 6-cylinder engine that was replaced by a 4.0L engine in '90. The V12 engine came out in 1994 and the Turbo XJR model was available the following year. In '99, two new V8 engines, including a turbo one, replaced the less "environmental-friendly" L6 and V12.

PROS

- **Its very classic look** and pristine design with leather and polished wood are hallmarks of its British origins.
- **With its cushy suspension** and superb soundproofing, it provides comfort that is hard to beat.
- **Top-notch materials**, perfect build craftsmanship and meticulous fit and finish.
- **Handling** is a dream because of the sophisticated suspension.
- **Steering is accurate**, but too over-assisted.
- **The well-calibrated** automatic transmission is great with its mixed shifting.
- **Fuel consumption** with the 4.0L engine is reasonable, considering vehicle weight and high aerodynamic coefficient.
- **A good outward view** and nicely arranged instrument panel make for pleasant driving.

CONS

- **Its high depreciation** that is the result of customer mistrust because of its poor reliability record and astronomical cost of upkeep.
- **The incredibly sky-high** gas consumption with the V12 engine or with the Turbo 6-cylinder on the XJR model. Even the new V8 that powers the '99 XJR isn't much more economical with its 16L/100km.
- **The driver's position** isn't perfect because the front seats don't provide much lumbar support.
- **Things to consider**: some complicated or inconveniently located controls, the noisy and awkward sliding roof and the air conditioner that is just impossible to adjust properly.

CONCLUSION

Before buying one of these dream cars, have it checked out by an expert and be very careful about making an investment that could cost you your shirt...

RECALLS

1998   Throttle cable may block throttle from opening completely. Potential fine cracks may be present between gear teeth inside the automatic transmission and may cause a "lock-up"

XJ — JAGUAR

RELIABILITY PROBLEMS

	1996	1997	1998	1999	2000	2001
Engine:	X	X	X	X	-	-
Transmission:	X	-	X	X	X	X
Suspension:	-	X	-	-	-	-
Steering:	-	-	-	-	-	-
Brakes:	X	X	X	X	X	X
Electricity:	X	X	X	X	X	X
Body:	-	-	X	X	-	-
Accessories:	X	X	X	X	X	X
Fit/finish:	-	-	-	-	-	-

POWERTRAIN

Year	Type/ L/Camshaft/bhp	Drivetrain & gearbox
96-98	L6/4.0/DOHC/223-290	rear-A4
1996	V12/6.0/SOHC/313	rear-A4
96-98	L6C/4.0/DOHC/322-370	rear-A4
99-01	V8/4.0/DOHC/290	rear-A5
	V8C/4.0/DOHC/370	rear-A5

PERFORMANCE

Acceler. 0/100 sec.	Top. speed km/h	Ave. Fuel consp. l./100 km
8.0	230	14.0
7.2	240	16.0
6.0	240	16.0
7.6	230	13.5
6.0	240	16.0

SPECIFICATIONS

Model 96-01	Wlb. mm	Lght. mm	Cb.wt kg	Brakes fr/rr	Steering type	Standard tires
sdn. 4dr. XJ6/8	2870	5024	1813	dc/ABS	pwr.r&p.	225/60R16
sdn. 4dr. VDP	2995	5149	1836	dc/ABS	pwr.r&p.	225/60R16
sdn. 4dr. XJR	2870	5024	1848	dc/ABS	pwr.r&p.	255/40R18
sdn. 4dr. V12	2870	5024	2005	dc/ABS	pwr.r&p.	225/60R16

PRICES

Model / version		1996	1997	1998	1999	2000	2001
sdn. 4dr. XJ6	mini	16800	21300				
	maxi	22700	26800				
sdn. 4dr. XJR	mini	24300	29700	42500	49300	58800	73500
	maxi	30100	35200	48300	54600	64200	77700
sdn. 4dr. VDP	mini	22350	27300	38300	48300	54300	66900
	maxi	28000	32500	44100	53500	59600	71400
sdn. 4dr. XJ12	mini	30700					
	maxi	36700					
sdn. 4dr. XJ8	mini			31100	39400	47200	64600
	maxi			36700	44600	53000	69300
sdn. 4dr. VDP S.E.	mini				52500	64200	80000
	maxi				57700	69800	84000

See page 7 to adapt these figures.

1999 JAGUAR XJ8

JAGUAR   XJS

1996 JAGUAR XJS

This large touring British coupe, powered by a huge V12 engine, came on the market in '75. The convertible model was launched in '88 and the 6-cylinder engine was added in '92.

PROS
- **The smooth, powerful V12** engine puts this heavy vehicle through its paces.
- **The convertible** is a classic, upper-crust car and it's fun to drive.
- **You feel pampered** when you're behind the wheel of this baby, for the suspension really absorbs road faults and noise level is very low.
- **Brakes are muscular** and well-balanced, and they're easy to control, thanks to the ABS.
- **The car handles** well for normal driving, but the rear end really swerves on tight curves when roads are slippery.
- **Overall construction quality** has improved on the last generation models and trim materials have become truly top-of-the-line.

CONS
- **The price and cost** of upkeep of such a vehicle are astronomical and the resale value isn't too great with such a high depreciation rate.
- **Cabin size** isn't in keeping with overall vehicle size, for hip room is tight up front and head room and leg room in the rear are terribly cramped.
- **Poorly designed** seats don't give proper support and the tiny rear seatbench is a poor excuse for a seat.
- **Driving** is no picnic with over-assisted, sensitive steering, a non-adjustable steering column, poor rearward view at quarterback and minuscule external rearview mirrors.

CONCLUSION
You have to be financially independent to purchase one of these models, and it's really more of a collector's item than a car you'd like to drive on a regular basis.

RECALLS
None over this period.

XJS — JAGUAR

RELIABILITY PROBLEMS

	1996	1997	1998	1999	2000	2001
Engine:	X					
Transmission:	-					
Suspension:	-					
Steering:	-					
Brakes:	X					
Electricity:	X					
Body:	X					
Accessories:	X					
Fit/finish:	-					

POWERTRAIN

Year	Type/ L/Camshaft/bhp	Drivetrain & gearbox
1996	L6/4.0/DOHC/237	rear-M5
		rear-A4

PERFORMANCE

Acceler. 0/100 sec.	Top. speed km/h	Ave. Fuel consp. l./100 km
8.5	220	13.0
9.0	210	14.0

SPECIFICATIONS

Model	Wlb. mm	Lght. mm	Cb.wt kg	Brakes fr/rr	Steering type	Standard tires
cpe. 2dr. (L6)	2591	4864	1730	dc/ABS	pwr.r&p.	215/70R15
con. 2dr. (L6)	2591	4864	1900	dc/ABS	pwr.r&p.	215/70R15
cpe. 2dr. (V12)	2591	4864	1920	dc/ABS	pwr.r&p.	225/55R16
con. 2dr. (V12)	2591	4864	1920	dc/ABS	pwr.r&p.	225/55R16

PRICES

Model / version		1996	1997	1998	1999	2000	2001
con. 2dr. 4.0L	mini	21000					
	maxi	26200					

See page 7 to adapt these figures.

1996 JAGUAR XJS

JAGUAR XK8

1998 JAGUAR XK8 coupe

The XK8, that replaced the XJS in 1997, is available as a 2+2 coupe and convertible in a single trim level. Both models are equipped with a 4L V8 engine that develops 290-hp and is driven by a 5-speed automatic with dual-mode shifter.

PROS
- **Driving pleasure** is due to the incredibly clean and crisp front and rear powertrain precision, the accurate steering and crisp brakes.
- **The V8 engine** is responsive and oozing with energy, besides being velvety smooth and discreet. It yields truly amazing output, thanks to a comfortable 5.74 kg/hp power to weight ratio.
- **Vehicle craftsmanship** has really come a long way, assembly is more well executed, finish details are very refined, but vehicle quality still isn't on a par with that of German or Japanese rivals. The lined convertible top is exquisitely made and its control mechanism is completely automatic.
- **Handling** is much better than that of the former XJS models. The XK8 exhibit great competence on wide curves and on slalom runs, even with their hefty weight and size.
- **Steering** is silky smooth, direct and precise, so controlling car path is very accurate both on the highway and in city traffic. The car maneuvers quite nicely in city snarls and tight spots.

CONS
- **The absence** of chrome that's so typical of a Jaguar; not a bit of the lovely shiny stuff to be seen either on the wheels, rearview mirrors, rear taillights or bumpers.
- **Outward view** is hampered by the high frame, thick windshield supports and there's a blind spot in rear view at quarterback because of the convertible hood, and the rear window is just too narrow.
- **The dashboard**, like the body itself, lacks accent details, the wooden panels on the dash are thick and massive and lack of ergonomics.
- **The rear seats** are useless, head and leg room are terribly tight and it would have been a neat idea to use this space for luggage storage.
- **To be improved upon**: no rear wiper on the coupe.

CONCLUSION
The XK8 is a very bright offspring of the former XJS, but it lacks of some nice chrome touches and inlaid work that are so characteristic of the British firm.

RECALLS
1997   The differential output shaft might detach itself.
1998   Throttle cable may block throttle from opening completely.
1999   Fine cracks may occur on the automatic transmission gears.

XK8 — JAGUAR

RELIABILITY PROBLEMS

	1996	1997	1998	1999	2000	2001
Engine:		X	X	X	-	-
Transmission:		X	-	X	X	-
Suspension:	-	-	-	-	-	-
Steering:	-	-	-	-	-	-
Brakes:		X	X	X	X	X
Electricity:		-	X	X	X	X
Body:	X	-	-	-	-	-
Accessories:	X	X	X	X	X	X
Fit/finish:	-	-	-	-	-	-

POWERTRAIN

Year	Type/ L/Camshaft/bhp	Drivetrain & gearbox
97-01	V8/4.0/DOHC/290	rear-A5
00-01	V8C/4.0/DOHC/370	rear-A5

PERFORMANCE

Acceler. 0/100 sec.	Top. speed km/h	Ave. Fuel consp. l./100 km
6.7	245	13.5
6.0	240	16.0

SPECIFICATIONS

Model 97-01	Wlb. mm	Lght. mm	Cb.wt kg	Brakes fr/rr	Steering type	Standard tires
cpe. 2dr.	2588	4760	1666	dc/ABS	pwr.r&p.	245/50R17
con. 2dr.	2588	4760	1754	dc/ABS	pwr.r&p.	245/50R17
cpe. 2dr. XKR	2588	4760	1666	dc/ABS	pwr.r&p.	245/50R17
con. 2dr. XKR	2588	4760	1754	dc/ABS	pwr.r&p.	245/50R17

PRICES

Model / version		1996	1997	1998	1999	2000	2001
cpe. 2dr. XK8	mini		33600	39900	47200	51400	66100
	maxi		38800	45100	52500	57800	70300
con. 2dr. XK8	mini		41000	49300	56200	61900	77700
	maxi		46200	54600	61400	68200	82400
cpe. 2dr. XKR	mini					65100	80300
	maxi					71400	84500
con. 2dr. XKR	mini					73500	90300
	maxi					79800	95000

See page 7 to adapt these figures.

1998 JAGUAR XK8

JEEP   Cherokee

1999 JEEP Cherokee

This sport utility dates back to 1984 as a 4x4 and as a 4x2 on the following year with a V6 engine which was replaced with an in-line 6-cylinder two years later.

PROS
- **Exceptional wheel function** (4X4) and the ability to get just about anywhere make the Cherokee a truly multi-purpose vehicle.
- **It's a comfortable vehicle** with a long wheelbase, well-adjusted suspension and nice and quiet 6-cylinder engine.
- **The 2.5L engine** on the 4X2 is very economical when coupled with a manual transmission, as is the V6 engine achieving high torque that's more suited to an automatic.
- **Wide choice of models**: 2 or 4-door, 4X2 or 4X4, sport utility or luxury trim levels, 2 engine models, 2 transmissions and 3 modes on the 4X4.

CONS
- **Expensive upkeep** and high gas consumption.
- **Poor maneuverability** crippled by a large steer angle diameter and light, sensitive steering that is over-assisted.
- **The cabin interior** is quite snug every which way and rear seat access is awkward with the narrow doors.
- **Driving isn't too pleasant** with a steering column that is too long, poorly designed seats and tiny external rearview mirrors.
- **Fit and finish** as well as build quality aren't what they should be and mechanical components aren't always reliable.

CONCLUSION
You need to have these vehicles inspected, for many of them have taken a lot of abuse and repairs aren't cheap by any means. Avoid the very frustrating 4-cylinder engine. Overall, a good value for the price.

RECALLS
1996   Risk of sparking near alternator fuse.
           Defective central seat belt on rear bench.
1997   Fuel level sending unit may degrade.
1998   Power brake booster is defective.
           Safety belt's anchors are defective.
1999   Defective spark plugs.

Cherokee   JEEP

RELIABILITY PROBLEMS

	1996	1997	1998	1999	2000	2001
Engine:	X	X	X	X	X	-
Transmission:	X	X	X	-	-	-
Suspension:	X	-	-	X	X	X
Steering:	-	-	X	X	-	-
Brakes:	X	X	X	X	X	X
Electricity:	X	X	X	X	X	X
Body:	-	-	X	X	X	-
Accessories:	X	X	X	X	X	X
Fit/finish:	X	-	X	X	X	-

POWERTRAIN / PERFORMANCE

Year	Type/ L/Camshaft/bhp	Drivetrain & gearbox	Acceler. 0/100 sec.	Top. speed km/h	Ave. Fuel consp. l./100 km
96-01	L4/2.5/OHV/121-125	rear/all-M4-M5	12.5	150	11.7
		rear/all-A3	13.5	145	13.1
	L6/4.0/OHV/177-190	rear/all-M5	9.0	180	13.3
		rear/all-A4	10.0	175	15.2

SPECIFICATIONS

Model 96-01	Wlb. mm	Lght. mm	Cb.wt kg	Brakes fr/rr	Steering type	Standard tires
wgn. 2dr. 4x2	2576	4254	1369	dc/dr	pwr.bal.	215/75R15
wgn. 4dr. 4x2	2576	4254	1431	dc/dr	pwr.bal.	225/70R15
wgn. 2dr. 4x4	2576	4254	1442	dc/dr	pwr.bal.	215/75R15
wgn. 4dr. 4x4	2576	4254	1521	dc/dr	pwr.bal.	225/75R15

PRICES

Model / version		1996	1997	1998	1999	2000	2001
4X2							
wgn. 2dr. SE	mini	3700	7900	10200	11650		
	maxi	7000	10300	12400	13650		
wgn. 2dr. Sport	mini.	4600	8400	11350	12900	15550	18900
	maxi	8100	10500	13350	14700	17650	21000
wgn. 4dr. SE	mini	5150	9450	11350	12600		
	maxi	8400	11550	13100	14700		
wgn. 4dr. Sport	mini.	6100	10300	12200	13650	18700	22000
	maxi	9650	12600	14300	15650	21000	24350
wgn. 4dr. Country	mini	8000	11350				
	maxi	11750	13650				
4X4							
wgn. 2dr. SE	mini	4700	9150	11450	13250		
	maxi	8100	11550	13650	15350		
wgn. 2dr. Sport	mini	5700	9650	12600	14500	17200	21000
	maxi	9150	11750	14600	16300	19300	23100
wgn. 4dr. SE	mini	6200	10700	12600	14200		
	maxi	9450	12800	14400	16300		
wgn. 4dr. Sport	mini	7150	11550	13450	15200	20400	24100
	maxi	10700	13850	15550	17200	22700	26450
wgn. 4dr. Country	mini	9000	12600				
	maxi	12800	14900				
wgn. 4dr. Classic	mini				13550	15350	18600
	maxi				15450	17650	21600
wgn. 4dr. LTD	mini				15450	16600	20250	24700
	maxi				17550	18900	23400	27300

See page 7 to adapt these figures.

JEEP   Grand Cherokee

1999 JEEP Grand Cherokee Laredo

The Grand Cherokee, first sold in '92, came equipped with the 4.0L 6-cylinder Cherokee engine and in '93, the 5.2L V8 engine was also available, followed in '98 by a 5.9L. In 1999, Jeep has remodeled its flagship by introducing a new platform, a rounder body design and two new engines: a 4.0L L6 and a 4.7L V8.

PROS
• **The stylish** Grand Cherokee is stunning.
• **Driving comfort** is akin to that of a luxury sedan, for the suspension is super smooth, seats are thickly upholstered and soundproofing is really effective.
• **Its off-the-road** capabilities are awesome with such high ground clearance, short overhang and the spare tire stored in the baggage compartment.
• **The vehicle handles** really well, in spite of a bit of sensitivity to strong crosswinds.
• **Both engine displacements** are exceptionally muscular and really have get up and go, given vehicle size and weight.
• **The cabin interior** is attractive, yet isn't too classy with the imitation wood on the instrument panel and the rather synthetic-looking leather trim.

CONS
• **Very expensive** to buy, insure, drive, keep in good running order and repair.
• **Some components** aren't too reliable, which spoils this vehicle's image, for if it weren't for these snags, this vehicle would be a perfect specimen of its breed.
• **Steering** is over-assisted, so it's inaccurate and vague.
• **Seats** aren't firm enough and don't provide adequate support.
• **You can't store** as much in the baggage compartment because of the spare tire.
• **The instrument panel** isn't ergonomic for controls on the center console are out of the driver's reach.

CONCLUSION
The Grand Cherokee is popular and in great demand, but it's costly to run, especially if all you really want is to be in style...

Grand Cherokee   JEEP

RECALLS
- **1996** The memory unit of the seats wiring harness may have to be moved.
Spare tire must be replaced by a normal-sized one.
- **1997** Inadvertent airbag deployment may occur.
Defective fuel gauge indicator.
- **1998** Power brake booster is defective.
- **98-99** Defective rear outboard seat belt retractors assemblies.
Wrong Vehicle Emission Control Information (VECI) label.
- **1999** Defective spark plugs.
- **99-00** The adjustable turning loop bolt of the shoulder belt will be replaced by a proper one.
- **2000** Some fuel tank may have a suspect vent tube welds. They will be inspected and replaced if necessary.
Some steering gear unit may have missed the heat treat process. They will be inspected and replaced if necessary.
Some passsenger-side airbag contains an incorrect inflator charge. The suspect module will be replaced.
- **2001** Steering gear assembly will be replaced on some vehicles.

RELIABILITY PROBLEMS

	1996	1997	1998	1999	2000	2001
Engine:	-	-	-	X	X	-
Transmission:	X	X	X	-	-	-
Suspension:	-	X	-	X	X	X
Steering:	-	X	X	X	-	-
Brakes:	X	X	X	X	X	X
Electricity:	-	X	X	X	X	X
Body:	-	X	X	X	-	-
Accessories:	-	X	X	X	X	X
Fit/finish:	-	-	-	-	-	-

POWERTRAIN / PERFORMANCE

Year	Type/ L/Camshaft/bhp	Drivetrain & gearbox	Acceler. 0/100 sec.	Top. speed km/h	Ave. Fuel consp. l./100 km
96-98	L6/4.0/OHV/185	rear/all-M5	9.0	190	15.0
		rear/all-A4	9.5	185	16.0
	V8/5.2/OHV/220	rear/all-A4	8.8	195	17.2
1998	V8/5.9/OHV/245	rear/all-A4	8.0	200	19.0
99-01	L6/4.0/OHV/195	rear/all-A4	9.5	190	15.0
	V8/4.7/SOHC/235	rear/all-A4	8.5	200	17.3

SPECIFICATIONS

Model	Wlb. mm	Lght. mm	Cb.wt kg	Brakes fr/rr	Steering type	Standard tires
96-98						
Grand Cherokee						
wgn. 4dr. SE	3690	4501	1637	dc/dr/ABS	pwr.bal.	215/75R15
wgn. 4dr. Lar/LTD	3690	4501	1781	dc/dr/ABS	pwr.bal.	225/70R16
99-01						
wgn. 4dr. Laredo	2691	4610	1696	dc/ABS	pwr.bal.	225/75R16
wgn. 4dr. Limited	2691	4610	1730	dc/ABS	pwr.bal.	245/70R16

PRICES

Model / version		1996	1997	1998	1999	2000	2001
Grand Cherokee 4x4							
wgn. 4dr. Laredo	mini	11250	13450	16800	22900	28000	31400
	maxi	13650	15750	19200	25200	30600	33600
wgn. 4dr. LTD	mini	15350	18000	22800	26000	30150	33600
	maxi	17850	19400	25200	28650	33100	37300
wgn. 4dr. Orvis	mini	15750	18900				
	maxi	18400	21300				
wgn. 4dr. LTD 5.9	mini			25000			
	maxi			27300			

See page 7 to adapt these figures.

JEEP   YJ/TJ

2000 JEEP TY

This all-terrain vehicle was redesigned in '86 and was equipped with Cherokee mechanical features, renamed the YJ in Canada, and powered by a 2.5L 4-cylinder or 4.0L 6-cylinder in-line engine.

PROS
- **Its neat-looking** body design is a real winner.
- **Its off-road capabilities** are really awesome when it's equipped with the right tires.
- **Steering** is crisp and smooth, but it's still a bit too sensitive because over-assisted, and you have to keep an eye on it.
- **Brakes** are over-sensitive with the optional ABS.

CONS
- **Road stability** is still iffy even with the longer wheel base and newly designed suspension.
- **Sudden stops** are hazardous, for they're very unstable even with ABS...
- **You're in for a pretty rough ride** with such a soft suspension, poorly designed cabin design and inadequate seats that finally never provided the proper support, even after its '97 face-lift.
- **Off-road maneuverability** is really crippled by the large steer angle diameter, vehicle width and really vulnerable front fenders.
- **Convenience** just isn't a priority on this vehicle, for there's next to no storage space, either inside the cabin or in the baggage compartment, boarding is awkward and opening or lowering the convertible top is a nightmare.
- **Poor fit** and finish and pretty basic trim materials that just don't jive with the hefty price tag.
- **It's an expensive** vehicle for what you don't get for your money, gas consumption is high and repairs cost a mint.
- **Things to consider**: uncomfortable cockpit, inconvenient instrument panel, limited visibility with the convertible top, poorly located external rearview mirrors and tiny windshield wipers.

CONCLUSION
The Jeep is popular because of its spirited adventurous look. This would explain the fact that it sells so much in spite of its hazardous behaviour, its lack of comfort and its impractical side.

RECALLS
1997   Inadvertent airbag deployment may occur.
97-98   Driver side airbag may become inoperative.
1998   Safety belt's anchors are defective.
           Power brake booster is defective.
1999   Defective spark plugs.
           Instrument wiring ground attachment screws may loosen.
2001   The driver seat belt retractor assembly will be replaced with a new constant force retractor.

YJ/TJ — JEEP

RELIABILITY PROBLEMS

	1996	1997	1998	1999	2000	2001
Engine:	X	X	X	X	X	-
Transmission:	-	X	X	X	-	-
Suspension:	-	X	-	-	X	X
Steering:	-	X	X	X	-	-
Brakes:	-	X	X	X	X	-
Electricity:	X	X	X	X	X	-
Body:	-	-	X	X	X	-
Accessories:	X	X	X	X	X	-
Fit/finish:	X	-	X	X	X	-

POWERTRAIN

Year	Type/ L/Camshaft/bhp	Drivetrain & gearbox
96-01	L4/2.5/OHV/117-120	rear/all-M5
		rear/all-A3
	L6/4.0/OHV/180-185	rear/all-M5
		rear/all-A3

PERFORMANCE

Acceler. 0/100 sec.	Top. speed km/h	Ave. Fuel consp. l./100 km
13.5	140	13.1
14.8	130	14.3
10.5	165	14.1
11.2	160	15.3

SPECIFICATIONS

Model	Wlb. mm	Lght. mm	Cb.wt kg	Brakes fr/rr	Steering type	Standard tires
YJ 1996						
con. 2dr.S	2373	3856	1403	dc/dr	bal.	205/75R15
con. 2dr.base	2373	3856	1465	dc/dr	bal.	215/75R15
con. 2dr.Sahara	2373	3856	1475	dc/dr	pwr.bal.	225/75R15
TJ 97-01						
con. 2dr.SE	2373	3886	1505	dc/dr	pwr.bal.	205/75R15
con. 2dr.Sport	2373	3886	1559	dc/dr	pwr.bal.	215/75R15
con. 2dr.Sahara	2373	3886	1570	dc/dr	pwr.bal.	225/75R15

PRICES

Model / version		1996	1997	1998	1999	2000	2001
con. 2dr. SE	mini	8500	10500	13650	15750	17800	20800
	maxi	11350	12600	15750	17850	19950	23100
con. 2dr.Sahara	mini	12000	14000	17300	18150	21400	24100
	maxi	14200	16300	18900	20400	23500	26250
con. 2dr. Sport	mini	10200	12900	15750	17850	19950	22800
	maxi	13700	14700	17850	19900	22000	25200

See page 7 to adapt these figures.

2000 JEEP TJ

KIA   Rio

2001 KIA Rio

Since 2001, the Rio constitutes Kia's base model on the Canadian market. It is based on the former Ford Festiva and Aspire models, that used to be built by this Korean auto maker.

PROS
- **The price/equipment ratio** is competitive. The RS and LS models are well-equipped and offer good value.
- **The brakes** are powerful, stable and easy to gauge even without ABS. However, they produce longer-than-average stopping distances.
- **The powerful headlights** and windshield wipers produce safe driving conditions even in the worst of weather.
- **Handling** is safe and predictable despite the simplistic technical solutions used for the suspension systems.
- **The cabin is roomy**, and the trunk offers a very respectable minimum in terms of space and access.
- **The quality** of the construction and finish are remarkable, approaching the standards set by the Japanese.
- **The presentation** is pleasing to the eye both inside and out. There is an obvious attention to esthetics and the materials look quite honestly good.

CONS
- **The 1.5-liter engine** cranks out timid performance levels. Its weight-to-power ratio works to its disadvantage, but the manual transmission nevertheless makes the most out of what's available.
- **The cabin** exudes a strong chemical smell when the car is new that persists for a long time.
- **The mediocre tires** do not provide very good grip on slippery surfaces and they are also quite noisy.
- **The inadequate soundproofing** results in a high noise level, punctuated by a symphony of engine, road and wind noise beyond 100 kph.
- **The weak shocks** combined with the soft springs and ample wheel travel make the car jumpy over undulated pavement.
- **The narrow trunk** opening makes it impossible to fit anything large.

VERDICT
The Rio is a good means of economical transportation. Most of its drawbacks could be easily corrected. However, its long-term reliability has yet to be demonstrated.

RECALLS
None over this period.

Rio KIA

RELIABILITY PROBLEMS

	1996	1997	1998	1999	2000	2001
Engine:						
Transmission:						
Suspension:						
Steering:						
Brakes:			Insufficient data			
Electricity:						
Body:						
Accessories:						
Fit/finish:						

POWERTRAIN / PERFORMANCE

Year	Type/ L/Camshaft/bhp	Drivetrain & gearbox	Acceler. 0/100 sec.	Top. speed km/h	Ave. Fuel consp. l./100 km
2001	L4/1.5/SOHC/96	front-M5	12.4	165	8.8
		front-A4	13.5	160	9.2

SPECIFICATIONS

Model 2001	Wlb. mm	Lght. mm	Cb.wt kg	Brakes fr/rr	Steering type	Standard tires
sdn. 4dr. base	2410	4215	944	dc/dr	r.&p.	175/70R13
sdn. 4dr. RS/LS	2410	4215	944	dc/dr	pwr.r.&p.	175/70R13

PRICES

Model / version		1996	1997	1998	1999	2000	2001
sdn. 4dr. 5 speed	mini						6300
	maxi						8900
sdn. 4dr. RS	mini						7900
	maxi						10500
sdn. 4dr. LS	mini						8400
	maxi						11000

See page 7 to adapt these figures.

2001 KIA Rio

KIA   Sephia

2000 KIA Sephia

The arrival of a new Korean manufacturer to the Canadian market opens up opportunities for new entry-level models. The Sephia is a 4-door sedan powered by a 1.8-liter engine.

PROS
- **Price** is the Sephia's strongest attraction, with the LS version representing the best value.
- **The 1.8-liter engine** inherited from the Protegé ensures interesting acceleration and pick-up, even with the automatic transmission.
- **The Sephia is relatively economical** in terms of fuel consumption, even though it does travel fewer kilometers per tank than some of its more modern competitors.
- **Careful fit and finish**, but the fabrics and plastics used are a throwback to another era.
- **The cabin can seat five occupants**, including three in the rear seat depending on their size.
- **The interior** is conservative and logical, with a well-organized dashboard and sufficient storage space up front.

CONS
- **The design** does date back some ten years, which explains the questionable presentation and mushy suspension and steering systems.
- **Braking** is mediocre and stopping distances are long, but the brakes' biggest drawbacks are their lack of stability and wheels that lock in emergency situations.
- **Reliability** remains to be proven given the questionable quality of some components.
- **The Sephia is far from quiet**, and a lot of engine and road noise seeps into the cabin. Furthermore, the seats are thinly padded and the suspension is stiff.
- **The trunk** is smaller than average for this category, and its floor is some 15 cm (6 inches) lower than the bumper.
- **Depreciation** will be higher than average as long as the model's reputation has not been clearly established.
- **The lack of storage space** in the rear, very small sideview mirrors and the lack of a gear indicator with the automatic transmission are some other flaws.

CONCLUSION
The Sephia will have earned the right to its billing as a good, cost-effective mode of transportation when it proves its reliability and when the efficiency of its manufacturer is demonstrated beyond a shadow of a doubt.

RECALLS
2000 A bilingual adhesive label will be fixed in compliance of the regulations.

Sephia — KIA

RELIABILITY PROBLEMS

	1996	1997	1998	1999	2000	2001
Engine:						
Transmission:						
Suspension:						
Steering:						
Brakes:			Insufficient data			
Electricity:						
Body:						
Accessories:						
Fit/finish:						

POWERTRAIN

Year	Type/ L/Camshaft/bhp	Drivetrain & gearbox
00-01	L4/1.8/DOHC/125	front-M5
		front-A4

PERFORMANCE

Acceler. 0/100 sec.	Top. speed km/h	Ave. Fuel consp. l./100 km
11.5	170	11.5
12.8	165	12.0

SPECIFICATIONS

Model 00-01	Wlb. mm	Lght. mm	Cb.wt kg	Brakes fr/rr	Steering type	Standard tires
sdn. 4dr. base	2560	4430	1124	dc/dr	pwr.r&p.	185/65R14
sdn. 4dr. LS	2560	4430	1157	dc/dr	pwr.r&p.	185/65R14

PRICES

Model / version		1996	1997	1998	1999	2000	2001
sdn. 4dr.	mini					8600	
	maxi					11000	
sdn. 4dr. L	mini						10500
	maxi						13100
sdn. 4dr. LS	mini					9150	12600
	maxi					11550	15200

See page 7 to adapt these figures.

2000 KIA Sephia

KIA Sportage

2000 KIA Sportage

The Sportage arrived at the same time as the Lada Niva bowed out and thus took over the title of the least expensive 4x4 sold on the market. It is a 4-door extended cab version powered by a 2.0-liter engine.

PROS
- **The competitive price** of this 4x4 makes it one of the least expensive vehicles in its class.
- **The sympathetic** styling and rounded lines please the eye.
- **Versatility** comes at a relatively economical price, and the Sportage is perfectly at home on both city and country roads.
- **There is enough room** on board for four adults and their luggage, and accessing the passenger and baggage compartments is relatively easy.
- **The soft suspension** is surprisingly comfortable and the seats are well-padded.
- **The brakes** are stable and resist well, but do not pack much bite.
- **The Sportage is remarkably maneuverable** in spite of its low-geared steering system.
- **For a vehicle sold at this price**, the Kia is consistent and provides good value.
- **Kudos** for the airbag designed to protect the driver's knees.

CONS
- **The poor weight/power ratio** translates into mediocre performance levels.
- **The brakes** are not very efficient, given the long distances required to make panic stops.
- **The recirculating ball** steering is a throwback to another era and is very mushy on centre.
- **The very high noise level** points to a serious lack of soundproofing.
- **The low ground clearance** limits off-road capabilities and makes the Sportage an all-road rather than all-terrain vehicle.
- **Oversights**: The spare tire hinders rear visibility, the hatch is hard to open in a hurry or in bad weather, and the windshield wipers are painfully slow.

CONCLUSION
The Sportage is by far the Kia model that offers the highest value for the moment, as long as it proves to be reliable.

RECALLS
None over this period.

Sportage   KIA

RELIABILITY PROBLEMS
                  1996 1997 1998 1999 2000 2001
Engine:
Transmission:
Suspension:
Steering:
Brakes: Insufficient data
Electricity:
Body:
Accessories:
Fit/finish:

POWERTRAIN   PERFORMANCE

Year	Type/ L/Camshaft/bhp	Drivetrain & gearbox	Acceler. 0/100 sec.	Top. speed km/h	Ave. Fuel consp. l./100 km
00-01	L4/2.0/DOHC/130	rr./all-M5	11.8	165	11.5
		rr.-all-A4	12.0	170	12.5

SPECIFICATIONS

Model 00-01	Wlb. mm	Lght. mm	Cb.wt kg	Brakes fr/rr	Steering type	Standard tires
wgn. 4dr. X	2649	4128	1520	dc/dr	pwr.ball	205/75R15
wgn. 4dr. EX	2649	4128	1540	dc/dr	pwr.ball	205/75R15

PRICES

Model / version		1996	1997	1998	1999	2000	2001
wgn. 4dr. X	mini					14000	17300
	maxi					16300	19950
wgn. 4dr. EX	mini					17200	21000
	maxi					19400	23600

See page 7 to adapt these figures.

2000 KIA Sportage

LADA   Niva

1996 LADA Niva

Imported from Russia since 1980, this all-terrain vehicle is powered by a 1.6L 4-cylinder engine. In 1995, it got a 1.7L fuel-injected engine and full-height rear hatch.

PROS
- **Its very competitive price** makes it the least expensive all-terrain vehicle on the market.
- **It's cleverly designed**, because it has effective Porsche suspension and transmission, it's the perfect shape and it's very practical, given the small vehicle size.
- **Its off-road capabilities** are even better than for Jeep vehicles because it's really much more maneuverable.
- **Convenience** has definitely not been overlooked, for the Niva provides comfortable seating for four, the trunk is adequate and there are enough storage compartments in the cabin.
- **It's sturdy and solidly built**, so it's a low-upkeep vehicle.
- **Handling** is safer compared to that of its rivals, thanks to permanent all-wheel drive, a well-adjusted suspension, relatively stable brakes without ABS and its good resistance to crosswinds. But tire quality is crucial, for it can definitely affect how it handles.
- **The 1.7L** fuel-injection engine performance are equivalent to those of the competition.

CONS
- **It's not the most comfortable** vehicle with its bouncy suspension, vinyl-trimmed seats with short back section (before '95) and shake, rattle and roll that assails passengers due to bad soundproofing.
- **Some poor-quality components**, slipshod build and fit and finish.
- **The bodywork is rust-prone** and the very poor-quality paint peels off prematurely.
- **The small gas tank** and high gas consumption limit road autonomy.
- **This old-design engine** is rough, noisy and shaky.
- **Brakes** are only fair to middling, but they're more stable than before.

CONCLUSION
The Niva is an excellent and sturdy vehicle, powerful and economic to use. That must be why they're so rare on the used car market.

RECALLS
None over this period.

Niva   LADA

RELIABILITY PROBLEMS

	1996	1997	1998	1999	2000	2001
Engine:	-	-	-			
Transmission:	-	-	-			
Suspension:	X	-	-			
Steering:	-	-	-			
Brakes:	X	X	X			
Electricity:	X	X	X			
Body:	X	X	X			
Accessories:	X	X	X			
Fit/finish:	X	X	X			

POWERTRAIN

Year	Type/ L/Camshaft/bhp	Drivetrain & gearbox
96-98	L4/1.7/SOHC/80	all-M5

PERFORMANCE

Acceler. 0/100 sec.	Top. speed km/h	Ave. Fuel consp. l./100 km
15.0	140	11.0

SPECIFICATIONS

Model 96-98	Wlb. mm	Lght. mm	Cb.wt kg	Brakes fr/rr	Steering type	Standard tires
wgn. 2dr. base	2200	3720	1100	dc/dr	w&r.	175/80R16
wgn. 2dr. Cossack	2200	3720	1150	dc/dr	w&r.	195/75R15
wgn. 2dr. SE	2200	3720	1150	dc/dr	w&r.	175/80R16

PRICES

Model / version		1996	1997	1998	1999	2000	2001
wgn. 2dr. base	mini	1600	2850	4400			
	maxi	3350	4400	5450			
wgn. 2dr. Cossack	mini	2100	3350	4950			
	maxi	3700	4750	6000			
wgn. 2dr. SE	mini			5450			
	maxi			6800			

See page 7 to adapt these figures.

1997 LADA Niva Cossack

LADA   Samara

1997 LADA Samara Sagona

These compact cars hail back to 1986. They come in a 3-door sedan model equipped with a 1.3L engine, a 5-door sedan model with 1.5L engine since '89 and a 4-door as well as the Sagona since 1993.

PROS
- **These very affordable** cars are the least expensive models on the Canadian market.
- **Driving** is safe and sure because of good wheel travel, firm shock absorbers, stable brakes and clean, crisp steering in spite of a high reduction ratio. Yet good-quality tires are a must.
- **The 1.5L fuel-injected engine** (GM) who is more powerful and quite economical, allows pleasant driving.
- **The cabin** is roomy and well-designed, the trunk is practical and there are some nice items, such as adjustable headlights, front and rear windshield wipers and headlight wipers.
- **It's quite comfortable** for such a low price car, since there isn't much vibration because of good tires, effective shock absorbers and comfortable seats.
- **High ground clearance** allows for hassle-free driving on bumpy roads.

CONS
- **The body design** isn't quite in style these days and overall design is bland and basic.
- **Reliability** isn't guaranteed with such sloppy build quality, loose fit and finish and some components that are problematic.
- **The 1.3L engine** is wimpy and it drinks up as much gas as the 1.5L engine.
- **The shifter layout** is confusing and you can easily mix up reverse with first gear.
- **Seats are quite** straight and there's a lot of noise, which is a sure sign of inadequate soundproofing.

CONCLUSION
Used Samara's are more reliable than brand new models, which explains why there are so few of them on the used car market and why they're so cheap.

RECALLS
None over this period.

Samara — LADA

RELIABILITY PROBLEMS

	1996	1997	1998	1999	2000	2001
Engine:	X	X	X			
Transmission:	-	-	-			
Suspension:	-	-	-			
Steering:	-	-	-			
Brakes:	-	X	-			
Electricity:	X	X	X			
Body:	X	X	X			
Accessories:	-	X	X			
Fit/finish:	X	X	X			

POWERTRAIN

Year	Type/ L/Camshaft/bhp	Drivetrain & gearbox
96-98	L4/1.3/SOHC/65	front-M5
	L4/1.5/SOHC/67-79	front-M5

PERFORMANCE

Acceler. 0/100 sec.	Top. speed km/h	Ave. Fuel consp. l./100 km
15.0	145	7.5
13.5	160	8.2

SPECIFICATIONS

Model 96-98	Wlb. mm	Lght. mm	Cb.wt kg	Brakes fr/rr	Steering type	Standard tires
sdn. 3dr. 1.3L	2460	4006	900	dc/dr	r&p.	165/70R13
sdn. 3dr. 1.5L	2460	4006	930	dc/dr	r&p.	165/70R14
sdn. 4dr. 1.5L	2460	4210	975	dc/dr	r&p.	165/70R14
sdn. 5dr. 1.5L	2460	4115	950	dc/dr	r&p.	165/70R14

PRICES

Model / version		1996	1997	1998	1999	2000	2001
sdn. 3dr. 1.3L	mini	1100					
	maxi	2750					
sdn. 3dr. 1.5L	mini	1300	1800	2400			
	maxi	3100	3700	4400			
sdn. 3dr. Sport	mini	1800	2100	3000			
	maxi	3350	4200	4700			
sdn. 4dr. 1.5L	mini	1700	2200	3150			
	maxi	3400	4400	5250			
sdn. 4dr. Sagona	mini	1900	2400	3350			
	maxi	3550	4800	5550			
sdn. 5dr. 1.5L	mini	1500	2100	2950			
	maxi	3200	4200	4700			

Note: Vehicles sold in 1998 were 1997 model year.

See page 7 to adapt these figures.

1997 LADA Samara

LEXUS ES

1999 LEXUS ES 300

The ES300 was first sold in '92 and replaced the Lexus entry-model ES250. Like its predecessor, this car was also inspired by the Toyota Camry. Its last generation was introduced in 1997 while the performance of its V6 was brought up to 210-bhp in '99, at the same time of the VVT-I (Variable Valve Timing) unveiling.

PROS

- **Reliability** and durability are outstanding which makes it a great buy!
- **The cabin interior** is quite spacious and can hold five adults and the trunk can accomodate them adequately.
- **The suspension** is smooth, seats are nicely shaped and upholstered and there's low noise level at cruising speed.
- **Driving** is pleasant with such well-calibrated controls and power and engine performance are exceptional.
- **Equipment** is quite extensive and plush, yet not quite as refined as that of some European cars.
- **Construction** quality, fit and finish and trim materials are definitely top-notch, but the car is blah and lacks personality.

CONS

- **The body design** isn't distinctive enough to make it stand out from other Japanese counterparts.
- **Steering** is vague because it's over-assisted, which makes it light and sensitive.
- **The initial price** is too expensive compared to that of the Camry V6 that tended to be as effective and almost as luxurious.

CONCLUSION

The ES 300 has been really very popular and it's become a sort of prize horse in this very competitive and high demand car category.

RECALLS

1997   Brake booster vacuum hose might freeze.

ES LEXUS

RELIABILITY PROBLEMS

	1996	1997	1998	1999	2000	2001
Engine:	-	X	-	-	-	-
Transmission:	X	X	-	-	-	-
Suspension:	-	-	-	X	-	-
Steering:	-	-	-	-	-	-
Brakes:	-	X	-	X	X	-
Electricity:	-	-	-	X	X	X
Body:	-	-	-	X	-	-
Accessories:	-	X	X	X	X	-
Fit/finish:	-	-	-	-	-	-

POWERTRAIN

Year	Type/ L/Camshaft/bhp	Drivetrain & gearbox
96-01	V6/3.0/DOHC/185-210	front-A4

PERFORMANCE

Acceler. 0/100 sec.	Top. speed km/h	Ave. Fuel consp. l./100 km
8.3	225	12.3

SPECIFICATIONS

Model	Wlb. mm	Lght. mm	Cb.wt kg	Brakes fr/rr	Steering type	Standard tires
1996						
sdn. 4dr.	2620	4770	1548	dc/ABS	pwr.r&p.	205/65R15
97-01						
sdn. 4dr.	2670	4831	1532	dc/ABS	pwr.r&p.	206/65VR15

PRICES

Model / version		1996	1997	1998	1999	2000	2001
sdn. 4dr.	mini	16800	20250	26800	29400	31500	35200
	maxi	19400	25200	29400	32550	35700	38800

See page 7 to adapt these figures.

1997 LEXUS ES 300

LEXUS   GS

1997 LEXUS GS 300

Mid-way between the ES300 and the LS400, the Lexus GS300 is a rear-wheel drive luxury sedan that was first sold in '93 and was renewed in 1998 where the 400's V8 was added to the 6-cylinder in-line engine of the 300.

PROS
- **Its look** is more stylish than that of the ES 300.
- **The engine purrs quietly**, controls work like a charm, the instrument panel is ergonomic, there's good visibility and the cockpit is really very comfy.
- **Performance** of the GS 400's V8 engine run alongside exotic models such as the BMW 540i.
- **You feel like** you're virtually being transported in a bubble with such top-notch shock absorbers, cushy seats and low noise and vibration.
- **Construction quality**, tight fit and finish and spiffy materials are what you've come to expect in a Toyota.
- **Safety is guaranteed** with the really rigid body, dual airbags and 4-disc brakes that come with standard ABS and anti-skid system.
- **The car is neutral**, even if the suspension is more geared to comfort and the GS models are quite frisky on curved roads.
- **The cabin interior** is nice and trim, but not as lavish as that of European rivals and the equipment is complete but there are no gadgets.

CONS
- **Resale value** of the 300 plummets because this car doesn't sell too well, either as a new or used car.
- **Engine performance** of the 300 are crippled by a definitely poor power to weight ratio, so driving is devoid of all zip and zoom.
- **The interior** isn't too roomy because only four passengers can be comfortably accommodated and the trunk capacity is limited.

CONCLUSION
Avoid this model because it isn't a good investment, unless of course, the price is a real steal...

RECALLS
96-97 Inadequate lubrication of the front suspension lower ball joints. (GS300)
1998 A new electronic command module must be installed. Defective speed sensor.

GS   LEXUS

RELIABILITY PROBLEMS

	1996	1997	1998	1999	2000	2001
Engine:	X	-	-	-	-	-
Transmission:	-	-	-	-	-	-
Suspension:	-	X	X	-	-	-
Steering:	X	-	-	-	-	-
Brakes:	-	X	X	X	-	-
Electricity:	X	-	X	X	X	-
Body:	-	-	X	X	X	-
Accessories:	-	-	X	X	X	-
Fit/finish:	-	-	-	-	-	-

POWERTRAIN

Year	Type/ L/Camshaft/bhp	Drivetrain & gearbox
96-01	L6/3.0/DOHC/220-225	rear-A5
98-01	V8/4.0/DOHC/300	rear-A5
2001	V8/4.3/DOHC/300	rear-A5

PERFORMANCE

Acceler. 0/100 sec.	Top. speed km/h	Ave. Fuel consp. l./100 km
8.0	220	12.1
6.8	240	13.7
6.5	240	12.9

SPECIFICATIONS

Model	Wlb. mm	Lght. mm	Cb.wt kg	Brakes fr/rr	Steering type	Standard tires
96-97						
sdn. 4dr. 300	2779	4950	1660	dc/ABS	pwr.r&p.	215/60VR16
98-01						
sdn. 4dr. 300	2799	4800	1649	dc/ABS	pwr.r&p.	215/60VR16
sdn. 4dr. 400	2799	4800	1674	dc/ABS	pwr.r&p.	225/55VR16 235/45ZR17

PRICES

Model / version		1996	1997	1998	1999	2000	2001
sdn. 4dr. 300	mini	21000	25500	30400	32500	35700	40900
	maxi	24600	29000	33600	35700	39900	46200
sdn. 4dr. 400	mini			41500	44600	47800	
	maxi			45100	48800	52500	
sdn. 4dr. 430	mini						52500
	maxi						57700

See page 7 to adapt these figures.

1998 LEXUS GS 400

LEXUS   LS & SC

1997 LEXUS LS 400

The LS400, first available in 1991, is the jewel of the Lexus model range. The SC400 coupe, that it inspired, was put on the market the following year. Both come equipped with a V8 engine.

PROS

- **The LS400** has a body design reminiscent of the lush Mercedes look, but the coupe is much more original and dashing, it's sporty but very classy.
- **The LS400** cabin can comfortably seat five passengers, but the coupe can only accommodate four passengers. The thick seats provide top-notch support and noise and vibration are barely felt at all, which makes for a pretty plush ride.
- **The V8 engine** is very muscular and whoops quite a torque, yet it runs so smoothly that you have to look at the instrument gauges to be sure it's really running.
- **Handling** is great with the power traction control. Yet handling is cleaner on the coupe with its stiffer suspension.
- **Trim finish** and build quality are simply perfect, equipment is extensive and sophisticated and overall design is superb. Moreover, these cars are extremely reliable and durable.

CONS

- **The short seat** on the seatbench has obviously been designed to provide more leg room.
- **The rear suspension** on the sedan is too soft and produces quite a sway on tight curves, and on the coupe, it's too stiff and can't be adjusted according to the driver's whim or fancy. A major flaw.
- **A small service network** can make upkeep and repairs problematic.
- **The narrow doors** on the SC400 make for awkward boarding.
- **The coupe** should be equipped with more crisp steering and with mixed shifting on the automatic transmission.

CONCLUSION

The lavish Lexus LS and SC models are equipped with both straight-forward and sophisticated features. Prices have jumped over the last years, compared with German rivals, and it makes you really wonder if the carmaker is offering these products at a fair price.

RECALLS

96-97   Magnetic switch of the starter motor must be replaced.
1998   A new electronic command module must be installed.

LS & SC LEXUS

RELIABILITY PROBLEMS

	1996	1997	1998	1999	2000	2001
Engine:	-	X	-	-	-	-
Transmission:	-	-	X	X	-	-
Suspension:	X	X	-	X	X	-
Steering:	-	-	-	-	-	-
Brakes:	X	X	-	-	-	-
Electricity:	-	-	-	-	-	-
Body:	-	-	-	X	-	-
Accessories:	-	X	X	-	-	-
Fit/finish:	-	-	-	-	-	-

POWERTRAIN

Year	Type/ L/Camshaft/bhp	Drivetrain & gearbox
96-00	V8/4.0/DOHC/250-290	rear-A5
2001	V8/4.3/DOHC/290	rear-A5

PERFORMANCE

Acceler. 0/100 sec.	Top. speed km/h	Ave. Fuel consp. l./100 km
7.2	230	12.7
7.5	240	12.8

SPECIFICATIONS

Model	Wlb. mm	Lght. mm	Cb.wt kg	Brakes fr/rr	Steering type	Standard tires
96-00						
sdn.4dr. LS400	2850	4996	1765	dc/ABS	pwr.r&p.	225/60R16
2001						
sdn. 4dr. LS430	2925	4995	1795	dc/ABS	pwr.r&p.	225/55R17
96-97						
cpe. 2dr.SC400	2690	4890	1635	dc/ABS	pwr.r&p.	225/55R16

PRICES

Model / version		1996	1997	1998	1999	2000	2001
cpe. 2dr. SC400	mini	33000	37800				
	maxi	37800	43000				
sdn. 4dr. LS400	mini	31200	34600	40400	46800	53500	
	maxi	34600	39400	45100	52000	58800	
sdn. 4dr. LS430	mini						59850
	maxi						65100

See page 7 to adapt these figures.

1997 LEXUS SC 400

LEXUS LX

1998 LEXUS LX 470

The LX is a dressed-to-kill Land Cruiser introduced in 1996 and sporting a 4.5L L6 engine and was given a tune up the year after with a 4.7L V8. In 1998, both engines were offered for a short time.

PROS

• **Impressive terrain** tackling capabilities and traction control make of the LX 450 a true off-roader.

• **The cabin** is quite versatile and can accommodate five to eight passengers depending on whether the optional seatbench is installed.

• **The cargo area** holds heaps of stuff, but loading luggage isn't a treat with the awkward rear hatch design and high door. The baggage compartment can be extended by folding the middle seatbench, but it's pretty skimpy with the third rear seatbench in there.

• **Getting aboard** is great with the running boards and handy handle-grips, but it's tough getting way back to the third seatbench.

• **The ride** is quite comfy, even with the two rigid-axle suspension, but even off-road bumps and ruts are a breeze with such good wheel travel. The suspension is soft as velvet on smooth highways.

• **Handling** is quite good with permanent all-wheel drive and with a more civilized suspension than the original Land Cruiser.

• **Engine response** is quite good, considering the 2,300 kg vehicle weight. Accelerations are zippier than pick-up, especially with a full load, but the big 6-cylinder powerplant has impressive torque, for standard trailering capacity is 2,250 kg.

• **The cockpit** is neat with the huge dashboard that houses most controls under a big visor. The driver is comfortable, but the seat doesn't offer much lateral support.

CONS

• **It's outrageously** priced and the greedy engine can guzzle up to 20 liters per 100 km on tough terrain.

• **Maneuverability** is not marvelous either in city traffic or out in the bush. This vehicle can be pretty clumsy at times.

• **Rear seat access** is no fun with those narrow doors and tight maneuvering room between the seats.

• **Steering** is smooth, but a high reduction ratio (3.4 turns) and large steer angle diameter make quick lane changes pretty hazardous.

CONCLUSION

The LX is like a Japanese-made Range Rover, meaning that adding to its purposeful side is reliability and durability.

RECALLS

98-99 Defective towing wire harness converter may cause the failure of the trailer and vehicle's rear lights.

LX — LEXUS

RELIABILITY PROBLEMS

	1996	1997	1998	1999	2000	2001
Engine:		-	-	-	-	-
Transmission:		X	-	X	-	-
Suspension:		X	-	-	-	-
Steering:		-	-	-	-	-
Brakes:		X	X	-	-	-
Electricity:		-	X	X	X	-
Body:		-	-	-	-	-
Accessories:		X	X	X	-	-
Fit/finish:		-	-	-	-	-

POWERTRAIN

Year	Type/ L/Camshaft/bhp	Drivetrain & gearbox
97-98	L6/4.5/DOHC/212	rear/all-A4
99-01	V8/4.7/DOHC/230	rear/all-A4

PERFORMANCE

Acceler. 0/100 sec.	Top. speed km/h	Ave. Fuel consp. l./100 km
11.4	175	18.4
10.5	175	18.4

SPECIFICATIONS

Model	Wlb. mm	Lght. mm	Cb.wt kg	Brakes fr/rr	Steering type	Standard tires
97-98						
wgn. 4dr. 450	2850	4821	2255	dc/ABS	pwr.bal.	275/70R16
99-01						
wgn. 4dr. 470	2850	4890	2450	dc/ABS	pwr.r&p.	275/70R16

PRICES

Model / version		1996	1997	1998	1999	2000	2001
wgn. 4dr. 450	mini		33600				
	maxi		37800				
wgn. 4dr. 470	mini			41000	52500	57700	68200
	maxi			44100	56700	62000	72400

See page 7 to adapt these figures.

1998 LEXUS LX 470

LEXUS RX

2000 LEXUS RX 300

The RX 300 is a compact SUV derived from the Camry platform and it's powered by the Camry's 3.0L V6.

PROS

• **Such elegant style** is a definite plus in the horde of rather plain-looking vehicles of this type.

• **Performance** are more car-like than SUV-ilk, since you can go from 0 to 100 km/h in about 10 seconds.

• **The ride** on smooth roads is wonderful with such a velvety suspension and thickly upholstered seats make for fatigue-free trips.

• **The cargo hold** is easy to get to and can be easily extended, there's lots of storage space and the air conditioner works like a charm.

• **The overall quality** of this vehicle surpasses that of its main rivals since build craftsmanship, finish job and trim materials are beyond reproach.

CONS

• **The overly soft suspension**, hard tires and insufficient wheel travel limit the RX 300 to road travel since even on the highway there's quite a bit of sway, so you're in for some unpleasant demeanor.

• **Brakes** aren't terrific, not with sudden stops that stretch to kingdom come and wishy-washy follow-through, even with ABS.

• **Maneuverability** is less smooth than that of the bulky LX 470, due to a wide steer angle diameter and visibility hampered by thick B- and C-pillars.

• **The instrument panel** is overdone with its massive wood appliqués and the screen that indicates ambient air readings (when there isn't a GPS system) is hard to decipher.

• **Noise interference** is high, a bit of a surprise for a vehicle of this breeding, and rear seat access is tricky with the narrow doors.

CONCLUSION

The RX 300 appeals to folks who'd like to own a 4X4, but who really don't need one...

RECALLS

1999 Defective automatic light control system that may not activate the headlights and the tail lights in low ambient light.

RX   LEXUS

RELIABILITY PROBLEMS

	1996	1997	1998	1999	2000	2001
Engine:				-	-	-	-
Transmission:			X	-	-	-
Suspension:				-	-	-	-
Steering:				-	-	-	-
Brakes:				-	X	X	-
Electricity:				X	X	X	X
Body:				-	-	-	-
Accessories:				X	X	-	-
Fit/finish:				-	-	-	-

POWERTRAIN

Year	Type/ L/Camshaft/bhp	Drivetrain & gearbox
98-01	V6/3.0/DOHC/220	front/all-A4

PERFORMANCE

Acceler. 0/100 sec.	Top. speed km/h	Ave. Fuel consp. l./100 km
10.4	180	13.0

SPECIFICATIONS

Model 98-01	Wlb. mm	Lght. mm	Cb.wt kg	Brakes fr/rr	Steering type	Standard tires
wgn. 4dr.	2616	4575	1769	dc/ABS	pwr.r&p.	225/70R16

PRICES

Model / version		1996	1997	1998	1999	2000	2001
wgn. 4dr.	mini			29000	32850	36700	42000
	maxi			32500	35700	39900	46200

See page 7 to adapt these figures.

2000 LEXUS RX 300

LINCOLN — Continental

2000 LINCOLN Continental

This luxury sedan became a front-wheel drive in 87, featuring a 3.8L V6 and a pneumatic suspension and was completely revamped in 95 with a 4.6L V8 and rear-wheel drive and then again in 1998.

PROS

- **Comfort** is excellent due to the air suspension, which makes even the roughest roads pleasant to drive on. The passenger compartment is noise-free.
- **Styling** is sober, in keeping with the tradition set by these prestige automobiles.
- **Steering** is precise, providing surprisingly good maneuvrability in spite of its low-gearing and a barely acceptable turning diameter.
- **Performance** of the V8 has enough power and torque to accelerate and pass safely.
- **Braking** is responsive and well-balanced, however it is a little difficult to control and the pedal should be approached with some caution.
- **Finishing** is rigorous and standard equipment is detailed.

CONS

- **The suspension** is too soft and causes left-to-right roll on curves and front-to-back rocking during acceleration and braking.
- **Seats** are spongey and don't provide enough support.
- **Steering** suffers from overgearing.
- **Interior design** is unworthy of a luxury car, there's a lot of plastic to be seen, the instrument panel is dull and the false inlaid wood looks dreadful.

CONCLUSION

A nice, well-behaved and conservative sedan, too American to compete effectively with its German cousins. With a V8 engine and a more international interior, things could change.

RECALLS

- **1996** Headlight's automatic ignition is defective.
  Gear shift does not lock properly.
- **1998** Defective fuel rail may leak and in the presence of an ignition source, a fire could result.
- **2000** In some vehicles lap and shoulder belts have an incorrect pin.

Continental   LINCOLN

RELIABILITY PROBLEMS

	1996	1997	1998	1999	2000	2001
Engine:	X	X	X	X	X	-
Transmission:	-	-	-	-	-	-
Suspension:	X	X	-	X	-	-
Steering:	-	-	-	-	-	-
Brakes:	X	X	X	X	X	X
Electricity:	X	X	X	X	X	X
Body:	-	-	X	X	X	X
Accessories:	-	X	X	X	X	X
Fit/finish:	X	-	-	-	-	-

POWERTRAIN

Year	Type/ L/Camshaft/bhp	Drivetrain & gearbox
96-01	V8/4.6/DOHC/260-275	front-A4

PERFORMANCE

Acceler. 0/100 sec.	Top. speed km/h	Ave. Fuel consp. l./100 km
8.3	200	13.9

SPECIFICATIONS

Model	Wlb.	Lght.	Cb.wt	Brakes	Steering	Standard
96-97						
sdn. 4dr.	2769	5240	1774	dc/ABS	pwr.r&p.	225/60R16
98-01						
sdn. 4dr.	2769	5296	1755	dc/ABS	pwr.r&p.	225/60R16

PRICES

Model / version		1996	1997	1998	1999	2000	2001
sdn. 4dr.	mini	10500	12600	19950	25700	33100	37800
	maxi	14700	17400	24100	29400	37800	43100

See page 7 to adapt these figures.

1998 LINCOLN Continental

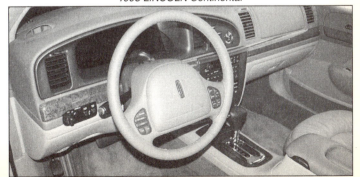

LINCOLN   LS

2000 LINCOLN LS

Before extending its market to the mid-size luxury niche, Lincoln created the LS to compete more aggressively against its Japanese and European rivals who have held a monopoly on this category since the dawn of the automotive era.

PROS
- **The original styling** leaves the beaten path and has character.
- **In terms of size**, the LS fits in between the Infiniti I30 and Lexus ES 300.
- **Ample comfort** is derived from the smooth suspension and well-padded seats that provide adequate lateral and lumbar support.
- **Both engines** produce adequate performance levels for this category.
- **The LS handles** with surprising assurance; it is well-balanced and has just enough bite to satisfy the Sportscar enthusiast.
- **The trunk** is large enough and can be extended into the cabin by folding down the rear 60/40 split bench.
- **The moisture-sensitive windshield wipers** do a good job and they position themselves automatically.

CONS
- **The interior presentation** is boring and was obviously inspired by the Lexus' lifeless centre console.
- **The materials** look cheap, and this is especially true of the fake wood inlays above the glove box.
- **The suspension** jumps a lot over poor road surfaces, which in turn affects the occupants' comfort.
- **Access** to the cabin is hindered by the narrow door openings, especially in the rear where the doors are not as long as in front.
- **Designers** could have done more in terms of practicality: storage spaces are ridiculously minuscule in front, while the back seat is practically devoid of any storage space at all.
- **The automatic transmission** makes its presence brutally known when changing gears.
- **It is impossible to adjust the front seat** while the vehicle is moving; there is simply not enough space to fit a hand in between the seat and the door.
- **The over-assisted steering** feels very light, which complicates certain maneuvres.

CONCLUSION
The Lincoln LS is the first Lincoln ever with an international flavour to it, which gives it an honest chance of being sold around the world.

RECALLS
2000 The output voltage of 9.6 volts the Daytime Running Lamps results in a brightness exceeding the requirements of the regulations. Dealers will install a revised EMF module.

2001 The front suspension lower ball joint may not have been tightened properly. It must be check, tightened or replaced.

LS LINCOLN

RELIABILITY PROBLEMS

	1996	1997	1998	1999	2000	2001
Engine:					-	-
Transmission:						
Suspension:					-	-
Steering:					-	-
Brakes:					-	-
Electricity:					X	X
Body:					X	-
Accessories:					X	X
Fit/finish:					-	-

POWERTRAIN

Year	Type/ L/Camshaft/bhp	Drivetrain & gearbox
00-01	V6/3.0/DOHC/210	rear-M5
		rear-A5
	V8/4.0/DOHC/252	rear-M5

PERFORMANCE

Acceler. 0/100 sec.	Top. speed km/h	Ave. Fuel consp. l./100 km
8.5	200	12.5
9.0	190	13.2
8.0	210	14.0

SPECIFICATIONS

Model 00-01	Wlb. mm	Lght. mm	Cb.wt kg	Brakes fr/rr	Steering type	Standard tires
sdn. 4dr. LS6	2908	4952	1632	dcABS	pwr.r&p.	215/60HR16
sed. 4dr. LS8	2908	4952	1675	dc/ABS	pwr.r&p.	215/60HR16

PRICES

Model / version		1996	1997	1998	1999	2000	2001
sdn. 4dr. V6 SP	mini					26200	32500
	maxi					30500	37300
sdn. 4dr. V6 AT	mini					29400	34700
	maxi					31500	39400
sdn. 4dr. V8 At	mini					31500	37300
	maxi					36700	41500

See page 7 to adapt these figures.

2000 LINCOLN LS

LINCOLN   Mark VIII

1996 LINCOLN Mark VIII

The Mark VIII coupe replaced the venerable Mark VII in '93 and the engine model went from a 5.0L V8 to a more technically advanced 4.6L engine.

PROS

- **The Mark VIII 4.6L engine** is much more muscular than the former 5.0L, which was anyway quite sprightly.
- **There's more stable** handling with the stiff suspension and crisper steering on the LSC.
- **Comfort** in this hefty car is a sure thing because of the highly sophisticated suspension.
- **The Mark VIII** is a safer car because its body structure has been beefed up and because it comes equipped with standard dual airbags.
- **Cabin design** and rear seat access have definitely improved on the latest generation models.
- **These cars** are quite stunning and do not go unnoticed.
- **Brakes** are powerful and stable on sudden stops, given the vehicle weight.

CONS

- **Poor construction** quality, slipshod fit and finish and some chintzy trim materials aren't at all what you'd expect on this caliber car and, consequently, the cabin design isn't too great.
- **The base model Mark VIII** suspension is too soft and causes a lot of swing and sway and it doesn't handle bumps and such in a civilized fashion.
- **Roof supports** are too wide and obstruct rearward view at quarterback.
- **It's too bad the spare tire** is stored in the trunk, which cuts down on luggage capacity and inside the cabin, storage compartments are few and far between.
- **Rear seat access** on the Mark VIII is a real chore and the low roof makes long trips uncomfortable.
- **The instrument panel** on the Mark VIII is high and massive.

CONCLUSION

Sport utility vehicles have stolen the show, so sports coupes are no longer in as great demand, and the same applies to the used car market.

RECALLS

None over this period.

Mark VIII LINCOLN

RELIABILITY PROBLEMS

	1996	1997	1998	1999	2000	2001
Engine:	X	X	X			
Transmission:	-	-	-			
Suspension:	X	X	-			
Steering:	-	-	-			
Brakes:	-	-	X			
Electricity:	X	-	X			
Body:	-	X	X			
Accessories:	X	X	X			
Fit/finish:	X	-	-			

POWERTRAIN

Year	Type/ L/Camshaft/bhp	Drivetrain & gearbox
96-98	V8/4.6/DOHC/280-290	rear-A4

PERFORMANCE

Acceler. 0/100 sec.	Top. speed km/h	Ave. Fuel consp. l./100 km
7.5	200	13.4

SPECIFICATIONS

Model 96-98	Wlb. mm	Lght. mm	Cb.wt kg	Brakes fr/rr	Steering type	Standard tires
cpe. 2dr. Mk VIII	2870	5255	1709	dc/ABS	pwr.r&p.	225/60R16
cpe. 2dr. LSC	2870	5265	1714	dc/ABS	pwr.r&p.	225/60R16

PRICES

Model / version		1996	1997	1998	1999	2000	2001
cpe. 2dr. Mk VIII	mini	13100	14500	26900			
	maxi	17750	19950	31000			
cpe. 2dr. LSC	mini		16100	29000			
	maxi		21500	33100			

See page 7 to adapt these figures.

1998 LINCOLN Mark VIII

LINCOLN — Navigator

1998 LINCOLN Navigator

The Navigator, the deluxe, top-of-the-line version of the Expedition, is animated by a standard 5.4L V8 which has seen its output being boosted to 300-bhp in '99.

PROS

- **Cabin size** is awesome since up to seven passengers can be accommodated with the three rows of seats.
- **The lavish interior** is equivalent to what Lincoln limos offer. The rear bucket seats make you feel like you're travelling inside a private jet.
- **General ride comfort** is a cut above that of other vehicles of this type, due to a well-honed suspension that's silky smooth, plush seat upholstery and super soundproofing.
- **Driving** is a dream with such a gutsy engine that yields zippy accelerations, albeit more impressive than on pick-up, for a vehicle that weighs in at nearly 3 tons when at full load capacity.
- **This bulky beast's** maneuverability is amazing, thanks to the steer angle diameter that's akin to that of a 4X4 compact...
- **The rear hatch** is really handy since it has a window that opens and rear seat passengers have loads of spacious spots to store stuff.

CONS

- **The Navigator** is a big brute of a vehicle, so it isn't a champion when it comes to getting around in city traffic and parking and such can be awkward.
- **Brakes** don't bite in as they should. Actually, only locomotive brakes could bring this heavyweight to a sudden stop...
- **Fuel bills** are high, especially for travel on rough terrain or when hauling a heavy trailer.
- **Getting aboard** is no picnic even with the running boards, since they're narrow and slippery.
- **The third seatbench** is tough to get to and is pretty snug, so it's really only suited to accommodate small children.

CONCLUSION

The Navigator is the all-round favorite with SUV customers. Sales have been a real surprise for everyone, even for the manufacturer, and resale value is currently a sure thing.

Navigator — LINCOLN

RECALLS
1999 Missing or partially installed retainer clip that holds the master cylinder pushrod to the brake pedal arm.
17-inch chrome steel wheels can separate from the vehicle due to insufficient wheel contact area with the hub and lack of lug nuts torque.
2000 The bolts of the trailer hitch assembly can become loose and the trailer hitch can potentialy separate from the vehicle.

RELIABILITY PROBLEMS

	1996	1997	1998	1999	2000	2001
Engine:			-	X	X	-
Transmission:			X	-	-	-
Suspension:			X	X	X	X
Steering:			X	-	-	-
Brakes:			X	X	-	-
Electricity:			X	X	X	X
Body:			-	-	-	-
Accessories:			X	X	X	X
Fit/finish:			-	-	-	-

POWERTRAIN

Year	Type/ L/Camshaft/bhp	Drivetrain & gearbox	Acceler. 0/100 sec.	Top. speed km/h	Ave. Fuel consp. l./100 km
1998	V8/5.4/SOHC/230	rear-A4	10.5	175	17.0
		rear/all-A4	11.0	170	18.2
99-01	V8/5.4/DOHC/300	rear-A4	9.8	180	18.8
		rear/all-A4	10.5	175	19.6

PERFORMANCE (see above)

SPECIFICATIONS

Model 98-01	Wlb. mm	Lght. mm	Cb.wt kg	Brakes fr/rr	Steering type	Standard tires
wgn. 4dr. 4x2	3025	5202	NA	dc/ABS	pwr.bal.	245/75R16
wgn. 4dr. 4x4	3025	5202	2444	dc/ABS	pwr.bal.	245/75R16

PRICES

Model / version		1996	1997	1998	1999	2000	2001
wgn. 4dr. 4x2	mini			28350	32000	40900	47200
	maxi			32500	37300	44600	50400
wgn. 4dr. 4x4	mini			30200	34000	43000	49400
	maxi			34400	39400	46200	52500

See page 7 to adapt these figures.

1998 LINCOLN Navigator

LINCOLN   Town Car

2000 LINCOLN Town Car

This big rear-wheel drive sedan, powered by a V8 engine, was upgraded in 1990. In '98, when Cadillac pulled its counterparts off the market, it monopolized the limousine market segment.

PROS

- **Its prestigious look** has become a symbol of the American luxury car.
- **Highway driving** is a dream with such a smooth suspension that gently rocks you as you sit in the superbly quiet cabin.
- **The big and spacious** cabin comfortably seats six passengers and holds their luggage.
- **Handling** on the latest generation models is much better because of the suspension that benefits from electronic ride control, thus controlling sway and nose-dive.
- **Equipment** is plush and includes scads of power assists and a very powerful climate control system.
- **The 4.6L engine** is almost economical with a 14 L/100 km yield.
- **The sensational climate control**, sound system, power assists and headlights.

CONS

- **Handling** isn't the greatest with such excessive vehicle weight, overly long wheelbase and steering that suffers from too high a reduction ratio.
- **The soft suspension** can really jostle passengers when it hits road faults.
- **The trunk** with it's sinuous design makes it hard to take advantage of and the lack of space impairs on its usefulness.
- **Seats** are poorly designed and don't provide adequate support.
- **The instrument clusters** are simplistic and insufficient in number, and the only storage compartment is the tiny glove compartment.

CONCLUSION

The Town Car is the favorite vehicle of limousine service companies and elderly car buyers, who consider it to be the best built car of its kind...

RECALLS

1996   Steering ball joints insufficiently greased at assembly. Defective power lock on driver's side.
96-99 Eventual cracking of the lower control arm ball joints. (Limo)
2000   Belt buckle assembly may not comply with standard and must be inspected and replaced if necessary.

Town Car — LINCOLN

RELIABILITY PROBLEMS

	1996	1997	1998	1999	2000	2001
Engine:	-	X	X	X	-	-
Transmission:	X	-	X	-	-	-
Suspension:	X	-	X	X	X	X
Steering:	X	-	-	-	-	-
Brakes:	-	X	X	X	X	X
Electricity:	-	X	X	X	X	X
Body:	-	X	-	-	X	-
Accessories:	X	X	X	X	X	-
Fit/finish:	-	-	-	-	-	-

POWERTRAIN

Year	Type/ L/Camshaft/bhp	Drivetrain & gearbox
96-01	V8/4.6/SOHC/190-220	rear-A4

PERFORMANCE

Acceler. 0/100 sec.	Top. speed km/h	Ave. Fuel consp. l./100 km
9.5	180	13.9

SPECIFICATIONS

Model	Wlb. mm	Lght. mm	Cb.wt kg	Brakes fr/rr	Steering type	Standard tires
96-97						
sdn. 4dr. Exec.	2982	5560	1828	dc/ABS	pwr.bal.	215/70R15
sdn. 4dr. Sign.	2982	5560	1837	dc/ABS	pwr.bal.	215/70R15
sdn. 4dr. Cartier	2982	5560	1847	dc/ABS	pwr.bal.	225/60R16
98-01						
sdn. 4dr. Exec.	2990	5469	1805	dc/ABS	pwr.bal.	225/60R16
sdn. 4dr. Sign.	2990	5469	1821	dc/ABS	pwr.bal.	225/60R16
sdn. 4dr. Cartier	2990	5469	1835	dc/ABS	pwr.bal.	235/60R16

PRICES

Model / version		1996	1997	1998	1999	2000	2001
sdn. 4dr. Executive	mini	10000	13400	20500	25500	33100	38800
	maxi	14100	17400	24100	29400	37300	43000
sdn. 4dr. Executive L	mini						39900
	maxi						44100
sdn. 4dr. Signature	mini	11000	16600	23100	28650	35200	41000
	maxi	15100	20500	27300	32500	39400	45100
sdn. 4dr. Designer	mini	12700	18400	24700	29700	37300	43000
	maxi	16800	21500	28400	33600	41500	47200
sdn. 4dr. Cartier L	mini						44100
	maxi						48300

See page 7 to adapt these figures.

1998 LINCOLN Town Car

MAZDA   Miata

2000 MAZDA Miata

Mazda had a bright idea when they launched the Miata convertible in 1989, for it created quite a sensation and really renewed interest in the roadster. In 1994, the 1.6L engine was replaced by the 1.8L engine that is much more spirited. In '99, its body style has dramatically changed for its headlights that are now part of the front grille. For its 10th anniversary, Mazda has also beefed up its 1.8L to push the engine to 140-bhp and has introduced a Nardi limited edition (7,500 units worldwide) with chrome alloy wheels, a special blue and a 6-speed manual transmission.

PROS

• **Its design**, reminiscent of those legendary British Sportscars of the sixties, was a smashing success.
• **Handling** is a dream with such crisp, frisky engines, transmission and steering.
• **Engines really unleash** a lot of power and make for a thrilling ride, even if they seem to be going faster than they really are.
• **The soft top** and the optional hard top handle easily and are very waterproof.
• **The 1.8L engine** is more muscular and smoother and gas consumption isn't any greater than for the former 1.6L engine.
• **Running this car** is quite economical because it's reliable, durable and upkeep is pretty straightforward.

CONS

• **The price of the Miata** is climbing, especially in good weather when you have to cough up more cash to buy one that's in good shape. Don't forget that some replacement parts are expensive...
• **Its Spartan comfort** level won't discourage the young at heart.
• **Cabin and trunk space** are at a minimum, so if you're bulky or hulky or have a lot of luggage, this car isn't the one for you.
• **There aren't too many storage** compartments in the cabin and the dashboard reflects into the windshield.
• **Things to consider**: poor rearward visibility at quarterback with either the soft top or the hard top, external rearview mirrors located too far back and not power-assisted, poor defrosting on side windows in cold weather.

CONCLUSION

In spite of its more upper-crust European rivals, the Miata is still the best small convertible Sportscar around.

RECALLS

1997 Injector harness may be damaged and should be replaced.

Miata   MAZDA

RELIABILITY PROBLEMS

	1996	1997	1998	1999	2000	2001
Engine:	-	X		X	X	X
Transmission:	X	-		-	-	-
Suspension:	-	-		-	-	-
Steering:	-	-		-	-	-
Brakes:	-	X		X	X	-
Electricity:	-	-		X	X	-
Body:	-	-		X	X	-
Accessories:	X	X		X	X	X
Fit/finish:	X	-		-	-	-

POWERTRAIN

Year	Type/ L/Camshaft/bhp	Drivetrain & gearbox
96-97	L4/1.8/DOHC/128-133	rear-M5
		rear-A4
99-01	L4/1.8/DOHC/140	rear-M5-M6
		rear-A4

PERFORMANCE

Acceler. 0/100 sec.	Top speed km/h	Ave. Fuel consp. l/100 km
9.0	190	10.8
10.4	180	10.8
8.2	200	11.4
9.5	185	10.6

SPECIFICATIONS

Model 96-97	Wlb. mm	Lght. mm	Cb.wt kg	Brakes fr/rr	Steering type	Standard tires
con. Soft top	2266	3948	1014	dc/dc	r&p.	185/60R14
con. Hard top	2266	3948	1070	dc/dc	pwr.r&p.	185/60R14
99-01						
con. base	2265	3945	1032	dc/dc	pwr.r&p.	185/60R14
con. leather/10th	2265	3945	1035	dc/ABS	pwr.r&p.	195/50R15

PRICES

Model / version		1996	1997	1998	1999	2000	2001
con. 2dr.	mini	11550	13650		17400	20250	23100
	maxi	14100	15750		19400	22600	26250
con. 2dr. 10th Ann.	mini				23100		
	maxi				25200		
con. 2dr. SE	mini					24700	
	maxi					27300	
con. 3dr. 6 speed	mini						24100
	maxi						27300

See page 7 to adapt these figures.

2000 MAZDA Miata

MAZDA — Millenia

2000 MAZDA Millenia S

The Millenia is the ultimate, top-end model of the Mazda choice range. It's available in the base model, powered by a 2.5L V6 borrowed to the 626, or S models driven by a Miller cycle engine.

PROS
- **The classic and elegant** body design that is also aerodynamic.
- **Engine performance** with the Miller cycle engine are sensational, considering displacement and engine weight.
- **The suspension** on the base model is smoother than on the S model.
- **Seats** are well-designed and soundproofing is effective.
- **Handling** is good, so there isn't much body movement and steering is quick, crisp and benefits from a good reduction ratio.
- **Equipment** is more than complete, for the only options are leather trim seats and sunroof.
- **The unusually deep trunk** is huge, but it can't be extended because the rear seatbench doesn't fold down.

CONS
- **This is a pricy car**, insurance isn't cheap and gas consumption isn't terribly economical.
- **The 2.5L V6 engine** from the 626 model isn't too frisky, for it has to carry an extra 216 kg, which affects power to weight ratio.
- **Brakes** aren't powerful enough for such muscular engines, and stops are longer than average.
- **The front suspension** on the S model is stiff and is crippled by poor wheel travel.
- **The futuristic cabin** interior design doesn't quite jive with the classic body design.
- **Rear seats** are tight, there isn't much head room or leg room and a third passenger would be pretty uncomfortable (and unwelcome).
- **There really** isn't enough storage space in the cabin, for the glove compartment has been replaced by the center console compartment.

CONCLUSION
Only the later Millenias are recommended as used cars, as long as mileage is low, and it's a good idea to avoid the engine on the 626 because it's less pleasant to drive.

RECALLS
None over this period.

Millenia — MAZDA

RELIABILITY PROBLEMS

	1996	1997	1998	1999	2000	2001
Engine:	X	X	X	X	-	-
Transmission:	-	-	-	-	-	-
Suspension:	-	X	X	X	X	-
Steering:	X	-	-	X	-	-
Brakes:	-	X	X	X	-	-
Electricity:	-	-	X	X	X	X
Body:	-	-	X	X	-	-
Accessories:	X	-	X	X	X	X
Fit/finish:	-	-	X	-	-	-

POWERTRAIN

Year	Type/ L/Camshaft/bhp	Drivetrain & gearbox
96-01	V6/2.5/DOHC/170	front-A4
	V6C/2.3/DOHC/210	front-A4

PERFORMANCE

Acceler. 0/100 sec.	Top. speed km/h	Ave. Fuel consp. l./100 km
10.2	200	12.2
8.2	220	12.2

SPECIFICATIONS

Model 96-01	Wlb. mm	Lght. mm	Cb.wt kg	Brakes fr/rr	Steering type	Standard tires
sdn. 4dr. base	2750	4820	1470	dc/ABS	pwr.r&p.	215/55R16
sdn. 4dr. S/ED	2750	4820	1522	dc/ABS	pwr.r&p.	215/50R17

PRICES

Model / version		1996	1997	1998	1999	2000	2001
sdn. 4dr. base	mini	11000	14500	17850	20800		
	maxi	14100	17300	20800	23600		
sdn. 4dr. S	mini	12600	16600	20500	23100	23600	28300
	maxi	15650	19400	22900	25700	26800	32000
sdn. 4dr. Mill. Ed.	mini					25700	
	maxi					28900	

See page 7 to adapt these figures.

2000 MAZDA Millenia S

MAZDA — MPV rwd

1996 MAZDA MPV RWD

The Mazda MPV 2WD made its debut in 1988 and one year later, the all-wheel drive came out of the factory. They're powered until '95 by a 2.6L 4-cylinder engine or a 3.0L V8. The MPV has not been actively commercialized in 1999 because its expected front wheel-drive replacement with dual sliding doors only hit the market very late in the season and is considered a Y2K model.

PROS

- **Its body design** is more that of a station wagon than a sport utility vehicle. It's too bad the latest model design was ruined with all those weird add-ons.
- **The suspension** is smoother than that of the competition for it provides for handling akin to that of a car.
- **The cockpit** is well designed, the instrument panel is straightforward, visibility is great and the automatic shifter is easy to control.
- **Construction quality** explains the excessive weight and fit. The finish is meticulous, even if some trim components look rather plain.
- **Practical touches**: the fourth door on the latest models, the numerous storage compartments and the rear windows that can be lowered.

CONS

- **For winter driving**, the all-wheel drive model is safer than the less predictable rear-wheel drive model.
- **Brakes** don't have enough grip, for stops are too long and they aren't predictable without ABS.
- **Gas consumption** is sky-high, especially on the 4X4, especially given that engine performance aren't anything out of the ordinary.
- **The side door** doesn't slide open and takes up more room.
- **Maneuverability** is crippled by too high a reduction ratio and too big a steer angle diameter.
- **These cars** aren't too reliable and repairs can be quite pricy.
- **Seats are hard** and don't provide much support, the elbowrests aren't adjustable height-wise up front. The main and rear seatbenches are hard to handle.

CONCLUSION

The MPV is more of a station wagon than a minivan and isn't the best used car to buy.

RECALLS

None over this period.

MPV rwd — MAZDA

RELIABILITY PROBLEMS

	1996	1997	1998	1999	2000	2001
Engine:	-	X	X			
Transmission:	X	-	-			
Suspension:	-	X	-			
Steering:	-	X	-			
Brakes:	X	-	X			
Electricity:	-	X	-			
Body:	-	-	-			
Accessories:	X	-	-			
Fit/finish:	-	-	X			

POWERTRAIN

Year	Type/ L/Camshaft/bhp	Drivetrain & gearbox	Acceler. 0/100 sec.	Top. speed km/h	Ave. Fuel consp. l./100 km
96-98	V6/3.0/SOHC/150-155	rear-A4	11.0	170	14.7
		rear/all-A4	11.8	165	17.0

SPECIFICATIONS

Model 96-98	Wlb. mm	Lght. mm	Cb.wt kg	Brakes fr/rr	Steering type	Standard tires
m.v. 4dr. base	2805	4660	1692	dc/ABS	pwr.r&p.	195/75R15
m.v. 4dr. LX	2805	4660	1719	dc/ABS	pwr.r&p.	215/65R15
m.v. 4dr. LX 4RM	2805	4660	1842	dc/ABS	pwr.r&p.	225/70R15

PRICES

Model / version		1996	1997	1998	1999	2000	2001
m.v. 4dr. 7 st. V6	mini	6300	7650	9450			
	maxi	8400	9650	11550			
m.v. 4dr. 7 st. LX	mini	8200	9650	11550			
	maxi	10500	11850	13650			
m.v. 4dr. 7 st. V6	mini	9650	13350	14400			
LX 4WD	maxi	12000	14700	16600			

See page 7 to adapt these figures.

1996 MAZDA MPV RWD

MAZDA   MPV fwd

2000 MAZDA MPV FWD

It took Mazda quite some time to replace its rear-wheel drive MPV with a front-wheel drive model. The newcomer is more modern and powered by a 2.5-liter V6 engine borrowed from Ford.

PROS
- **The styling** is exciting and in keeping with the philosophy recently adopted by Mazda.
- **Passenger room** has increased, the seats are roomy and passengers do not feel cramped.
- **The dashboard** is simple, highly functional and its ergonomic design is remarkable, because all controls are within easy reach.
- **The seat organization** is very clever: the rear bench folds into the floor where it can be used as a storage bin. Also, the middle seats slide to the sides to form a bench and can be moved to the rear to nestle passengers under the hatch.
- **The ride** is pleasant thanks to the excellent position of the steering wheel, good visibility and the very practical handbrake.
- **The power windows** on the sliding doors are a rare feature in the minivan world.

CONS
- **The poor weight/power ratio** translates into inadequate performance levels.
- **The firmly padded** and relatively flat seats are uncomfortable and offer very little in terms of support.
- **Access** to the cabin is hindered by front doors that do not open up wide enough and sliding doors that are too narrow.
- **The engine** consumes as much fuel as a larger V6.
- **The base model** takes the bare-bones approach, which may make it difficult to resell.
- **Flaws**: the high rear ratio, the impractical gear shift lever, the fixed hatch window and the minimal number of storage spaces available to middle-seat passengers.

CONCLUSION
The latest MPV is more universal than its predecessor, but its engine is clearly marginal and its seats are uncomfortable.

RECALLS
2000 The tire pressure information is incorrect on the label and the tires too. Both will be replaced on some vehicles.
On some vehicles the Powertrain Control Module will be reprogrammed.
The rear-door childproof locking doesn't work properly and will be modified.
The lower intake manifold doesn't match the fuel injectors and will be replaced.

MPV fwd — MAZDA

RELIABILITY PROBLEMS

	1996	1997	1998	1999	2000	2001
Engine:					X	X
Transmission:					-	-
Suspension:					-	-
Steering:					-	-
Brakes:					X	-
Electricity:					X	X
Body:					-	-
Accessories:					X	-
Fit/finish:					-	-

POWERTRAIN

Year	Type/ L/Camshaft/bhp	Drivetrain & gearbox
00-01	V6/2.5/DOHC/170	front-A4

PERFORMANCE

Acceler. 0/100 sec.	Top. speed km/h	Ave. Fuel consp. l./100 km
12.0	180	13.5

SPECIFICATIONS

Model 00-01	Wlb. mm	Lght. mm	Cb.wt kg	Brakes fr/rr	Steering type	Standard tires
m.v. 4dr.	2840	4750	1665	dc/dr	pwr.r&p.	205/65R15

PRICES

Model / version		1996	1997	1998	1999	2000	2001
m.v. 4dr. 7st. DX	mini					16300	20150
	maxi					19100	23600
m.v. 4dr. 7st. LX	mini					19400	23400
	maxi					22250	26800
m.v. 4dr. 7st. ES	mini					22800	26600
	maxi					26100	29900

See page 7 to adapt these figures.

2000 MAZDA MPV FWD

MAZDA — MX-3 Precidia

1996 MAZDA MX-3

In 1992, the MX-3, a small sports coupe inspired by the 323, was put on the market. It's powered either by a 1.6L 4-cylinder or by the smallest V6 engine available, a 1.8L.

PROS
- **Its stocky**, thickset look is very much like that of the Honda CRX that was prematurely taken off the market.
- **The V6 engine** runs smoothly and quietly.
- **The car is stable** with such a solid frame and good shock absorbers, so there isn't much sway and understeering is predictable and can be easily controlled.
- **Steering** on the GS model is quicker and more accurate than that on the base model that is too vague, since it suffers from too high a reduction ratio.
- **The rear seat** area is very roomy, much more so than on several other coupes that really look bigger.

CONS
- **Brakes** aren't great and don't have much lasting power, achieving long and unpredictable stops, and ABS only comes as an option.
- **Engines performance** are only fair to middling with such a heavy engine and the V6 doesn't have much torque under 4000 rpm.
- **The V6 may** be an innovative engine model but it's far from economical with the automatic.
- **Rear seat access** is tricky because of low roof clearance, but the nicely shaped doors help a bit.
- **The cabin design** is very plain, equipment on the base model is at a bare minimum, since it doesn't include an airbag, not even as an option.

CONCLUSION
This small sports coupe with 4-cylinder engine has been very popular with the ladies, but the gents prefer the more innovative V6 engine.

RECALLS
1996 Alternator may short-circuit and cause a fire. (V6 engine)

MX-3 Precidia   MAZDA

RELIABILITY PROBLEMS

	1996	1997	1998	1999	2000	2001
Engine:	-					
Transmission:	-					
Suspension:	-					
Steering:	-					
Brakes:	X					
Electricity:	-					
Body:	-					
Accessories:	X					
Fit/finish:	-					

POWERTRAIN

Year	Type/ L/Camshaft/bhp	Drivetrain & gearbox
1996	L4/1.6/DOHC/105	front-M5
		front-A4
	V6/1.8/DOHC/128-130	front-M5
		front-A4

PERFORMANCE

Acceler. 0/100 sec.	Top. speed km/h	Ave. Fuel consp. l./100 km
9.8	175	8.5
11.0	170	9.5
8.7	195	10.0
10.0	180	11.0

SPECIFICATIONS

Model 1996	Wlb. mm	Lght. mm	Cb.wt kg	Brakes fr/rr	Steering type	Standard tires
cpe. 3dr. RS	2455	4208	1062	dc/dr	pwr.r&p.	185/65R14
cpe. 3dr. GS	2455	4208	1151	dc/dc	pwr.r&p.	205/55R15

PRICES

Model / version		1996	1997	1998	1999	2000	2001
cpe. 3dr. RS	mini	7550					
	maxi	9450					
cpe. 3dr. GS V6	mini	9450					
	maxi	11550					

See page 7 to adapt these figures.

1996 MAZDA MX-3

MAZDA   Protegé

1999 MAZDA Protegé

These small front-wheel drive subcompact and compact cars replaced the GLC models in 1989 and got a face-lift in 1995. In 1999, Mazda has completely revamped its body design, improved the suspension, brought 14-in. wheels on all models, enhanced the capabilities of the two engines (DOHC) and updated the automatic transmission. All of this to make sure the Protegé remains the most popular Mazda sold in North America.

PROS
• **Vehicle size** is well distributed, for the cabin is one of the most spacious in this car category.

• **Handling** is clean with such a long wheel base, good-quality tires and shock absorbers. Handling on the Protegé LX is even more stable on curves because of a stiffer suspension.

• **Engines** are powerful and run smoothly, especially the last generation DOHC engines which are quite economical.

• **The shifter** is well-calibrated, especially on the sports models, and it's clean and smooth.

• **Really comfortable** cars with nicely contoured, thick seats and smooth suspension.

• **Wide choice** of car sizes, finish levels, engines and transmissions.

• **Remarkably reliable**, but bodywork is prone to rust.

CONS
• **Brakes** lack grip on sudden stops, that are long (except on the models equipped with 4-disc brakes) and without ABS, there's almost immediate wheel lock.

• **There's a lot** of constant noise, for the body is poorly soundproofed and the engines are very boisterous.

• **The cabin interior** is terribly bleak for everything is a dreary gray.

• **The rear seatbench** on base model is flat and hard and very uncomfortable.

CONCLUSION
The Protegé are practical and fun to drive and they're quite economical to run and they're both elegant and dependable.

RECALLS
1999 Possible short circuit in the audio system.

Protegé — MAZDA

RELIABILITY PROBLEMS

	1996	1997	1998	1999	2000	2001
Engine:	X	X	X	-	-	-
Transmission:	-	-	-	-	X	-
Suspension:	-	-	-	-	-	-
Steering:	-	-	-	-	-	-
Brakes:	-	-	-	X	-	-
Electricity:	-	-	-	X	-	-
Body:	X	X	-	X	X	-
Accessories:	X	-	-	X	X	X
Fit/finish:	-	-	-	-	-	-

POWERTRAIN

Year	Type/ L/Camshaft/bhp	Drivetrain & gearbox
97-98	L4/1.5/DOHC/92	front-M5
		front-A4
96-98	L4/1.8/DOHC/122-125	front-M5
1996	L4/1.6/SOHC/82	front-M5
		front-A4
	L4/1.8/SOHC/103	front-M5
		front-A4
99-01	L4/1.6/DOHC/105	front-M5
		front-A4
	L4/1.8/DOHC/122	front-M5
		front-A4

PERFORMANCE

Acceler. 0/100 sec.	Top. speed km/h	Ave. Fuel consp. l./100 km
11.0	165	7.7
12.3	160	9.1
8.5	190	10.5
11.0	170	8.0
12.5	165	8.5
9.0	180	9.0
10.5	175	9.5
11.6	175	8.5
13.5	165	9.3
10.5	190	8.9
12.6	175	9.7

SPECIFICATIONS

Model	Wlb.	Lght.	Cb.wt	Brakes	Steering	Standard
Protegé 96-98						
sdn. 4dr. SE/S	2605	4440	1145	dc/dc	pwr.r&p.	185/65R14
sdn. 4dr. LX	2605	4440	1145	dc/dc	pwr.r&p.	185/65R14
Protegé 99-01						
sdn. 4dr.DX/LX/SE	2610	4420	1105	dc/dr	pwr.r&p.	185/65R14

PRICES

Model / version		1996	1997	1998	1999	2000	2001
sdn. 4dr. DX	mini				10500	12300	
	maxi				12300	14400	
sdn. 4dr. LX	mini	6800	7900	9750	12100	14400	15900
	maxi	8600	9750	11550	13850	16500	18700
sdn. 4dr. SE	mini	5800	6800	8600	11000	13300	14900
	maxi	7350	8700	10500	12800	15400	17650
sdn. 4dr. ES	mini						17100
	maxi						19850

See page 7 to adapt these figures.

1999 MAZDA Protegé

MAZDA 626 / MX-6

1998 MAZDA 626 LX V6

First launched in 1988, they got a face-lift in '93 and a new 2.5L V6 engine, and later in 1998.

PROS
- **Wide choice** of body designs, mechanical features and trim levels for both the sedans and the coupes.
- **All engines are powerful**, whether it be the conventional 4-cylinder model or the V6 which is undoubtedly one of the best in its generation.
- **The slick rear suspension** eliminates sway and provides for neutral road stability.
- **The cabin** is nice and roomy, seats are comfy (except on the DX) and noise level is very tolerable at cruising speed.
- **Fit and finish** are clean as a whistle and construction quality is really top-notch.

CONS
- **The anonymous body design** which does not stand out compared to its rivals.
- **Older models** aren't too reliable and must be thoroughly inspected before purchase.
- **The unsettling performance** of the 4-cylinder engine loses its appeal with the automatic transmission.
- **Brakes** aren't wonderful and gas consumption with the V6 on the latest generation is terribly high.
- **The stiff suspension** on the 626 and MX-6 is harsh when it hits bumps.
- **Cabin design** is bland, controls are inconveniently located and equipment is pretty plain and simple on base models.

CONCLUSION
The Mazda 626 and MX-6 models are good cars, they're nice and stable on the road, but they're terribly unreliable, which is a real problem.

RECALLS
96-97 Minor undercarriage impacts can result in unnecessary airbag deployment.
Defective fuel cap that allows fuel vapor to leak from the pipe.
1997 Engine may stall if a spring in the tensioner breaks.
1998 Powertrain control module is not properly programmed.
1999 Possible condensation entering the audio unit and causing a short circuit. Aluminum tape must be affixed over the audio unit to prevent water from entering.
2000 The brake master cylinder cap doesn't have ventilation hole.

626 / MX-6 — MAZDA

RELIABILITY PROBLEMS

	1996	1997	1998	1999	2000	2001
Engine:	-	X	X	X	-	-
Transmission:	-	-	X	X	-	-
Suspension:	X	X	X	X	-	-
Steering:	-	X	X	X	-	-
Brakes:	-	-	X	X	X	X
Electricity:	X	X	-	-	X	X
Body:	-	X	X	X	X	-
Accessories:	X	-	-	X	X	-
Fit/finish:	-	-	-	-	-	-

POWERTRAIN

Year	Type/ L/Camshaft/bhp	Drivetrain & gearbox
96-01	L4/2.0/DOHC/114-125	front-M5
		front-A4
	V6/2.5/DOHC/164-170	front-M5
		front-A4

PERFORMANCE

Acceler. 0/100 sec.	Top. speed km/h	Ave. Fuel consp. l./100 km
10.0	180	9.0
12.2	175	10.7
8.0	210	11.7
10.4	200	12.2

SPECIFICATIONS

Model	Wlb. mm	Lght. mm	Cb.wt kg	Brakes fr/rr	Steering type	Standard tires
626 96-97						
sdn. 4dr. SE	2610	4685	1247	dc/dr	pwr.r&p.	195/70SR14
sdn. 4dr. ES	2610	4685	1315	dc/ABS	pwr.r&p.	205/55VR15
MX-6 96-97						
cpe. 2dr. RS	2610	4615	1190	dc/dr	pwr.r&p.	195/65R14
cpe. 2dr. LS	2610	4615	1270	dc/dc	pwr.r&p.	205/55R15
98-01						
sdn. 4dr. DX/LX	2670	4745	1269	dc/dr	pwr.r&p.	185/70R14
sdn. 4dr. ES	2670	4745	1358	dc/ABS	pwr.r&p.	205/60R15

PRICES

Model / version		1996	1997	1998	1999	2000	2001
626							
sdn. 4dr. DX	mini	6700	8400	10300	12100		
	maxi	8800	10500	12600	14200		
sdn. 4dr. LX	mini	7750	9450	11550	13300	15400	18150
	maxi	9850	11550	13650	15200	17850	21000
sdn. 4dr. ES V6	mini	9450	11000	13100	15400	17500	19700
	maxi	11550	13100	15200	17300	19950	22600
sdn. 4dr. LX V6	mini	11000	12600	14700	17500	19600	23950
	maxi	13000	14700	16800	19400	22000	25700
MX-6							
cpe. 2dr. RS	mini	10500	12600				
	maxi	12600	14700				
cpe. 2dr. LS V6	mini	12500	14700				
	maxi	14700	16800				

See page 7 to adapt these figures.

2000 MAZDA 626

MAZDA — Tribute

2001 MAZDA Tribute

The Tribute is the Ford Escape's twin brother. They differ only with respect to a few presentation and equipment details.

PROS

- **The compact size** is current and practical, and the youthful styling is highly successful within the otherwise very conservative lineup.
- **The Tribute handles** as safely as a car, to the great delight of female drivers.
- **The overall comfort** level is quite adequate for a utility vehicle, thanks to efficient seats and soundproofing.
- **The brakes** are powerful and easy to modulate. Stops are short and straight, even without ABS.
- **The V6** cranks out honorable performance levels, and output is quite reasonable under load.
- The simple and efficient **all-wheel traction system** requires no driver intervention.
- **The Tribute's off-road capabilities** are adequate to allow it to travel over quite hilly terrain, but it's not a real 4x4.
- **The powerful headlights** provide good visibility even in poor weather.

CONS

- **The 4-cylinder's** limited performance is adequate only with front-wheel drive and the manual transmission.
- **Rear-seat roominess** is limited. Indeed, rear accessibility and legroom are at a premium.
- **The standard tires** are of poor quality because their provide mediocre grip even on dry roads.
- **The suspension** reacts harshly on poor roads where the occupants get jostled around without mercy.
- **Ford's plastics look very cheap** and give the dashboard a very utilitarian look to it.
- **The windshield wipers** operate too slowly to ensure adequate visibility in rainy conditions.

VERDICT
The Tribute is a more luxurious version of the Ford Escape, which explains its popularity with female buyers.

RECALLS
None over this period.

MAZDA — Tribute

RELIABILITY PROBLEMS

	1996	1997	1998	1999	2000	2001
Engine:						
Transmission:						
Suspension:						
Steering:						
Brakes:			Insufficient data			
Electricity:						
Body:						
Accessories:						
Fit/finish:						

POWERTRAIN / PERFORMANCE

Year	Type/ L/Camshaft/bhp	Drivetrain & gearbox	Acceler. 0/100 sec.	Top. speed km/h	Ave. Fuel consp. l./100 km
2001	L4/2.0/SOHC/125	ft./all-M5	12.0	160	10.0
	V6/3.0/OHV/200	ft./all-A4	10.0	175	13.0

SPECIFICATIONS

Model 2001	Wlb. mm	Lght. mm	Cb.wt kg	Brakes fr/rr	Steering type	Standard tires
wgn. 4dr. 4x2	2620	4395	1402	dc/dr	pwr.r.&p.	225/70R15
wgn. 4dr. 4x4	2620	4395	1567	dc/dr	pwr.r.&p.	235/70R15

PRICES

Model / version	1996	1997	1998	1999	2000	2001
wgn. 4dr. DX 4cyl. mini						20500
AWD maxi						23100
wgn. 4dr. DX V6 mini						21800
maxi						32000
wgn. 4dr. LX V6 mini						25000
AWD maxi						27800
wgn. 4dr. ES V6 mini						28000
AWD maxi						31000

See page 7 to adapt these figures.

2001 MAZDA Tribute

MERCEDES-BENZ   C Class

1998 MERCEDES-BENZ C230 Classic

The C-Class was first sold in 1984 and is the entry-level Mercedes model range. These cars are powered by 4 and 6-cylinder gas engines and also by the latest 2.8L V6. Since '99, the lineup has been given a compressed 2.3L and, finally, a 4.3L V8 to power the exciting C43 AMG.

PROS
- **Good resale value** because they're solidly built, fit and finish are clean, and trim components are attractive.
- **C-Class cars handle** beautifully and are quite insensitive to crosswinds, because they come equipped with very sophisticated suspensions that stabilize the vehicles in most situations.
- **The 6-cylinder** engine is more skittish and is more economical because of a better power to weight ratio and because of smoother functioning. Engine performance on the C36 and the C43 with its V8 are like those of a big, exotic touring car.
- **Brakes** are smooth and effective, achieving short, straight stops.
- **The cockpit** is adequate in spite of the large steering wheel which still isn't adjustable.
- **Steering** is smooth and precise and makes for superb maneuverability, even with a slightly high reduction ratio.
- **The instrument panel** is well-designed, gauges are easy to read, controls are within easy reach, though a few of them are unusual and outward view is simply perfect.
- **The suspension** handles bumps and such smoothly and the seats provide adequate support.

CONS
- **This is an expensive** car, it costs a bundle, insurance premiums aren't cheap and running and maintaining this baby can be pretty costly...
- **Gas consumption** is high.
- **The rear seat area** is cramped, there isn't much leg room and access isn't great with the narrow doors.
- **Trunk size** is good, but it's impossible to store large items because of its small opening.

CONCLUSION
C-Class Mercedes cars are fun to drive, they're reliable, luxurious and comfy, but they take a bit out of your pocketbook. Nevertheless, they're a blue chip investment.

RECALLS
2001 Headlamp function will be checked and incorrect Signal Acquisition Active Module unit will be replaced.

C Class — MERCEDES-BENZ

RELIABILITY PROBLEMS

	1996	1997	1998	1999	2000	2001
Engine:	-	X	-	-	-	X
Transmission:	X	-	X	X	X	-
Suspension:	-	-	-	-	-	-
Steering:	-	-	-	-	-	-
Brakes:	X	X	X	X	X	X
Electricity:	-	-	-	X	-	-
Body:	-	-	-	X	X	-
Accessories:	X	X	X	X	X	X
Fit/finish:	-	-	-	-	-	-

POWERTRAIN / PERFORMANCE

Year	Type/ L/Camshaft/bhp	Drivetrain & gearbox	Acceler. 0/100 sec.	Top. speed km/h	Ave. Fuel consp. l./100 km
96-00	L4/2.2/DOHC/147	rear-A4	10.5	210	11.0
96-97	L6/2.8/DOHC/162	rear-A4	9.0	230	12.0
	L6/3.6/DOHC/268	rear-A4	7.0	250	13.3
1998	V6/2.8/SOHC/194	rear-A5	8.2	210	11.8
99-01	L4C/2.3/DOHC/185	rear-A5	NA	NA	NA
	V6/2.8/SOHC/194	rear-A5	8.2	210	11.8
	V8/4.3/SOHC/302	rear-A5	NA	NA	NA
2001	V6/2.6/SOHC/168	rear-A5	10.7	220	12.3
	V6/3.2/SOHC/215	rear-A5	8.2	220	12.9

SPECIFICATIONS

Model	Wlb. mm	Lght. mm	Cb.wt kg	Brakes fr/rr	Steering type	Standard tires
sdn. 4dr. Diesel	2665	4447	1345	dc/dc	pwr.bal.	185/65R15
sdn. 4dr. 2.2	2665	4447	1315	dc/ABS	pwr.bal.	185/65R15
sdn. 4dr. 2.6	2665	4447	1370	dc/ABS	pwr.bal.	185/65R15
sdn. 4dr. 2.2/2.3	2690	4507	1474	dc/ABS	pwr.bal.	205/60R15
sdn. 4dr. 2.8	2690	4507	1504	dc/ABS	pwr.bal.	205/60R15
sdn. 4dr. 3.6/4.3	2690	4507	1610	dc/ABS	pwr.bal.	225/45ZR17 245/40ZR17
2001						
sdn. 4dr. C240	2715	4528	1524	dc/ABS	pwr.r.&p.	205/55R16
sdn. 4dr. C320	2715	4528	1585	dc/ABS	pwr.r.&p.	205/55R16

PRICES

Model / version		1996	1997	1998	1999	2000	2001
sdn. 4dr. C280	mini			30450	35700	39900	
	maxi			33900	39000	43000	
sdn. 4dr. C230 Sport	mini				31100	33800	
	maxi				34400	37800	
sdn. 4dr. C220	mini	18700					
	maxi	22000					
sdn. 4dr. C220 SE	mini	14700					
	maxi	18000					
sdn. 4dr. C280	mini	23800	27200	29400	35900	38800	
	maxi	27300	30650	32500	39400	42700	
sdn. 4dr. C36	mini	33000	40750				
	maxi	37000	44700				
sdn. 4dr. 230 SE	mini	17850					
	maxi	24500					
sdn. 4dr. 230	mini	22600					
	maxi	26000					
sdn. 4dr. Classic C230	mini			19100	24900	29100	
	maxi			22700	28400	33100	
sdn. 4dr. Elegance C230	mini			24100	29900	34100	
	maxi			27700	33400	38000	
sdn. 4dr. C43 AMG	mini				45100		
	maxi				48300		
sdn. 4dr. CLS240	mini						33600
	maxi						37800
sdn. 4dr. C240 ELG	mini						37800
	maxi						44100
sdn. 4dr. C240	mini						41000
	maxi						47200
sdn. 4dr. C320	mini						45100
	maxi						51450
sdn. 4dr. 320 Sport	mini						47200
	maxi						52500

See page 7 to adapt these figures.

MERCEDES-BENZ　　　　CLK Class

2000 MERCEDES-BENZ CLK430

The CLK coupe is a spin-off of the C-Class platform. It was launched in 1997 and is equipped with a 3.2L V6 engine. Later in 1999, it got the brand new 4.3L V8 to inspire a newcomer in the serie, the CLK 430. Since 1999, the CLK is available in two body style, a 2-door coupe and convertible.

PROS

- **The car's gorgeous style** is proof that a car can be elegant and compact as well.
- **The overall value** for your buck makes it an interesting alternative to some coupes that are a lot pricier.
- **Active and passive** safety features are the feather in the cap of this car manufacturer.
- **Zippy performance** with the initial V6 that had never been put on the market by the builder yield awesome accelerations and pick-up without overly straining mechanical components.
- **Driving pleasure** derives from super overall balanced demeanor and from this coupe's dual personality that can be comfy or sporty, depending on the driver's whim.
- **The trunk** is unusually spacious for a model of this type. Besides, it can be extended towards the cabin and includes a ski-sized passthrough.

CONS

- **The constantly** pervasive high noise level doesn't jive with the lavish character of this model and exhaust noise isn't anything to write home about.
- **Steering** suffers from a poor reduction ratio, so lively, moves are tricky due to lack of accuracy in this department.
- **The rear seats** aren't any more roomy than inside the C-Class and upholstery is really too firm.
- **Vehicle stability** is sometimes jeopardized by wind and road surface conditions, so the awful sway effect can only be due to poor tire quality.
- **Storage spots** are few and far between and the glove and console compartments are tiny.
- **Power windows** are annoyingly slow to function and headlights are less than up to par on low beam.

CONCLUSION

The CLK coupe has assets that will convince parents whose children have left home to exchange their minivan for this wee gem that will put new zest into their life...

RECALLS

1998 Front seat belt shoulder anchor bolts must be reinforced.

CLK Class — MERCEDES-BENZ

RELIABILITY PROBLEMS

	1996	1997	1998	1999	2000	2001
Engine:			X	X	X	X
Transmission:			-	-	-	-
Suspension:			-	-	-	-
Steering:			X	-	-	-
Brakes:			X	X	X	-
Electricity:			X	X	X	X
Body:			-	-	X	X
Accessories:			X	X	X	X
Fit/finish:			-	-	-	-

POWERTRAIN

Year	Type/ L/Camshaft/bhp	Drivetrain & gearbox
98-01	V6/3.2/SOHC/215	rear-A5
99-01	V8/4.3/SOHC/275	rear-A5
2001	V8/5.5/SOHC/342 AMG	rear-A5

PERFORMANCE

Acceler. 0/100 sec.	Top speed km/h	Ave. Fuel consp. l./100 km
7.8	210	11.2
7.0	210	11.0
6.0	250	13.5

SPECIFICATIONS

Model	Wlb. mm	Lght. mm	Cb.wt kg	Brakes fr/rr	Steering type	Standard tires
98-01						
cpe. 2dr. (320)	2690	4577	1470	dc/ABS	pwr.bal.	205/55R16
99-01						
con. 2dr.	2690	4577	1618	dc/ABS	pwr.bal.	205/55R16
cpe. 2dr. (430)	2690	4577	1525	dc/ABS	pwr.bal.	225/45ZR17 245/40ZR17
2001						
cpe. 2dr. 55AMG	2690	4577	1562	dc/ABS	pwr.bal.	225/45R17 245/45R17

PRICES

Model / version		1996	1997	1998	1999	2000	2001
cpe. 2dr. 320	mini			33600	39600	42700	52500
	maxi			38300	44600	47800	57700
cpe. 2dr. 430	mini				46900	50600	57700
	maxi				52000	55650	63000
con. 2dr. 320	mini				46200	49550	55650
	maxi				50400	54600	60900
con. 2dr. 430	mini					56300	61900
	maxi					60900	66100
con. 2dr. 55	mini						65100
	maxi						70300

See page 7 to adapt these figures.

2000 MERCEDES-BENZ CLK

MERCEDES-BENZ   E Class

1998 MERCEDES-BENZ E 430

The E-Class sedan hails back to 1984, the TD station wagon came out in 86, all-wheel drive models in 90 and V8 engines in 92. The latest generation cars were first available in 1996. In '99, the 4.2L has been traded for an improved 4.3L and air curtains that offset head injuries now come standard on all the E sedans.

PROS

- **Construction quality**, components and fit and finish are among the best in this car category.
- **Handling** is a cut above, for these cars are stable, neutral and very safe at all times.
- **Gas engine** performance is terrific, allowing for Sportscar zip and zoom.
- **Steering** is almost perfect, even with the huge steering wheel.
- **The appealing body** design of the latest models is also quite aerodynamically efficient.
- **The instrument panel** is loaded and gauges are very easy to read, and outward view is just great.
- **Power brakes** are muscular, well-calibrated and smooth, but they're quite over-assisted.
- **The cabin is spacious** and comfortable, the suspension is well-adjusted and noise level is low at cruising speed.
- **There are lots of storage** compartments in the cabin interior and there's easy access to the huge trunk.

CONS

- **These cars** don't come cheap, they're expensive to buy and upkeep, and fuel consumption on gas engine models are costly.
- **The Diesel engine** is economical but not worth the hassles (wimpy power, noise and a lot of shake, rattle and roll).
- **Some items** need to be improved on older models, for example, the non-adjustable steering column and some inconveniently located controls.
- **Rearward view** at quarterback isn't great because of the thickness of the C-pillar.

CONCLUSION

The E-Class is without a doubt the most practical Mercedes model range, both for size and for overall performance.

RECALLS

1999 Defective window bag that may not fully deploy in the event of a side impact collision.

E Class — MERCEDES-BENZ

RELIABILITY PROBLEMS

	1996	1997	1998	1999	2000	2001
Engine:	X	X	X	X	X	-
Transmission:	X	X	X	X	-	-
Suspension:	-	X	X	X	X	X
Steering:	-	-	-	-	-	-
Brakes:	X	-	-	-	-	-
Electricity:	-	X	X	X	X	X
Body:	-	-	-	-	-	-
Accessories:	-	-	X	X	X	X
Fit/finish:	-	-	-	-	-	-

POWERTRAIN

Year	Type/ L/Camshaft/bhp	Drivetrain & gearbox
96-98	L6D/3.0/DOHC/134	rear-A4
	L6/3.2/DOHC/217	rear-A4
	V8/4.2/DOHC/275	rear-A4
99-01	L6TD/3.0/DOHC/174	rear-A5
	V6/3.2/SOHC/221	rear-A5
		all-A5
	V8/4.3/DOHC/275	rear-A5
2001	V8/5.5/DOHC/349 AMG	rear-A5

PERFORMANCE

Acceler. 0/100 sec.	Top speed km/h	Ave. Fuel consp. l./100 km
12.5	205	8.5
8.2	210	12.4
7.5	210	13.3
9.0	210	8.9
7.5	210	11.3
7.8	210	11.8
6.5	210	15.2
6.0	250	13.6

SPECIFICATIONS

Model 96-01	Wlb.	Lght.	Cb.wt	Brakes	Steering	Standard
sdn. 4dr. E300D	2833	4810	1605	dc/ABS	pwr.r&p.	215/55R16
sdn. 4dr. E320	2833	4810	1570	dc/ABS	pwr.r&p.	215/55R16
wag.4dr. E320 AWD	2833	4825	1755	dc/ABS	pwr.r&p.	215/55R16
sdn.4dr. E320/ 430	2833	4810	1715	dc/ABS	pwr.r&p.	215/55R16
ber. 4 p. 55 AMG	2833	4810	1649	d/ABS	crém.ass.	275/35R18

PRICES

Model / version		1996	1997	1998	1999	2000	2001
sdn. 4dr. E320	mini	28800	34900				
	maxi	32750	38850				
sdn. 4dr. 300D	mini	21600	28650				
	maxi	25500	32550				
sdn. 4dr. E420	mini		41200				
	maxi		45350				
sdn. 4dr. 300 TD	mini			29400	35700		
	maxi			33500	39500		
sdn. 4dr. 320W	mini			35000	40300	46100	51500
	maxi			38850	44000	50400	56700
sdn. 4dr. 4Matic	mini			38300	43450	49250	54600
	maxi			42000	47100	53500	59900
sdn. 4dr. E430W	mini			43000	49350	55200	65100
	maxi			47000	53100	59850	77700
sdn. 4dr.E430	mini						69300
4Matic	maxi						80800
sdn. 4dr. E55	mini				61100	70200	77700
	maxi				64800	74500	83000
wgn. 4dr. E320 S	mini			36200	41350	47100	53500
	maxi			40100	45100	51400	58800
wgn. 4dr. 4Matic	mini			39400	42400	50300	56700
	maxi			43200	48300	54600	61900

See page 7 to adapt these figures.

MERCEDES-BENZ   M Class

1999 MERCEDES-BENZ ML430

In 1998, Mercedes-Benz introduced the ML320 powered by a 3.2L V6 and one year later, the ML 430 equipped with a powerful 268-bhp 4.3L V8 and the 342-bhp 55 AMG. All-wheel drive is achieved by electronically controlled locking differentials.

PROS

- **The social status** associated with owning an affordable vehicle sporting the Stuttgart star made this model as rare as hen's teeth, at least in the first production years.
- **The style** mid-way between that of a 4X4 and a minivan created a whole new breed and the body's aerodynamic efficiency is the reason behind such economic fuel consumption for a heavy vehicle.
- **The ML320**'s appealing value explains why new or used models are hard to come by and they don't come cheap either.
- **This model** behaves very much like a car, so it's unique and quite different from its rivals, due to sophisticated, state-of-the-art technical applications.
- **The vehicle format** is really neat, since it offers really airy cabin space yet it's quite compact.
- **Performance** is comparable to those of much bigger and brawnier engines, in spite of vehicle weight, namely more than 2 tons when at full load capacity. Of course, the performance of the V8 is even better and its towing capacities are way above average. The ML55 AMG is a real sports truck.
- **Ride comfort** is terrific due to the well-honed suspension, nicely contoured seats and reasonable noise interference at cruising speed.
- **Headlights** provide safe driving and the luggage cover design is really clever.

CONS

- **Some trim materials** such as the plastic components aren't up to snuff, considering the German automaker's reputation, which explains in part the fairly affordable price.
- **This vehicle** is load-sensitive and the all-wheel drive function seemed taxed on the first models.
- **The rear seatbench** is tough to get to due to the narrow doors and the complicated seat removal device is hard to decipher, in short, a real nightmare.
- **Weird features:** the control for cruise control, the location of the CD player inside the cargo, hold and missing shifter position indicator on the dashboard.

CONCLUSION

Mercedes-Benz came onto the SUV stage with great assurance and poise, since the ML320 and ML 430 are equipped with some innovative handling and ride comfort features.

RECALLS

None over this period.

M Class   MERCEDES-BENZ

RELIABILITY PROBLEMS

	1996	1997	1998	1999	2000	2001
Engine:			X	X	X	X
Transmission:			X	X	-	-
Suspension:			-	-	-	-
Steering:			-	-	-	-
Brakes:			X	X	X	-
Electricity:			X	X	X	X
Body:			X	X	X	X
Accessories:			X	X	X	X
Fit/finish:			X	X	X	-

POWERTRAIN   PERFORMANCE

Year	Type/ L/Camshaft/bhp	Drivetrain & gearbox	Acceler. 0/100 sec.	Top. speed km/h	Ave. Fuel consp. l./100 km
98-01	V6/3.2/SOHC/215	rear/all-A5	9.0	180	14.0
99-01	V6/4.3/SOHC/268	rear/all-A5	7.5	200	16.0
00-01	V8/5.5/SOHC/342 AMG	rear/all-A5	6.0	240	20.0

SPECIFICATIONS

Model 98-01	Wlb. mm	Lght. mm	Cb.wt kg	Brakes fr/rr	Steering type	Standard tires
wgn. 4dr. CLassic	2820	4587	1905	dc/ABS	pwr.r&p.	255/65R16
wgn. 4dr. Elegance	2820	4587	1922	dc/ABS	pwr.r&p.	255/65R16
wgn. 4dr. ML430	2820	4587	2010	dc/ABS	pwr.r&p.	275/55R17
wgn. 4 p. M55AMG	2820	4587	2110	dc/ABS	pwr.r&p.	285/50R18

PRICES

Model / version		1996	1997	1998	1999	2000	2001
wgn. 4dr. 320 Classic	mini			26500	29400	33400	38800
	maxi			29400	32800	37300	42000
wgn. 4dr. 320 Elegance	mini			32500	36000	41100	46200
	maxi			35700	39400	45100	50400
wgn. 4dr. 430	mini				39400	44300	49300
	maxi				42700	48300	53500
wgn. 4dr. 55 AMG	mini					58800	66100
	maxi					63000	70900

See page 7 to adapt these figures.

1998 MERCEDES-BENZ ML320

MERCEDES-BENZ S Class Sedans

2000 MERCEDES-BENZ Classe S

The big S-Class cars that replaced the former models in 1992 are available in two body styles with different wheel base, and are powered by 6, 8 and 12-cylinder gas and Diesel engines. A new smaller model was inaugurated in 2000.

PROS
- **State-of-the-art gadgetry,** and such, on these cars that are among the most technically advanced vehicles on the market.
- **Safety** is more than guaranteed with such a very robust and rigid body, and dual frontal and side-mounted airbags, so you feel very safe indeed behind the wheel of such a car.
- **The V8 and V12** engines really unleash the power, considering hefty vehicle size and weight.
- **Handling** is a dream because of the sophisticated suspension, muscular brakes, clean steering and impressive road stability that really only sheer vehicle weight can sometimes affect.
- **Construction quality,** fit and finish and trim components are among the best in the world.
- **Comfort** is assured with such an airy, spacious cabin and trunk, adjustable suspension, better-designed seats and efficient soundproofing that is enhanced by the dual-pane windows, luxurious controls and accessories.
- **The Diesel** engine is more economical.

CONS
- **You're so comfy** inside this car that you can lose a feel for the road and the outside world, for that matter, so you have to remember to be careful on slippery roads.
- **This is an expensive**, upper-crust car that costs a mint and the subsequent price of insurance premium, gas, upkeep and repairs can be astronomical.
- **The 6-cylinder** engines are much less lively than the others.
- **Maneuverability and quick moves** are crippled by excessive vehicle weight and size.
- **Driving** is less fun with all the power assists and self-adjusting systems.

CONCLUSION
Mercedes S Class cars are the nec plus ultra as far as automobile technology is concerned, but they're just too plush and really too out-of-sight costly.

RECALLS
1996 Friction between the front wheels and the brake conduits might cause them to rupture.
2000 The blower motor regulator of the climate control system can be defective and replaced.

S Class Sedans — MERCEDES-BENZ

RELIABILITY PROBLEMS

	1996	1997	1998	1999	2000	2001
Engine:	-	X	X	X	X	X
Transmission:	X	-	-	-	-	-
Suspension:	-	X	-	-	-	-
Steering:	-	-	-	-	-	-
Brakes:	X	X	X	X	X	-
Electricity:	-	X	-	X	X	X
Body:	-	X	-	-	-	-
Accessories:	X	X	X	X	X	X
Fit/finish:	-	-	-	-	-	-

POWERTRAIN

Year	Type/ L/Camshaft/bhp	Drivetrain & gearbox	Acceler. 0/100 sec.	Top. speed km/h	Ave. Fuel consp. l./100 km
96-98	L6TD/3.5/SOHC/148	rear-A4-A5	13.6	180	11.0
96-99	L6/3.2/DOHC/228	rear-A4-A5	9.3	210	13.0
	V8/4.2/DOHC/275	rear-A4-A5	8.5	210	15.3
	V8/5.0/DOHC/315	rear-A4-A5	7.8	210	15.9
	V12/6.0/DOHC/389	rear-A4-A5	7.0	250	18.5
00-01	V8/4.3/SOHC/275	rear-A5	7.0	210	15.2
	V8/5.0/SOHC/302	rear-A5	6.5	210	16.0
2001	V8/5.4/SOHC/354 AMG	rear-A5	6.0	250	17.0
	V12/5.8/SOHC/362 s600	rear-A5	NA		

SPECIFICATIONS

Model 96-99	Wlb. mm	Lght. mm	Cb.wt kg	Brakes fr/rr	Steering type	Standard tires
S320/ 320V/ S350D	3040	5113	2090	dc/ABS	pwr.bal.	225/60R16
S420 / 400V	3140	5113	2150	dc/ABS	pwr.bal.	235/60R16
S500 / 500V	3140	5213	2190	dc/ABS	pwr.bal.	235/60R16
S600 / 600V	3140	5213	2310	dc/ABS	pwr.bal.	235/60R16
00-01						
sdn. 4dr. S430	2965	5038	1855	dc/ABS	pwr.r&p.	225/60R16
sdn. 4dr. S430L	3085	5158	1875	dc/ABS	pwr.r&p.	225/60R16
sdn. 4dr. S500L	3085	5158	1875	dc/ABS	pwr.r&p.	225/60R16
sdn. 4 p. S55	3086	5159	1899	dc/ABS	pwr.r&p.	275/40R18
sdn. 4 p. S600	3086	5159	2036	dc/ABS	pwr.r&p.	225/55R17

PRICES

Model / version		1996	1997	1998	1999	2000	2001
sdn. 4dr. S320	mini	34600	41500				
	maxi	38800	46000				
sdn. 4dr. 320V	mini	35700	42300	43300	48600		
	maxi	40300	46900	47700	53000		
sdn. 4dr. 320W	mini			42000	46700		
	maxi			46200	51100		
sdn. 4dr. S420	mini	42000	47700				
	maxi	46800	52800				
sdn. 4dr. 420V	mini			50700	58200		
	maxi			55800	63200		
sdn. 4dr. 430V	mini					72100	82900
	maxi					78200	88200
snd. 4dr. S430L	mini					66900	78700
	maxi					72900	85000
sdn. 4dr. S500	mini	48100	54400				
	maxi	53500	59800				
sdn. 4dr. 500V	mini			60900	66100	74300	86100
	maxi			66100	71700	80300	91300
sdn. 4dr. S55	mini						117600
	maxi						126000
sdn. 4dr. S600	mini	64600	75600				
	maxi	70300	81900				
sdn. 4dr. 600V	mini			80600	91300		122800
	maxi			86600	97100		131200

See page 7 to adapt these figures.

MERCEDES-BENZ　　　　　　　　CL-SL

2000 MERCEDES-BENZ CL500

The upper-crust SL convertible was first sold in 1990. Inspired by the S-Class model range, it's powered by a 6, 8 and 12-cylinder engine.

PROS
- **High-tech vehicle** in many respects, it's equipped with sophisticated safety features and everything is electronic when it comes to mechanical components. Safety is top-notch with such a solid structure, front and side-mounted airbags and all the electronic assists.
- **The V8 engine** and especially the V12 have incredible get up and gusto, given the outrageously excessive vehicle weight (two tons!).
- **Handling** is very safe and sure, thanks to an elaborately designed suspension, good tires and various systems, such as ABS and anti-skid system, that will keep even the worst driver from going off the road...
- **Steering** is accurate and brakes are powerful and smooth, which makes for zoomy, zesty driving.
- **Build quality**, tight finish and very spiffy trim components are what you'd expect for such an expensive car.

CONS
- **The preposterously** high price, upkeep and repairs for such a car, even used.
- **Excessive weight** really affects maneuverability and ease on curved roads and all the electronic gizmos can be frustrating for keen Sportscar drivers.
- **Pick-up** is anemic on the 320SL with its much poorer power to weight ratio than that of the 500SL and 600SL models.

CONCLUSION
The Mercedes SL convertible is the symbol par excellence of social status and so it appeals to people who place social standing above all else. So it's perfectly normal that such a ritzy car is expensive.

RECALLS
2000 The blower motor regulator of the climate control system can be defective and replaced.
2001 Heated windshield washer bottle hose will be replaced on some vehicles.

RELIABILITY PROBLEMS

	1996	1997	1998	1999	2000	2001
Engine:	X	X	X	X	X	-
Transmission:	-	-	-	-	-	-
Suspension:	-	-	-	-	-	-
Steering:	X	-	X	-	-	-
Brakes:	-	-	-	-	-	-
Electricity:	X	-	X	X	X	X
Body:	-	X	-	-	-	-
Accessories:	X	-	X	X	X	X
Fit/finish:	-	-	-	-	-	-

CL-SL   MERCEDES-BENZ

POWERTRAIN

Year	Type/ L/Camshaft/bhp	Drivetrain & gearbox
96-98	L6/3.0/DOHC/228	rear-A4-A5
96-99	V8/5.0/DOHC/315-322	rear-A4-A5
	V12/6.0/DOHC/389	rear-A4-A5
2000	V8/5.0/SOHC/339	rear-A5
2001	V8/5.0/SOHC/302	rear-A5
	V8/5.4/SOHC/355	rear-A5
	V12/5.8/SOHC/362	rear-A5

PERFORMANCE

Acceler. 0/100 sec.	Top. speed km/h	Ave. Fuel consp. l./100 km
9.5	220	15.0
7.1	230	16.0
6.5	240	18.0
6.0	240	17.0
6.8	240	14.5
6.0	250	15.0
5.8	250	15.2

SPECIFICATIONS

Model	Wlb. mm	Lght. mm	Cb.wt kg	Brakes fr/rr	Steering type	Standard tires
96-99						
con. 2dr.SL 320	2515	4470	1820	dc/ABS	pwr.bal.	225/55R16
con. 2dr.SL 500	2515	4499	1889	dc/ABS	pwr.bal.	245/45R17
con. 2dr.SL 600	2515	4599	2021	dc/ABS	pwr.bal.	245/40R18
98-00						
cpe. 2dr.CL500	2945	5065	2130	dc/ABS	pwr.bal.	235/60R16
cpe. 2dr.CL600	2945	5065	2250	dc/ABS	pwr.bal.	235/60R16
2001						
cpe. 2dr.CL500	2885	4994	1846	dc/ABS	pwr.r.&p.	225/55R17
cpe. 2dr.CL55	2885	4994	1851	dc/ABS	pwr.r.&p.	245/45R18 275/40R18
cpe. 2dr.CL600	2885	4994	1950	dc/ABS	pwr.r.&p.	225/55R17

PRICES

Model / version		1996	1997	1998	1999	2000	2001
con. 2dr. SL 320	mini	44100	47250				
	maxi	49000	52500				
con. 2dr. SL 500	mini	51200	56400	61900	67400	78500	89400
	maxi	56700	62000	67400	72950	85000	100200
con. 2dr. SL 600	mini	59500	70850	80800	87900	103300	117600
	maxi	65500	76600	86800	93800	110200	131250
cpe. 2dr. S 500	mini	50800	57400				
	maxi	56500	63000				
cpe. 2dr. CL500	mini			62500	67700	77700	88200
	maxi			68150	73200	83500	94500
cpe. 2dr. CL 55	mini						98700
	maxi						105000
cpe. 2dr. S 600	mini	66700	79800				
	maxi	72750	85000				
cpe. 2dr. CL600E	mini			85200	91300		109200
	maxi			91300	99600		119700

See page 7 to adapt these figures.

1999 MERCEDES-BENZ SL

MERCEDES-BENZ SLK

2001 MERCEDES-BENZ SLK 320

The SLK coupe was first sold in 1997 and is Mercedes-Benz's contender against the BMW Z3. But it's unique with its removable hard top and supercharged 2.3L engine. As an option in '99, AMG performance equipment and a manual transmission are offered.

PROS

- **This versatile model** is useful for longer periods during the year than it is the case for a conventional convertible.
- **It's a real eye-catcher**, since the swish and original body design is a real beauty.
- **The cleverly** designed top is this vehicle's main drawing card and lowering or raising the hard top always attracts a throng of admirers.
- **The engine** musters really impressive power and pick-up even if the supercharger is a bit slow to kick in, namely beyond 3,000 rpm.
- **This car handles** beautifully, thanks to the well-calibrated suspension, accurate steering and brakes, so everything is always under full control.
- **This car** is really safe to drive with its roll bar and four airbags.
- **Overall craftsmanship** is flawless and partly justifies the retail price.
- **Nice features:** great headlights, wipers, climate control and rear defroster.

CONS

- **The driver** won't be terribly comfy when seated behind the wheel and the poorly suited engine seems to strain and sputter.
- **The trunk** is snug and awkward to get to when the top is folded down.
- **Rear visibility** isn't the greatest with the headrests and wind deflector that obstruct the driver's view in the main mirror range and lateral mirrors are too tiny.
- **The complicated mechanism** that controls the hard top may cause potential buyers to ask themselves if it's really dependable and upkeep for this gorgeous gadget may be more expensive than usual.
- **Some practical items** like the skimpy-sized sun visors.

CONCLUSION

The SLK is a good buy for it's a rather rare bird and so is in great demand, especially during the summertime.

RECALLS

None over this period.

SLK — MERCEDES-BENZ

RELIABILITY PROBLEMS

	1996	1997	1998	1999	2000	2001
Engine:			X	X	X	-
Transmission:			X	-	-	-
Suspension:			-	-	-	-
Steering:			-	-	-	-
Brakes:			X	-	-	-
Electricity:			X	X	X	X
Body:			-	-	-	-
Accessories:			X	X	X	X
Fit/finish:			X	X	X	-

POWERTRAIN

Year	Type/ L/Camshaft/bhp	Drivetrain & gearbox
98-99	L4C/2.3/DOHC/185	rear-A5
99-00		rear-M5
2001	V6/3.2/SOHC/215	rear-A5
		rear-M6

PERFORMANCE

Acceler. 0/100 sec.	Top speed km/h	Ave. Fuel consp. l./100 km
7.8	230	10.8
NA	NA	11.2
7.2	225	11.4
NA	NA	13.0

SPECIFICATIONS

Model	Wlb. mm	Lght. mm	Cb.wt kg	Brakes fr/rr	Steering type	Standard tires
98-00						
cpe. 2dr. 230	2400	3995	1377	dc/ABS	pwr.bal.	fr.205/55R16 rr. 225/50R16
2001						
cpe. 2dr. 230	2400	4010	1406	dc/ABS	pwr.bal.	ft.205/55R16 rr.225/50R16
cpe. 2dr. 320	2400	4010	1430	dc/ABS	pwr.bal.	ft.205/55R16 rr.225/50R16

PRICES

Model / version		1996	1997	1998	1999	2000	2001
cpe. 2dr.	mini			34600	37800	41500	
	maxi			38300	41500	45700	
cpe. 2dr. 230	mini						47200
	maxi						52500
cpe. 3dr. 320	mini						53500
	maxi						57750

See page 7 to adapt these figures.

2001 MERCEDES-BENZ SLK 320

NISSAN Altima

1998 NISSAN Altima SE

The Altima replaced the Stanza in 1993. This small sedan is available in XE, GXE and GLE trim levels and all models are powered by a 2.4L 4-cylinder engine and has been retouched in '98 by its manufacturer.

PROS
- **It's very stylish** and has a lavish luxury car look.
- **The 2.4L engine** is quite lively and steering is quick as a flash and right on.
- **The SE and GLE** models handle better because of the sturdier suspension, while the soft suspension on the XE and GXE models causes more swing and sway.
- **The car is quite comfy**, for the suspension is never harsh, the seats provide good support, soundproofing is effective at cruising speed and the cabin is roomier on the latest version.
- **This is a solidly built** vehicle, with an immaculate fit and finish and attractive trim components and the cabin interior is well-designed and quite spiffy.

CONS
- **Built with such a sturdy frame,** the Altima is heavy, which affects engine efficiency, of course. There's a poorer power to weight ratio and higher fuel consumption than is the case for the competition.
- **Pick-up** is less lively than accelerations, because first and second gears are too closely spaced on the manual transmission.
- **The manual transmission** can be a hassle to operate because of its lack of precision and sluggish feedback.
- **The cabin** on 96-97 models aren't as roomy as that of some rivals.
- **Brakes** are effective, but they heat up with intensive use, and stops are unpredictable, so ABS is a real must.
- **Some controls** are awkwardly located and rearward view at quarterback isn't perfect.

CONCLUSION
The Altima and the Maxima share the compact market segment that is beating the pants off luxury and Sportscars, as far as sales go. A nice niche that attracts a lot of buyers.

RECALLS
None over this period.

Altima — NISSAN

RELIABILITY PROBLEMS

	1996	1997	1998	1999	2000	2001
Engine:	X	X	X	X	X	-
Transmission:	-	X	-	-	-	-
Suspension:	X	-	-	-	-	-
Steering:	-	-	-	-	-	-
Brakes:	-	-	-	X	X	-
Electricity:	-	-	X	X	X	-
Body:	-	X	-	X	-	-
Accessories:	-	-	X	X	X	X
Fit/finish:	-	-	X	X	-	-

POWERTRAIN

Year	Type/ L/Camshaft/bhp	Drivetrain & gearbox
96-01	L4/2.4/DOHC/150	front-M5
		front-A4

PERFORMANCE

Acceler. 0/100 sec.	Top. speed km/h	Ave. Fuel consp. l./100 km
9.0	190	9.7
10.2	180	10.6

SPECIFICATIONS

Model	Wlb. mm	Lght. mm	Cb.wt kg	Brakes fr/rr	Steering type	Standard tires
96-97						
sdn. 4dr. XE	2620	4585	1283	dc/dr	pwr.r&p.	205/65R15
sdn. 4dr. GXE	2620	4585	1333	dc/dr	pwr.r&p.	205/65R15
sdn. 4dr. SE	2620	4585	1373	dc/ABS	pwr.r&p.	205/65R15
sdn. 4dr. GLE	2620	4585	1403	dc/ABS	pwr.r&p.	205/65R15
98-01						
sdn. 4dr. XE	2619	4661	1304	dc/dr	pwr.r&p.	195/65R15
sdn. 4dr. GXE	2619	4661	1324	dc/dr	pwr.r&p.	195/65R15
sdn. 4dr. SE	2619	4661	1325	dc/dc	pwr.r&p.	205/60R15
sdn. 4dr. GLE	2619	4661	1335	dc/dr	pwr.r&p.	195/65R15

PRICES

Model / version		1996	1997	1998	1999	2000	2001
sdn. 4dr. XE	mini	5800	7350	10000	12300	14700	16600
	maxi	7900	9450	11850	14200	16800	19400
sdn. 4dr. GXE	mini	7900	9250	11550	13700	15200	17100
	maxi	9450	11000	13450	15750	17300	19950
sdn. 4dr. SE	mini	9150	10800	13450	15200	16300	18150
	maxi	11000	13100	15500	17300	18400	21000
sdn. 4dr. GLE	mini	9450		13850	15650	16800	18800
	maxi	12300		15750	17850	18900	21500

See page 7 to adapt these figures.

1998 NISSAN Altima SE

NISSAN   Maxima

1996 NISSAN Maxima GLE

Inaugurated in 1984 (front-wheel drive), the Maxima was upgraded in '86, '89 and in '95 and it's powered by a 3.0L V6 engine. The addition in 1999 of the EuroSport (ES) version won't go unnoticed, for that trim level will only be available in Canada. Moreover, the anti-skid control system will become standard on model equipped with the automatic transmission and anti-lock brakes.

PROS

- **The frisky and fiery V6** engine is thrilling, especially on the lighter-weight base model.
- **The GXE** model is less expensive than its rivals, the Accord, 626 and Camry.
- **The sleek,** classy look of the latest models.
- **The better-adjusted suspension** has improved handling on the SE model that is more agile than the GXE/Brougham.
- **Maneuverability** is good because of smooth, accurate, quick as a flash steering.
- **The rear "Multilink"** suspension makes for superb road stability on curves and quite a smooth ride.
- **The powerful V6** is the most economical engine in its category, thanks to a good power to weight ratio.
- **Construction quality** and fit and finish are definitely top-notch but the overall look is plain and not at all plush.

CONS

- **The cabin interior** on the GXE is terribly chintzy-looking.
- **Poorly designed seats** don't provide adequate support because they're so sunken-in and they're hard with such firm upholstery.
- **The manual shifter** on the SE isn't at all in keeping with the character of this model, for it's inaccurate and stubborn.
- **The instrument panel** isn't too ergonomic, for the controls located on the center console aren't within easy reach for the driver.
- **There aren't too many storage** compartments and there are no niceties that you find on rival models.
- **Just unbelievable**: no automatic shifter indicator on the instrument panel, crummy windshield wiper and washer system and horrible rear defroster.

CONCLUSION

The Maxima is a sturdy and reliable car that is comfortable to drive and fun to put through its paces.

RECALLS

None over this period.

Maxima — NISSAN

RELIABILITY PROBLEMS

	1996	1997	1998	1999	2000	2001
Engine:	X	X	X	-	-	-
Transmission:	X	X	-	-	-	-
Suspension:	-	-	-	-	-	-
Steering:	-	X	-	-	-	-
Brakes:	-	-	X	X	X	-
Electricity:	X	X	X	X	X	-
Body:	X	X	X	-	X	-
Accessories:	-	X	X	X	-	-
Fit/finish:	-	X	-	X	-	-

POWERTRAIN

Year	Type/ L/Camshaft/bhp	Drivetrain & gearbox
96-01	V6/3.0/DOHC/190-222	front-M5
		front-A4

PERFORMANCE

Acceler. 0/100 sec.	Top. speed km/h	Ave. Fuel consp. l./100 km
8.0	220	10.9
8.5	210	11.3

SPECIFICATIONS

Model	Wlb.	Lght.	Cb.wt	Brakes	Steering	Standard
96-99						
sdn. 4dr. GXE	2700	4810	1369	dc/dc	pwr.r&p.	205/65R15
sdn. 4dr. SE/ES	2700	4810	1396	dc/ABS	pwr.r&p.	215/55R16
sdn. 4dr. GLE	2700	4810	1399	dc/ABS	pwr.r&p.	205/65R15
00-01						
sdn. 4dr. GXE	2751	4839	1450	dc/ABS	pwr.r&p.	205/65R15
sdn. 4dr. SE	2751	4839	1448	dc/ABS	pwr.r&p.	255/50R17
sdn. 4dr. GLE	2751	4839	1496	dc/ABS	pwr.r&p.	215/55R16

PRICES

Model / version		1996	1997	1998	1999	2000	2001
sdn. 4dr. GXE	mini	8900	11300	13250	15750	21000	23800
	maxi	11950	14700	16600	18900	23600	26200
sdn. 4dr. SE	mini	13300	16600	19200	22350	24700	
	maxi	16800	19950	22350	25700	28400	
sdn. 4dr. GLE	mini	12900	16000	18900	21850	25400	28100
	maxi	16300	19400	22000	25200	28350	31000
sdn. 4dr. ES	mini				18700		
	maxi				22000		
sdn. 4dr. SE Ann.	mini						27800
	maxi						31500

See page 7 to adapt these figures.

1996 NISSAN Maxima GLE

NISSAN Pathfinder

1998 NISSAN Pathfinder Chilkoot

The Pathfinder has been on the market since 1986. It was originally powered by a 2.4L 4-cylinder engine. The 3.0L V6 engine came out in '87 and the vehicle was revamped in 1996. It's interesting to know that the Chilkoot trim level is exclusively sold in Canada.

PROS
- **The bold body style** of the 95 models was a real crowd pleaser.
- **Highway driving** is very smooth and comfy.
- **The cabin is very spacious**, especially in the rear seat area with its more generous leg room than the competition.
- **Handling** is safe and sure for there's only moderate sway and the combined springs and shock absorbers are well-calibrated.
- **Brakes** have become very muscular, balanced and easy to ajust and smooth power steering provides good maneuverability.
- **The instrument panel** is simple, straightforward and ergonomic.
- **Construction quality** and finish details are good and equipment is complete.

CONS
- **The look** of the latest model has disappointed a lot of fans because it isn't as brassy and virile as before.
- **Engine performance** has improved, but not enough to make for really fun driving, for the V6 still lacks torque.
- **The gears** aren't well-calibrated, especially on the automatic whose electronic unit should be readjusted.
- **Side view** is obstructed by the spare tire mounted on the rear blocks rearward view.
- **Seats** on older models are hard because they're thinly upholstered and they're poorly designed so they don't provide adequate lateral or lumbar support.
- **Fuel consumption** is never economical, especially off-the-road.
- **Ground clearance** on the latest models is lower with the smaller tires, which can be a real pain on rough terrain.

CONCLUSION
This all-terrain vehicle is reliable and quite nice-looking, but its overall design is beginning to look dusty and needs sprucing up.

RECALLS
1996 Floor rug may block gas pedal function.

Pathfinder NISSAN

RELIABILITY PROBLEMS

	1996	1997	1998	1999	2000	2001
Engine:	X	-	-	-	-	-
Transmission:	X	X	X	X	X	-
Suspension:	-	-	X	X	-	-
Steering:	-	-	-	-	-	-
Brakes:	-	-	-	-	-	-
Electricity:	X	X	X	X	X	-
Body:	-	X	-	-	-	-
Accessories:	X	-	X	X	X	-
Fit/finish:	-	X	X	X	X	-

POWERTRAIN

Year	Type/ L/Camshaft/bhp	Drivetrain & gearbox
96-00	V6/3.3/SOHC/168	rear/all-M5
		rear/all-A4
2001	V6/3.5/SOHC/250	rr./all-M5
		rr./all-A4

PERFORMANCE

Acceler. 0/100 sec.	Top. speed km/h	Ave. Fuel consp. l./100 km
10.3	165	14.7
11.6	160	15.4
9.5	180	14.7
10.2	175	15.6

SPECIFICATIONS

Model	Wlb.	Lght.	Cb.wt	Brakes	Steering	Standard
96-98 4x2						
wgn. 5dr. XE	2700	4529	1667	dc/ABS	pwr.r&p.	235/70R15
wgn. 5dr. SE	2700	4529	1712	dc/ABS	pwr.r&p.	235/70R15
96-01 4x4						
wgn. 5dr. XE	2700	4529	1803	dc/dr/ABS	pwr.r&p.	265/70R15
wgn. 5dr. SE	2700	4529	1844	dc/dr/ABS	pwr.r&p.	265/70R15
wgn. 5dr. LE	2700	4529	1830	dc/dr/ABS	pwr.r&p.	235/70R15

PRICES

Model / version		1996	1997	1998	1999	2000	2001
96-99							
wgn. 5dr. XE	mini	12600	14300	15950	16800	23600	25900
	maxi	14700	16500	18000	18900	26000	28650
wgn. 5dr. SE	mini	18400	21000	22600	24250	30000	32500
	maxi	20700	23300	24900	26500	32750	35500
wgn. 5dr. LE	mini	18800	21500	23100	25000	31400	33600
	maxi	21000	23800	25400	27300	34100	36550
wgn. 4dr. Klondike	mini		17300				
	maxi		19600				
wgn. 4dr. Chilkoot	mini			18900	20350		
	maxi			21200	23000		
1999.5-2000							
wgn. 5dr. XE	mini				18700		
	maxi				20800		
wgn. 5dr. SE	mini				25600		
	maxi				27900		
wgn. 5dr. LE	mini				26350		
	maxi				28600		

See page 7 to adapt these figures.

1998 NISSAN Pathfinder Chilkoot

NISSAN Quest

1996 NISSAN Quest

The Quest is identical to the Mercury Villager and was first sold in 1993. It's built on the former Maxima platform and is equipped with the Maxima 3.0L V6 engine. In '99, the Quest has been overhauled and it now offers a second sliding door and a new 3.3L V6 engine.

PROS
- **The modern**, shapely body design is very appealing and the cabin interior design is attractive as well.
- **Modular rear seats** can be modified according to 14 different arrangements and are really surprisingly easy to manipulate.
- **Good wheel travel** and well-adjusted shock absorbers on the rear end enhance driving comfort.
- **The vehicle** is neutral even if the suspension and rear end are of simple, rather rustic design.
- **The GXE** is a safe vehicle with its robust frame, dual airbags, standard headrests on every seat and ABS brakes. This equipment comes standard as well as on all models built after '99.
- **Spiffy trim components**, construction quality and tight finish are typical of Japanese products.

CONS
- **Excessive vehicle weight** affects performance and fuel consumption.
- **The disc-drum brakes** on the XE lack grip and lasting power, so vehicle path is unpredictable.
- **The rear seat** area and baggage compartment are limited with seven adults on board.
- **Maneuverability** isn't the greatest with such a large steer angle diameter and steering is vague at the center and a bit over-assisted.
- **Better soundproofing** would sure make for a more pleasant ride.
- **Some storage compartments** and controls aren't very convenient.
- **Road, engine and wind noise** is almost deafening.

CONCLUSION
The Quest is more of a station wagon than a minivan, for its hefty weight is more suited to travel than to real work, and buyers who prefer cars to minivans won't be disappointed.

RECALLS
1996 Delay feature of power windows may be malfunctioning.
1998 Battery could be defective.
99-00 The retaining bolts for the steering rack mounting may not have been torqued to the proper specifications.
The seatblet buckle assembly are defective and must be replaced.

Quest — NISSAN

RELIABILITY PROBLEMS

	1996	1997	1998	1999	2000	2001
Engine:	X	X	-	-	-	-
Transmission:	-	X	X	X	-	-
Suspension:	-	-	-	-	-	-
Steering:	-	-	-	-	-	-
Brakes:	X	X	X	X	X	-
Electricity:	-	X	X	X	X	X
Body:	-	-	-	-	X	-
Accessories:	-	X	-	X	X	X
Fit/finish:	-	X	X	X	-	-

POWERTRAIN

Year	Type/ L/Camshaft/bhp	Drivetrain & gearbox
96-98	V6/3.0/SOHC/151	front-A4
99-01	V6/3.3/SOHC/170	front-A4

PERFORMANCE

Acceler. 0/100 sec.	Top. speed km/h	Ave. Fuel consp. l./100 km
13.3	160	12.5
11.0	180	13.8

SPECIFICATIONS

Model 96-01	Wlb. mm	Lght. mm	Cb.wt kg	Brakes fr/rr	Steering type	Standard tires
m.v. 4dr. GXE	2850	4948	1798	dc/dr/ABS	pwr.r&p.	215/70R15
m.v. 4dr. SE	2850	4948	1756	dc/dr/ABS	pwr.r&p.	225/60R15
m.v. 4dr. GLE	2850	4948	1798	dc/dr/ABS	pwr.r&p.	215/70R15

PRICES

Model / version		1996	1997	1998	1999	2000	2001
m.v. 4dr. XE	mini	9150	11800	13750	15550		
	maxi	11200	14000	15750	17500		
m.v. 4dr. GXE	mini	11550	15000	17650		20700	23100
	maxi	14300	17100	19750		23100	25900
m.v. 4dr. SE	mini				17850	23700	26200
	maxi				20100	26200	29100
m.v. 4dr. GLE	mini				21300		
	maxi				23600		

See page 7 to adapt these figures.

1999 NISSAN Quest

NISSAN Sentra/200SX 96-98

1997 NISSAN Sentra

Inspired by the former generation, the Sentra as well as the NX coupe were redesigned in 1991. In spite of the added coupe in '94, Nissan weeded out this model range, and with good reason. However, the new SE version introduced in '99 has good chances to boost the vitality of this model, for its numerous standard items it offers, such as 140-bhp 2.0L, air conditioner, ABS brakes, 15-inch alloy wheels, rear spoiler and fog lights.

PROS
- **These cars aren't unattractive**, but they're terribly ordinary.
- **Handling** has improved for there's less swing and sway, but the base model tires are too narrow to be as effective as those that equip the more elaborate models.
- **Power steering** is more pleasant to use than the manual that is sluggish and inaccurate, because it suffers from too high a reduction ratio.
- **The 1.6L engine** is livelier and more muscular than before, but the 2.0L engine that powers the 1999 Sentra SE is the most spectacular.
- **The ride is quite comfortable** with the upgraded suspension, more spacious cabin interior, better contoured seats and lower noise level.
- **Equipment** and fit and finish are adequate for such economical cars and only the instrument panel seems to be really lacking.

CONS
- **Rear seats** on the Sentra are narrow and hard to get into and only children will be comfortably seated in them.
- **The spongy brake** pedal makes it difficult to control stops with any accuracy.

CONCLUSION
The Sentra and 200 SX models don't have a look that makes you sit up and take notice, but they're solid, reliable cars and, depending on the engine model, they're fun to drive.

RECALLS
1996 Corroded front coil springs can break damaging the tires on Sentra 2-door models.
96-97 Moisture may penetrate into throttle chamber and freeze. Light bulbs are not bright enough for brake signal.
1997 Vehicle identification number might be incorrect.
96-98 Mechanism of the windshield wipers must be inspected and replaced if necessary.
2001 Dealers will replace the lower control arm attachment bolts. Odometer that record in miles will be replaced with ones that record in kilometers.
Dealers will inspect for cracks and replace the faulty wheels.

Sentra/200SX 96-98 — NISSAN

RELIABILITY PROBLEMS

	1996	1997	1998	1999	2000	2001
Engine:	X	X	X	X	X	X
Transmission:	X	-	-	-	-	-
Suspension:	X	-	-	-	-	-
Steering:	-	-	-	-	-	-
Brakes:	-	-	X	X	X	-
Electricity:	X	X	X	X	X	-
Body:	X	-	X	X	X	X
Accessories:	X	X	X	-	X	X
Fit/finish:	-	-	-	X	-	-

POWERTRAIN

Year	Type/ L/Camshaft/bhp	Drivetrain & gearbox
96-01	L4/1.6/DOHC/110-115	front-M5
		front-A4
	L4/2.0/DOHC/140	front-M5
		front-A4

PERFORMANCE

Acceler. 0/100 sec.	Top. speed km/h	Ave. Fuel consp. l./100 km
10.0	165	8.0
11.5	160	8.8
9.0	180	9.0
NA	NA	NA

SPECIFICATIONS

Model	Wlb. mm	Lght. mm	Cb.wt kg	Brakes fr/rr	Steering type	Standard tires
Sentra 96-98						
cpe. 2dr.	2430	4326	1064	dc/dr	r&p.	155/80R13
sdn. 4dr.	2430	4326	1090	dc/dr	pwr.r&p.	175/70R13
Sentra 99-01						
sdn. 4dr. base	2535	4343	1050	dc/dr	r&p.	155/80R13
sdn. 4dr. XE/GXE	2535	4343	1080	dc/dr	pwr.r&p.	175/70R13
sdn. 4dr. SE	2535	4343	1188	dc/ABS	pwr.r&p.	175/70R13
200SX 96-98						
cpe. 2dr. base	2535	4321	1065	dc/dr	pwr.r&p.	175/70R13
cpe. 2dr. SE	2535	4321	1145	dc/dc	pwr.r&p.	175/65R14
cpe. 2dr. SE-R	2535	4321	1175	dc/dc	pwr.r&p.	195/55R15

PRICES

Model / version		1996	1997	1998	1999	2000	2001
Sentra 96-99							
cpe. 2dr. DLX	mini	4400					
	maxi	6300					
cpe. 2dr. XE	mini	6000					
	maxi	8200					
sdn. 4dr. XE	mini	5450	6600	8500	9750		13100
	maxi	7900	8400	10300	11550		15750
sdn. 4dr. GXE	mini	7000	8200	10100	11150		14700
	maxi	8900	10100	11650	12600		17300
sdn. 4dr. GLE	mini	7500	8700				
	maxi	9450	10600				
sdn. 4 dr. SE	mini				13450		17850
	maxi				15200		20500
sdn. 4dr. 5 speed	mini	3700	4950	6400			
	maxi	5250	6800	8400			
200SX 96-98							
cpe. 2dr.	mini	6100					
	maxi	7350					
cpe. 2dr. SE	mini	6800		8500			
	maxi	8400		10500			
cpe. 2dr. SE-R	mini	7650		10500			
	maxi	9450		12600			

See page 7 to adapt these figures.

NISSAN XTerra

2000 NISSAN Xterra

Nissan derived its Xterra from the Pathfinder's chassis and mechanical components to create a smaller SUV with more youthful styling. In 2000, a single version was introduced with a 3.3-liter V6 engine. Since 2001, it's available in a choice of three models.

PROS

- **The large tubular roof rack** adds to the original styling.
- **The Xterra is surprisingly roomy** for such a compact vehicle, especially in the spacious rear seats.
- **The cargo bay** is roomy and features a modular configuration.
- The Xterra is surprisingly **maneuverable** for an SUV.
- **Performance levels** are honorable despite the fact that the weight-to-power ratio is somewhat hindered by a gross weight of close to 2 tons.
- **The brakes are easy to gauge**, which makes for pleasant everyday driving.
- **The numerous front storage spaces** as well as running boards and roof rack emphasize this vehicle's practical side.

CONS

- **The rustic suspension** is uncomfortable on poor roads where it becomes very jumpy partially because of the large bouncy tires.
- **The high center of gravity** makes the Xterra unstable in curves where moderation must be exercised at all times.
- **This vehicle's large engine** requires more fuel than the average.
- **The brakes** are not powerful enough, and stopping distances are above-average.
- **Access** to the rear seats and cargo bay is hindered by the high ground clearance.
- **The headlights** are too dim to be efficient in poor weather conditions.
- **The overassisted steering** feels light and vague on center. This hinders driving precision.

VERDICT

The Xterra is experiencing a good level of commercial success because of the way it defines itself as well as its great looks.

RECALLS

None over this period.

NISSAN   XTerra

RELIABILITY PROBLEMS

	1996	1997	1998	1999	2000	2001
Engine:					-	-
Transmission:					-	-
Suspension:					-	-
Steering:					-	-
Brakes:					-	-
Electricity:					-	-
Body:					-	-
Accessories:					X	-
Fit/finish:					-	-

POWERTRAIN

Year	Type/ L/Camshaft/bhp	Drivetrain & gearbox	Acceler. 0/100 sec.	Top. speed km/h	Ave. Fuel consp. l./100 km
00-01	V6/3.3/SOHC/170	rr./all-M5	11.0	175	14.3
		rr./all-A4	11.8	170	15.2

SPECIFICATIONS

Model 00-01	Wlb. mm	Lght. mm	Cb.wt kg	Brakes fr/rr	Steering type	Standard tires
wgn. 5dr.	2649	4521	1841	dc/dr/ABS	pwr.bal.	265/70R15
wgn. 5dr. XE	2649	4521	1860	dc/dr/ABS	pwr.bal.	265/70R15
wgn. 5dr. SE	2649	4521	1897	dc/dr/ABS	pwr.bal.	265/70R15

PRICES

Model / version		1996	1997	1998	1999	2000	2001
wgn. 5dr.	mini					23100	
	maxi					27100	
wgn. 5dr. XE	mini						26250
	maxi						29600
wgn. 5dr. SE	mini						28350
	maxi						31700

See page 7 to adapt these figures.

2000 NISSAN Xterra

NISSAN 240SX

1997 NISSAN 240SX

This rear-wheel drive sports coupe replaced the 200SX in 1989 and is available in 2 or 3-door models driven by a 2.4L engine. It has been redesigned in 1995 and finally disappeared in 1998.

PROS

- **This model is stylish** either with or without the rear hatch.
- **The cockpit is comfy**, instrument gauges are easy to read, but who really needs the Eyecue head-up display on the windshield?
- **Road stability** is good, thanks to the rear end that really sticks to the road. But the front end tends to get light at high speeds.
- **Brakes** are muscular, but there's almost immediate rear wheel lock, so ABS is an absolute must.
- **The trunk** on the hatchback is bigger than on the conventional coupe, but it's more awkward to get to.
- **The LE coupe** is more fun to drive with its good visibility, greater stability and lower noise level.

CONS

- **The 2.4L engine** isn't too hot and it seems to sputter and strain, especially with the automatic transmission that saps its power even more.
- **The stiff rear axle** jumps a lot and seats are poorly designed, so comfort isn't what it should be.
- **Outward view** is obstructed by the thick roof support and the low-angled rear window on the hatchback that gets murky at the first raindrop that falls.
- **Cabin size** is cut down by the huge tunnel that runs down the middle.
- **The insufficiently rigid** frame on the SE cracks a lot.

CONCLUSION

The 240SX coupe is economical and fun for Sportscar driving fans, but all in all, engine performance isn't too much out of the ordinary.

RECALLS

None over this period.

240SX — NISSAN

RELIABILITY PROBLEMS

	1996	1997	1998	1999	2000	2001
Engine:	X	-	-			
Transmission:		-	-			
Suspension:		-	-			
Steering:		X	-			
Brakes:		X	-			
Electricity:		-	X			
Body:		-	-			
Accessories:		X	X			
Fit/finish:		-	-			

POWERTRAIN

Year	Type/ L/Camshaft/bhp	Drivetrain & gearbox
96-98	L4/2.4/DOHC/155	rear-M5
		rear-A4

PERFORMANCE

Acceler. 0/100 sec.	Top speed km/h	Ave. Fuel consp. l./100 km
8.6	200	10.7
9.8	195	11.4

SPECIFICATIONS

Model	Wlb. mm	Lght. mm	Cb.wt kg	Brakes fr/rr	Steering type	Standard tires
96-98						
cpe. 2dr. base	2525	4501	1270	dc/dc	pwr.r&p.	195/60R15
cpe. 3dr. SE	2525	4501	1276	dc/dc	pwr.r&p.	205/55R16
cpe. 3dr. LE	2525	4501	1304	dc/ABS	pwr.r&p.	205/55R16

PRICES

Model / version		1996	1997	1998	1999	2000	2001
cpe. 2dr. base	mini		11550	12900			
	maxi		13650	15000			
cpe. 3dr. SE	mini	9250	13550	14400			
	maxi	11550	14700	16600			
cpe. 3dr. LE	mini	10700	14000	15750			
	maxi	14200	16300	18150			

See page 7 to adapt these figures.

1997 NISSAN 240SX

NISSAN 300ZX

1996 NISSAN 300ZX

The popular 240Z was first available in 1969. It was replaced by the 260Z in '74, the 280Z Turbo in '78 and the 300ZX with V6 engine in '90. It was available until '96 in four body styles and came equipped with two engine models.

PROS

• **With such a gutsy** look and unique body shape, this car is sure to make heads turn, especially the latest models that are very stylish.

• **The 3.0L V6 Turbo** sure is an exotic one, but the conventional engine is also very powerful.

• **The car handles** well with such a sophisticated suspension design, especially with the HICAS system on the latest generation that links the rear wheels to the steering function.

• **Steering** is clean and quick and the driver has all the controls and instruments needed for a pleasant ride.

• **Comfort** is exceptional with such cushy, nicely contoured seats and a firm, but smooth suspension.

CONS

• **Fuel economy** isn't the greatest with such a heavy car.

• **You have to know** what you're doing when you're at the wheel of these fast cars, especially on slippery roads and you have to accelerate gradually, especially with Turbo engine power at your toetip.

• **Brakes** could have more grip for stopping distances are long and even with ABS, there's some wheel lock.

• **The steering** column isn't adjustable, which isn't at all in keeping with the caliber and cost of such a car.

• **The small trunk** isn't too useful, nor are all the storage compartments scattered here and there throughout the cabin.

CONCLUSION

The last generation Nissan 300ZX is by far the best purchase choice, but the car should be inspected from stem to stern.

RECALLS

None over this period.

300ZX — NISSAN

RELIABILITY PROBLEMS

	1996	1997	1998	1999	2000	2001
Engine:	X					
Transmission:	-					
Suspension:	--					
Steering:	-					
Brakes:	X					
Electricity:	-					
Body:	-					
Accessories:	X					
Fit/finish:	-					

POWERTRAIN

Year	Type/ L/Camshaft/bhp	Drivetrain & gearbox
1996	V6/3.0/DOHC/222	rear-M5
		rear-A4
	V6T/3.0/DOHC/300	rear-M5

PERFORMANCE

Acceler. 0/100 sec.	Top. speed km/h	Ave. Fuel consp. l./100 km
7.0	230	12.0
8.1	220	13.0
6.2	250	13.5

SPECIFICATIONS

Model 1996	Wlb. mm	Lght. mm	Cb.wt kg	Brakes fr/rr	Steering type	Standard tires
con. 2dr.	2451	4305	1567	dc/ABS	pwr.r&p.	225/50R16
cpe. 3dr. base	2451	4305	1430	dc/ABS	pwr.r&p.	225/50R16
cpe. 3dr. 2+2	2570	4521	1470	dc/ABS	pwr.r&p.	225/50R16
cpe. 3dr. Biturbo	2451	4305	1485	dc/ABS	pwr.r&p.	225/50R16
						rr. 245/45R16

PRICES

Model / version		1996	1997	1998	1999	2000	2001
cpe. 3dr. base	mini	22350					
	maxi	24800					
cpe. 3dr. 2+2	mini	24700					
	maxi	27500					
cpe. 3dr. BiTurbo	mini	27700					
	maxi	30650					

See page 7 to adapt these figures.

1996 NISSAN 300ZX

SAAB 900-9³

1999 SAAB 900³

This Swedish front-wheel drive car was first sold way back in 1969. It was upgraded in 1978, in '84 (Turbo), in '85 (convertible) and redesigned in 1993 when a V6 engine was also available, along with the traditional 4-cylinder engine. Its name change in '99 has also been a good reason for Saab to "clean the house" in terms of engine. Since, its 2.0LTurbo ouput an honorable 200-bhp.

PROS
- **The Turbo and V6** engines are more muscular and economical.
- **The cockpit** and instrument panel are nicely designed.
- **Handling** is good in most situations, but there's oversteering when car is pushed to the limit.
- **Brakes** are strong and reliable.
- **This car has a nice personality**, it's well-built and fitted, it's well equipped and the Turbo has real character.
- **The huge trunk** may be extended or modified as needed.

CONS
- **The body design** is getting a bit dusty and dingy-looking, the convertible could be more robust, the rear end is stiff and it's an overhang engine system.
- **Engine performance** isn't too hot on the base model even with its good power to weight ratio and aerodynamic efficiency.
- **Gears are more** tailored to economy than to performance.
- **The cabin interior** is cramped because rear seats are very tight and the front wheel wells take up a lot of room.
- **Comfort isn't great** with such hard seats, harsh suspension, high noise level, especially on the poorly soundproofed convertible model.
- **Things to consider**: brake pads wear out in no time, rear wheels lock almost immediately without ABS and the engine tends to overheat.

CONCLUSION
In spite of modifications and a more modern design, the 900 and the 9³ hasn't broken any sales records, because they are too expensive.

RECALLS
1996 Defective safety belt anchorage.
96-97 Throttle control lever bushings may corrode.
96-98 Missing instructions regarding the setting of the headlights.

900- 9³   SAAB

POWERTRAIN / PERFORMANCE

Year	Type/ L/Camshaft/bhp	Drivetrain & gearbox	Acceler. 0/100 sec.	Top. speed km/h	Ave. Fuel consp. l./100 km
96-98	L4/2.0/DOHC/185	front-M5	7.5	220	11.0
	L4/2.3/DOHC/150	front-A4	11.0	180	11.5
	V6/2.5/DOHC/170	front-M5	8.5	190	11.0
		front-A4	9.2	185	12.0
99-01	L4/2.0/DOHC/185	front-M5	10.2	205	11.9
		front-A4	11.0	200	12.4
	L4T/2.0/DOHC/200	front-M5	7.5	220	12.2
		front-A4	8.3	210	13.6
Viggen	L4T/2.0/DOHC/200	front-M5	7.5	220	12.2

SPECIFICATIONS

Model	Wlb. mm	Lght. mm	Cb.wt kg	Brakes fr/rr	Steering type	Standard tires
900 96-99						
con. 2dr. S	2600	4637	1415	dc/ABS	pwr.r&p.	195/60R15
cpe. 2dr. S	2600	4637	1356	dc/ABS	pwr.r&p.	195/60R15
sdn. 5dr. S	2600	4637	1335	dc/ABS	pwr.r&p.	195/60R15
sdn. 5dr. SE	2600	4637	1495	dc/ABS	pwr.r&p.	195/60R15
9³ 99-01						
con. 2dr. S	2605	4629	1450	dc/ABS	pwr.r&p.	195/60R15
cpe. 2dr. S	2605	4629	1355	dc/ABS	pwr.r&p.	205/50R16
cpe. 3dr. Viggen	2605	4629	1355	dc/ABS	pwr.r&p.	205/50R16
sdn. 5dr. S	2605	4629	1375	dc/ABS	pwr.r&p.	195/60R15
con. 2dr. SE	2605	4629	1450	dc/ABS	pwr.r&p.	205/50R16
sdn. 5dr. SE	2605	4629	1375	dc/ABS	pwr.r&p.	205/50R16
sdn. 5dr. Viggen	2605	4629	1375	dc/ABS	pwr.r&p.	205/50R16

PRICES

Model / version		1996	1997	1998	1999	2000	2001
900							
con. 2dr. S	mini	15300	19100	24100			
	maxi	19100	22700	27500			
con. 2dr. Turbo SE	mini	18700	25200	30000			
	maxi	22350	29000	33400			
con. 2dr. SE V6	mini	18600	24100				
	maxi	22350	27900				
sdn. 3dr. S	mini	7150	9250	11250			
	maxi	9850	11850	13950			
sdn. 3dr. SE V6	mini	9450					
	maxi	11950					
sdn. 3dr. SE Turbo	mini	10000	15000	16300			
	maxi	13450	17650	18900			
sdn. 3dr. S Turbo	mini	9000	10700	12600			
	maxi	11750	13450	15750			
sdn. 5dr. S	mini	6500	9250	11200			
	maxi	9000	11750	13950			
sdn. 5dr. S V6	mini	6300					
	maxi	8900					
sdn. 5dr. SE V6	mini	8700	15450				
	maxi	11550	18100				
sdn. 5dr. SE Tbo	mini	9450	15350	16800			
	maxi	12200	18150	19400			
9³							
sdn. 3dr.	mini				17300	20700	25200
	maxi				19950	23600	28550
sdn. 3dr. Viggen	mini					35200	40100
	maxi					38000	43250
con. 2dr.	mini				28900	34300	38850
	maxi				31500	37300	42200
con. 2dr. SE	mini				32500	39000	43900
	maxi				35200	42000	47000
con. 2dr. Viggen	mini					46200	50200
	maxi					49000	53350
sdn. 5dr.	mini				17300	22600	27100
	maxi				19950	24900	30250
sdn. 5dr. SE	mini				23100	27000	31300
	maxi				25700	29400	34450
sdn. 5dr. Viggen	mini					36400	40750
	maxi					38850	43900

See page 7 to adapt these figures.

SAAB 9000-9⁵

2000 SAAB 9^5 wagon

The 9000 is a top-of-the-line sports sedan that began its career in 1984 and was powered by a Turbo 16 engine. The multi-valve S model came out in '85 and the 9000 SPG sports model hit the market in '88. Engine models include the 4-cylinder, conventional or Turbo, or the V6. And then Saab decided in 1999 to call it the 9^5. By the same token, they tried to make it look a little more modern, just to make sure it goes unnoticed.

PROS

- **Its classic and elegant body** design, like that of the model with separate trunk, is more attractive than that of the hatchback.
- **The Turbo** engine really moves this car and puts it through its paces without a hitch, especially with the new V6 Turbo.
- **Handling** is quite safe and stable but the car tends to go into understeering and there's frequent loss of wheel function.
- **Visibility** is just great, the instrument panel is well-designed and steering is quick and accurate.
- **Brakes** are effective and stable with ABS, but they're hard to control with the stiff pedal.
- **The cabin interior** is nice and spacious, and easy to climb into.
- **The suspension** is effective, but a bit stiff, so the ride isn't always silky smooth. Fabric trim on the seats is preferable to leather seats.
- **Construction quality**, finish and trim components are impeccable and equipment is very extensive.

CONS

- **Conventional engines** coupled with the automatic are less frisky and feisty and they suffer from a poor power to weight ratio.
- **The Turbo engine** is a real gas-guzzler.
- **On Turbo models**, torque affects steering on strong accelerations.
- **These cars are expensive** to buy, and upkeep is costly because of a small service network, so resale value isn't great.
- **The manual transmission** is poorly calibrated and there's a gap between 3rd and 4th gear.

CONCLUSION

The Saab 9000 and the 9^5 are outstanding cars, but you shouldn't buy one used unless you're absolutely sure of what shape it's in, for maintenance and any major repairs can really deplete your bank account.

RECALLS

None over this period.

9000-9⁵ — SAAB

RELIABILITY PROBLEMS

	1996	1997	1998	1999	2000	2001
Transmission:	X	X	X	X	X	X
Suspension:	-	-	-	-	-	-
Steering:	-	-	-	-	-	-
Brakes:	X	X	X	X	-	-
Electricity:	X	-	X	X	X	X
Body:	-	X	-	X	X	-
Accessories:	X	X	X	X	X	-
Fit/finish:	-	-	-	-	-	-

POWERTRAIN

Year	Type/ L/Camshaft/bhp	Drivetrain & gearbox
96-98	L4/2.3/DOHC/150-170	front-M5
		front-A4
	L4T/2.3/DOHC/200-225	front-M5
		front-A4
	V6/3.0/OHV/210	front-A4
99-01	L4T/2.3/DOHC/170	front-M5
		front-A4
	V6/3.0/DOHC/200	front-A4

PERFORMANCE

Acceler. 0/100 sec.	Top. speed km/h	Ave. Fuel consp. l./100 km
9.9	210	10.5
11.0	200	11.5
8.5	225	11.5
9.2	215	12.5
9.0	220	13.0
10.6	220	11.9
11.7	210	13.5
9.4	220	13.3

SPECIFICATIONS

Model	Wlb. mm	Lght. mm	Cb.wt kg	Brakes fr/rr	Steering type	Standard tires
9000						
sdn. 5dr. S	2672	4620	1410	dc/ABS	pwr.r&p.	195/65R15
sdn. 5dr. Turbo	2672	4761	1420	dc/ABS	pwr.r&p.	205/60R15
sdn. 5dr. CSE	2672	4761	1440	dc/ABS	pwr.r&p.	205/60R15
9⁵						
sdn. 4dr. base	2703	4805	1490	dc/ABS	pwr.r&p.	215/55R16
sdn. 5dr. SE	2703	4805	1615	dc/ABS	pwr.r&p.	215/55R16
sdn. 4dr. Aero	2703	4805	1565	dc/ABS	pwr.r&p.	225/45R17
wgn. 4dr.	2703	4808	1705	dc/ABS	pwr.r&p.	215/55R16

PRICES

Model / version		1996	1997	1998	1999	2000	2001
9000							
sdn. 4dr. CDE	mini	12600	17000				
	maxi	16400	20600				
sdn. 5dr. CS	mini	8300	13350				
	maxi	11250	16400				
sdn. 5dr. CS Aero	mini	15650	19400				
	maxi	18900	23100				
sdn. 5dr. Tbo CSE	mini	13650					
	maxi	17200					
sdn. 5dr. CSE V6	mini	14600					
	maxi	17850					
sdn. 4dr. CSE An.	mini			18400	21000		
	maxi			21850	24350		
9⁵							
sdn. 4dr. 2.3	mini				22000	28750	33300
	maxi				24900	32000	36550
sdn. 4dr. 3.0	mini				23300	30000	34850
	maxi				26250	33400	38100
sdn. 4dr. 2.3 SE	mini				28550		
	maxi				31500		
sdn. 4dr. 3.0 SE	mini				29600	36300	42200
	maxi				32500	39800	45450
sdn. 4dr. Aero	mini					37900	42850
	maxi					41150	46000
wgn. 4dr. 2.3	mini					29300	33400
	maxi					32500	36500
wgn. 4dr. 3.0	mini					32100	36550
	maxi					35500	39700
wgn. 4dr. Aero	mini						39000
	maxi						42300

See page 7 to adapt these figures.

SATURN L

2000 SATURN LS

To widen its market, Saturn has decided to compete with Honda Accord and Toyota Camry. An ambitious enterprise which hasn't pay back yet. The L models are available as 4-door sedans and wagons animated by 4- and 6-cylinder engines.

PROS

- **Styling is plain**, but it does have the advantage of making these models immediately identifiable as members of the Saturn family.
- **The principle** of a structure supporting body panels, including side polymer panels is a good one.
- **Suspension** is an excellent compromise between comfort and handling. Smooth but not soft, it's relatively neutral when cornering at average speeds and it provides a comfortable ride.
- **Performance** level is very respectable with both engines, the 3.0L and 2.2L and manual transmission.
- **Brakes** are reliable, efficient and consistent, but ABS is only optional.
- **Trunk** is roomy in all directions and the rear seat folds down for extra space.
- **The careful assembly** and nice-looking materials provide a solid feel and look for both the body and the passenger compartment.

CONS

- **Noise level** is strangely high because of engine and tire noise and wind that leaks in around the top of the windshield.
- **The 4-cylinder engine** is weak when teamed with the automatic transmission and doesn't justify its fuel consumption.
- **Maneuverability** is mediocre and some parking maneuvers are painful.
- **Wagon cargo space** can barely take on as much as the sedan's trunk, because its height is limited by the glasses design.
- **Storage spaces** are limited to the minimum in front and rear.
- **The Firestone Affinity tires** aren't the best choice for these models - they lack grip and generate noise.
- **Forgotten:** front seats armrests, shifter indicator for the automatic transmission and dummy pedal for the driver's comfort.

CONCLUSION

The Saturn L haven't encountered a big success and those who take the risk will soon discover that the resale value is low and resale time fairly long.

RECALLS

2001 Dealers will inspect the shift cable retainer clip, verify proper installation and if necessary replace the cable.

L   SATURN

RELIABILITY PROBLEMS

	1996	1997	1998	1999	2000	2001
Engine:					X	-
Transmission:					-	-
Suspension:					-	-
Steering:					-	-
Brakes:					-	-
Electricity:					X	X
Body:					X	-
Accessories:					X	X
Fit/finish:					X	-

POWERTRAIN

Year	Type/ L/Camshaft/bhp	Drivetrain & gearbox	Acceler. 0/100 sec.	Top. speed km/h	Ave. Fuel consp. l/100 km
00-01	L4/2.2/DOHC/137	front-M5	10.0	175	10.0
		front-A4	11.0	170	10.5
	V6/3.0/DOHC/182	front-A4	8.8	180	12.0

SPECIFICATIONS

Model 00-01	Wlb. mm	Lght. mm	Cb.wt kg	Brakes fr/rr	Steering type	Standard tires
sdn. 4dr. LS	2705	4836	1320	dc/dr	pwr.r&p.	195/65R15
sdn. 4dr. LS1	2705	4836	1369	dc/dr	pwr.r&p.	195/65R15
sdn. 4dr. LS2	2705	4836	1430	dc/dc	pwr.r&p.	205/65R15
wgn. 4dr. LW1	2705	4836	1395	dc/dr	pwr.r&p.	195/65R15
wgn. 4dr. LW2	2705	4836	1465	dc/dc	pwr.r&p.	205/65R15

PRICES

Model / version		1996	1997	1998	1999	2000	2001
sdn. 4dr. LS	mini					14200	16300
	maxi					16300	18900
sdn. 4dr. LS1	mini					15200	17300
	maxi					17300	19950
sdn. 4dr. LS2	mini					18900	22000
	maxi					20500	24700
wgn. 4dr. LW1	mini					15750	17850
	maxi					17850	21000
wgn. 4dr. LW2	mini					16800	19400
	maxi					18900	22600

See page 7 to adapt these figures.

2000 SATURN LW2

SATURN

2000 SATURN SL2

Under GM's wing, Saturn has developed pretty awesome products and amazing P.R. with customers. These sedans and station wagons were first sold in 1990 and were freshened up in '96. Since '99, the Saturn has corrected some very well-know flaws by receiving improved engine components for both models, better fuel efficiency and much less noise and vibration.

PROS
- **A distinctive style** that is unmistakably that of a Saturn.
- **An original design** with a metallic cage structure on which are mounted polymer panels that are rust-proof and resistant to light impacts.
- **Dealership service** is second to none and makes up for the occasional reliability problems.
- **Handling** is clean with such a well-adjusted suspension.
- **Power brakes** and steering are smooth, so the car moves all of a piece and emergency stops are safe and sure.
- **Build and finish** quality is quite good, but still doesn't compare with that of upper-end Japanese cars.

CONS
- **The snug sedan** cabin only seats four adults, and the tiny seatbench on the coupe isn't too comfortable.
- **Engines** are noisy and rough around the edges and gears on the manual transmission are poorly calibrated.
- **Braking** could have more grip and power, for stopping distances are longer than average.
- **Performance** are by no means sensational, even with the more muscular engines that seem to sputter and strain.
- **There's a heck** of a racket during strong accelerations, but the noise level is more tolerable at cruising speed.
- **The trunk** as well as the baggage compartment on the station wagon aren't roomy, because of the large suspension wells. Luckily the rear seatbench folds down and both can be extended.
- **The plastic trim** in the cabin is far from chic.

CONCLUSION
The Saturns are good used cars, for they're quite stylish and are durable with their straightforward mechanical components.

RECALLS
1997 Correction to the owner's manual about headlamps adjusting.
Defective passenger and front passenger seat belts.
Pinion bearing cage is defective on manual steering.
Key could be removed while in the "Run" position.
Defective horn assembly that could generate an underhood fire.

S — SATURN

2001 Dealers will check the automatic transaxle park lock cable assembly operation and if necessary adjust the cable. Dealers will inspect and if necessary replace the fuel tank assembly.

RELIABILITY PROBLEMS

	1996	1997	1998	1999	2000	2001
Engine:	X	X	X	-	-	-
Transmission:	X	X	-	X	-	-
Suspension:	-	X	X	-	X	-
Steering:	-	-	-	-	-	-
Brakes:	X	X	X	X	-	-
Electricity:	X	X	X	-	X	-
Body:	X	-	-	-	-	-
Accessories:	X	X	X	X	X	X
Fit/finish:	X	-	-	-	X	-

POWERTRAIN

Year	Type/ L/Camshaft/bhp	Drivetrain & gearbox	Acceler. 0/100 sec.	Top. speed km/h	Ave. Fuel consp. l./100 km
96-01	L4/1.9/SOHC/85-100	front-M5	11.0	165	8.0
		front-A4	12.2	160	8.5
	L4/1.9/DOHC/124	front-M5	8.7	185	8.5
		front-A4	9.8	180	9.5

SPECIFICATIONS

Model 96-01	Wlb. mm	Lght. mm	Cb.wt kg	Brakes fr/rr	Steering type	Standard tires
cpe. 2dr. SC1	2520	4400	1035	dc/dr	pwr.r&p.	175/70R14
cpe. 2dr. SC2	2520	4434	1084	dc/dr	pwr.r&p.	195/60R15
cpe. 3dr. SC1/2	2601	4574	1052	dc/dr	pwr.r&p.	195/60R15
sdn. 4dr. SL/SL1	2601	4493	1055	dc/dr	r&p.	175/70R14
sdn. 4dr. SL2	2601	4493	1084	dc/dr	pwr.r&p.	185/65R15
wgn. 4dr. SW1	2601	4493	1085	dc/dr	pwr.r&p.	175/70R14
wgn. 4dr. SW2	2601	4493	1111	dc/dr	pwr.r&p.	185/65R15

PRICES

Model / version		1996	1997	1998	1999	2000	2001
cpe. 2dr. SC1	mini	6500	7650	8700	10300		
	maxi	8400	9550	10600	12100		
cpe. 2dr. SC2	mini	7550	8700	10100	11000		
	maxi	9450	10600	11650	12900		
cpe. 3dr. SC1	mini				10800	12100	14200
	maxi				12600	14200	16800
cpe. 3dr. SC2	mini				11350	13650	15750
	maxi				13100	15750	18400
sdn. 4dr. SL	mini	2800	4000	5350	6600	8400	10500
	maxi	5250	6300	7150	9250	10500	13100
sdn. 4dr. SL1	mini	4950	6100	7450	8600	11000	13100
	maxi	6800	8000	9250	11000	13100	15750
sdn. 4dr. SL2	mini	6000	7150	8500	10300	13100	15200
	maxi	7900	9000	10300	12100	15200	17850
wgn. 4dr. SW1	mini	6500	7700	9000	10800		
	maxi	8400	9650	10600	12600		
wgn. 4dr. SW2	mini	7550	8300	9550	11350	12600	14200
	maxi	9450	10500	11550	13100	14700	16800

See page 7 to adapt these figures.

SUBARU   Forester

2001 SUBARU Forester

The Forester is built on the Impreza platform and shares its mechanical features. It was first available in 1998.

PROS
- **The automatic all-wheel drive** makes for smooth moves in all kinds of weather and on dirt roads in the middle of... the forest.
- **The vehicle** handles well in spite of high ground clearance. Cornering into curves is no problem at all and demeanor is neutral at normal speeds.
- **Maneuverability** is great due to a tight steer angle diameter and trim overall size.
- **The cargo hold** is spacious and easy to get to with the rear hatch that opens nice and wide and lowers to just the right loading level.
- **Long trips** are fatigue-free with such a civilized suspension, nicely shaped front seats and relatively low noise interference.
- **Nice feature:** storage spots for front seat travelers and luggage cover.

CONS
- **Off-road rambles** are no picnic, a reminder that the Forester is more of a high-perched car than a true grit 4X4.
- **Accelerations** are nothing to rave about with the automatic transmission and pick-up is strained with a full load.
- **The manual transmission** is sensitive to cold conditions and the shifter grinds and isn't always reliable.
- **The engine** is raucous, gets the shakes and yields only average power and torque even with its impressive displacement.
- **Rear seat** passengers don't have enough leg and elbowroom and boarding is tricky with such slim doors.
- **Seats** are terribly firm, especially the rear seatbench that's flat as blazes and offers only a short seat cushion.
- **Some dashboard trim materials** look rather chintzy and don't jive with the overall cabin look.
- **Tires** are poorly suited to this vehicle, so they're disappointing both on the highway and on less traveled roads.
- **To be mentioned:** lack of storage spots in the rear seat area, really awful radio with terribly low-slung dials.

CONCLUSION
The Forester isn't a true 4X4, but the all-wheel drive feature provides safe travel and the vehicle is right in fashion...

RECALLS
1998 A reinforcement bar had to be installed behind the front bumper.
Oil leaks on the exhaust manifold.
98-99 Defective brake master cylinder on vehicles equipped with ABS.

Forester — SUBARU

RELIABILITY PROBLEMS

	1996	1997	1998	1999	2000	2001
Engine:			-	-	X	-
Transmission:			X	X	-	-
Suspension:			-	-	-	-
Steering:			X	X	-	-
Brakes:			X	X	X	-
Electricity:			X	X	X	-
Body:			X	X	-	-
Accessories:			X	X	X	X
Fit/finish:			X	X	-	-

POWERTRAIN

Year	Type/ L/Camshaft/bhp	Drivetrain & gearbox
98-01	H4/2.5/DOHC/165	all-M5
		all-A4

PERFORMANCE

Acceler. 0/100 sec.	Top. speed km/h	Ave. Fuel consp. l./100 km
9.2	165	11.5
10.4	160	11.5

SPECIFICATIONS

Model 98-01	Wlb. mm	Lght. mm	Cb.wt kg	Brakes fr/rr	Steering type	Standard tires
wgn. 4dr. L	2525	4450	1379	dc/dr/ABS	pwr.r&p.	205/70R15
wgn. 4dr. S	2525	4450	1379	dc/ABS	pwr.r&p.	215/60R16

PRICES

Model / version		1996	1997	1998	1999	2000	2001
wgn. 4dr. L	mini			17300	19400	21400	23600
	maxi			19200	21200	23600	26200
wgn. 4dr. S	mini			18500	21300	24550	27300
	maxi			19950	23100	26250	29900
wgn. 4dr. LTD	mini				23000	25700	28900
	maxi				24700	28000	31500
wgn. 4dr. Spe.Ed.	mini						24700
	maxi						27300

See page 7 to adapt these figures.

2001 SUBARU Forester

SUBARU Impreza

2000 SUBARU Impreza RS

The Impreza replaced the Loyale in 1993. It's available in various body styles: coupes, sedans and station wagons, in 2- and 4-door models, with front-wheel and all-wheel drive and all are powered by either a 1.8L, 2.2L or a 2.5L 4-cylinder engine.

PROS

- **Its unusual design**, especially the shapely lines of the station wagon that resembles the Pacer.
- **Driving** is enhanced by a muscular engine that whoops quite a torque, by well-calibrated gears and safe all-wheel drive.
- **Handling** on the all-wheel drive model is more impressive than the model equipped with front-wheel drive whose softer suspension causes more swing and sway.
- **Solid build** and clean finish.
- **Steering** is smooth and benefits from a good reduction ratio, which allows for excellent maneuverability, thanks to a small steer angle diameter.
- **The suspension** provides for a more smooth ride than that of the Loyale that was rather primitive by comparison.
- **Brakes** are effective and stable, even without the optional ABS.
- **Standard equipment** is quite adequate and includes an airbag and an AM/FM radio/cassette.

CONS

- **Cabin space** is quite snug, especially in the rear seats and they aren't easy to climb into because of tight leg room.
- **The base engine** coupled with all-wheel drive is anemic and accelerations and pick-up are pretty sluggish and frustrating.
- **The trunk** on the sedan and the baggage compartment on the station wagon are smaller than average for this car category.
- **The center console** isn't too ergonomic with controls out of the driver's reach.
- **Interior trim** is very synthetic looking and some shades are weird.

CONCLUSION

The Impreza is only really to be commended in the all-wheel drive model, for the front-wheel drive model has a lot of rivals that are far more competent.

RECALLS

None over this period.

Impreza — SUBARU

RELIABILITY PROBLEMS

	1996	1997	1998	1999	2000	2001
Engine:	X	X	-	-	-	-
Transmission:	-	-	-	-	-	-
Suspension:	-	-	-	-	-	-
Steering:	-	-	X	-	-	-
Brakes:	-	X	X	X	X	-
Electricity:	X	X	X	X	X	X
Body:	-	-	X	X	-	-
Accessories:	X	-	X	X	X	X
Fit/finish:	-	-	X	X	X	-

POWERTRAIN

Year	Type/ L/Camshaft/bhp	Drivetrain & gearbox
96-01	H4/2.2/SOHC/135-137	all-M5
		all-A4
98-01	H4/2.5/DOHC/165 (RS)	all-M5

PERFORMANCE

Acceler. 0/100 sec.	Top speed km/h	Ave. Fuel consp. l./100 km
10.0	170	10.5
11.4	160	10.8
9.0	175	11.5

SPECIFICATIONS

Model 96-01	Wlb. mm	Lght. mm	Cb.wt kg	Brakes fr/rr	Steering type	Standard tires
cpe. 2dr. AWD	2520	4374	1281	dc/ABS	pwr.r&p.	205/55R16
sdn. 4dr. AWD	2520	4374	1220	dc/dr	pwr.r&p.	195/60R15
wgn.5dr. AWD	2520	4374	1286	dc/dr	pwr.r&p.	175/70R14
sdn. 4dr. AWD	2520	4374	1134	dc/dr/ABS	pwr.r&p.	205/60R15
sdn. 4dr. RS	2520	4374	1150	dc/ABS	pqw.r&p.	205/55R16
wgn.5dr. Outback	2520	4374	1286	dc/ABS	pwr.r&p.	205/55R16

PRICES

Model / version		1996	1997	1998	1999	2000	2001
cpe. 2dr. RS	mini			17400	19200	21000	23100
	maxi			19200	21000	23100	25700
cpe. 2dr. L AWD	mini	6100	9450				
	maxi	8000	11150				
sdn. 4dr. L AWD	mini	7150	9750	12200			
	maxi	8900	11550	13950			
sdn. 4dr. TS	mini				15000	17300	19400
	maxi				16800	19400	22000
sdn. 4dr. RS	mini					20500	22600
	maxi					22600	25200
wgn. 4dr. L AWD	mini	7550	11350				
	maxi	9450	13250				
wgn. 4dr. Brighton	mini		7350	10500	12400	14700	16300
	maxi		9000	11950	14200	16800	18900
wgn. 4dr. Outback	mini	11250	13250	17850	19750	22600	24700
	maxi	13100	15300	19750	21500	24700	27300

See page 7 to adapt these figures.

SUBARU — Legacy

1998 SUBARU Legacy wagon

Subaru first put the Legacy on the market in 1990. The Turbo came out in '91, the Touring station wagon in '93 and the Outback as well as the 2.5L engine in '96. Without a doubt, the Legacy is by far the Subaru that sells the most in North America, for its AWD transmission and its numerous body styles and trim levels.

PROS
- **All-wheel drive** is the first drawing card of a Subaru vehicle for it makes for safe driving all year round.
- **Handling** is clean and stable with such a robust frame, competent suspension and optimal wheel function, no matter what the road conditions.
- **Fuel consumption** is a bit more economical with the 2.5L engine that benefits from a better power to weight ratio, especially on the front-wheel drive model.
- **The cabin is roomy**, as is the trunk; four adults and all their luggage can be accommodated by this car.
- **Steering is accurate**, smooth and even with its slightly high reduction ratio, it provides for good maneuverability, thanks to its small steer angle diameter.

CONS
- **Brakes** aren't too hot for they don't really grip as they should and even the 4-disc brakes are tough to control with such a soft pedal.
- **Excessive** vehicle weight cripples the 2.2L engine that really has to puff and strain on the all-wheel drive models.
- **Driving** would be more pleasant if the frame design wasn't so high and if the driver wasn't seated so low.
- **Steering** is too light, because it's over-assisted.
- **Equipment** is very Spartan on base models and every little nicety comes as an option.
- **Noise level** is chronic and loud with such a boisterous engine, road noise and wind whistling around the cabin.

CONCLUSION
The Legacy is the best choice at Subaru, because of its practical size and its more refined mechanical features.

RECALLS
96-97 Front transverse links may break and must be inspected.
1997 The hazard light switch might be defective.
Bearing in throttle assembly may be missing.
97-98 Automatic shift lever assembly may fail.
1998 Defective oil filter.
98-99 Defective brake master cylinder on vehicles equipped with ABS.
2000 The bolts of the transverse link will be retorqued.
The low beam bulbs will be reequipped with DOT marked units.
2001 Suspect inner-front seat rails will be replaced.
Vehicles will be inspected and all fuel hoses under lot number 0804 and 0806 will be replaced.
Affected right front bearing housings will be replaced.
Alla beige coloured rear center lap/shoulder belts with lot number 0171 will be replaced.

Legacy   SUBARU

RELIABILITY PROBLEMS

	1996	1997	1998	1999	2000	2001
Engine:	X	X	X	X	-	-
Transmission:	-	-	-	-	-	-
Suspension:	X	-	X	X	-	-
Steering:	-	-	X	-	-	-
Brakes:	-	-	X	-	-	-
Electricity:	X	X	X	X	-	-
Body:	-	-	-	-	-	-
Accessories:	X	X	X	X	X	-
Fit/finish:	X	-	-	-	-	-

POWERTRAIN

Year	Type/ L/Camshaft/bhp	Drivetrain & gearbox
96-00	H4-2.2/SOHC/130-137	front/all-M5
		front/all-A4
96-01	H4-2.5/DOHC/155-165	front/all-M5
		front/all-A4
2001	H6-3.0/SOHC/212	front/all-A4

PERFORMANCE

Acceler. 0/100 sec.	Top. speed km/h	Ave. Fuel consp. l./100 km
11.0	180	10.5
12.2	175	10.1
10.0	190	11.5
NA	NA	NA
8.8	200	11.6

SPECIFICATIONS

Model	Wlb. mm	Lght. mm	Cb.wt kg	Brakes fr/rr	Steering type	Standard tires
96-99						
sdn. 4dr. Brighton	2629	4686	1318	dc/dr	pwr.r&p.	185/70R14
sdn. 4dr. L	2629	4610	1309	dc/ABS	pwr.r&p.	185/70R14
wgn. 4dr. L	2629	4686	1349	dc/ABS	pwr.r&p.	185/70R14
sdn. 4dr. GT	2629	4610	1402	dc/ABS	pwr.r&p.	205/55R16
wgn. 4dr. GT	2629	4686	1442	dc/ABS	pwr.r&p.	205/55R16
wgn. 4dr. Outback	2629	4719	1431	dc/ABS	pwr.r&p.	205/70R15

PRICES

Model / version		1996	1997	1998	1999	2000	2001
sdn. 4dr. L	mini	8600				18900	21000
	maxi	10900				21500	24150
sdn. 4dr. L AWD	mini	10700	12400	14800			
	maxi	13000	14800	17100			
sdn. 4dr. LS AWD	mini	12500	3450				
	maxi	14700	5850				
sdn. 4dr. LSi AWD	mini	13350	17100				
	maxi	15750	19500				
sdn. 4dr. GT AWD	mini	13350	15200	19000	21850	23100	25200
	maxi	15650	17950	21300	24150	25700	28350
sdn. 4dr. L Ann.	mini			17100			
	maxi			19400			
sdn. 4dr. GT LTD AWD	mini			21100	25500	26800	28350
	maxi			23400	27300	29400	31500
sdn. 4dr. Outback LTD	mini				21850	24150	26250
	maxi				24700	27300	29400
wgn. 4dr. L	mini	9150				19400	22000
	maxi	11550				22000	24900
wgn. 4dr. Ann.	mini			17650			
	maxi			19950			
wgn. 4dr. L AWD	mini	10700	12900	15550			
	maxi	13100	15350	18150			
wgn. 4dr. LS AWD	mini	12300	14500				
	maxi	14700	16900				
wgn. 4dr. Bri. AWD	mini	7000	8200	10600	12400	16500	18400
	maxi	9450	10600	12900	14700	19100	21200
wgn. 4dr. Bri.SE AWD	mini			12200	15000		
	maxi			14500	17300		
wgn. 4dr. LSi AWD	mini	15950	17650				
	maxi	18400	20000				
wgn. 4dr. GT AWD	mini	13850	16600	20300	22350	24100	26200
	maxi	16350	19000	22900	24700	26800	29200
wgn. 4dr. Outback AWD	mini	13850	16600	20600	23400	25700	28250
	maxi		16800	19500	23200	26250	28900	31500
wgn. 4dr. Out. LTD	mini			18700	22150	24450	27300	29900
	maxi			21600	25000	27300	30450	33100
wgn. 4dr. H6 3.0	mini						32550
	maxi						36200
wgn. 4dr. H6 3.0 VOC	mini						36750
	maxi						40400

See page 7 to adapt these figures.

SUBARU   SVX

1997 SUBARU SVX

The SVX sports coupe replaced the XT in 1992. It's equipped with all-wheel drive and is powered by a 3.3L flat-6 engine.

PROS

- **Its unique Giugiaro** design makes it stands out from its rivals, but it hasn't helped sales anyway.
- **The SVX benefits** from good wheel function and a smooth engine, but accelerations and pick-up aren't at all Sportscar like.
- **The cabin interior** and trunk are roomy enough to accommodate four passengers and all their belongings.
- **Brakes** are good and tough, stable and smooth, but stops are longer than the average because of excessive vehicle weight.
- **Handling** is quite good in spite of vehicle weight, because the suspension keeps the frame on track.
- **Practical year-round** car and there are lots of convenient storage compartments distributed throughout the interior. All in all, equipment is complete and plush.
- **The cabin design** is quite original and fabrics and trim are exceptionally attractive.

CONS

- **Its wild**, rakish look and treated door windows that aren't too practical but let the driver enjoys fresh air without being blowed.
- **The sluggish SVX** suffers from poor maneuverability and lack of agility on curves, which really takes the fun out of driving.
- **High gas consumption** that is by far more than that of V6 engines with equivalent displacement.
- **Its lack of popularity** may make it possible to buy it at a good price, but the car will be worth even less on the used car market...

CONCLUSION

The SVX didn't sell as well as expected, but at least there aren't too many of them out there and it's a good buy for what it has to offer.

RECALLS

None over this period.

SVX   SUBARU

RELIABILITY PROBLEMS

	1996	1997	1998	1999	2000	2001
Engine:	X	X				
Transmission:	X	X				
Suspension:	-	-				
Steering:	-	-				
Brakes:	X	X				
Electricity:	X	-				
Body:	-	-				
Accessories:	X	X				
Fit/finish:	-	-				

POWERTRAIN

Year	Type/ L/Camshaft/bhp	Drivetrain & gearbox
96-97	H6/3.3/DOHC/230	all-A4

PERFORMANCE

Acceler. 0/100 sec.	Top. speed km/h	Ave. Fuel consp. l./100 km
9.0	220	13.5

SPECIFICATIONS

Model	Wlb. mm	Lght. mm	Cb.wt kg	Brakes fr/rr	Steering type	Standard tires
cpe. 2dr.	2610	4652	1625	dc/ABS	pwr.r&p.	225/50VR16

PRICES

Model / version		1996	1997	1998	1999	2000	2001
cpe. 2dr. LSI	mini	22000	25200				
	maxi	25200	28350				

See page 7 to adapt these figures.

1996 SUBARU SVX

SUZUKI — Esteem

2001 SUZUKI Esteem

In 1996, Suzuki introduced a model inspired by the Swift, but bigger, sturdier and driven by a 1.6L 4-cylinder engine. For its '99 harvest, Suzuki has presented a more muscular GLX powered by a 121-bhp L1.8L engine.

PROS
- **A surprisingly spacious** cabin interior, considering the overall trim size of the car. There's generous head and leg room, and according to exact measurements, the Esteem boasts of a larger interior than its main rivals.
- **Controls** are silky smooth and responses are rarely harsh.
- **The well-adjusted suspension**, nicely designed seats and effective soundproofing make for a comfy ride.
- **The GLX** is a better buy than the competition, considering the equipment you get for the going price.
- **Assembly is solid**, fit and finish are meticulous and trim components look just great.
- **As far as convenience goes**, there's a practical and convertible trunk and sufficient storage compartments throughout the cabin interior.

CONS
- **Driving is vague** because of the rear end that is hard to control and slides off track. The Esteem is very sensitive to crosswinds, road ruts and quick lane changes.
- **The original tires** are undersized and they squeal on the slightest curve taken at higher speed.
- **Its plain** and simple body design isn't at all spectacular but some people find it attractive.
- **The manual shifter** is inaccurate and sluggish and the automatic shifter is rough.
- **Aerodynamic efficiency** can't be the greatest (unpublished), for there's constant wind noise whistling around the windshield.
- **Rear seat** access isn't a piece of cake for heftier individuals, because the narrow doors don't open too wide.

CONCLUSION
The Esteem isn't recommended as a used car, because its real value is an unknown factor, given that sales are confidential.

RECALLS
1998 Defective accessory engine block heater that may experience an electrical short circuit.

Esteem — SUZUKI

RELIABILITY PROBLEMS

	1996	1997	1998	1999	2000	2001
Engine:	X	X	X	X	-	-
Transmission:	X	-	-	-	-	-
Suspension:	-	-	-	-	-	-
Steering:	X	-	X	X	-	-
Brakes:	X	X	-	-	-	-
Electricity:	-	X	X	X	X	-
Body:	-	-	-	-	-	-
Accessories:	X	X	X	X	X	-
Fit/finish:	X	-	-	-	-	-

POWERTRAIN

Year	Type/ L/Camshaft/bhp	Drivetrain & gearbox
96-01	L4/1.6/SOHC/98	front-M5
		front-A4
99-01	L4/1.8/DOHC/121	front-M5
		front-A4

PERFORMANCE

Acceler. 0/100 sec.	Top. speed km/h	Ave. Fuel consp. l./100 km
11.0	160	7.7
12.2	150	8.5
NA	NA	NA
NA	NA	NA

SPECIFICATIONS

Model 96-01	Wlb. mm	Lght. mm	Cb.wt kg	Brakes fr/rr	Steering type	Standard tires
sdn. 4dr. GL	2480	4195	990	dc/dr	pwr.r&p.	175/70R13
sdn. 4dr. GLX	2480	4195	1016	dc/dr	pwr.r&p.	185/60R14
wgn. 4dr. GL	2480	4345	1070	dc/dr	pwr.r&p.	175/70R13
wgn. 4dr. GLX	2480	4345	1080	dc/dr	pwr.r&p.	185/60R14

PRICES

Model / version		1996	1997	1998	1999	2000	2001
sdn. 4dr. GL	mini	3700	4700	6000	7350	8500	10000
	maxi	5800	6400	7650	8900	10500	12600
sdn. 4dr. GLX	mini	4700	5600	7100	8400	10100	12100
	maxi	6300	7450	8700	10000	12100	14700
wgn. 4dr. GL 1.6	mini			7550	8400		
	maxi			9250	10000		
wgn. 4dr. GLX 1.6	mini			8500	9450		
	maxi			10300	11100		
wgn. 4dr. GL 1.8	mini					9550	11550
	maxi					11550	14200
wgn. 4dr. GLX 1.8	mini				9850	11550	13100
	maxi				11550	13650	15750

See page 7 to adapt these figures.

2001 SUZUKI Esteem wagon

SUZUKI-GEO-PONTIAC

Sidekick
Tracker
Sunrunner

1998 SUZUKI Sidekick convertible

The Sidekick was available as a convertible and 2-door sedan in 1989, the 4-door station wagon came out in '91 and the DOHC engine in '92.

PROS
- **Its fun body style** is playful and the interior design is very spiffy.
- **There's a wide choice** of models, trim levels and mechanical features.
- **Handling** is better than that of the former Samurai because of the independent suspension up front, wider wheel tracks, more accurate steering and because the leaf springs have been replaced by coil springs.
- **The 1.8L engine** has more gusto and good manners than the base 1.6L engine and gears on the manual transmission are nicely calibrated.
- **Nice practical items**: the folding seatbench and the handy to use soft top.

CONS
- **Brakes** aren't great with such long and unpredictable stops, due to almost immediate wheel lock.
- **With the automatic**, engine performance are anemic and gears aren't as well spaced on as on the manual.
- **High sensitivity** to crosswinds on the 4-door model.
- **Thin bodywork** is vulnerable to impact and to corrosion.
- **Low ground clearance** cripples performance on rough terrain.
- **Engine roar**, tire thump, hum and whistling wind sure make for a tiring ride.
- **The trunk holds** next to nothing when the rear seats are occupied on the 2-door.
- **Some trim components** look flimsy and bodywork is fragile and rust-prone.

CONCLUSION
These minivans are legion and prices vary with the shape they're in, so it's a good idea to check the vehicle over and really think things over carefully.

RECALLS
1999 Steering column shaft coupling could break resulting in loss of steering control. (Tracker)
Miscalibration of the powertrain control module could result in a no-start condition in cold weather.

Sidekick
Tracker
Sunrunner

PONTIAC-GEO-SUZUKI

RELIABILITY PROBLEMS

	1996	1997	1998	1999	2000	2001
Engine:	X	X	-	X	-	-
Transmission:	-	-	-	-	-	-
Suspension:	-	-	-	-	-	-
Steering:	-	-	-	X	-	-
Brakes:	X	X	X	X	-	-
Electricity:	--	X	X	X	X	X
Body:	X	X	X	-	X	-
Accessories:	X	X	X	X	X	X
Fit/finish:	-	-	-	-	-	-

POWERTRAIN

Year	Type/ L/Camshaft/bhp	Drivetrain & gearbox	Acceler. 0/100 sec.	Top. speed km/h	Ave. Fuel consp. l./100 km
96-01	L4/1.6/SOHC/80-97	rear/all-M5	12.2	165	10.5
		rear/all-A3/A4	16.3	135	9.5
1996	L4/1.6/DOHC/95 (4 door)	rear/all-M5	13.3	145	9.0
		rear/all-A4	15.5	140	10.0
96-98	L4 1.8/DOHC/120	rear/all-M5	12.8	155	10.5
		rear/all-A4	14.4	155	10.7
99-01	L4/2.0/DOHC/127	rear/all-M5	11.7	160	10.5
		rear/all-A4	12.8	155	11.5

SPECIFICATIONS

Model 96-01	Wlb. mm	Lght. mm	Cb.wt kg	Brakes fr/rr	Steering type	Standard tires
con. 2dr.	2200	3650	1085	dc/dr	bal.	205/75R15
sdn. 3dr.	2200	3650	1100	dc/dr	bal.	205/75R15
wgn. 5dr.	2480	4030	1240	dc/dr	pwr.bal.	215/65R16

PRICES

Model / version		1996	1997	1998	1999	2000	2001
SUZUKI Sidekick							
con. 2dr. JA 4x4	mini	3200	4200	5800			
	maxi	5250	6100	7650			
con. 2dr. JX 4x4	mini	4200	5150				
	maxi	6300	7150				
wgn. 4dr. JX 4x4	mini	5250	6300	7350			
	maxi	6800	7900	9250			
wgn. 4dr. JX Sport 4x4	mini	7350	8400	10900			
	maxi	9450	10500	12800			
wgn. 4dr. JLX Sport 4x4	mini	9150	10700	12400			
	maxi	11000	13100	14400			

GEO/CHEVROLET Tracker - PONTIAC Sunrunner

Model / version		1996	1997	1998	1999	2000	2001
con. 2dr. 4x2	mini	2850	5250				
	maxi	4700	7150				
con. 2dr. 4x4	mini	4400	6300				
	maxi	6300	8200				
con. 2dr. GT 4x4	mini	5250					
	maxi	7350					
con. 2dr. 4x2	mini	3700	5650				
	maxi	5350	7550				
con. 2dr. 4x4	mini	5000	6600	9750	10800	12600	15200
	maxi	6950	8500	12100	13000	15100	18400
con. 2dr. LSi 4X4	mini	5450					
	maxi	7350					
wgn. 2dr. 4X4	mini		7550	10500	11600	13650	16300
	maxi		9550	12600	13850	16300	19400
wgn. 2dr. LSi 4X4	mini		9150				
	maxi		10500				

See page 7 to adapt these figures.

SUZUKI   Swift

1999 SUZUKI Swift

The Swift was first sold in 1989 as a 3 and 5-door sedan, then as a 4-door in '92. It's powered by a 1.6L 4-cylinder engine. It was redesigned and upgraded in '95 and the DLX, a 3-door sedan, is the only trim level available since then.

PROS
- **These small city slicker** cars are attractive.
- **Four adults** can be accommodated in the cabin, in spite of the small vehicle size.
- **The engine** is more efficient with the manual transmission.
- **The car handles well**, for there isn't much sway and understeering is easy to control.
- **It's quite a comfortable car**, for the suspension is quite smooth and the noise level is reasonable at cruising speed.

CONS
- **Brakes** just don't do their job on sudden stops, because almost immediate wheel lock stretches stopping distances to the limit.
- **Steering** is vague and with such a light vehicle, it's hard to stay on track in crosswinds and on rough roads, especially with the small tires that put up a fuss when they hit road ruts.
- **The automatic transmission** saps the power of the engines.
- **On the hatchback**, the trunk is teeny tiny, but it can be extended by lowering the rear seatbench.
- **Thin bodywork** is vulnerable to impact and to rust.

CONCLUSION
These small cars are practical and fun to drive in the city, but they're not quite at home on the highway. They don't hold up too well over time and replacement parts are expensive.

RECALLS
1997 Defective shifter assembly that allows automatic transmission to be moved from the Park position without the use of the key, transmission lever detent button, or depressing the brakes.

Swift — SUZUKI

RELIABILITY PROBLEMS

	1996	1997	1998	1999	2000	2001
Engine:	X	X	X	X	-	-
Transmission:	-	X	-	-	-	-
Suspension:	X	-	-	-	-	-
Steering:	-	-	-	-	-	-
Brakes:	X	X	X	X	-	-
Electricity:	-	X	X	X	-	-
Body:	X	X	X	X	X	X
Accessories:	X	X	X	X	X	X
Fit/finish:	-	-	-	-	-	-

POWERTRAIN

Year	Type/ L/Camshaft/bhp	Drivetrain & gearbox
96-98	L4/1.0/SOHC/55	front-M5
96-01	L4/1.3/SOHC/70-79	front-M5
		front-A3

PERFORMANCE

Acceler. 0/100 sec.	Top. speed km/h	Ave. Fuel consp. l./100 km
13.8	145	5.4
12.8	160	6.1
14.0	150	7.9

SPECIFICATIONS

Model 96-01	Wlb. mm	Lght. mm	Cb.wt kg	Brakes fr/rr	Steering type	Standard tires
sdn. 3dr.	2365	3795	860	dc/dr	r&p.	155/80R13

PRICES

Model / version		1996	1997	1998	1999	2000	2001
sdn. 3dr. DLX	mini	3200	4200	4750	5650	7350	9450
	maxi	4700	5800	6300	7350	9450	12100

See page 7 to adapt these figures.

2000 SUZUKI Swift

The Canadian Used Car Guide 2002-20023 305

SUZUKI Vitara-Grand Vitara-XL7

1999 SUZUKI Grand Vitara

The Vitara and Grand Vitara have replaced the Sidekicks. These 4x4 are available in a 2-door convertible or 4-door station wagon in JA, JX or JLX trim level. The two firsts are driven by a 2.0L 4-cylinder engine and the station wagon gets a new 2.5L V6. The stretch version XL7 appears in 2001 powered by a 2.7-liter V6.

PROS
• **Space cabin** is roomier because they're longer and wider, mostly in the XL7 which offers a 3rd row of seats.
• **Affordable prices**, explain why they aren't loaded with equipment. But it's nice to buy a convertible or station wagon without wincing.
• **The V6 engines**, gives the JLX station wagon and XL7 better performance than the 2.0L engine. Too bad the 2.6-liter isn't available in the convertible.
• **Handling** is a lot more competent with the more rigid platform and more accurate rack-and-pinion steering.
•**The rack-and-pinion steering** has cut down on the steer angle diameter for both vehicles, so they offer better maneuverability.
• **The inside presentation** has a modern and functional new look; it feels more like a car than a SUV.
• **Well-planned storage** compartments and the baggage compartment on the 4-door wagon can be extended by lowering the rear seatbench.

CONS
• **Stability** still really depends on the road surface, wind and tire grip. The convertible can reserve some surprises...
•**The fuel economy** is disappointing because these engines are not strong enough to hoist these vehicles to decent performance levels.
• **Off-the-road capabilities** is questionable because entrance and exit angles as well as ground clearance have been reduced.
• **The ride** is far from comfy with such a suspension that reacts badly to the least road flaw, seat upholstery is pretty hard and sound dampening is next to nil.
• **The brakes** are still not up to par, yielding the same long stretches on sudden stops. But vehicle path is more predictable with standard ABS assistance.
• **Access** to the rear seats is limited inside the convertible because of lack of space and missing running boards.
• **The convertible** suffers its very jittery suspension, the near-stingy heater, the cramped rear seat and inadequate luggage compartment, and some trim material still looks a bit cheap...

CONCLUSION
Attractive bodies seek skilled engines to power two very thirsty vehicles.

RECALLS
2000 Correct label regarding GAWR will replace the wrong one.

Vitara-Grand Vitara -XL7　　　SUZUKI

RELIABILITY PROBLEMS

	1996	1997	1998	1999	2000	2001
Engine:				X	-	-
Transmission:				-	-	-
Suspension:				X	-	-
Steering:				-	-	-
Brakes:				X	X	X
Electricity:				X	X	-
Body:				X	X	-
Accessories:				X	X	X
Fit/finish:				-	-	-

POWERTRAIN / PERFORMANCE

Year	Type/ L/Camshaft/bhp	Drivetrain & gearbox	Acceler. 0/100 sec.	Top speed km/h	Ave. Fuel consp. l./100 km
99-01	L4/2.0/DOHC/127	rear/all-M5	NA	NA	10.5
		rear/all-A4	NA	NA	10.5
	V6/2.5/DOHC/155	rear/all-M5	NA	NA	12.3
		rear/all-A4	NA	NA	12.6
2001	V6/2.7DOHC/183	rear.all-A4	10.7	170	13.8

SPECIFICATIONS

Model 99-00	Wlb. mm	Lght. mm	Cb.wt kg	Brakes fr/rr	Steering type	Standard tires
Vitara						
con. 2dr.	2200	3855	1235	dc/dr	pwr.bal.	205/75R15
wgn. 4dr.	2480	4135	1355	dc/dr	pwr.bal.	215/65R16
Grand Vitara						
wgn. 4dr.	2480	4180	1450	dc/dr	pwr.bal.	235/60R16
XL7						
wgn. 4dr.	2800	4665	1680	dc/dr	pwr.bal.	235/60R16

PRICES

Model / version		1996	1997	1998	1999	2000	2001
Vitara							
con. 2dr. JA 1.6	mini				10000	11450	15450
	maxi				11750	13850	18100
con. 2dr. JA 2.0	mini				12100		
	maxi				13850		
con. 2dr. JX 2.0	mini					13550	15950
	maxi					15950	18600
con. 2dr. JLX 2.0	mini					14400	
	maxi					16800	
wgn. 2dr. JX H.T.	mini				12300	14600	17750
	maxi				14100	17000	20500
Grand Vitara							
wgn. 4dr. JX H.T.	mini				15750	17400	20900
	maxi				17750	19850	23600
wgn. 4dr. JLX H.T.	mini				18000	19750	22900
	maxi				20150	22100	25700
wgn. 4dr. Ltd H.T.	mini					22350	25500
Aut.	maxi					24800	28300
XL7							
wgn. 4dr. Base	mini						27300
	maxi						30300
wgn. 4dr. Plus	mini						28350
	maxi						31400

See page 7 to adapt these figures.

SUZUKI X-90

1996 SUZUKI X-90

The X-90 hit the market in 1996, and no one blinked an eye. It is based on the body design and powertrain of the defunct Sidekick.

PROS

- **This is an innovative**, fun vehicle, combining all-terrain capabilities with those of a year-round roadster.
- **The X-90** is just loaded with equipment, but costs much less than the Miata that has fewer bells and whistles.
- **Road stability** is quite reasonable, but it's not a good idea to make quick lane changes with steering that suffers from a higher than average reduction ratio. And the X-90 is sensitive to crosswinds, road ruts and extension joints.
- **This small vehicle** is amazingly adaptable, for it can go off the highway and head happily for the open fields, beaches and mountains, in good weather or bad.
- **It maneuvers marvelously** well, for it combines a really short wheel base with quick as a flash steering, so it can get to any spot it pleases.
- **It's convenient too**, for there are lots of storage compartments in the interior and the trunk is practical and easy to get to.

CONS

- **Excessive vehicle weight** affects engine performance, for the Sidekick engine has to strain to pull the extra 250 kg.
- **Brakes** aren't great, achieving stops that are far too long, even if they're nice and predictable with ABS.
- **This vehicle is appealing**, but it's a mixed bag as far as body design goes and looks a bit weird.
- **Comfort** is non-existent, for the suspension jumps around every which way and there's quite a bit of noise and roar.
- **The engine** isn't economical, for mileage stays around 11L/100 km.
- **The cockpit** isn't too comfortable with such a low seat, non-adjustable steering wheel, inaccurate steering and lack of a foot rest.

CONCLUSION

The X-90 is an innovative concept, but driving isn't fun because the deficient engine and suspension don't optimize the full potential of the vehicle.

RECALLS

None over this period.

X-90 SUZUKI

RELIABILITY PROBLEMS

	1996	1997	1998	1999	2000	2001
Engine:	X	X	X			
Transmission:	X	X	X			
Suspension:	-	-	-			
Steering:	X	-	-			
Brakes:	X	X	-			
Electricity:	-	-	-			
Body:	-	-	-			
Accessories:	X	X	X			
Fit/finish:	X	X	-			

POWERTRAIN

Year	Type/ L/Camshaft/bhp	Drivetrain & gearbox
96-98	L4/1.6/SOHC/95	rear/all-M5
		rear/all-A4

PERFORMANCE

Acceler. 0/100 sec.	Top speed km/h	Ave. Fuel consp. l./100 km
NA	NA	NA
15.0	140	9.9

SPECIFICATIONS

Model	Wlb. mm	Lght. mm	Cb.wt kg	Brakes fr/rr	Steering type	Standard tires
cpe. 2dr.	base	2200	3710	dc/dr/ABS	pwr.bal.	195/65R15

PRICES

Model / version		1996	1997	1998	1999	2000	2001
cpe. 2dr.	mini	3200	4200	5800			
	maxi	4750	5800	7550			

See page 7 to adapt these figures.

1996 SUZUKI X-90

The Canadian Used Car Guide 2002-20023

TOYOTA   Avalon

1998 TOYOTA Avalon XLS

The Avalon replaced the Cressida in 1995. It's built on the Camry platform and shares its 3.0L V6 engine. For 1999, the Avalon XLS gets as standard equipment a lot of bells and whistles: traction control, leather-clad heated seats, sunroof and memory driver's seat. Almost more American than Japanese...

PROS
- **The engine** is spectacular for it can accelerate from 0 to 100 km/h in 8.5 seconds with the automatic.
- **The cabin** can comfortably seat five passengers, not six, which is the number of occupants according to Toyota.
- **Brakes** are effective, stable, long-lasting and easy to adjust.
- **The ride** is exceedingly comfortable because of the smooth suspension, nicely contoured, thick seats that provide good support.
- **Assembly, fit and finish** and main trim components are top-notch, but the overall look isn't really lavish.
- **Equipment** is extensive, since ABS is now standard on the XL base model.

CONS
- **Its plain body design** that isn't in keeping with such advanced technical features or such a high price tag.
- **This upper-end** Camry is very pricy indeed, which proves that the renowned Toyota quality and dependability don't come cheap.
- **The six-passenger** model with the shifter located on the steering wheel is a caricature of the big American car, for you can't even seat a child in the middle of the rearbench up front because of the ever so tight leg room.
- **Fuel consumption** is a bit higher than average for equal displacement engines.
- **Steering** is devoid of character, it gets vague at times and you have to keep an eye on it in crosswinds.
- **The noise level** is strangely higher than on counterpart vehicles, especially road noise.
- **Not too convenient**: no storage compartment in the center console, trunk release button inside the glove compartment.

CONCLUSION
This is a nice car, but it isn't terribly popular. It's a good buy all-round, but you have to be willing to put up the cash to own one.

RECALLS
1997 Moisture may seep and freeze in the brake booster vacuum hose and disable the brakes altogether.
2000 Rear axle hub will be inspected and replaced if necessary.

Avalon — TOYOTA

RELIABILITY PROBLEMS

	1996	1997	1998	1999	2000	2001
Engine:	-	-	-	-	-	-
Transmission:	-	-	-	-	-	-
Suspension:	-	X	X	X	-	-
Steering:	-	-	-	-	-	-
Brakes:	X	-	-	-	-	-
Electricity:	-	X	X	X	X	X
Body:	-	-	-	X	X	-
Accessories:	X	-	X	-	X	X
Fit/finish:	-	X	X	X	-	-

POWERTRAIN

Year	Type/ L/Camshaft/bhp	Drivetrain & gearbox
96-01	V6/3.0/DOHC/192-210	front-A4

PERFORMANCE

Acceler. 0/100 sec.	Top. speed km/h	Ave. Fuel consp. l./100 km
8.5	200	11.2

SPECIFICATIONS

Model	Wlb. mm	Lght. mm	Cb.wt kg	Brakes fr/rr	Steering type	Standard tires
96-99						
sdn. 4dr. XL	2720	4875	1560	dc/ABS	pwr.r&p.	205/65R15
sdn. 4dr. XLS	2720	4875	1560	dc/ABS	pwr.r&p.	205/65R15
00-01						
sdn. 4dr. XL	2720	4874	1560	dc/ABS	pwr.r&p.	205/65R15
sdn. 4dr. XLS	2720	4874	1570	dc/ABS	pwr.r&p.	205/60R16

PRICES

Model / version		1996	1997	1998	1999	2000	2001
sdn. 4dr. XL	mini	11000	12600	14700	18400	22000	26800
	maxi	13650	16300	18400	21500	25700	30500
sdn. 4dr. XLS	mini	12600	14700	16800	20500	24700	29900
	maxi	15750	17850	20500	23600	28300	33600

See page 7 to adapt these figures.

2000 TOYOTA Avalon XLS

TOYOTA Camry-Solara

1999 TOYOTA Camry LE

The Camry was upgraded in 1992. The station wagon and coupe were available in '93 and '94 respectively. These cars are powered by a 2.2L 4-cylinder engine or a 3.0L V6. The addition of the Solara SE and SE V6 in '99 is broadening the product line with a youth touch. Toyota is somehow playing very safe by preparing the path of the "post-utility vehicles" era, in the same fashion as Honda did with its Accord coupe.

PROS
- **The larger cabin** and trunk can accommodate five passengers and their luggage.
- **The suspension** provides a super blend of plush, Germanic comfort and neutral, stable handling at normal speeds.
- **The cockpit boasts** of a nicely designed instrument panel, provides adequate visibility and driving is great with such clean, crisp, just right steering.
- **Solidly built**, neatly assembled and very spiffy, but the overall design lacks character and imagination.
- **The 4-cylinder engine** runs smoothly and is easy on the gas, but the V6 is more popular with its whopping 194-bhp.
- **Steering** is accurate, visibility is good and the instrument panel is super ergonomic, so driving is pleasant.

CONS
- **Brakes** aren't the best with such long stops with or without ABS, but this feature at least stabilizes vehicle path on V6 models that are equipped with standard ABS.
- **The coupe** isn't terribly comfy with its hard seats, harsh suspension and chronically high noise level.
- **Both engines** aren't too efficient because of excessive vehicle weight.
- **The hard seats** are uncomfortable and they're poorly designed and don't provide adequate support.
- **The interior design** is blah and bland.

CONCLUSION
The Camry is a good buy either as a new or used car and it's become the most sought-after, reliable family car in North America.

RECALLS
1997 Moisture may seep and freeze in the brake booster vacuum hose and disable the brakes altogether.
Ignition module is defective resulting in a possibility that the key could be removed while the car is in "Drive".

Camry-Solara — TOYOTA

RELIABILITY PROBLEMS

	1996	1997	1998	1999	2000	2001
Engine:	X	X	X	-	-	-
Transmission:	-	-	-	-	-	-
Suspension:	-	X	X	X	-	-
Steering:	-	-	-	-	-	-
Brakes:	-	X	X	X	X	-
Electricity:	-	X	X	X	X	X
Body:	X	-	-	-	-	-
Accessories:	-	X	X	X	X	-
Fit/finish:	X	-	-	-	-	-

POWERTRAIN

Year	Type/ L/Camshaft/bhp	Drivetrain & gearbox
96-01	L4/2.2/DOHC/125-139	front-M5
		front-A4
	V6/3.0/DOHC/185-194	front-M5
		front-A4

PERFORMANCE

Acceler. 0/100 sec.	Top. speed km/h	Ave. Fuel consp. l./100 km
10.5	180	10.0
11.8	175	10.4
7.8	210	11.4
8.4	200	11.9

SPECIFICATIONS

Model 1996	Wlb. mm	Lght. mm	Cb.wt kg	Brakes fr/rr	Steering type	Standard tires
cpe. 2dr. base	2620	4770	1320	dc/dr	pwr.r&p.	195/70R14
cpe. 2dr. LE V6	2620	4770	1390	dc/dc	pwr.r&p.	205/65R15
sdn. 4dr. base	2620	4770	1330	dc/dr	pwr.r&p.	195/70R14
sdn. 4dr. V6	2620	4770	1400	dc/dc	pwr.r&p.	205/65R15
wgn. 4dr. base	2620	4810	1440	dc/dr	pwr.r&p.	195/70R14
wgn. 4dr. V6	2620	4810	1540	dc/dc	pwr.r&p.	205/65R15
97-01						
sdn. 4dr. CE	2670	4785	1360	dc/dr	pwr.r&p.	195/70R14
sdn. 4dr. CE V6	2670	4785	1415	dc/ABS	pwr.r&p.	205/65R15
sdn. 4dr. LE	2670	4785	1415	dc/dr/ABS	pwr.r&p.	195/70R14
sdn. 4dr. XLE V6	2670	4785	1475	dc/ABS	pwr.r&p.	205/65R15
99-01						
cpe. 2dr. Solara	2670	4825	1440	dc/dr/ABS	pwr.r&p.	205/65R15
cpe. 2dr. Sol.V6	2670	4825	1465	dc/ABS	pwr.r&p.	205/60R16

PRICES

Model / version		1996	1997	1998	1999	2000	2001
cpe. 2dr. base	mini	8400					
	maxi	10500					
cpe. 2dr. LE	mini	9450					
	maxi	12100					
cpe. 2dr. LE V6	mini	11000					
	maxi	13650					
cpe. 2 dr. Solara SE	mini				16300	19400	21200
	maxi				17850	21200	24100
cpe. 2 dr. Solara SE V6	mini				18400	22000	23100
	maxi				19950	23900	26200
con. 2dr. Solara SLE V6	mini					31000	32750
	maxi					32750	35700
sdn. 4dr. base	mini	9450					
	maxi	11550					
sdn. 4dr. LE	mini	10500	13350	14200	16300	17300	21200
	maxi	13100	15200	16800	18400	19950	24700
sdn. 4dr. CE	mini		12400	13450	15200	16300	19950
	maxi		14200	15750	17300	18900	23100
sdn. 4dr. base V6	mini	11200					
	maxi	13650					
sdn. 4dr. CE V6	mini		13850	15200	17300	18400	23100
	maxi		16300	17850	19400	21000	26200
sdn. 4dr. XLE V6	mini		15750	17300	18900	19950	23100
	maxi		17850	19950	21000	22600	26700
wgn. 4dr. LE	mini	11000					
	maxi	13650					
wgn. 4dr. LE V6	mini	12100					
	maxi	14700					

See page 7 to adapt these figures.

TOYOTA — Celica

2000 TOYOTA Celica GTS

The Celica was first sold in 1970, underwent modifications in '77, '81 and '85, the year it was first equipped with front-wheel drive. The all-wheel drive model was on the market in '89 and the more recent model came out in 2000.

PROS
- **The unusual Celica look** appeals to some and not to others, year after year. But the latest model seems to be the most popular.
- **Handling** is just super with the cushy independent suspension, especially on the GT-S model.
- **The GT** model is really zoomy, but because of its cohesive overall design, the GT-S seems to be a better choice.
- **The really nice** cockpit and variable assist power steering make for very pleasant driving.
- **Fuel consumption** is economical, no matter the transmission type.
- **The front seats** on the GT-S model are incredibly ergonomic with the side cushions and lumbar sections.

CONS
- **Torque effects** on some models on strong accelerations.
- **Brakes** are inadequate and on sudden stops, they're unpredictable. Only the brakes on the latest GT-S generation are really effective.
- **The 2.2L engine** isn't too hot, for it only unleashes its power at high rpm, that is, at illegal speeds.
- **The cabin interior** is cramped in the rear seat area and boarding is tricky.
- **Gauges** are hard to read and the instrument panel is plain and unattractive.
- **The suspension** on the GT-S model is firm, that is, it's very stiff.
- **The trunk** doesn't hold much and luggage handling is inconvenient with such a high opening.
- **Some models** are pretty sensitive to crosswinds.

CONCLUSION
The Celica coupe is really solidly built, well equipped and affordable. But it doesn't have a real Sportscar character as far as looks go.

RECALLS
None over this period.

Celica TOYOTA

RELIABILITY PROBLEMS

	1996	1997	1998	1999	2000	2001
Engine:	X	X	-	-	-	-
Transmission:	X	-	-	-	X	-
Suspension:	-	-	-	-	-	-
Steering:	-	-	-	-	-	-
Brakes:	X	X	X	X	-	-
Electricity:	X	X	X	X	X	X
Body:	-	-	-	-	X	-
Accessories:	X	X	X	X	X	-
Fit/finish:	-	-	-	X	-	-

POWERTRAIN

Year	Type/ L/Camshaft/bhp	Drivetrain & gearbox	Acceler. 0/100 sec.	Top. speed km/h	Ave. Fuel consp. l./100 km
96-99	L4/2.2/DOHC/130 GTS	front-M5	9.0	200	10.8
		front-A4	10.2	190	10.6
00-01	L4/1.8/DOHC/140 GT	front-M5	8.8	175	9.0
		front-A4	11.0	170	9.5
	L4/1.8/DOHC/180 GTS	front-M5	8.0	185	10.5

PERFORMANCE

(see POWERTRAIN table)

SPECIFICATIONS

Model	Wlb. mm	Lght. mm	Cb.wt kg	Brakes fr/rr	Steering type	Standard tires
96-99						
cpe. 3dr. GT	2540	4425	1095	dc/dr/ABS	pwr.r&p.	185/70R14
cpe. 3dr. GT-S	2540	4425	1170	dc/ABS	pwr.r&p.	205/55R15
00-01						
cpe. 3dr. GT	2540	4425	1095	d/t/ABS	pwr.r&p.	185/70R14
cpe. 3dr. GT-S	2540	4425	1170	d/ABS	pwr.r&p.	205/55R15

PRICES

Model / version		1996	1997	1998	1999	2000	2001
cpe. 3dr. GT	mini	11000	13650			19500	22000
	maxi	13650	16300			22000	25200
cpe. 3dr. GT-S	mini			16100	18900	22700	25200
	maxi			17850	21500	25200	28300

See page 7 to adapt these figures.

1997 TOYOTA Celica GT

TOYOTA   Corolla

1998 TOYOTA Corolla

This front-wheel compact was launched in 66 and modified in 70, 74, 79, 83, 88, 93 and 98. It truly represents the Toyota bread and butter, for it's the most global modern car, being built in such a huge quantity throughout the most impressive number of countries simultaneously.

PROS
- **Choice** is extensive in this range, which offers a wide selection of body styles and trims, two engines and transmission types, depending on the model year.
- **Comfort** improved drastically in 98, with the introduction of new suspensions.
- **Safety** has been enhanced on the latest edition, with a more rigid body shell, a driver's airbag and more powerful braking.
- **Roominess** and trunk size is good on sedans and wagons, but rear seats on some of these are narrower than average and not easily accessible.

CONS
- **Interior design** is depressing and trims are obviously very inexpensive.
- **The 1.6L engine** has always been timid when coupled with an automatic transmission.
- **Multi-valve engines** last longer if the valves are adjusted on a regular basis.
- **Braking** lacks bite and stopping distances are long.
- **Comfort** would be superior if seats were not as hard and if soundproofing was better on simpler versions.
- **Steering** is imprecise at the center and the driver must compensate constantly to maintain a straight trajectory.
- **Road adherence** on the old base model Corolla is average, but although marked, the roll is rarely dangerous.

CONCLUSION
The Corolla models boast enviable reliability and their handling and appearance have improved noticeably over the years. They are good buys in the used car market, but are available at higher than average prices.

Corolla   TOYOTA

RECALLS
1997 Airbag computer may be defective.

RELIABILITY PROBLEMS

	1996	1997	1998	1999	2000	2001
Engine:	X	X	X	X	-	-
Transmission:	-	X	-	-	-	-
Suspension:	-	-	X	X	X	-
Steering:	X	X	-	-	-	-
Brakes:	-	-	X	X	X	-
Electricity:	-	X	X	X	-	-
Body:	X	X	-	X	-	-
Accessories:	-	-	-	X	-	-
Fit/finish:	X	-	-	-	-	-

POWERTRAIN

Year	Type/ L/Camshaft/bhp	Drivetrain & gearbox	Acceler. 0/100 sec.	Top. speed km/h	Ave. Fuel consp. l./100 km
96-97	L4/1.6/DOHC/90-105	front-M5	11.8	170	9.0
		front-A4	12.5	165	10.0
96-01	L4/1.8/DOHC/105-120	front-M5	9.5	185	7.7
		front-A4	11.2	180	8.3

SPECIFICATIONS

Model	Wlb. mm	Lght. mm	Cb.wt kg	Brakes fr/rr	Steering type	Standard tires
96-97						
sdn. 4dr. SD	2465	4369	1055	dc/dr	pwr.r&p.	175/65R14
sdn. 4dr. DX	2465	4369	1085	dc/dr	pwr.r&p.	185/65R14
wgn. 4dr. SD/DX	2465	4369	1100	dc/dr	pwr.r&p.	185/65R14
98-01						
sdn. 4dr. VE	2465	4420	1095	dc/dr	pwr.r&p.	175/65R14
sdn. 4dr. CE	2465	4420	1110	dc/dr	pwr.r&p.	175/65R14
sdn. 4dr. LE	2465	4420	1145	dc/dr	pwr.r&p.	185/65R14

PRICES

Model / version		1996	1997	1998	1999	2000	2001
sdn. 4dr. base	mini	6300					
	maxi	8400					
sdn. 4dr. DX 1.8	mini	8100	9650				
	maxi	10000	11350				
sdn. 4dr. DX	mini	7600	9450				
	maxi	9450	11000				
sdn. 4dr. LE	mini			12600	14200	14700	16300
	maxi			14200	15750	17300	18900
sdn. 4dr. SD	mini		8400				
	maxi		10500				
sdn. 4dr. VE	mini			10500	11550	12600	
	maxi			12100	13650	15200	
sdn. 4dr. CE	mini			11550	12600	13650	14700
	maxi			13100	14700	16300	17300
sdn. 4dr. Sport	mini						15200
	maxi						17850
wgn. 5dr. DLX	mini	8400					
	maxi	10000					

See page 7 to adapt these figures.

TOYOTA   Echo

2000 TOYOTA Echo

In 2000, the Echo replaced the Tercel as Toyota's low-end model in North America. The Echo comes with 2 or 4 doors and a 1.5-liter 4-cylinder engine.

PROS

- **The styling**, inspired by the Prius' lines, is refreshing and features bold lines and oversized headlights.
- **The passenger compartment** and trunk are unusually roomy for a model in this category.
- **The Echo's good weight-power ratio** (9.9 kg/hp) makes it fun to drive, even when equipped with the automatic transmission.
- **Good fuel economy** considering its performance capabilities.
- The Echo offers **better value** than its predecessor, for its equipment list is much more extensive.
- **A lot of storage space**, located mainly in the front, including two adjacent glove boxes.
- **Comfort** is surprisingly good for a car of this size. The suspension never reacts brutally, the seats are well-upholstered and the noise level is reasonable at cruising speeds.
- **The instrument panel** is resolutely modern and distinctive because of its instrument cluster positioned dead centre and at the foot of the windshield.
- **The rear windows** roll down all the way, much to the joy of kids who enjoy feeling the wind on their faces.
- **The windshield wipers** are efficient; their rythm and reach keep the windshield clean even in pouring rain.

CONS

- **The rear seats** are more difficult to access because of the narrower rear doors that do not open up as widely as in the front.
- **The radio** and air-conditioning controls are inverted.
- **The optional 14-inch** tires provide better handling than the standard 13-inchers.
- **The trunk's presentation** could be improved. The trim fabric is flimsy and clumsily attached to the bench's seatback.

CONCLUSION

Toyota is convinced that young buyers will be the ones to revive the small-car market. It is undoubtedly right on the money.

RECALLS

2000   The vacuum port of the PCV valve will be repaired on some vehicles.

Echo — TOYOTA

RELIABILITY PROBLEMS

	1996	1997	1998	1999	2000	2001
Engine:					-	-
Transmission:					-	-
Suspension:					-	-
Steering:					-	-
Brakes:					-	-
Electricity:					-	-
Body:					X	-
Accessories:					X	-
Fit/finish:					-	-

POWERTRAIN

Year	Type/ L/Camshaft/bhp	Drivetrain & gearbox
00-01	L4/1.5/DOHC/108	front-M5
		front-A4

PERFORMANCE

Acceler. 0/100 sec.	Top. speed km/h	Ave. Fuel consp. l./100 km
10.0	165	7.5
11.5	160	8.5

SPECIFICATIONS

Model 00-01	Wlb. mm	Lght. mm	Cb.wt kg	Brakes fr/rr	Steering type	Standard tires
sdn. 2dr.	2370	4145	1077	dc/dr	pwr.r&p.	155/80R13
sdn. 4dr.	2370	4145	1090	dc/dr	pwr.r&p.	155/80R13

PRICES

Model / version		1996	1997	1998	1999	2000	2001
sdn. 2dr.	mini					11000	13100
	maxi					13350	15750
sdn. 4dr.	mini					11550	13650
	maxi					13850	16300

See page 7 to adapt these figures.

2000 TOYOTA Echo

TOYOTA — Highlander

2001 TOYOTA Highlander

To keep up with the SUV market, Toyota came up with the Highlander, based on the platform and mechanics of the Lexus RX 300, itself derived from the Camry. The Highlander comes with a 2.2-liter L4 and 2-wheel drive or a 3.0-liter V6 with 4-wheel drive. Only an automatic transmission is available.

PROS

- **The interesting midsize format** provides a practical amount of space and uses powerful yet economical mechanics.
- **Rear-seat roominess** is surprising given the amount of available legroom. Access is facilitated by a reasonable level of ground clearance as well as large doors that open wide.
- **The relatively low center of gravity** is conducive to safe handling, and the Highlander handles more like an automobile than a utility vehicle thanks to its suspension design.
- **The brakes** are powerful in both normal situations and emergency stops. Decelerations are quick and straight.
- **The body's reasonable dimensions** and the short turning radius make the Highlander extremely maneuverable.
- **The vast trunk** and practical storage spaces will make daily life easier for the typical young family.
- **The powerful headlights** produce great visibility in all conditions.
- The overall **attention to quality** is reminiscent more of what can be found in a Lexus than a Toyota. This is especially true of the high-end model equipped with leather trim.

CONS

- **The stiff suspension** reacts harshly on poor pavement.
- **Road defects** pass easily through the steering column all the way to the driver. This is quite rare to be worthy of mention.
- **The windshield wipers** are not the most efficient out there. There are rather slow and clear only 75% of the windshield's surface.
- **The massive dashboard** is borrowed straight from the Lexus RX 300, and the gear shift lever is rather unpractical.

VERDICT

The Highlander is undoubtedly one of the best buys in its category, and chances are it will make for a rare and expensive find on the used-car market.

RECALLS

None over this period.

Highlander — TOYOTA

RELIABILITY PROBLEMS

	1996	1997	1998	1999	2000	2001
Engine:						
Transmission:						
Suspension:						
Steering:						
Brakes:			Insufficient data			
Electricity:						
Body:						
Accessories:						
Fit/finish:						

POWERTRAIN

Year	Type/ L/Camshaft/bhp	Drivetrain & gearbox
2001	L4/2.4DOHC/155 2WD	front-A4
	V6/3.0/SOHC/220 AWD	front/all-A4

PERFORMANCE

Acceler. 0/100 sec.	Top. speed km/h	Ave. Fuel consp. l./100 km
NA		
10.1	175	13.0

SPECIFICATIONS

Model 2001	Wlb. mm	Lght. mm	Cb.wt kg	Brakes fr/rr	Steering type	Standard tires
wgn. 4dr. FWD	2715	4685	1580	dc/ABS	pwr.r.&p.	225/70R16
wgn. 4dr. AWD	2715	4685	1760	dc/ABS	pwr.r.&p.	225/70R16

PRICES

Model / version		1996	1997	1998	1999	2000	2001
wgn. 4dr. 2WD	mini						24150
	maxi						28350
wgn. 4dr. AWD	mini						27300
	maxi						33600

See page 7 to adapt these figures.

2001 TOYOTA Highlander

The Canadian Used Car Guide 2002-2003

TOYOTA — Previa

1996 TOYOTA Previa

Introduced in '91, the Previa is offered in two trims, base or LE and is powered by a 2.4L 4-cylinder engine which is also available with a turbo compressor, coupled on a 2- or 4-wheel drive transmission, depending on the model year and trim level.

PROS
- **Futuristic lines** give the Previa a very special personality.
- **The engine** is supple enough when equipped with a manual transmission; an automatic transmission is the better alternative on the 4x4.
- **The passenger compartment** is very roomy, easily accessible and well laid out. The baggage compartment is big enough to store luggage for seven passengers.
- **A high driving position** provides excellent visibility.
- **Maneuverability** is enhanced by a short wheelbase and a reduced turning radius.
- **Steering** is well-balanced although imprecise at center.
- **Fuel consumption** is reasonable despite very ordinary engine performance.
- **The 4WD** is very efficient and its stability is above-average.
- **Handling** is safer on the 4WD in winter driving conditions than on the rear-wheel drive, which is quite unstable on icy roads.
- **The instrument panel** on the Previa suffers from wretched excess, but is nevertheless very functional.

CONS
- **The mechanical system** is oddly positioned underneath the front seats.
- **Outrageous selling prices** don't make them very appealing, either as a used vehicle or brand new, while other modern realizations don't suffer from this handicap.
- **Sensitivity** to cross winds, evident on these vehicles, calls for cautious driving and a lot of foresight.
- **Braking** is not efficient enough, but is stable and shows endurance.
- **A V6 engine** would be a welcome feature on the Previa, where the clanking noises of the 4-cylinder engine are a major drawback at cruising speed. The addition in '95 of the turbo compressor doesn't make it punchier than what it would be on any typical V6.
- **The large windows** seriously reduces the effectiveness of the air-conditioning unit in summer time.

CONCLUSION
The Previa is a good vehicle, but its special mechanical system, cabin and price are incompatible with market requirements.

RECALLS
1997 An oil leak might occur at the air breather plug at highway speeds.

Previa — TOYOTA

RELIABILITY PROBLEMS

	1996	1997	1998	1999	2000	2001
Engine:	X	-				
Transmission:	-	X				
Suspension:	X	X				
Steering:	-	-				
Brakes:	-	-				
Electricity:	-	-				
Body:	-	-				
Accessories:	-	-				
Fit/finish:	-	-				

POWERTRAIN

Year	Type/ L/Camshaft/bhp	Drivetrain & gearbox
1996	L4/2.4/DOHC/138	rear-M5
		rear-A4
96-97	L4C/2.4/DOHC/161	rear/all-A4

PERFORMANCE

Acceler. 0/100 sec.	Top speed km/h	Ave. Fuel consp. l./100 km
11.5	175	10.5
12.5	165	11.5
12.1	170	13.5

SPECIFICATIONS

Model 96-97	Wlb. mm	Lght. mm	Cb.wt kg	Brakes fr/rr	Steering type	Standard tires
m.v. 4dr.	2865	4750	1703	dc/dr	pwr.r&p.	205/75R14
m.v. 4dr. AWD	2865	4750	1857	dc/dr	pwr.r&p.	215/65R15

PRICES

Model / version		1996	1997	1998	1999	2000	2001
m.v. 4dr. S/C	mini	7350	9350				
	maxi	9350	11200				
m.v. 4dr. S/C LE	mini	9000	10500				
	maxi	11000	12600				
m.v. 4dr. S/C AWD	mini	10500	12100				
	maxi	12600	14200				

See page 7 to adapt these figures.

1997 TOYOTA Previa SC

The Canadian Used Car Guide 2002-2003

TOYOTA   Prius

2001 TOYOTA Prius

The Prius was the second hybrid vehicle to be sold in Canada after the Insight. It is equipped with a thermal engine that produces the electricity required to recharge the batteries which in turn enables the electric motor to provide traction in various modes.

PROS
- **State-of-the-art technology** becomes less of a cause for concern when it's marketed by Japanese auto makers, especially Toyota whose models are renowned for being reliable.
- **The excellent fuel economy** and ultra-low emissions are the two main advantages of this avant-garde model.
- **The ride is comfortable** given the soft suspension and well-contoured and padded seats.
- **The Prius is practical** and maneuverable given its compact dimensions, but is nevertheless capable of seating up to 5 people.
- **The modern dashboard** reflects the out-of-the-ordinary spirit of this model.
- **Overall quality** is excellent, whether it be with respect to the solid construction, rigorous finish or simple yet elegant presentation of certain details.

CONS
- The Prius is so **technically complex** that the average small-town mechanic will not be able to assist you in the event of a failure.
- **New and therefore rare technology** comes with a high price tag. Nevertheless, certain environmentalists will undoubtedly make the effort to help reduce emissions of pollutant gases.
- **Performance** is timid when compared to that of a diesel engine, although the Prius has the advantage of being less noisy and smelly.
- **Handling** is average due to the narrow tires used to reduce rolling resistance. Furthermore, the supple suspension encourages body motions in curves.
- **The dashboard's** ergonomics leave to be desired because some elements were designed with right-side driving in mind.
- **There are not enough practical storage spaces**. The existing space is limited to a console bin and a small glove box.

VERDICT
The Prius is a realistic vehicle that is fun to drive. And it's a much better buy that the Insight whose capacities are limited. Calling out to all Martians . . .

RECALLS
None over this period.

Prius · TOYOTA

RELIABILITY PROBLEMS

	1996	1997	1998	1999	2000	2001
Engine:						
Transmission:						
Suspension:						
Steering:						
Brakes:			Insufficient data			
Electricity:						
Body:						
Accessories:						
Fit/finish:						

POWERTRAIN

Year	Type/ L/Camshaft/bhp	Drivetrain & gearbox
2001	L4/1.5+elec.mot./70	CVT

PERFORMANCE

Acceler. 0/100 sec.	Top. speed km/h	Ave. Fuel consp. l./100 km
13.8	160	4.5

SPECIFICATIONS

Model 2001	Wlb. mm	Lght. mm	Cb.wt kg	Brakes fr/rr	Steering type	Standard tires
sdn. 4dr.	2550	4305	1640	dc/dr/ABS	pwr.r.&p.	175/65R14

PRICES

Model / version		1996	1997	1998	1999	2000	2001
sdn. 4dr.	mini						20150
	maxi						23950

See page 7 to adapt these figures.

2001 TOYOTA Prius

TOYOTA — RAV4

1997 TOYOTA RAV4

The RAV4 is available in either a short wheelbase 2-door model or in a long wheelbase 4-door model, as front-wheel or all-wheel drive, equipped with a 16-valve 2.0L DOHC 4-cylinder engine. Since 1999, only the AWD is available due to the poor demand on the front-wheel drive. It was redefined in 2001 on the same mechanical basis.

PROS

- **Performance** is very much like a car, thanks to a good power to weight ratio of 9.5 kg/hp and the smooth engine yields pretty gutsy pick-up at low rpm, even with the automatic gearbox.
- **Behind the wheel**, you're sitting nice and high, so you can see in all directions. The dashboard is logical and controls are easy to reach.
- **Roadhandling** is competent even on the short model that flits about like a little car, but you do have to be careful negotiating tight curves at zippy speeds.
- **Ride comfort** is more cushy on the 4-door model than is the case for some competitors, that are rustic and old-fashioned by comparison.
- **Pepier engine** provides a more fun to drive (2001).
- **Build quality** is Toyota standards. Assembly and fit and finish are superior, and trim components aren't at all plain.
- **Very convenient,** there are loads of storage spots everywhere and the trunk can be extended.

CONS

- **This fun-loving vehicle** isn't cheap, and a good old brawny Cherokee looks like a bargain beside the RAV4.
- **The transfer box** is sorely missed when tackling tough terrain that's ridden with major obstacles, for adherence is very iffy.
- **Equipment** isn't as extensive as on some other same-ilk vehicles and you have to check out the options to butter things up a bit.
- **The ride** isn't too great for long hauls, since seating doesn't offer much support and the Jolly Jumper suspension gets pretty tiring,
- **The retractable roofs** will never give you the free, let-your-hair-down feeling you get in a Jeep or a Sidekick.
- **Rearward view** is poor because of the spare tire and headrests.
- **To be improved upon:** the rear hatch that opens the wrong way from the sidewalk, because in Japan, people drive on the left side of the road...

CONCLUSION

The RAV4 is a treat to drive, but it's a pretty expensive toy for what you get, for it's neither a comfy car nor a tough, let-me-at-it 4X4.

RECALLS

None over this period.

RAV4   TOYOTA

RELIABILITY PROBLEMS

	1996	1997	1998	1999	2000	2001
Engine:	-	-	X	X	X	-
Transmission:	-	-	X	-	-	-
Suspension:	-	-	-	-	-	-
Steering:	-	-	-	-	-	-
Brakes:	-	-	X	X	X	-
Electricity:	-	X	-	-	X	-
Body:	-	-	-	X	X	-
Accessories:	-	-	-	X	X	-
Fit/finish:	-	X	-	-	-	-

POWERTRAIN

Year	Type/ L/Camshaft/bhp	Drivetrain & gearbox
97-01	L4/2.0/DOHC/120-148	front/all-M5
		front/all-A4

PERFORMANCE

Acceler. 0/100 sec.	Top. speed km/h	Ave. Fuel consp. l./100 km
11.5	165	10.7
13.0	160	10.8

SPECIFICATIONS

Model	Wlb. mm	Lght. mm	Cb.wt kg	Brakes fr/rr	Steering type	Standard tires
4x2 (97-98)						
wgn. 2dr.	2200	3749	1145	dc/dr	pwr.r&p.	215/70R16
wgn. 4dr.	2410	4150	1210	dc/dr	pwr.r&p.	215/70R16
4x4 (97-00)						
wgn. 2dr.	2200	3749	1225	dc/dr	pwr.r&p.	235/60R16
wgn. 4dr.	2410	4161	1290	dc/ABS	pwr.r&p.	235/60R16
2001						
wgn. 4dr.	2490	4195	1310	dc/dr	pwr.r&p.	215/70R16

PRICES

Model / version		1996	1997	1998	1999	2000	2001
con. 2dr. FWD	mini			12100	14700		
	maxi			13850	16500		
wgn. 2dr. FWD	mini		7900	9900			
	maxi		10000	11750			
wgn. 4dr. FWD	mini		9450	11350			
	maxi		11300	13350			
wgn. 2dr. AWD	mini			12300	15450	17550	
	maxi			14400	17500	20500	
wgn. 4dr. AWD	mini		11450	13200	16500	19100	23100
	maxi		13450	15450	18600	21850	26000

See page 7 to adapt these figures.

2001 TOYOTA RAV4

TOYOTA — Sequoia

2001 TOYOTA Sequoia

The Sequoia is the largest SUV available in Toyota's lineup. It borrows the Tundra pickup's chassis and mechanical components as well as the front end of its body. It's driven by a 4.7-liter V8 engine.

PROS
- **The immense cabin and cargo bay** are roomy enough to carry up to 7 individuals and their luggage.
- **The muscular V8 engine** provides this behemoth with acceleration and pick-up worthy of an automobile's.
- **The ride comfort** is appreciable on the highway, where the suspension and seats combine to produce a comfortable ride.
- **The Sequoia's off-road capabilities** are surprising for a vehicle of this size. In fact, its size is its only limit.
- **Fuel consumption** is relatively reasonable given the overall weight and large engine displacement.
- **The large fuel tank** gives the Sequoia a good travelling range, especially useful when leaving the beaten path.
- **The grab handles** and numerous storage spaces of this vehicle are testimony to Toyota's attention to detail.

CONS
- **The Sequoia** is bland to drive and devoid of sensationalism.
- The center console controls are not very practical because they out of the reach of the driver's and passenger's hands.
- **The high weight** and large size limit the Sequoia's ability to access tight spots.
- **The long stopping distances** are a result of the hefty weight. Trajectories can sometimes be unpredictable and fade resistance is average.
- **The interior** has a distinctively utilitarian look to it given the price, especially when you consider that the presentation of certain competitive models rivals that of a Cadillac.
- **The overhead console**, with its numerous bins, is a little ridiculous.

VERDICT
The Sequoia is the equivalent of the Land Cruiser, which was never sold in Canada during its first years. It's a serious competitor to the large SUVs offered by the domestic auto makers.

RECALLS
None over this period.

Sequoia — TOYOTA

RELIABILITY PROBLEMS

	1996	1997	1998	1999	2000	2001
Engine:						
Transmission:						
Suspension:						
Steering:						
Brakes:			Insufficient data			
Electricity:						
Body:						
Accessories:						
Fit/finish:						

POWERTRAIN

Year	Type/ L/Camshaft/bhp	Drivetrain & gearbox
2001	V8/4.7/SOHC/240	rr./all-A4

PERFORMANCE

Acceler. 0/100 sec.	Top. speed km/h	Ave. Fuel consp. l./100 km
10.0	175	17.4

SPECIFICATIONS

Model 2001	Wlb. mm	Lght. mm	Cb.wt kg	Brakes fr/rr	Steering type	Standard tires
wgn. 4dr. SR5	3000	5180	2390	dc/ABS	pwr.ball.	265/70R16
wgn. 4dr. Limited	3000	5180	2402	dc/ABS	pwr.ball.	265/70R16

PRICES

Model / version		1996	1997	1998	1999	2000	2001
wgn. 4dr SR5 V8	mini						34650
	maxi						39900
wgn. 4dr. Ltd V6	mini						50400
	maxi						55650

See page 7 to adapt these figures.

2001 TOYOTA Sequoia

The Canadian Used Car Guide 2002-2003

TOYOTA Sienna

2000 TOYOTA Sienna

The Sienna replaced the Previa in 1998. It has a more conventional shape and build, is based on the Camry platform and is powered by a 3.0L V6.

PROS
- **Ride comfort** derives from well-adjusted suspensions and nicely soundproofed, sturdy body.
- **Performance** is pretty impressive due to a good power to weight ratio, so accelerations and pick-up are on a par with those achieved by a station wagon.
- **This vehicle** is nicely priced for such a good equipment array, even the entry-level CE version that's perfectly acceptable.
- **Cabin space** is better adapted to accommodating seven passengers than is the case for short wheelbase rivals, yet the Sienna doesn't have rigidity problems that often affect and afflict extended models.
- **Roadability** is competent; the vehicle stays on the straight and narrow normal runs and on curves or tight bends taken at a good clip.
- **Steering** is responsive, precise and gradual, so there isn't torque fallout on strong accelerations.

CONS
- **The ho-hum design** is too similar to that of the Villager-Quest and the slide-rail for the sliding doors isn't as neatly integrated as on other models.
- **Choice** is limited to a single overall and wheelbase length.
- **Seats** are quite flat, hard and thinly upholstered and the rear seatbench is hard to get to.
- **The parking brake** is the most awkward on the market.
- **Visibility** is hindered at rear quarterback due to the bulky C-pillar, slim rear window shape and rear headrests.
- **The overly cushy** suspension generates a lot of swish and sway, so you have to slow down and the front end bottoms out when travelling on less than perfect pavement.
- **Maneuverability** suffers from a wide steer angle diameter.
- **Brakes** are stable, but take forever to bring the vehicle to a full stop.
- **The cabin design** is pretty plain with the shiny finish on some plastic parts that look more trashy than classy.
- **Tires** are pretty crummy when it comes to grip and a smooth ride.
- **The instrument panel** isn't too ergonomic. The center console is really low and some accessories are poorly located.

CONCLUSION
The Sienna is more humdrum when it comes to looks, but it's also more run-of-the-mill than the Previa that it replaced and model choice is too limited.

RECALLS
None over this period.

Sienna   TOYOTA

RELIABILITY PROBLEMS

	1996	1997	1998	1999	2000	2001
Engine:			-	-	-	-
Transmission:			-	-	-	-
Suspension:			X	X	-	-
Steering:			-	-	-	-
Brakes:			-	X	-	-
Electricity:			X	X	X	X
Body:			-	-	-	-
Accessories:			X	X	X	X
Fit/finish:			X	X	X	-

POWERTRAIN

Year	Type/ L/Camshaft/bhp	Drivetrain & gearbox
98-01	V6/3.0/DOHC/194-210	front-A4

PERFORMANCE

Acceler. 0/100 sec.	Top speed km/h	Ave. Fuel consp. l./100 km
10.5	180	12.9

SPECIFICATIONS

Model 98-01	Wlb. mm	Lght. mm	Cb.wt kg	Brakes fr/rr	Steering type	Standard tires
m.v. 3/4dr. CE	2900	4915	1705	dc/dr/ABS	pwr.r&p.	205/70R15
m.v. 3/4dr. LE	2900	4915	1765	dc/dr/ABS	pwr.r&p.	205/70R15

PRICES

Model / version		1996	1997	1998	1999	2000	2001
wgn. 3dr. Cargo	mini			11550	13100		
	maxi			13450	15200		
wgn. 3dr. CE	mini			13950	15550	19400	
	maxi			16100	17850	22250	
wgn. 3dr. LE	mini			15750			
	maxi			18150			
wgn. 4dr. CE	mini			14700	16100	20500	24100
	maxi			17100	18400	22900	27800
wgn. 4dr. LE	mini			16800	18900	21500	25700
	maxi			19200	21500	24150	29400
wgn. 4dr. XLE	mini			18600	20600	23400	27800
	maxi			20700	23100	26000	31500

See page 7 to adapt these figures.

2000 TOYOTA Sienna

TOYOTA   Supra

1997 TOYOTA Supra

Unveiled in 1978, the GT Supra coupe was built on the Celica platform and was equipped with Cressida mechanical features. It became a model in its own right in '85 and was upgraded in '90 and again in '94.

PROS
- **The Sportscar** character and look of the latest generation.
- **The turbo engine** musters up impressive power given the excessive vehicle weight and it achieves stunning accelerations and pick-up worthy of a true blue Sportscar.
- **Handling is great**, no matter what the situation. Only road faults and vehicle weight can affect road stability.
- **The engine keeps** its Sportscar zip with the manual transmission, but the automatic saps it of such capabilities.
- **Power steering** is accurate and quick on the draw and the cockpit is super, even though the seat is a bit low-slung.
- **Gas consumption** is reasonable, considering engine power and vehicle weight.
- **Build and finish** details are very top-notch.
- **The out-of-ordinary look** of the rear spoiler, for its muscular size and shape that will for sure not go unnoticed.

CONS
- **Excessive vehicle weight** really kills all spontaneity and agility on curved roads.
- **The cabin interior** is blah and just too synthetic-looking to have any real class, yet it's well-designed.
- **Major blind spots** reduce outward view towards the rear and sides.
- **Brakes** are powerful and smooth, making for straight stops, but with ABS, sudden stops take longer to achieve.
- **The poorly designed** seats don't provide adequate lateral and lumbar support.
- **Rear seats** are almost non-functional and this space is more suited for storing excess baggage.
- **Storage compartments** are skimpy and few and far between.

CONCLUSION
The Supra coupe has come a long way and is now a high-caliber car that can boast of stunning performance. Its price is definitely less popular nowadays, now that personal and social values have changed, which explains why sales are so dismally low.

RECALLS
None over this period.

Supra — TOYOTA

RELIABILITY PROBLEMS

	1996	1997	1998	1999	2000	2001
Engine:						
Transmission:						
Suspension:						
Steering:						
Brakes:			Insufficient data			
Electricity:						
Body:						
Accessories:						
Fit/finish:						

POWERTRAIN

Year	Type/ L/Camshaft/bhp	Drivetrain & gearbox
96-97	L6T/3.0/DOHC/320	rear-M5
		rear-A4

PERFORMANCE

Acceler. 0/100 sec.	Top. speed km/h	Ave. Fuel consp. l./100 km
5.0	250	13.6
5.7	250	12.8

SPECIFICATIONS

Model	Wlb. mm	Lght. mm	Cb.wt kg	Brakes fr/rr	Steering type	Standard tires
96-97						
cpe. 2dr. Turbo	2550	4515	1594	dc/ABS	pwr.r&p.	235/45R17 255/40R17

PRICES

Model / version		1996	1997	1998	1999	2000	2001
cpe. 2dr. Turbo	mini		31500				
	maxi		35700				

See page 7 to adapt these figures.

1997 TOYOTA Supra

TOYOTA — Tercel-Paseo

1996 TOYOTA Paseo

The tiny Tercel hails back to 1978. It was redesigned in '82 and '87 and upgraded in '91 and in '95. The Paseo coupe, which is an offshoot of the Tercel, was launched in 1992 and got a face-lift in 1996.

PROS

- **The Tercel is reliable** and inexpensive to run, which explains why there aren't many on the used car market and resale value is so high.
- **The Paseo design** appeals mainly to the ladies.
- **The 1.5L engine** is quite efficient, for it performs adequately and doesn't burn too much gas.
- **Handling** is sure and predictable, except on the base model equipped with small tires. The car hugs the road quite well, but it's sensitive to road faults and to crosswinds.
- **The roomy cabin** on the sedan can comfortably accommodate four adults and there's room for their luggage as well.
- **The driver's seat** is firm and high, providing good outward view.
- **Power steering** is a better choice for city driving.
- **The cabin** and trunk are bigger since 1995.

CONS

- **Brakes** aren't too effective, for sudden stops are long to achieve.
- **The narrow tires** that equip the base model don't grip well on slippery roads.
- **Manual steering** is stiff at slow speed and inaccurate at higher speed because of too high a reduction ratio.
- **The suspension** can be very harsh and bumpy on bad roads, the seats are hard and soundproofing is poor, all of which affect overall comfort.
- **Rear seats** on the Paseo are next to non-existent and are really only serve as extra storage space when the trunk is extended.
- **The instrument panel** is terribly plain and the cabin interior isn't really too attractive.

CONCLUSION

The Tercel started out as a simple means of transportation, but it has become quite a classy little car, and the Paseo coupe has added good looks to its list of winning traits.

RECALLS

None over this period.

Tercel-Paseo — TOYOTA

RELIABILITY PROBLEMS

	1996	1997	1998	1999	2000	2001
Engine:	-	-	-	-		
Transmission:	X	X	X	X		
Suspension:	-	-	-	-		
Steering:	X	X	-	-		
Brakes:	-	-	-	-		
Electricity:	X	-	-	-		
Body:	-	-	-	-		
Accessories:	-	-	-	-		
Fit/finish:	-	X	X	X		

POWERTRAIN / PERFORMANCE

Year	Type/ L/Camshaft/bhp	Drivetrain & gearbox	Acceler. 0/100 sec.	Top. speed km/h	Ave. Fuel consp. l./100 km
96-99	L4/1.5/DOHC/93(Tercel)	front-M5	11.0	165	7.2
		front-A4	13.5	165	8.4
	L4/1.5/DOHC/100	front-M5	10.5	160	7.8
		front-A3-A4	11.8	165	8.7

SPECIFICATIONS

Model 96-99	Wlb.	Lght.	Cb.wt	Brakes	Steering	Standard
sdn. 2dr. base	2380	4110	889	dc/dr	r&p.	155/80R14
sdn. 2dr. DX-CE	2380	4110	912	dc/dr	pwr.r&p.	155/80R14
sdn. 4dr. DX-CE	2380	4110	923	dc/dr	pwr.r&p.	155/80R13
cpe. 3dr. Paseo	2380	4155	986	dc/dr	pwr.r&p.	185/60R14

PRICES

Model / version		1996	1997	1998	1999	2000	2001
Tercel							
sdn. 2dr. base / S	mini	4700					
	maxi	6300					
sdn. 2dr. DX	mini	5250					
	maxi	6800					
sdn. 2dr. CE	mini		5800	7350	8900		
	maxi		7900	8900	11000		
sdn. 4dr. DX	mini	5800					
	maxi	7350					
sdn. 4dr. CE	mini		6300	7900	9450		
	maxi		8400	9450	11550		
Paseo							
cpe. 3dr.	mini	6300	7350	8400	9450		
	maxi	7900	8900	10000	11550		

See page 7 to adapt these figures.

1998 TOYOTA Tercel CE

TOYOTA 4Runner

2000 TOYOTA 4Runner

This sport utility vehicle was introduced in 1985 as a 3-door model driven by a 4-cylinder engine and it got a V6 in 1988 and a 5-door body style in '90. Revamped in 1995, it was given in '99 a bunch of small improvements, and especially a vitamine shot that the 4Runner was lacking of to sustain the strong competition in this market segment.

PROS

- **The vehicle is neutral** on the road and well-balanced on rough terrain and out in the rough, it can get just about anywhere with such high ground clearance.
- **The V6 engine** is more muscular but it lacks torque at low rpm in some situations. The 4-cylinder engine has less vim and vitality, but it does its job in a nice, hassle-free way.
- **Construction quality** is very good, for the vehicle is solid and finish is tight and clean.
- **It's a very practical vehicle**, because it's midway between a station wagon and a pickup truck, and it comes equipped with all-wheel drive.
- **Driving comfort** is really above average, with such well-contoured front seats, smooth and civilized suspension and reasonable noise level with the V6, even though there is some wind noise.

CONS

- **The 4Runner is reliable** and durable, which explains its high price tag and why these models are hard to find on the used vehicle market.
- **Boarding** this vehicle with such a high ground clearance is difficult without a step to climb onto.
- **The V6 engine** really guzzles the gas, especially when carrying a heavy load or going over rough terrain.
- **Steering** is light because it's over-assisted. This may be an advantage on rough terrain, but it sure complicates things on the highway when there are crosswinds.
- **The overall look** is very basic and plain before 1997, even on the luxurious upper-end SR5. The Limited edition has truly corrected this annoying situation.

CONCLUSION

The 4Runner is a good, all-purpose vehicle that's reliable and efficient. The only disadvantage is how much it costs to keep it on the road, so its attributes may be impressive, but there's a hefty price tag attached.

RECALLS

None over this period.

4Runner — TOYOTA

RELIABILITY PROBLEMS

	1996	1997	1998	1999	2000	2001
Engine:	-	X	-	-	X	X
Transmission:	X	-	X	-	-	-
Suspension:	-	X	X	X	X	-
Steering:	-	-	-	X	-	-
Brakes:	-	X	-	-	-	-
Electricity:	X	-	X	X	X	-
Body:	-	-	-	-	-	-
Accessories:	X	-	-	X	X	-
Fit/finish:	-	-	-	X	-	-

POWERTRAIN / PERFORMANCE

Year	Type/ L/Camshaft/bhp	Drivetrain & gearbox	Acceler. 0/100 sec.	Top speed km/h	Ave. Fuel consp. l./100 km
1996	L4/2.4/SOHC/116	rear/all-M5	12.8	160	12.0
		rear/all-A4	13.7	155	13.5
	V6/3.0/SOHC/150	rear/all-M5	12.0	165	14.0
		rear/all-A4	13.3	160	14.5
97-01	L4/2.7/DOHC/150	rear/all-M5	NA	NA	13.7
		rear/all-A4	NA	NA	12.6
	V6/3.4/DOHC/183	rear/all-M5	10.0	165	14.4
		rear/all-A4	11.5	160	14.1

SPECIFICATIONS

Model	Wlb. mm	Lght. mm	Cb.wt kg	Brakes fr/rr	Steering type	Standard tires
1996						
wgn. 4dr. SR5	2625	4486	1844	dc/dr	pwr.bal.	225/75R15
wgn. 4dr. V6	2625	4486	1889	dc/dr	pwr.bal.	225/75R15
97-01						
wgn. 4dr. SR5	2675	4540	1690	dc/dr	pwr.r&p.	225/75R15
wgn. 4dr. V6	2675	4540	1762	dc/dr/ABS	pwr.r&p.	265/70R16
wgn. 4dr. LTD	2675	4540	1803	dc/dr/ABS	pwr.r&p.	265/70R16

PRICES

Model / version		1996	1997	1998	1999	2000	2001
wgn. 4dr. 4x4 V6	mini						29400
	maxi						32550
wgn. 4dr. 4x4 SR5	mini	11350	14700	17850	21850		
	maxi	13650	17300	20000	24150		
wgn. 4dr. 4x4 V6 SR5	mini	15200	17850	21000	24150	26200	31500
	maxi	17850	19950	23100	27000	29400	34650
wgn. 4dr. 4x4 V6 LTD	mini	20500	23600	26650	29300	32750	38300
	maxi	23100	26200	28750	32500	36700	41600

See page 7 to adapt these figures.

VOLKSWAGEN Eurovan

1999 VOLKSWAGEN Eurovan

The Eurovan replaced the Vanagon in 1992. It became a front-wheel drive vehicle driven by a 2.5L 5-cylinder gas engine, or a Diesel engine since '93 and a camper model is still available. In '99, the Eurovan has been reintroduced after a year spent at the fountain of Youth and shows up with a VR6 engine and a 4 speed automatic transmission that can haul a mere 2,000kg ! Offered in three different trim levels, including a practical camper, the Eurovan is surely a phoenix of its own.

PROS
- **The cabin interior** is absolutely huge, even on the shorter model and there's unusually generous space every which way which makes for exceptional freedom of movement and access.
- **Handling** is outstanding for a vehicle of this type, for the independent suspension stabilizes and balances the van to a remarkable degree, controlling sway and vehicle path.
- **Build quality**, finish and trim components are flawless, but the overall design is rather plain and simple.
- **Equipment** is more extensive on the more attractive GL and GLS.
- **The cockpit** is perfect, for it provides excellent visibility and good vehicle control.
- **The side door** is light and easy to open and close and rear windows slide open.
- **The very practical baggage** compartment is huge and it opens nice and low, storage compartments are well distributed throughout the cabin and there are headrests for all seats.
- **The economical yield** of the Diesel engine.

CONS
- **The Eurovan looks** more like a van than a real family vehicle.
- **Both Audi L5 engines** are anemic because of a poor power to weight ratio, that 's why VW has brought in the VR6.
- **Gas consumption** on the gas fed L5 engine is comparable to that of a 3.0L V6, without the muscle or torque.
- **The brake pedal** is really soft and makes it hard to slow down with any accuracy and stops are a long time coming.
- **Steering** is vague and doesn't go back to center on its own and needs to be constantly readjusted in crosswinds, for the Eurovan sure doesn't like wind.

CONCLUSION
The old Eurovan weren't powered by the right engine before '99, which is too bad, for it's a superbly designed, very practical vehicle.

RECALLS
None over this period.

Eurovan — VOLKSWAGEN

RELIABILITY PROBLEMS

	1996	1997	1998	1999	2000	2001
Engine:	X	X		X	-	
Transmission:	-	-		-	-	
Suspension:	-	X		-	-	
Steering:	-	-		-	-	
Brakes:	X	-		X	-	
Electricity:	-	-		-	-	
Body:	X	-		-	-	
Accessories:	X	X		X	-	
Fit/finish:	-	-		-	-	

POWERTRAIN

Year	Type/ L/Camshaft/bhp	Drivetrain & gearbox
96-97	L5/2.5/SOHC/110	front-M5
		front-A4
	L5D/2.4/SOHC/77	front-M5
99-01	V6/2.8/DOHC/140	front-A4

PERFORMANCE

Acceler. 0/100 sec.	Top. speed km/h	Ave. Fuel consp. l./100 km
14.5	160	12.5
15.5	155	13.0
18.5	140	8.0
NA	NA	15.8

SPECIFICATIONS

Model	Wlb. mm	Lght. mm	Cb.wt kg	Brakes fr/rr	Steering type	Standard tires
95-97						
m.v. 4dr. CL	2920	4740	1730	dc/dr	pwr.r&p.	205/65R15
m.v. 4dr. GL	2920	4740	1780	dc/dr	pwr.r&p.	205/65R15
m.v. 4dr. CV	2920	4740	1890	dc/dr	pwr.r&p.	205/65R15
99-01						
m.v. 4dr. GLS	2920	4789	1914	dc/ABS	pwr.r&p.	205/65R15
m.v. 4dr. MV	2920	4789	1972	dc/ABS	pwr.r&p.	205/65R15
m.v. 4dr. Camper	3320	5189	2375	dc/ABS	pwr.r&p.	205/65R15

PRICES

Model / version		1996	1997	1998	1999	2000	2001
m.v. 4dr. CV	mini	15200	21000				
	maxi	18900	25000				
m.v. 4dr. Diesel	mini	11550					
	maxi	13650					
m.v. 4dr. GLS Auto	mini	10500			22800	30000	32500
	maxi	12900			25200	32500	35700
m.v. 4dr. MV Auto	mini				24150	31100	33600
	maxi				26250	33600	36750
m.v. 4dr. Camper	mini				28750		
	maxi				31100		

See page 7 to adapt these figures.

2000 VOLKSWAGEN Eurovan

VOLKSWAGEN — Golf

1996 VOLKSWAGEN Golf GL

Launched under this name in 1985, the Golf is available as a 3- or 5-door sedan or as a 2-door convertible. The GTI 16V came out in 1987, the VR6 engine in '94 and the latest body design in '95. In '99, two type of Golf were sold in the marketplace: the "Classic" Golf and the New Golf.

PROS
- **The huge cabin and trunk** give space in all directions and access is very easy from side and rear.
- **Handling** is clean and the sports models literally stick to the road, for they exhibit no sway or lean.
- **The last VR6** engine provides strong accelerations and pick-up.
- **Driving** is pleasant with such a nice cockpit, good visibility, crisp, sensitive steering and the straightforward, ergonomic instrument panel that has become quite attractive, by the way.
- **The economical,** remarkably sturdy Diesel engine that simply refuses to die.
- **Convenience** hasn't been overlooked, for the rear seat area has modular seats and storage compartments are well distributed throughout the cabin.

CONS
- **The Volkswagen reputation** for fool-proof reliability is no longer what it once was, for bodywork is quite prone to rust and mechanical features aren't really dependable, and we might add, the quality of some components is pretty wishy washy.
- **Driving competence** varies with the years, models, the shape the original equipment or replacement parts are in, and tire quality.
- **High noise** really affects driving comfort.
- **The cabin interior** is smaller than average for this car category, because of the narrow body.
- **Gas engines** aren't economical, mostly the least VR6 which guzzles just like its american competitors.

CONCLUSION
The Golf lost its pristine reputation when it began to be built in Mexico, and in spite of technical improvements, it's less economical and less efficient than its rivals.

RECALLS
1996 Securing bolts of the hood latches may loosen.

Golf — VOLKSWAGEN

RELIABILITY PROBLEMS

	1996	1997	1998	1999	2000	2001
Engine:	X	X	X	X		
Transmission:	X	-	-	-		
Suspension:	-	-	-	-		
Steering:	-	-	-	-		
Brakes:	X	X	-	-		
Electricity:	X	X	-	-		
Body:	X	-	-	-		
Accessories:	-	-	X	X		
Fit/finish:	X	-	-	-		

POWERTRAIN

Year	Type/ L/Camshaft/bhp	Drivetrain & gearbox	Acceler. 0/100 sec.	Top. speed km/h	Ave. Fuel consp. l./100 km
96-99	L4/1.8/SOHC/90-123	front-M5	11.8	175	9.3
		front-A3-A4	13.0	165	10.0
	L4/2.0/SOHC/115-133	front-M5	10.9	180	10.1
		front-A4	12.0	175	10.8
	L4D/1.9/SOHC/75-90	front-M5	13.0	170	5.9
	V6/2.8/DOHC/174-201	front-M5	8.0	210	12.2
		front-A4	8.8	200	12.6

SPECIFICATIONS

Model 96-99	Wlb. mm	Lght. mm	Cb.wt kg	Brakes fr/rr	Steering type	Standard tires
con. 2dr.	2475	4020	1225	dc/dr	pwr.r&p.	195/60R14
sdn. 3dr. CL	2475	4075	1117	dc/dr	pwr.r&p.	195/60R14
sdn. 3dr. GTI	2475	4075	1043	dc/dc	pwr.r&p.	185/60R14
sdn. 3dr. GTI v6	2475	4075	1252	dc/ABS	pwr.r&p.	205/50R15
sdn. 5dr. CL	2475	4075	1173	dc/dr	pwr.r&p.	195/60R14

PRICES

Model / version		1996	1997	1998	1999	2000	2001
con. 2dr. Cabriolet	mini	10800	12600	14700	16300		
	maxi	13200	15100	16800	18300		
con. 2dr. Highline	mini		15200				
	maxi		17850				
con. 2dr. GLS	mini			17850	19400		
	maxi			19850	21400		
sdn. 3dr. CL	mini	6500	7900				
	maxi	8100	9650				
sdn. 3dr. GTI	mini	9750	11350	13350			
	maxi	11550	13350	15750			
sdn. 3dr. GTI VR6	mini	11750	13350	16150	18900		
	maxi	13550	15400	18900	21000		
sdn. 5dr.	mini				9650		
	maxi				12000		
sdn. 5dr. CL	mini	7250	8400				
	maxi	8600	10200				
sdn. 5dr. GL	mini	8200	9400	10000	11550		
	maxi	9650	11100	12100	13550		
sdn. 4dr. K2	mini			9450	10200		
	maxi			11250	12300		
sdn. 5dr. GL TDI	mini	8900	9650				
	maxi	9750	11450				
sdn. 5dr. Jazz	mini			10200			
	maxi			12300			
sdn. 5dr. Trek	mini			10400			
	maxi			12200			
sdn. 5dr. Wolfsburg	mini			12800	13750		
	maxi			15100	16000		
sdn. 5dr. 2.0L	mini				10700		
	maxi				13000		

See page 7 to adapt these figures.

VOLKSWAGEN   Jetta

1996 VOLKSWAGEN Jetta GL

The Jetta, that's inspired by the Golf, was first sold in 1975 and the GLX with VR6 engine was first available in '94. It comes in 2- and 4-door models, powered by gas or Diesel engines. In '99, two type of Jetta were sold in the marketplace: the "Classic" Jetta and the New Jetta.

PROS

- **Handling** on the models equipped with a 4-cylinder engine is clean, for there isn't much sway or swing.
- **The VR6 engine** is remarkable and yields very spirited accelerations and pick-up.
- **Driving** is enhanced by the nicely designed cockpit, good visibility, crisp and sensitive steering and a convenient, ergonomic and nice-looking instrument panel.
- **The Diesel engine** is economical and so robust that it just never dies.
- **The huge trunk** is characteristic of the Jetta and can hold heaps and heaps of luggage.

CONS

- **The Volkswagen reputation** for fool-proof reliability is no longer what it once was, for bodywork is quite prone to rust and mechanical features aren't really dependable, and we might add, the quality of some components is pretty hit and miss.
- **Handling** on the GLX is very touchy with the VR6 engine that is just too muscular for this type of frame and undercarriage. So there's whopping torque and responses are rough around the edges, which could be problematic for an inexperienced driver.
- **High noise** really affects driving comfort on long trips.
- **The cabin interior** is smaller than average for this car category, because of the narrow body.
- **The 3-speed** automatic is poorly calibrated.
- **Gas engines** aren't economical.

CONCLUSION

The Jetta lost its credibility when it began to be built in Mexico, and in spite of improvements, it's less economical and less roomy than its rivals.

RECALLS

1999   A sound absorbing mat inside of the B-pillar side trim may have been improperly installed and could ignite in the event of a collision, resulting in vehicle fire.

Jetta — VOLKSWAGEN

RELIABILITY PROBLEMS

	1996	1997	1998	1999	2000	2001
Engine:	X	X	X	X		
Transmission:	X	X	X	X		
Suspension:	X	-	X	X		
Steering:	-	-	-	-		
Brakes:	-	X	X	-		
Electricity:	X	X	-	-		
Body:	-	-	-	-		
Accessories:	X	X	X	X		
Fit/finish:	X	-	X	X		

POWERTRAIN

Year	Type/ L/Camshaft/bhp	Drivetrain & gearbox
1996	L4/1.8/SOHC/90-123	front-M5
		front-A3-A4
96-98	L4/2.0/SOHC/115-133	front-M5
		front-A4
	L4D/1.9/SOHC/75-90	front-M5
96-99	V6/2.8/DOHC/174	front-M5
		front-A4

PERFORMANCE

Acceler. 0/100 sec.	Top. speed km/h	Ave. Fuel consp. l./100 km
11.8	175	9.3
13.0	165	10.0
10.9	180	10.1
12.0	175	10.8
13.0	170	5.9
8.0	210	12.2
8.8	220	12.6

SPECIFICATIONS

Model 96-99	Wlb. mm	Lght. mm	Cb.wt kg	Brakes fr/rr	Steering type	Standard tires
sdn. 4dr. GL	2513	4376	1279	dc/ABS	pwr.r&p.	195/65R15
sdn. 4dr. GLS	2513	4376	1283	dc/ABS	pwr.r&p.	195/65R15
sdn. 4dr. GLX	2513	4376	1369	dc/ABS	pwr.r&p.	195/65R15
sdn. 4dr. TDI	2475	4404	1254	dc/dr	pwr.r&p.	205/50R15

PRICES

Model / version		1996	1997	1998	1999	2000	2001
sdn. 4dr. GL	mini	8100	9650	12300	13550		
	maxi	10100	11650	14200	15400		
sdn. 4dr. GL TDI	mini	8600	9250	13350	15100		
	maxi	11150	11150	15200	17000		
sdn. 4dr. TDI DSL	mini		10200				
	maxi		12200				
sdn. 4dr. GLX VR6	mini	12600	15400	17850			
	maxi	14800	17550	19750			
sdn. 4dr. GT	mini		10200	12800			
	maxi		12200	14900			
sdn. 4dr. GLS	mini	9150	10600	13300			
	maxi	13250	12700	15200			
sdn. 4dr. Jazz/Treck	mini		10800				
	maxi		12900				
sdn. 4dr. K2	mini			13350			
	maxi			15200			
sdn. 4dr. Wolfburg	mini			13850	15650		
	maxi			15750	17500		

See page 7 to adapt these figures.

VOLKSWAGEN — New Beetle

2000 VOLKSWAGEN New Beetle

The Beetle is a Golf spin-off and its launch in 1998 was the automobile industry highlight of the year. Since that day, the New Beetle has won its right to be equipped with the sophisticated 150-bhp 1.8L turbo, borrowed from the Audi A4 mainly in order to create, once more, a bit of excitment for the brand's enthusiasts.

PROS
- **The style** is utterly irresistible, so this car sure gets noticed, thanks to the array of bright body shades.
- **Ultra-modern** technical features are real assets when it comes to safety and comfort, such as effective heating and air conditioning that do their stuff when it counts and the four airbags.
- **Safe travel** derives from clean follow-through, smooth and precise steering and brakes that really grip in most situations.
- **Front seats** are comfy and accessible, offer lots of toe, hip and headroom, seats are beautifully contoured and upholstered and the suspension is quite velvety.
- **The performance** of the 1.8L turbo engine is just so exemplary and truly dictates the selection of this engine above others.
- **The cabin design** is very plush and includes top-notch trim and neat finish touches, so the overall look is quite unique.
- **The rear hatch** is well integrated and meticulously crafted with the lock hidden under the brand crest, a real work of art!
- **The manual gearbox** is a driver's dream with such an accurate and well-honed shifter, a true VW beauty.

CONS
- **Convenience-wise**, there aren't enough storage spots, the rear seats are snug and hard to get to and the trunk holds enough luggage only when the seatbench is folded down.
- **Performance** is wimpy and breathless with both the 2.0L and 1.9L Diesel engines, linked to either the manual or automatic transmission.
- **Outward view** is hampered by the high body belt that cuts down on window size, massive roof supports and tiny mirrors.
- **Noise** is stereophonic due to the noisy, shaky engine, whistling mirrors and roaring tires.
- **It's hard getting comfy** behind the wheel and the driver feels really far removed from the windshield and from what's going on up front...
- **The dashboard** is absolutely huge for what it holds, so it makes the cabin look tinier than it actually is.
- **Disappointing:** rear windows that can't be opened, small sun-visors, insufficiently bright headlights, awkwardly located clock and the hardly practical cup-holders.

CONCLUSION
The Beetle is a winner due to its nostalgic style rather than for its overall practicality or fair performance.

RECALLS
1998 Wiring inspection and installation of modified battery casing.

New Beetle — VOLKSWAGEN

RELIABILITY PROBLEMS

	1996	1997	1998	1999	2000	2001
Engine:			X	X	-	-
Transmission:			-	-	-	-
Suspension:						
Steering:			-	-	-	-
Brakes:			-	-	-	-
Electricity:			X	X	X	X
Body:			X	X	X	-
Accessories:			X	X	-	-
Fit/finish:			X	-	-	-

POWERTRAIN

Year	Type/ L/Camshaft/bhp	Drivetrain & gearbox
98-01	L4TD/1.9/SOHC/90	front-M5
		front-A4
	L4/2.0/SOHC/115	front-M5
		front-A4
99-01	L4T/1.8/DOHC/150	front-M5
		front-A4

PERFORMANCE

Acceler. 0/100 sec.	Top. speed km/h	Ave. Fuel consp. l./100 km
13.0	170	5.6
14.2	165	6.9
10.6	180	9.9
11.8	175	10.5
8.0	210	10.2
NA	NA	NA

SPECIFICATIONS

Model 08-01	Wlb. mm	Lght. mm	Cb.wt kg	Brakes fr/rr	Steering type	Standard tires
sdn. 2dr. 2.0	2512	4092	1230	dc/dc	pwr.r&p.	205/55R16
sdn. 2dr. TDI	2512	4092	1260	dc/dc	pwr.r&p.	205/55R16
sdn. 2dr. 1.8T	2512	4092	1290	dc/dc	pwr.r&p.	205/55R16

PRICES

Model / version		1996	1997	1998	1999	2000	2001
sdn. 2dr. 2.0	mini			12200			
	maxi			14700			
sdn. 2dr. GL	mini				13650	16300	19100
	maxi				15950	18700	22250
sdn. 2dr. GLS	mini				14700	17300	20500
	maxi				17000	19650	23300
sdn. 2dr. TDI	mini			13650			
	maxi			16300			
sdn. 2dr. GLS TDI	mini				16300	18900	22000
	maxi				18600	21200	25000
sdn. 2dr. GLS 1.8T	mini				17850	19400	22600
	maxi				20150	21700	25400
sdn. 2dr. GLX 1.8T	mini				19950	22800	27000
	maxi				22250	25000	29700

See page 7 to adapt these figures.

2000 VOLKSWAGEN New Beetle

VOLKSWAGEN — New Golf

2000 VOLKSWAGEN New Golf GTI

The last Golf derived from the former one. It is available as 3- or 5-door sedans with TDI or 2.0L 4-cylinder or 2.8L V6 gas engine.

PROS
- **Performance** of the GTi and GLX's VR6 is the most exciting. It provides the kind of acceleration and pick-up that makes you hate the sluggish 2.0L on the pretentious GTI GLS.
- **Handling** is stable and predictable thanks to efficient and sophisticated suspensions that result in precision driving. Although they tend to understeer, it's easy to control and are ideal for sporty drivers.
- **Steering** is precise and responsive. Assistance is just right and it makes driving on winding roads a very pleasant experience.
- **The fuel economy** of the Diesel engine's is more noteworthy than levels recorded for the less economical gasoline engines.
- **The presentation** is not as severe now that materials come in colors other than grey and black. Plastics and fabrics look significantly better than they did on previous models.
- **The standard anti-theft** system is far from a luxury. It's now part of standard equipment and will no doubt serve to decrease the number of thefts that once reached virtually epidemic levels.
- **The convertible** is the only one of its kind, with four seats, a roll bar and a lined top including a glass rear windshield featuring a defroster, a definite asset for problem-free in winter driving.
- **Bonus**: high praise for the diesel models' range and automatic windshield wipers that spring into action as soon as it begins to rain.

CONS
- **The price** of the Golf is yet high compared to some of their less problematic Japanese competitors.
- **The rear bench** is wider, but it isn't still long enough and only smaller passengers will feel comfortable.
- **Few exasperating problems** continue to plague Golf owners. Once you get past the product's good looks, you soon see that some manufacturing details could use improvement.
- **The performance** of the 2.0L engine is mediocre and acceleration and pick-up are both unenthusiastic.
- **Comfort** is no picnic; this car remains noisy, the engine and drivetrains vibrate, the suspension is very firm and seats are very hard.
- **Dashboard** wastes a lot of space and is a hazard for kneecaps.
- **To be fixed:** very weak headlights and slow windshield wipers, are dangerous, especially on the high-performance GLX versions

CONCLUSION
Improvements aside, the Golf are overvalued. Their reliability has not yet been proven undeniably and their performance levels and warranties fail to justify their price.

RECALLS
2000 One of the two brackets used to bolt the front control arm to the body structure may not have been welded properly and must be inspected and replaced if necessary.

00-01 One of two brackets use to bolt the front control arm to the body structure may have not been welded to specifications.

New Golf — VOLKSWAGEN

RELIABILITY PROBLEMS

	1996	1997	1998	1999	2000	2001
Engine:				X	-	-
Transmission:				X	-	-
Suspension:				-	-	-
Steering:				-	-	-
Brakes:				X	-	-
Electricity:				X	X	X
Body:				-	-	-
Accessories:				X	X	X
Fit/finish:				X	-	-

POWERTRAIN

Year	Type/ L/Camshaft/bhp	Drivetrain & gearbox
99-01	L4/2.0/SOHC/115	front-M5
		front-A4
	V6/2.8/DOHC/174	front-M5
		front-A4
	L4D/1.9/SOHC/90	front-M5
00-01	L4/1.8T(S)HC/150	front-M5

PERFORMANCE

Acceler. 0/100 sec.	Top speed km/h	Ave. Fuel consp. l./100 km
10.9	180	10.1
12.0	175	10.8
8.0	210	12.2
8.8	200	12.6
13.0	170	5.9
9.0	200	10.0

SPECIFICATIONS

Model 99-01	Wlb. mm	Lght. mm	Cb.wt kg	Brakes fr/rr	Steering type	Standard tires
con. 2dr. Cabrio	2474	4074	1398	dc/dr/ABS	pwr.r&p.	195/60R14
sdn. 2dr. GTI GLS	2511	4149	1253	dc/dr/ABS	pwr.r&p.	195/65R15
sdn. 2dr. GTI GLX	2511	4149	1311	dc/ABS	pwr.r&p.	205/55R16
sdn. 4dr. TDI GLS	2511	4149	1304	dc/dr/ABS	pwr.r&p.	195/65R15
sdn. 4dr. GL 2.0L	2511	4149	1235	dc/dr/ABS	pwr.r&p.	195/65R15
sdn. 4dr. GLS	2511	4149	1279	dc/dr/ABS	pwr.r&p.	195/65R15

PRICES

Model / version		1996	1997	1998	1999	2000	2001
sdn. 2dr. GL 2.0L	mini				13000	15100	17850
	maxi				15100	17750	20900
sdn. 2dr. GL TDI	mini				14200	16150	18900
	maxi				16300	18800	21950
sdn. 2dr. GLS 1.8	mini					19300	22000
	maxi					21950	25100
sdn. 2dr. GTI GLS 2.0L	mini				16700	17900	
	maxi				18800	20700	
sdn. 2dr. GTI GLX 2.8L	mini				19600	22450	24900
	maxi				21750	25100	27600
sdn 4dr. 1.8T	mini					17950	21000
	maxi					20900	24000
sdn. 4dr. GLS 2.0L	mini				15100	17200	19950
	maxi				17200	19850	23000
sdn. 4dr. GLS TDI	mini				16200	17450	20700
	maxi				18300	20400	23400

See page 7 to adapt these figures.

VOLKSWAGEN — New Jetta

2000 VOLKSWAGEN New Jetta GL

The new Jetta derived from the former one. It is available as 4-door sedan with 2.0L 4-cylinder or 2.8L V6 gas engine.

PROS

- **Performance** of the GLX's VR6 is the most exciting. It provides the kind of acceleration and pick-up that makes you hate the sluggish 2.0L on the GLS.
- **Handling** is stable and predictable thanks to efficient and sophisticated suspensions that result in precision driving. Although they tend to understeer, it's easy to control and are ideal for sporty drivers.
- **Steering** is precise and responsive. Assistance is just right and it makes driving on winding roads a very pleasant experience.
- **The presentation** is not as severe now that materials come in colors other than grey and black. Plastics and fabrics look significantly better than they did on previous models.
- **The standard anti-theft** system is far from a luxury. It's now part of standard equipment and will no doubt serve to decrease the number of thefts that once reached virtually epidemic levels.
- **The trunk** is smaller than on the previous model, but it has a respectable capacity and can be extended by lowering the backrest of the rear
- **Bonus**: high praise for the automatic windshield wipers that spring into action as soon as it begins to rain.

CONS

- **The price** of the Jetta is yet high compare to some of their less problematic Japanese competitors.
- **The fuel economy** of the gasoline engines is not obvious mostly if they are driven on the sports mode.
- **The rear bench** is wider, but it isn't still long enough and only smaller passengers will feel comfortable.
- **Few exasperating problems** continue to plague the Jetta owners. Once you get past the good looks of the product, you soon see that some manufacturing details could use improvement.
- **The performance** of the 2.0L engine is mediocre and acceleration and pick-up are both unenthusiastic.
- **Comfort** is no picnic; this car remains noisy, the engine and drivetrains vibrate, the suspension is very firm and seats are very hard.
- **Dashboard** wastes a lot of space and is a hazard for kneecaps.
- **To be fixed:** weak headlights and slow windshield wipers are dangerous, especially on the high-performance GLX versions

CONCLUSION

Improvements aside, the Jetta are overvalued. Their reliability has not yet been proven undeniably and their performance levels and warranties fail to justify their price.

RECALLS

None over this period.

New Jetta — VOLKSWAGEN

RELIABILITY PROBLEMS

	1996	1997	1998	1999	2000	2001
Engine:				X	-	-
Transmission:				X	X	-
Suspension:				X	-	-
Steering:				-	-	-
Brakes:				-	-	-
Electricity:				X	X	X
Body:				X	X	-
Accessories:				X	X	X
Fit/finish:				X	-	-

POWERTRAIN

Year	Type/ L/Camshaft/bhp	Drivetrain & gearbox	Acceler. 0/100 sec.	Top. speed km/h	Ave. Fuel consp. l./100 km
99-01	L4/2.0/SOHC/115	front-M5	10.9	180	10.1
		front-A4	12.0	175	10.8
	V6/2.8/DOHC/174	front-M5	8.0	210	12.2
		front-A4	8.8	200	12.6
	L4D/1.9/SOHC/90	front-M5	13.0	170	5.9
00-01	L4T/1.8/SOHC/150	front-M5	9.0	200	10.0

SPECIFICATIONS

Model 99-01	Wlb. mm	Lght. mm	Cb.wt kg	Brakes fr/rr	Steering type	Standard tires
sdn. 4dr. GLS TDI	2513	4376	1311	dc/dr	pwr.r&p.	195/65R15
sdn. 4dr. GL	2513	4376	1279	dc/dc	pwr.r&p.	195/65R15
sdn. 4dr. GLS	2513	4376	1283	dc/ABS	pwr.r&p.	195/65R15
sdn. 4dr. GLX 2.8L	2513	4376	1369	dc/dr	pwr.r&p.	195/65R15

PRICES

Model / version		1996	1997	1998	1999	2000	2001
sdn. 4dr. GL	mini				16150	17450	19400
	maxi				18100	19600	22250
sdn. 4dr. GL TDI	mini				17850	19950	22250
	maxi				19750	22250	25100
sdn. 4dr. GLS	mini				17300	19400	21750
	maxi				19200	21700	24350
sdn. 4dr. GLS TDI	mini				18400	20500	22800
	maxi				20250	22800	25400
sdn. 4dr. Wolfburg	mini						21750
	maxi						24450
sdn. 4dr. G:S 1.8	mini					18900	21200
	maxi					22250	23900
sdn. 4dr. GLS 2.8L	mini				19400	22000	24350
	maxi				21400	24350	27100
sdn. 4dr. GLX 2.8L	mini				22600	25700	28150
	maxi				24550	28100	30600

See page 7 to adapt these figures.

VOLKSWAGEN New Passat

2001 VOLKSWAGEN New Passat

The Passat has been extensively redesigned while awaiting a full revamp. It remains available as a sedan or wagon with either a 1.8-liter L4 or a 2.8-liter V6. The 4Motion all-wheel drive system is optional.

PROS

- **The cabin and trunk** are roomy and make for a spacious and comfortable vehicle.
- **The V6** provides spicy performance and energetic full-stop and pick-up accelerations.
- **The Passat handles** with exemplary rigor, a Volkswagen trademark and one of the model's main advantages.
- **Ride comfort** is appreciable, although somewhat firm as is often the case with German automobiles.
- **The efficient brakes** are easy to gauge and work gradually to bring the car to a stop in a short and straight line.
- **The solid construction** and attentive finish are part of the quality image that Volkswagen is seeking to market.
- **The 4Motion** all-wheel drive system gives a whole new dimension to the mid-range family wagon, which is not as expensive as an Audi yet more prestigious than a Subaru.

CONS

- **The Passat doesn't come cheap** and is far from being an economy car.
- **The vague steering** feels disappointingly elastic in this otherwise rigorous package. This is mainly because of the poor-quality Continental tires that come as standard equipment.
- **The Continental Contact tires** do not provide adequate grip, even on dry roads. In the rain, they are prone to aquaplaning and are very noisy.
- **The Tiptronic transmission** is tiresome to use and is very less practical that equivalent systems developed by other auto makers.
- When coupled to the automatic transmission, the 1.8T produces timid performance given the high weight-to-power ratio.
- **The center console** is no model of ergonomics, with several out-of-reach controls.
- **The instruments** are lit in such a way that makes them difficult to read at night. The small digital screen lacks contrast and is impossible to decipher during the day.

VERDICT

The Passat remains the family wagon of choice for European car aficionados. It is built according to strict German construction standards but is far from economical.

RECALLS

None over this period.

New Passat — VOLKSWAGEN

RELIABILITY PROBLEMS
	1996	1997	1998	1999	2000	2001
Engine:						
Transmission:						
Suspension:						
Steering:						
Brakes:			Insufficient data			
Electricity:						
Body:						
Accessories:						
Fit/finish:						

POWERTRAIN

Year	Type/ L/Camshaft/bhp	Drivetrain & gearbox	Acceler. 0/100 sec.	Top. speed km/h	Ave. Fuel consp. l./100 km
2001	L4T/1.8/DOHC/170	front-M5	9.2	200	10.5
	V6/2.8/SOHC/190 FWD	front-A5	9.7	220	13.1
	V6/2.8/SOHC/190 AWD	all-A5	10.5	200	13.7

SPECIFICATIONS

Model 2001	Wlb. mm	Lght. mm	Cb.wt kg	Brakes fr/rr	Steering type	Standard tires
sdn. 4dr. FWD	2703	4703	1452	dc/ABS	pwr.r.&p.	195/65R15
wgn. 4dr. FWD	2703	4703	1591	dc/ABS	pwr.r.&p.	195/65R15
sdn. 4dr. AWD	2703	4703	1634	dc/ABS	pwr.r.&p.	195/65R15
wag. 4dr. AWD	2703	4703	1704	dc/ABS	pwr.r.&p.	195/65R15

PRICES

Model / version		1996	1997	1998	1999	2000	2001
sdn. 4dr. GLS	mini						24700
	maxi						27500
sdn. 4dr. GLS V6	mini						27300
	maxi						30100
sdn. 4dr. GLS V6 4M	mini						31500
	maxi						34350
sdn. 4dr. GLX V6	mini						28350
	maxi						31200
sdn. 4dr. GLX 4M	mini						35700
	maxi						38550
wgn. 4dr. GLS	mini						26800
	maxi						29600
wgn. 4dr. GLS V6	mini						30450
	maxi						33300
wgn. 4dr. GLS 4M	mini						36750
	maxi						39600
wgn. 4dr. GLX	mini						31500
	maxi						34350
wgn. 4dr. GLX 4M	mini						36750
	maxi						39600

See page 7 to adapt these figures.

2001 VOLKSWAGEN New Passat

VOLKSWAGEN — Passat

1996 VOLKSWAGEN Passat

First launched in Europe in 1980, these compact sedans and station wagons were equipped with 4-cylinder gas engines, for the Diesel and VR6 were only installed before these cars were revamped in '95. The Syncro all-wheel drive and the Tiptronic 5-speed automatic transmission made their debut in 1999. Would the new model objective be that the Passat will, from now on, "compete" against its more expensive sister, the Audi A4?

PROS

- **The cabin** is very roomy, considering the compact size of the car and the trunk is huge and can be extended.
- **The instrument panel** is practical, the cockpit is comfortable and there's good all-round outward view.
- **Power steering** is quick and accurate and with such a small steer angle, the Passat maneuvers in superb fashion.
- **Brakes** are muscular, but they're easier to control at high speed for the pedal is stiff at lower speed.
- **Handling** on curves is amazing for the car stays neutral before going gradually into understeer.
- **The 2.0L engine** is competent, but the VR6 is a better choice, even if it's not as spectacular as on the Golf/Jetta.
- **The all-wheel drive** on the Syncro models makes for safer winter driving.

CONS

- **Hit and miss reliability** has tarnished the reputation of this model and sales are confidential, even if it's been remarkably improved in many respects.
- **The 2.0L G60 and Diesel** engines aren't too economical because of excessive vehicle weight.
- **Poorly calibrated** gears force the driver to downshift all the time in order to get pick-up of any momentum.
- **The big headrests** obstruct rearward view.

CONCLUSION

The Passat doesn't deserve its sad lot, for the latest generation models are very state-of-the-art, but there's a price to pay for all the frustrations that besieged owners of former models.

RECALLS

1998 Air flow meter screen may be damaged.
98-99 A control valve in the vacuum hose connecting the brake booster to the intake manifold may cause loss of power brake assist at low temperatures.
2000 Fuel sending unit will be replaced by a redesigned one.

Passat — VOLKSWAGEN

RELIABILITY PROBLEMS

	1996	1997	1998	1999	2000	2001
Engine:	X	X	X	X	X	-
Transmission:	-	-	-	-	-	-
Suspension:	X	-	X	X	X	-
Steering:	-	-	-	-	-	-
Brakes:	-	X	X	X	X	-
Electricity:	X	X	X	X	X	X
Body:	X	-	X	X	-	-
Accessories:	-	-	X	X	X	X
Fit/finish:	-	-	-	-	-	-

POWERTRAIN

Year	Type/ L/Camshaft/bhp	Drivetrain & gearbox	Acceler. 0/100 sec.	Top. speed km/h	Ave. Fuel consp. l./100 km
96-98	L4/2.0/DOHC/110	front-M5	11.8	200	10.0
96-01	L4T/1.8/DOHC/150	front-M5	9.0	220	11.3
		front-A5	10.5	210	NA
	V6/2.8/DOHC/172-190	front-M5	8.0	225	12.4
		front-A4/A5	9.3	220	13.2
	L4TD/1.9/SOHC/75-90	front-M5	14.5	175	6.2

SPECIFICATIONS

Model 96-01	Wlb. mm	Lght. mm	Cb.wt kg	Brakes fr/rr	Steering type	Standard tires
sdn. 4dr. GLS	2705	4675	1200	dc/dc	pwr.r&p.	185/60R14
sdn. 4dr. GLX VR6	2705	4675	1250	dc/ABS	pwr.r&p.	215/50R15
sdn. 4dr. TDI	2705	4675	NA	dc/dc	pwr.r&p.	195/60R14
sdn. 4dr. 4Motion	2707	4669	1624	dc/ABS	pwr.r&p.	195/65R15
wgn. 4dr. GLX VR6	2623	4569	1480	dc/ABS	pwr.r&p.	215/50R15
wgn. 4dr. TDI	2623	4569	1450	dc/dc	pwr.r&p.	195/60R14
wgn. 4dr. 4Motion	2707	4669	1657	dc/ABS	pwr.r&p.	195/65R15

PRICES

Model / version		1996	1997	1998	1999	2000	2001
sdn. 4dr. TDI	mini	10700	12600				
	maxi	13200	14700				
sdn. 4dr. GLS VR6	mini			17650	21200	23800	25200
	maxi			19750	23300	26250	28150
sdn. 4dr. GLS	mini	9750		16500	19600	21750	22800
	maxi	11750		18600	21700	24150	25400
sdn. 4dr. GLS 4Motion	mini					28000	29400
	maxi					30450	32350
sdn. 4dr. GLX	mini	13650	15650	19100			
	maxi	15950	17850	21300			
sdn. 4dr. GLX VR6	mini				24900	24900	26250
	maxi				27000	27300	29200
sdn. 4dr. GLX VR6 Syncro	mini				26500		
	maxi				28550		
sdn. 4dr. GLX 4Motion	mini					32250	33600
	maxi					34650	36550
wgn. 4dr. TDI	mini	11150	13000				
	maxi	13350	15350				
wgn. 4dr. GLX	mini	14400	17650				
	maxi	16500	18900				
wgn. 4dr. GLS 4Motion	mini					29100	34650
	maxi					31500	37500
wgn. 4dr. GLS VR6	mini				21750	27000	28350
	maxi				23850	29400	31200
wgn. 4dr. GLX VR6 Syncro	mini				26800		
	maxi				28900		
wgn. 4dr. GLS	mini				20150	23800	24900
	maxi				22250	26250	27500
wgn. 4dr. GLX 4Motion	mini					34100	
	maxi					37500	
wgn. 4dr. GLX V6	mini					28100	29400
	maxi					30450	32350

See page 7 to adapt these figures.

VOLVO 40 Series

2001 VOLVO S40

Volvo finally found a successor to the former 240 to fill in its bottom end and attract a younger clientele. The 40 has been around in Europe for several years now, and it is the fruit of collaborative efforts between the Swedish auto maker and Mitsubishi.

PROS
- **The dimensions** are interesting, especially in the case of the wagon which is practical and highly appreciated by young families.
- **The impressive** list of passive security features are in keeping with Volvo's traditional philosophy.
- **The sure handling** can be attributed to an efficient rear-end geometry and good-quality shock absorbers.
- **Performance** is quite respectable given the vehicle's weight and the engine's displacement. Fuel consumption remains reasonable.
- **Presentation** has been polished to the slightest details. Also thanks to rigorous construction standards, the 40 is a small luxury car that stands in a class all its own.
- **The excellent** overall comfort results from the soft suspension, great seats and hushed cabin.
- **The 40's extensive equipment** list allows it to rival other established models.

CONS
- **The hefty overall weight** is the result of the body's structural rigidity capable of resisting high impacts.
- **Body roll** leads to important body motion, and the 40 models are sensitive to crosswinds.
- **The rear seats** are difficult to access and were designed more with children than with football players in mind.
- **The headlights** and windshield wipers are inefficient and make for uncomfortable driving in poor weather conditions.
- **The ergonomics** of the center console need to be improved. The window and radio controls are ill-located. Furthermore, there is no gear reminder for the automatic transmission.
- **Rearward** visibility is mediocre and hindered by the thick roof pillars and rear-seat headrests.
- **There is an inadequate number of storage spaces**, which takes away from this compact's practical side and reveals the age of its design.

VERDICT
The small Volvo will need to be slightly redesigned before it can truly conquer the North American market, where its name is not enough to ensure its success.

RECALLS
None over this period.

40 Series — VOLVO

RELIABILITY PROBLEMS

	1996	1997	1998	1999	2000	2001
Engine:						
Transmission:						
Suspension:						
Steering:						
Brakes:			Insufficient data			
Electricity:						
Body:						
Accessories:						
Fit/finish:						

POWERTRAIN

Year	Type/ L/Camshaft/bhp	Drivetrain & gearbox
2001	L4T/1.9/DOHC/165	front-A5

PERFORMANCE

Acceler. 0/100 sec.	Top. speed km/h	Ave. Fuel consp. l./100 km
8.8	200	10.5

SPECIFICATIONS

Model 2001	Wlb. mm	Lght. mm	Cb.wt kg	Brakes fr/rr	Steering type	Standard tires
sdn. 4dr.	2562	4541	1255	dc/ABS	pwr.r.&p.	195/60R15
wgn. 4dr.	2562	4541	1280	dc/ABS	pwr.r.&p.	195/60R15

PRICES

Model / version		1996	1997	1998	1999	2000	2001
sdn. 4dr. 2.4L	mini						28900
	maxi						32300
sdn. 4dr. 1.8L	mini						30450
	maxi						32550

See page 7 to adapt these figures.

2001 VOLVO V40

Volvo   60 Series

2001 VOLVO S60

The S60 replaces the S70 sedans. Its components are borrowed from the former S70 and the current S80.

PROS
- **The lines** are very pleasing to the eye and are in keeping with Volvo's metamorphosis: from straight to rounded in the space of a few short years.
- **The array of mechanical options** to choose from offers an interesting range of choices that makes it easy to adapt the vehicle's character to that of its owner.
- **The T5** is capable of breathtaking performance and is a sports car in its own right, with muscular acceleration and pick-up.
- **Handling** is more sure than ever with the refined suspension components.
- **The excellent front and rear seats** are Volvo strong points, because they make for fatigue-free travelling over long distances.
- **Overall quality** has been improved once again. This in turn increases this model's resale value a little bit more.
- **The rear ventilation ducts** contribute to improving the comfort of rear-seat occupants.

CONS
- **Legroom and shoulder room** are at a premium in the rear sears, where access is not as easy as on previous models.
- **Maneuverability** suffers from the wide turning radius that forces the driver to sometimes attempt certain maneuvers several times before being successful.
- **There are too many options** to choose from, revealing a sales system that is typical to Ford.
- **The poorly designed steering wheel** is massive and uncomfortable to grasp.
- **Front and rear storage space** has been reduced to the strict minimum, which is unacceptable in a car of this price and status.
- **The wide center console** and the position of the hand brake take up previous front-seat space.
- **The spare tire** is located far under the trunk floor and is difficult to get at.

VERDICT
Although very refined and elegant, the latest Volvo is not as practical or roomy as its predecessor, a fact reflected by its declining sales figures.

RECALLS
None over this period.

60 Series　　　　　　　　　　　　　　　　VOLVO

RELIABILITY PROBLEMS
	1996	1997	1998	1999	2000	2001
Engine:						
Transmission:						
Suspension:						
Steering:						
Brakes:			Insufficient data			
Electricity:						
Body:						
Accessories:						
Fit/finish:						

POWERTRAIN / PERFORMANCE

Year	Type/ L/Camshaft/bhp	Drivetrain & gearbox	Acceler. 0/100 sec.	Top. speed km/h	Ave. Fuel consp. l./100 km
2001					
2.4	L5T/2.4/DOHC/168	front-M5	8.8	210	11.0
2.4T	L5T/2.4/DOHC/197	front-A5	8.5	210	11.4
T5	L5T/2.4/DOHC/247	front-A5	6.8	210	11.8

SPECIFICATIONS

Model 2001	Wlb. mm	Lght. mm	Cb.wt kg	Brakes fr/rr	Steering type	Standard tires
sdn. 4dr. 2.4	2715	4576	1427	dc/ABS	pwr.r.&p.	195/65R16
sdn. 4dr. 2.4T	2715	4576	1435	dc/ABS	pwr.r.&p.	205/55R16
sdn 4dr. T5	2715	4576	1450	dc/ABS	pwr.r.&p.	215/55R16

PRICES

Model / version		1996	1997	1998	1999	2000	2001
sdn. 4dr. 2.4L	mini						35700
	maxi						38850
sdn. 4dr. 2.4T	mini						37800
	maxi						40950
sdn. 4dr. TS	mini						40950
	maxi						44400

See page 7 to adapt these figures.

2001 VOLVO S60

VOLVO   70 Series

1998 VOLVO C70

The 70 Series replaced the 850 lineup in 1998. It's a fresh remake of the previous models, but based on the same mechanical features. It's sold as a C coupe and convertible, S sedan and V station wagon.

PROS
- **The AWD version** opens up new vistas, since you can benefit from this feature without being at the wheel of a truck.
- **The fuller, rounder shape** is in keeping with traditional traits that give it an unmistakable Volvo look.
- **The superb Turbo engine** provides really thrilling sporty moves. The base model engine is less awesome, but fairly impressive even with the automatic gearbox.
- **Brakes** are among the best tested on a mass-produced car, yielding really trim stopping distances in spite of hefty vehicle weight and anti-lock system.
- **Handling** has been seriously improved with the really rigid structure and better suspension travel. The AWD is amazing on slippery surfaces and the vehicle holds the road just beautifully.
- **Cabin and trunk space** comfortably accommodate five passengers and their luggage.
- **Ride comfort** is super with the supple suspension of conventional engine models, the remarkable seat design, reasonable noise level at cruising speed and air conditioner that's easy to adjust as needed, no matter what the season.
- **The instrument panel** is more esthetic and ergonomic than on previous models.
- **Construction quality, finish job and trim materials** are comparable to those of some Japanese products and equipment is top of the line.

CONS
- **Upkeep** isn't cheap and resale value fluctuates quite a bit, so fans of these Swedish beauties have to cough up the cash to enjoy such a privilege.
- **The automatic shifter** is rougher around the edges with the base model engine than with the Turbo.
- You're in for a **far from smooth ride** on the sporty versions equipped with a stiffer suspension that faithfully transmits every single bump and crack.
- **Some components** seem to be poorly and loosely put together, since you can hear some strange squeaks and rattles.
- **Unusual controls** take some getting used to, such as for windows, mirrors, cruise control and low-slung sound system dials. The steering wheel is still too big and awfully wide.

CONCLUSION
The 70 Series models have a shapelier exterior and more ergonomic cabin design, yet boast of the zippy performance range of the 850 lineup.

RECALLS
1998 Incorrect "Vehicle Emission Control Information" label.(S&V)
98-99 Users of the third seat (V70) may come in contact with the tailpipe when entering or exiting the vehicle due to its location and the variability in its lenght.
1999 A fuel filter bracket must be installed on affected AWD vehicles.
2000 Defective tail gate locking mechanism will be replaced.

70 Series — VOLVO

RELIABILITY PROBLEMS

	1996	1997	1998	1999	2000	2001
Engine:			X	X	X	X
Transmission:			-	-	-	-
Suspension:			X	X	-	-
Steering:			-	-	-	-
Brakes:			X	X	X	-
Electricity:			X	X	X	X
Body:			-	-	-	-
Accessories:			X	X	X	X
Fit/finish:			-	-	-	-

POWERTRAIN

Year	Type/ L/Camshaft/bhp	Drivetrain & gearbox
98-01	L5T/2.3/DOHC/240 (T5)	front-M5
	L5/2.4/DOHC/168	front-M5
		front-A4
	L5T/2.4/DOHC/190	front-A4
	L5T/2.4/DOHC/190 AWD	front/all-M5
	L5/2.3/DOHC/236 C70	front-A4
		front-M5

PERFORMANCE

Acceler. 0/100 sec.	Top speed km/h	Ave. Fuel consp. l./100 km
7.8	235	12.3
8.9	205	11.9
9.2	200	11.7
9.0	220	12.0
9.6	210	12.3
6.8	235	11.9
NA	NA	11.9

SPECIFICATIONS

Model 98-01	Wlb. mm	Lght. mm	Cb.wt kg	Brakes fr/rr	Steering type	Standard tires
con. 2dr.Cabrio.	2664	4720	1647	dc/ABS	pwr.r&p.	225/45R17
cpe. 2dr.	2664	4720	1458	dc/ABS	pwr.r&p.	205/55R16
sdn. 4dr. base	2664	4660	1413	dc/ABS	pwr.r&p.	195/60R15
sdn. 4dr. GLT	2664	4660	1450	dc/ABS	pwr.r&p.	195/60R15
wgn. 4dr. T-5R	2664	4710	1536	dc/ABS	pwr.r&p.	205/55R16
wgn. 4dr. AWD	2664	4710	1480	dc/ABS	pwr.r&p.	205/65R15

PRICES

Model / version		1996	1997	1998	1999	2000	2001
cpe. 2dr.	mini			28750	31800	37300	42550
	maxi			32750	35700	41500	46200
con. 2dr.	mini			33600	36000	41500	50400
	maxi			37500	39900	45700	54100
sdn. 4dr.	mini			17000	21750	27800	
	maxi			21000	25400	32000	
sdn. 4dr. SR	mini			18300			
	maxi			22000			
sdn. 4dr. SE	mini			18700			
	maxi			22450			
sdn. 4dr. GLT	mini			19950	25400	31000	
	maxi			23850	29100	35200	
sdn. 4dr. T5	mini			21500	26550	33600	
	maxi			25400	30450	37800	
sdn. 4dr. T5 SE	mini			22600			
	maxi			26550			
sdn. 4dr. T5 AWD	mini				29400	34100	
	maxi				33300	38300	
wgn. 4dr.	mini			18000	24450	30100	
	maxi			22000	28350	34300	
wgn. 4dr. SR	mini			19100			
	maxi			23100			
wgn. 4dr. SE	mini			20150			
	maxi			24150			
wgn. 4dr. GLT	mini			22250	28350	32750	
	maxi			26200	32200	36900	
wgn. 4dr. T5	mini			24150	30450		43600
	maxi			28000	34350		46700
wgn. 4dr. AWD	mini			25200			
	maxi			29100			
wgn. 4dr. XC AWD	mini			29400	32350	37300	45150
	maxi			33300	36200	41500	48300
wgn. 4dr. R AWD	mini			33300			
	maxi			36950			
wgn. 4dr. TBO AWD	mini				35700	41150	
	maxi				39600	45400	
wgn. 4dr. 2.4L	mini						36200
	maxi						39700
wgn. 4dr. 2.4T	mini						39400
	maxi						42800

See page 7 to adapt these figures.

VOLVO   80 Series

2000 VOLVO S 80

The S80 has replaced the 900 Series as the top model of the Volvo lineup. It is available with a tranversal 6-cylinder in line engine, 2.9L atmospheric in the base or 2.8L turbo in theT6 version.

PROS
- **The styling** differs greatly from previous models that have been around for generations. With a more sculptured shape, the S80 is very similar to the 1992 ECC prototype.
- **The bucket seats** in the S80, as in all Volvos, demonstrate what comfort should be. The high back and well-shaped seat provide excellent support. And they're heated.
- **The trunk** is very deep and flat. Because of the 60/40 rear folding seat, storage space can nearly double.
- **Accelerating** and passing is highly inspiring in the bi-turbo version.
- **Handling** is very smooth. The suspension dampens any roll and minimizes bumps.
- **The rear bench** is very comfortable. There's enough room for heads, shoulders and legs. Headrests are adjustable, improving rear window visibility slightly, as long as no one is sitting there.
- **Bonus**: for detailed equipment, a logically laid out dashboard and powerful headlamps whose brightness and reach are both excellent.

CONS
- **The large turning radius** due to the transverse-mounted 6-cylinder in line engine, seriously hampers maneuverability.
- **Braking efficiency** is disappointing and emergency stopping distances are longer than average for this category.
- **Rear visibility** is seriously limited. The high trunk makes backing up an uneasy undertaking in this large car.
- **Steering** is over-assisted and quickly becomes light and imprecise at center, to please the typical North American driver.
- **Performance** of the base S80 is uninspiring since both acceleration and passing are mediocre at best.
- The same tires equipped the base model and the T6 who delivered superior performance.
- **Minus**: wipers are too slow to keep up with heavy rain and a flat emergency tire that has no place in a car sold at this price.

CONCLUSION
This model has some fine qualities, but it has been created to please more the American than the Swedish...

RECALLS
99-00 Both front ball joint will be replaced with a reinforced version.

80 Series VOLVO

RELIABILITY PROBLEMS

	1996	1997	1998	1999	2000	2001
Engine:				X	-	-
Transmission:				X	-	-
Suspension:				X	X	X
Steering:				X	-	-
Brakes:				X	X	-
Electricity:				X	X	X
Body:				-	-	-
Accessories:				X	X	X
Fit/finish:				-	-	-

POWERTRAIN

Type/ L/Camshaft/bhp	Drivetrain & gearbox
99-01 L6/2.9/DOHC/201	front-A4
L6T/2.8/DOHC/268	front-A4

PERFORMANCE Year

Acceler. 0/100 sec.	Top. speed km/h	Ave. Fuel consp. l./100 km
9.0	200	13.2
7.2	240	14.2

SPECIFICATIONS

Model 99-01	Wlb. mm	Lght. mm	Cb.wt kg	Brakes fr/rr	Steering type	Standard tires
sdn. 4dr. 2.9L	2791	4822	1552	dc/ABS	pwr.r&p.	215/55R16
sdn. 4dr. T6	2791	4822	1552	dc/ABS	pwr.r&p.	225/55R16

PRICES

Model / version		1996	1997	1998	1999	2000	2001
sdn. 4dr. 2.9L	mini				31000	34850	43600
	maxi				34800	39150	47000
sdn. 4dr. T6	mini				34100	39000	47800
	maxi				38000	43350	51250
sdn. 4dr. T6 Exec.	mini						49900
	maxi						53500

See page 7 to adapt these figures.

2000 VOLVO S 80

VOLVO — 850 Series

1997 VOLVO 850

The first front-wheel drive in Volvo history, the 850 came in 1993 as a sedan powered by a 2.4L 5-cylinder conventional engine. The station wagon and the Turbo engine were available in '94 and the T-5R model was sold in '95. In Sweden in '97, Volvo has revised its style in perspective of a total model rename that will take place the following year.

PROS
- **High-level safety** features with a very robust, reinforced body that has been imitated since, ABS brakes, standard dual airbags and front-wheel drive.
- **The typical Volvo** body design is still the same, but the angular lines have been softened and streamlined, especially with aerodynamics in mind.
- **The base model** is adequate, but not at all like the Turbo that really has get up and go.
- **Brakes** are strong and stable on sudden stops.
- **The cabin** accommodates five adults and the trunk holds all their baggage. The baggage compartment on the station wagon is more spacious and can be extended by lowering the rear seatbench.
- **Build is solid**, finish is impeccable and trim materials are spiffy.

CONS
- **The base engine** loses a lot of power with the automatic transmission and gears are sometimes cantankerous.
- **There's swing and sway** on the base model because of the soft suspension, so handling isn't great.
- **Some controls** aren't too ergonomic, like those for the windows, cruise control, rearview mirrors and sound system that are too low; and lastly, the steering wheel diameter is too wide.
- **Safety belts** are awkward on some models.

CONCLUSION
The 850 models are a good buy because they're really practical and they benefit from "à la carte" performance, depending on the engine model chosen.

RECALLS
None over this period.

850 Series — VOLVO

RELIABILITY PROBLEMS

	1996	1997	1998	1999	2000	2001
Engine:	-	X				
Transmission:	X	-				
Suspension:	-	X				
Steering:	-	X				
Brakes:	X	-				
Electricity:	-	X				
Body:	-	-				
Accessories:	X	X				
Fit/finish:	-	-				

POWERTRAIN

Year	Type/ L/Camshaft/bhp	Drivetrain & gearbox
1996	L5T/2.3/DOHC/222 (T5)	front-M5
	L5/2.4/DOHC/168	front-M5
		front-A4
1997	L5T/2.3/DOHC/250 (R)	front-M5
	L5/2.4/DOHC/190	front-A4

PERFORMANCE

Acceler. 0/100 sec.	Top speed km/h	Ave. Fuel consp. l./100 km
7.8	220	12.5
9.0	210	11.5
9.8	200	12.0
7.8	235	12.3
9.6	200	11.6

SPECIFICATIONS

Model 96-97	Wlb. mm	Lght. mm	Cb.wt kg	Brakes fr/rr	Steering type	Standard tires
sdn. 4dr.	2664	4661	1446	dc/ABS	pwr.r&p.	195/60R15
sdn. 4dr. Turbo	2664	4661	1450	dc/ABS	pwr.r&p.	205/50R16
wgn. 4dr.	2664	4710	1480	dc/ABS	pwr.r&p.	195/60R15
wgn. 4dr. T-5R	2664	4710	1536	dc/ABS	pwr.r&p.	205/50R17

PRICES

Model / version		1996	1997	1998	1999	2000	2001
sdn. 4dr.	mini		12100				
	maxi		16000				
sdn. 4dr. Tbo	mini	15450					
	maxi	19500					
sdn. 4dr. GLT	mini	11550	14100				
	maxi	15400	18150				
sdn. 4dr. GLE	mini	9650					
	maxi	13650					
sdn. 4dr. Plat.Edit.	mini	17500					
	maxi	21500					
sdn. 4dr. T5	mini		18150				
	maxi		22350				
sdn. 4dr. R	mini	18900	21750				
	maxi	23100	26000				
wgn. 4dr. Turbo	mini	17000					
	maxi	21000					
wgn. 4dr.	mini		13550				
	maxi		17450				
wgn. 4dr. GLT	mini	13350	15000				
	maxi	17300	19100				
wgn. 4dr. GLE	mini	11200					
	maxi	15200					
wgn. 4dr. Plat.Edit.	mini	19500					
	maxi	23700					
wgn. 4dr. T5	mini		18600				
	maxi		22700				
wgn. 4dr. AWD	mini		22000				
	maxi		26600				
wgn. 4dr. R	mini	20150	22250				
	maxi	24350	26800				

See page 7 to adapt these figures.

VOLVO 900/90 Series

1998 VOLVO S90

The 900 Series is inspired by the former 700 Series and was powered by a 4-cylinder engine when it was first sold in '91. The 6-cylinder in-line engine came out in '92. The 90 Series took over in 1998 with the same powertrain.

PROS
- **There's a wide variety** of choices in this model range that includes two body styles, three engine models, two suspension designs, two transmissions and six trim levels.
- **Preventive safety** features, body design and top-notch quality typical of Volvo products.
- **The efficiency** of the 2.3L multi-valve engine, the Turbos and the 6-cylinder in-line engine.
- **Driving is really** enjoyable because of the well-designed cockpit, excellent outward view, well-organized instrument panel, clean and smooth steering that also benefits from a small steer angle diameter, resulting in superb maneuverability.
- **Brakes are powerful**, predictable and stable, especially with ABS.
- **The cabin interior** has a nice lay-out, seat trim is attractive and the noise level is exceptionally low.
- **The luggage capacity** of the 900 models is generous, especially on the station wagon with its trunk that can be extended by lowering the rear seatbench.

CONS
- **The independent suspension** on the 960 really shows the deficiencies of the front end, that doesn't quite stick to the road.
- **The unimpressive** performance of the 4-cylinder conventional engine that shakes and roars as soon as it's solicited to do its job.
- **The interior cabin** design isn't very plush, considering the hefty price of the vehicle.

CONCLUSION
These are very classic cars, but they have a charm of their own and they're quite comfortable, especially with the 6-cylinder in-line engine that is silky smooth.

RECALLS
None over this period.

900/90 Series — VOLVO

RELIABILITY PROBLEMS

	1996	1997	1998	1999	2000	2001
Engine:	X	-	X			
Transmission:	-	X	-			
Suspension:	-	-	-			
Steering:	-	-	-			
Brakes:	-	X	X			
Electricity:	-	-	X			
Body:	X	X	-			
Accessories:	-	X	X			
Fit/finish:	-	X	-			

POWERTRAIN

Year	Type/ L/Camshaft/bhp	Drivetrain & gearbox
96-98	L6/2.9/DOHC/181	rear-A4

PERFORMANCE

Acceler. 0/100 sec.	Top. speed km/h	Ave. Fuel consp. l./100 km
8.8	215	12.5

SPECIFICATIONS

Model 96-98	Wlb. mm	Lght. mm	Cb.wt kg	Brakes fr/rr	Steering type	Standard tires
sdn. 4dr.	2770	4872	1570	dc/ABS	pwr.r&p.	205/55R16
wgn. 4dr.	2770	4862	1609	dc/ABS	pwr.r&p.	195/65R15

PRICES

Model / version		1996	1997	1998	1999	2000	2001
sdn. 4dr.	mini	14200	18600	21300			
	maxi	18050	22900	25400			
wgn. 4dr.	mini	15750	19500	23350			
	maxi	18600	23950	26450			

See page 7 to adapt these figures.

1997 VOLVO 960

NOTES

NOTES